Milton's English Poetry

Being Entries from *A Milton Encyclopedia*

With an Introduction by
William B. Hunter

and a Bibliography by
John T. Shawcross

Lewisburg
Bucknell University Press
London and Toronto: Associated University Presses

Associated University Presses
440 Forsgate Drive
Cranbury, NJ 08512

Associated University Presses
25 Sicilian Avenue
London WC1A 2QH, England

Associated University Presses
2133 Royal Windsor Drive
Unit 1
Mississauga, Ontario
Canada L5J 1K5

The paper used in this publication meets the
requirements of the American National Standard
for Permanence of Paper for Printed
Library Materials Z39.48-1984.

Library of Congress Cataloging-in-Publication Data

Milton encyclopedia. Selections.
 Milton's English poetry.

 Bibliography: p.
 1. Milton, John, 1608–1674—Criticism and interpreta-
tion. I. Hunter, William Bridges, 1915–
II. Title.
PR3588.M484 1986   821'.4   85-47666
ISBN 0-8387-5096-6 (alk. paper)

Printed in the United States of America

CONTENTS

SHORT FORMS USED IN THIS COLLECTION

AdP	Ad Patrem
Animad	Animadversions upon the Remonstrant's Defense
Apol	An Apology
Arc	Arcades
Areop	Areopagitica
BrM	Bridgewater Manuscript
BN	Brief Notes upon a Late Sermon
Brit	The History of Britain
Bucer	The Judgement of Martin Bucer
CarEl	Carmina Elegiaca
Carrier 1, 2	On the University Carrier; Another on the Same
CharLP	Character of the Long Parliament
Circum	Upon the Circumcision
CD	De Doctrina Christiana
CM	*The Works of John Milton* (New York: Columbia University Press, 1931–38). 18 vols. The so-called Columbia Milton.
Colas	Colasterion
CivP	A Treatise of Civil Power
DDD	The Doctrine and Discipline of Divorce
1Def	Pro Populo Anglicano Defensio
2Def	Defensio Secunda
3Def	Pro Se Defensio
Educ	Of Education
Eikon	Eikonoklastes
El	Elegia
EpDam	Epitaphium Damonis
Epistol	Epistolarum Familiarium
EpWin	Epitaph on the Marchioness of Winchester
FInf	On the Death of a Fair Infant
French, *Life Records*	J. Milton French. *The Life Records of John Milton* (New Brunswick, N.J.: Rutgers University Press, 1949–58). 5 vols.
Hire	Considerations Touching the Likeliest Means to Remove

7

	Hirelings out of the Church
Hor	The Fifth Ode of Horace
IlP	Il Penseroso
L'Al	L'Allegro
Lyc	Lycidas
Logic	Artis Logicae
Mask	A Mask (Comus)
Masson, *Life*	David Masson, *The Life of John Milton* (London, 1859–1880). 6 vols. plus Index.
Nat	On the Morning of Christ's Nativity
New F	On the New Forcers of Conscience
Parker, *Milton*	William Riley Parker. *Milton: A Biography* (Oxford: Clarendon Press, 1968). 2 vols.
PL	Paradise Lost
PR	Paradise Regained
PrelE	Of Prelatical Episcopacy
PresM	The Present Means
Prol	Prolusion
Ps	Psalm
RCG	Reason of Church Government
Ref	Of Reformation
Rous	Ad Ioannem Rousium
SA	Samson Agonistes
Shak	On Shakespeare
SolMus	At a Solemn Music
Sonn	Sonnet
Tenure	The Tenure of Kings and Magistrates
Tetra	Tetrachordon
Time	Of Time
TM	Trinity Manuscript
TR	Of True Religion
Vac	At a Vacation Exercise
Variorum Commentary	*A Variorum Commentary on the Poems of John Milton.* 4 vols. to date (New York: Columbia University Press, 1970–).
Way	The Ready and Easy Way to Establish a Free Commonwealth
Yale *Prose*	*Complete Prose Works of John Milton.* 8 vols. (New Haven, Conn.: Yale University Press, 1953–82).

INTRODUCTION

Milton is famous today—many, especially in England, would say notorious—as a revolutionary. His independence from society's norms may have been unequaled by any of his contemporaries as he reexamined the organization of the leading institutions of his age: the English Church in his pamphlets attacking the bishopric; the family in the pamphlets on divorce; political institutions in his several attacks upon King Charles I and his defenses of the Commonwealth, as well as his constant questioning of Erastianism; traditional theology in his longest work, *Of Christian Doctrine*. Some individual contemporaries were more extreme than he in some of these areas, but no one was a revolutionist in all of them or even in most. It should come as no surprise, then—although the fact may no longer be generally appreciated—to find that Milton was also a revolutionary in his English poetry.

Such an idea is unexpected in part because Milton's poetry is so well known and assimilated into the mainstream of our literature. But even more it is because the traditional background against which he was reacting is often overlooked today. A good example is the form of blank verse that he developed in *Paradise Lost*—a form which, because of its extraordinary influence upon later poets from James Thomson to the Romantics to the Victorians to Robinson, Frost, and Eliot, everyone unquestioningly accepts as the natural medium for the long narrative poem. Before Milton was born blank verse had, of course, been firmly established as the primary medium for drama. What is not so generally recognized is that as far as Milton and most of his readers were concerned, it had rarely been employed for nondramatic material. Even today few know that the sole such examples before *Paradise Lost* are the excerpt from the *Aeneid* translated by the Earl of Surrey early in the sixteenth century and a section of George Gascoigne's *Steele Glass* done a generation or so later. Milton certainly knew what dramatic blank verse was and wrote a good deal of it in his play, *Mask*. But later he developed his narrative medium independently of the dramatic tradition with significantly different rules. He never allows himself, for example, an extra syllable within a line except as permitted by a system of

elisions by which any two syllables with adjacent vowels or separated by the letters *l, n,* and *r* can be read as one. In comparison with playwrights, he tolerates almost no feminine endings; only about 1 percent of the lines fall into this category. In such ways he composed a much more regular ten-syllable line than any of the playwrights ever did. On the other hand, his development of the variation of the number of stresses within the line from only three ("Immútable, immórtal, ínfinite") to eight ("Rócks, cáves, lákes, féns, bógs, déns, and shádes of déath") has no equivalence at all on the stage, nor does his freedom to position stresses on the odd-numbered syllables of his line. No playwright was as daring as he in placing the caesura at any point in the line. Although he compared this verse with that of the English dramatists, he never called it "blank verse" but claimed that he was doing things "unattempted yet in prose or rhyme," as indeed is true. In sum, he developed a revolutionary new narrative medium from the traditional dramatic one, but it was so unexpected to his readers that Samuel Simmons, his publisher, had to procure an explanation from him for "that which stumbled many . . . , why the poem rimes not."

Having achieved success in this new medium, he allowed himself to use it once again, but only once, in *Paradise Regained,* and characteristically experimented with yet another innovation in *Samson Agonistes,* which he published in the same volume. Even today no one is quite sure of what the prosodic principles of this drama are, although many attempts have been made to explain them; but every reader agrees that whatever they are they are successful, for the verse finds a ready reception everywhere.

If Milton was thus revolutionary in his poetic medium, he was even more so in the contents of his English poetry, though once again he always worked within the strictest limits of each form as he applied it in ways hitherto undreamed of. To refer again to *Paradise Lost,* it is, of course, the best example in any modern language of the epic as it had been written by Homer and Virgil, with its beginning *in medias res,* invocations to a goddess (not to a god), its opening statement of theme, its epic question ("what cause / Mov'd our Grand Parents . . . to fall off / From their Creator?") epic similes, epic catalogue, and so on. But for those who know the tradition, the innovations within its pattern are startling. Never in the *Iliad, Odyssey,* or *Aeneid* is there a description of the make-up of the universe and of its creation such as those which occupy Books II and VII and which find their ancient poetic authority in Lucretius's *De Rerum Natura.* Milton alone developed the use of sonorous lists of proper names, an achievement which has not had a successful imitation in English. Never before had there been a structural feature like that which informs the echoing of the Holy Trinity of Father, Son, and Holy Spirit in the unholy one of Satan, Sin, and Death. Classical commentators had never had to call for analogies for such topics as philosophy in all its aspects; theology with its dogmas, its mysteries, its heresies, and its subordinate divisions of angelology and demonology; history both ancient and modern; science, especially geography and astronomy; and political theory. To read Milton's poem is to become at

a bound one of his self-defining "fit audience," who enjoy the pleasure and privilege of being set apart in a special universe of discourse with its author.

What has been suggested here in brief about the revolutionary quality of Milton's epic is equally true of the rest of his poetry, when one sees it in its seventeenth-century context rather than in the one which its influence created. An early example, as Milton recognized in his proud verse letter to his friend Diodati, is the *Nativity Ode*. Here was a new employment of the ancient Pindaric and Horatian form, which it follows in formal definition with its regular stanza structure and elevated subject matter. Its English background shows in its archaisms consciously imitated from Spenser. But completely original are the stanza form of the *Hymn* itself, which had never been written before in English and perhaps because of its intrinsic difficulty would not be again in any significant work, its employment of proper names as sonorous support to the sense, and its control of verse texture: "The wakefull trump of doom must thunder through the deep."

Then, in a limited group of works, Milton outdid the smooth and lyric Jonson in the application of what is essentially a four-stress verse form to the English lyric, climaxing in the perfection of *L'Allegro* and *Il Penseroso*. What has been insufficiently appreciated is the fact that critics have had a hard time identifying poetry of others from whom Milton (probably still a master's candidate at Cambridge) might have developed these most mellifluous of works. Jonson has been properly considered, though all of his four-stress poems are short. A longer example of this meter, in dialogue form, is the eighth "nimphall" of Michael Drayton's *Muses' Elysium*, published in 1630. The song "Hence, all you vain delights" in John Fletcher's play *The Nice Valour* has been suggested as akin to part of *Il Penseroso* as it rejects "vain delights" and hails "sweetest melancholy," but the verse form is different and the play was not printed until 1647. Yet another possibility is the verse of "Democritus Junior" prefixed to Robert Burton's *Anatomy of Melancholy*, but its length and its relatively pedestrian quality leaves it well behind Milton's two great companion poems. In them, rather, Milton again has taken a form well established by others and produced within its constraints a new and universally admired creation. At the same time, he has had to practice in order to get there, and he typically shows us how he did so in the brief "Song: On May Morning" and the more fully developed "Epitaph on the Marchioness of Winchester."

Having been graduated from Cambridge, Milton continued to investigate new ways to write poetry. It is hard to show that this is true of the "Entertainment" *Arcades* because there is no recognizable form to which one can assign it, but *Mask* is another matter. The fact is that Milton called it a masque, so a masque it must be (the title *Comus* came almost exactly a hundred years later); but everyone has had trouble fitting it into this well-known Stuart genre. It is too long. It is too serious. Three of its main characters (the Lady and her two brothers) were probably not masked. No previous noble participant had ever been subjected to the physical coercion that the Lady had to endure, for the

attack upon her chastity was more brutally close to rape than any masque had dared picture. Milton probably had never actually seen a court masque and relied upon his friend and producer Henry Lawes for guidance about how to fit it to the sponsor's wishes. But the author does technically remain within the bounds of the form with the two antimasque dances—one grotesque, the second some kind of country clog—with the several songs, with the near-allegorical treatment of the subject matter, and with the stage spectacle, especially the appearance of Sabrina with her nymphs.

Just as Milton had practiced stress verse leading to *L'Allegro* and *Il Penseroso*, at some time after the performance of *Arcades* he moved to another form new to him in English and in itself relatively irregular, the Italian short song or *canzone*. In *On Time, At a Solemn Music*, and *Upon the Circumcision* he produced his first poems of this genre in English (he had written one in Italian while still at college), characteristically exploring its potential for original treatment. In the first two of these poems he experimented with sustaining very long sentences through many lines of irregular length and irregular rhyme; in the third, *Upon the Circumcision*, he managed the same within two matching (but metrically irregular) fourteen-line stanzas. English poetry had never seen anything like this, and such five-finger exercises led directly to the metrical achievements of *Lycidas*.

That great monody follows perfectly the form of the classical pastorals of Theocritus, Bion, Moschus, and Virgil; as scholars have noted, Milton even translates specific lines from them and, of course, adopts the Greek names of their characters. What is revolutionary is the new and nonpastoral content of *Lycidas* and its prosodic construction. Ostensibly a lament over the death by drowning of his fellow student at Christ's College, Edward King, it perfectly fits the classical pattern of a shepherd mourning in song the death of an associate. But the real subject of Milton's poem is his self-concerns: his poetic aspirations, his problems with a career, the corruption that he sees in the contemporary Anglican establishment by then dominated by Archbishop Laud. Mingled with this is the shock about a death caused by the same medium, water, which gives life to the communicant at baptism, ending with the great promise of resurrection through the sacrifice of "him that walked the waves." At the conclusion, Milton ends with a promise to himself and to his readers that he will move on to other kinds of poetry or of occupation: "Tomorrow to fresh fields and pastures new." And, indeed, he would never write another English pastoral.

Equally striking about *Lycidas* is the unusual prosody, the like of which had never been seen in any English writer. For lack of a better model critics point to Spenser's *Epithalamium* with its irregular stanzas and lines of varying length, but the comparison is not very enlightening. For one thing, *Lycidas* is not in stanzas, has no refrain lines, and never employs the twelve-syllable line which was such a favorite with Spenser and which Milton himself had often used before. Rather, the construction is in irregularly rhymed verse paragraphs until the final one in which the shepherd takes his leave in a perfectly regular stanza

of ottava rima. The opening paragraph could be called a sonnet in one sense—it has fourteen lines—but there the resemblance stops. Irregularly occurring throughout the poem's ten-syllable lines are short ones of six syllables, which always rhyme with an adjacent long one. Appearing with similar irregularity are ten lines which do not rhyme with anything (the first is an example). The effect that one feels upon reading the poem aloud is much the same as that derived from blank verse or even good free verse; most people are surprised when the rhymes are pointed out to them. Only in certain places does the rhyme spring into prominence, as in the jolt that joins a long line with a short one, or in the few couplets which mark the end of some but not all of the verse paragraphs. Everywhere are the long sentences spanning the irregular rhymes and those of varying length. Indeed, the only English models for this revolutionary technique are Milton's own *On Time, Upon the Circumcision,* and *At a Solemn Music.* But he was never to create another poem like these.

Indeed, at the early age of twenty-nine, with the composition of *Lycidas,* Milton essentially stopped writing poetry in English, having published so far a 16-line piece on Shakespeare prefixed to the Second Folio of 1632, *Mask* in 1637, and *Lycidas* in 1638. All were shrouded in anonymity. Had he died on his trip to Italy we might still be wondering who was the gifted "I.M." who wrote all three. Speculation as to why he stopped is probably not profitable. But at any rate he turned to prose which he produced in prodigious quantities in the next fifteen years until blindness finally forced him to desist, and he returned again to the composition of poetry, this time of a very different kind from that which he collected and published, at last with his name attached, in 1645.

During these poetically lean years, however, he did write some verse at quite irregular intervals, which he dictated after he became blind: his sonnets. While still at Cambridge he had tried his hand at six of them—one in English, the rest in Italian. In those days, the late 1620s, the form had become pretty much exhausted and old-fashioned in England; Milton probably thought of himself as imitating Italians models rather than native ones like those of Sidney or Drayton or Shakespeare. They were written, as all twenty-three of them would ultimately be, in the strict Italian form, and the subject of this initial half-dozen was likewise traditional—love, especially its disappointments. They are in no significant sense revolutionary or worthy of especially close attention. But with the seventh he moved permanently into English, which he endowed with new life as he explored in a strictly traditional form a whole new series of subjects: his twenty-third birthday, the possibility of an attack on his London home during the Civil War, some problems facing the victorious Cromwell, invitations to dinner, his blindness, and others. Only one concerns love, but here too is a revolutionary treatment: the final one is a tender poem to his deceased wife who had appeared to him in a dream. But as she lovingly leaned over him, "I waked, she fled, and day brought back my night" of blindness. The Romantics were to be the next group of great writers of sonnets, and to a man they followed Milton's lead rather than that of the Elizabethans.

The only other poetry that we know he completed during these years when

prose dominated his life and he "wrote with his left hand" were two sets of translations of the Psalms into English, done in April 1648 and in August 1653, (the only poems that he dated so specifically). Like all the rest of his mature poetry, the eight translations done in 1653 are radical experiments in verse form. Within the limits of the more or less unalterable content of the psalms, he explored English stanzaic verse in ways not to be found again until the nineteenth century. They may be practice poems (for the revolutionary verse found in *Samson?*) like his English *canzones*. Dictated at the rate of one a day, few collections of English lyrics can match them in their experimental prosody, fixed though they are in their subject matter.

The nine translations done in the spring of 1648, on the other hand, are unique in Milton's mature poetry in that in them alone he broke no new ground whatsoever. They are in the omnipresent common meter of the other contemporary metrical psalters, and they even contain several lines either exactly quoted or closely paraphrased from the others; indeed, to call them "translations" is not very accurate. What Milton seems to have found interesting was the few dozen words which he printed in italics with their Hebrew originals transliterated in the margins so that a "curious" reader could check upon his accuracy. Otherwise these psalms are the sole example of the mature Milton as a pure traditionalist.

The originality of *Paradise Regained* is almost impossible to determine because of the fact that there are no other examples with which one may compare it. Perhaps this is one of the reasons for its lesser popularity than that of its longer companion, *Paradise Lost*. Milton himself suggested the book of Job as an example of such a shorter epic, but the comparison is not very enlightening beyond the fact that both poems rely heavily on long speeches delivered in dialogue. Comparison with Virgil's *Georgics* reveals little except that both works are divided into four books. Perhaps Milton's real originality here consists in his having invented a completely new form of English poetry, the short epic, but if so the lack of other examples for comparison obscures its revolutionary significance.

Finally (whenever it was written), *Samson Agonistes*. Enough has been said above to establish the revolutionary character of its verse, unmatched anywhere else in our literature but completely satisfying, whether it is read silently or aloud. Equally startling are its contents. Milton has melded Matthew Arnold's "Hebraism and Hellenism" into a single whole which follows the strictest rules of Greek drama, such as the chorus, the unities of time, place, and action, the report by a messenger of violence offstage, and limitation of stage dialogue to that between only two characters in the stark fashion of Aeschylus. Dr. Johnson indeed complained that the play does not have a "middle"—that is, nothing much happens between Samson's original entry and his final departure to become a spectacle for the Philistines. But in terms of inner action a great deal goes on: Samson is tempted by Manoa with the offer to have his atonement through suffering bought off, by Harapha (treated as a comic character, atypical

of classical traditions) to retreat into acceptance of his apparently defenseless stance, and by Dalila with her offer of personal care (and what a victory it would have been for her, to destroy her husband as she had and then by her charms to win him back). Like the Lady in *Mask* and the Son in *Paradise Regained* Samson proves himself able to reject all temptations, as he had not been before his suffering began with his being blinded. He even resists the officer's command to go to the Philistine celebration until some "inward motion," which he interprets as originating with God, sends him away to his victorious death. Milton himself may have experienced similar "inward motions" which directed him to attack the bishops, to support divorce on the grounds of incompatibility (to his everlasting contemporary disgrace), to defend the execution of King Charles, and to argue futilely for the "Good Old Cause" even as it was collapsing in final ruin. *Samson Agonistes*, indeed, follows the rules of classical drama as laid down by Aristotle and elaborated in the Italian renaissance; and yet it is a completely original play within these limits which Milton has reformulated to suit himself.

So it was that Milton was a revolutionary in almost all of the poetry which he wrote in his maturity, difficult though the fact is to appreciate today in the face of the total acceptance and absorption of that poetry into our culture over three and a half centuries. Yet one further fact distinguishes him from all other English poets earlier or later. This is the observation that, having once mastered the traditional form into which as has been seen he introduced his own original developments, and having written what is often regarded as the supreme example of it in English, he was then apparently satisfied with such mastery, and turned to a different form in which he produced yet another single masterpiece. *Lycidas* is simply the best pastoral poem in English (he would write one more, though it would be in Latin and follow somewhat different rules). *Comus* is the best, though hardly most representative, masque. *Paradise Lost* is the only good example that English has of the classical epic, *Paradise Regained* the only example of the "brief epic," and *Samson Agonistes* our outstanding classical tragedy. The *Nativity Ode* is arguably comparable to the great odes of Keats and Shelley, though here for once Milton indeed tried to imitate himself, only to fail badly with the *Passion*. Even Dr. Johnson could find nothing bad to say about *L'Allegro* and *Il Penseroso*, and they remain perennially satisfying though Milton never wrote another stress line beyond a few in *Arcades* and *Mask*. Only in the sonnets was he to find a medium to which he would return again and again, whose possibilities he would explore for a quarter of a century and the sole form which engaged his attention beyond the production of one or at most two examples.

In such a brief survey as this, one may discover Milton as he saw himself and come to recapture some of his originality which has been forgotten. The selections from *A Milton Encyclopedia* which follow were all written by experts in each subject, generally in the earlier part of the 1970s. Some of the entries

have been revised for publication in this volume. In the decade since then Milton scholarship of the previous thirty-four decades has not been radically revised despite the insurgence of structuralists, deconstructionists, and feminists. None of the contributors received any money for any contribution (nor did any editor); the esteem which Milton's work holds today finds eloquent testimonial in these thoughtful entries which were written only because their authors believed in the importance of their subject. To all of them are due again our thanks for helping convey to our contemporaries the excitement yet inherent in the poetry of John Milton.

[WBH]

Milton's
English Poetry

BIOGRAPHY, MILTON'S. Milton was born on Friday, December 9, 1608, in his father's home on Bread Street, London, at 6:30 in the morning, and was baptized at All Hallows, Bread Street, on December 12. His father, John Milton, was a scrivener, whose family came from Stanton St. John, Oxon. The Miltons were Roman Catholics, but John, Sr., in the early 1580s, espoused Protestantism, and the poet was thus brought up in a Calvinistic household. His mother, Sara Jeffrey, of St. Swithin's parish, London, came from a family apparently related to Bradshaws, Castons, and Haughtons, names formerly assigned to her. John, Sr., came to London around 1583, and married Sara some time between 1590 and 1600. One older sister and one younger brother survived infancy. Because of his father's various business ventures, in some of which Milton himself became involved, Milton did not have to pursue gainful employment during his life, although he did receive a salary as a secretary to the Council of State.

Through the year 1632 Milton was being educated ostensibly to become a minister. In his early years he was tutored privately, but the name of only one teacher is known, Thomas Young. Young, a minister originally from Scotland, may have served as tutor around 1618–1620. He was an important influence on Milton in religious matters and may have been the major link in Milton's entry into pamphleteering during the episcopal controversy. During this period of study at home, Milton seems to have read a great deal, and late-night study may have contributed to the weakening of his eyes. Around 1620 Milton began attending Alexander Gill's St. Paul's School, located only a few blocks from his home. Perhaps the decision to attend a formal school was prompted as much by Young's removal to Hamburg because of difficulties with the Church authorities as it was by Milton's level of learning. Milton remained at St. Paul's until early 1625. Here his friends included Charles Diodati and Alexander Gill, Jr., one of the instructors, though not Milton's.

Next Milton attended Christ's College, Cambridge, where he was admitted on February 12, 1625, and where he would matriculate on April 9. Why he chose Christ's College over others is not known, but its reputation was high and its faculty well known. Milton received the Bachelor of Arts degree on March 26, 1629, and the Master of Arts degree on July 3, 1632. He was constantly in Cambridge from 1625 through 1632, except for vacations spent, apparently, at his family's home or homes, and except for two other periods. During these years the family still lived on Bread Street, until 1631 when they

moved to Hammersmith, then a suburb to the west of Westminster. It is possible that Milton sojourned at some country place during a vacation or two, with or without his family, but there is no evidence. It may be that *L'Al* and *IlP* reflect a country vacation, and the Seventh Prolusion alludes to such a vacation, but this may be a reference to being in Hammersmith in the summer of 1631. The two further periods when Milton was not in Cambridge were the Lent Term of 1626 (until April 19) and the period when the university was closed due to the plague, from April 17, 1630, to around January 1631. In the first instance Milton was rusticated because of a disagreement with his tutor William Chappell. Upon his return he was placed under Nathaniel Tovey, who remained his tutor through his remaining years at Christ's. This arrangement proved successful and Milton, upon graduation as Bachelor of Arts, was fourth on the University honors list and first from his College.

During his years at Christ's Milton produced various academic exercises in prose, seven of which survive, and various poems, some of which are "academic" (i.e., the result of some occurrence in the college community such as the death of an official). Whether Milton rejected a clerical career for himself while still at Christ's (specifically around the end of 1629, when he was beginning his graduate studies and when he produced *El6* and *Nat*, or later) is debated. At least his continued study through 1632 aimed at a clerical career, and the period thereafter until around the summer of 1637 seems to make no firm commitment one way or another. It has been argued that disillusionment with the ministry had grown during these years after graduation, but that a decision against a clerical career had not really been made (or admitted) until around the summer of 1637. Any decision in favor of a poetical career (rather than simply a continuance of poetic writing) is dependent upon the foregoing, and thus has been dated around 1629, around 1632, or around summer 1637.

Despite the honors as an undergraduate and a successful graduate career, Milton did not receive a fellowship in 1632. Perhaps he did not seek one, and perhaps his removal to his father's house from 1632 through 1638 was necessitated by the age and increasing infirmity of his parents rather than reaction to a lack of academic preferment. The reasons for Milton's actions from 1632 through 1638 have been debated by scholars through the years, with arguments ranging from disappointment at not receiving a fellowship to rejection of a clerical career, from familial duties to pursuit of a poetical career. Normally a graduate of Milton's social status would have proceeded to further study at a college (often the same one), sometimes leading to a divinity degree, or at one of the Inns of Court, sometimes leading to a law degree, or to a sojourn abroad, roughly for about a year. Milton's actions in 1632 to 1638 encompass all these courses in a way, since he retired to his father's home for study, considered removal to one of the Inns of Court in November 1637, and traveled on the Continent from around April 1638 through August 1639.

From July 1632 through around the middle of 1635 Milton lived with his parents at their home in Hammersmith. At this time he wrote *Arc* and *Mask*,

and perhaps other poems. The last two works indicate Milton's acquaintance with the Bridgewater (or Egerton) family, probably through their music teacher, Henry Lawes, who wrote the music for both works and took part in them. In 1635 the Miltons moved to Horton, Bucks, and here Milton resided until he left for the Continent. He worked through his studies chronologically and geographically so that by November 1637 he had reached the thirteenth century and had begun an investigation of independent Italian city-states. The Horton period, which was once thought to date from 1632 through 1638, saw the death of Milton's mother on April 3, 1637, a culmination in the soul-searching *Lyc* in November 1637, and finally a move to independency by traveling to the Continent. What other poems were written during the Hammersmith-Horton studious retirement and their exact order are debated. *TM,* Milton's poetic workbook, was begun during the period (although a suggestion that it may have been begun before Milton's graduation is still sometimes heard), but specifically when is uncertain. Usually proposed has been 1632 or 1633, on the basis of the redating of *Arc,* which begins the notebook, and on the omission of *L'Al* and *IlP,* generally accepted as 1631. The dating of a letter to an unknown friend, which includes a copy of *Sonn 7,* is likewise pertinent. The recent dating of *Arc* in May 1634 nullifies some of the arguments for an early date. On the other hand, one suggestion dates the manuscript from around autumn 1637 and accordingly raises questions concerning the dates of the letter and such poems as the three English odes *(Time, Circ,* and *Sol Mus).* Milton's rejection of a clerical life and acceptance of a poetical career is significant for which dating is preferred. A question that all of this raises is, Does *TM* reflect work contemporary with the original composition of the poems it records or does it reflect later recording for revision and for a single repository of poems of a given period? (Of the poems entered earliest, only *SolMus* is not a transcription from some earlier copy.)

During this studious retirement (1632–1638) Milton also began his extant *CB,* which records ideas and points of view from his reading and which seems to aim at preservation of such ideas for future use in his own writing. The date at which Milton began to keep this miscellany is likewise uncertain: the usual date has been around 1635 with suggestions before that time and even during his university days and after that time in autumn 1637 on the basis of career decision. A few entries have been dated on the basis of position on the page and handwriting as 1635–1637? and many others as 1637?–1638? or, of course, later, even after Milton became totally blind. The date of *AdP* has likewise been placed anywhere from 1631 through March 1638 on the basis of the answers to the preceding question about Milton's biography. By March 1638 Milton's publications were only *Shak* in the Shakespeare Second Folio (1632) and *Mask* in 1637 or early 1638, with *Lyc* following sometime in 1638 (and whatever was meant in a letter to Alexander Gill, Jr., concerning "printed" ghost-written material).

Sometime by the beginning of April Milton had decided to travel to the

Continent and spoke of his trip with Sir Henry Wotton. The Italian journey, as it is called, concentrated on stays in Florence, Rome, Naples, and Venice, although other Italian areas were visited as were France (particularly Paris) and Switzerland (particularly Geneva). The period was to be one of the most important in Milton's biography because of the encouragement it yielded for a poetic career, because of the friends met and discussions held, and because of his immediate contact with the culture of Italy. Several Latin poems were also composed during this trip. Milton seems to have returned to England in August 1639. During his travels his good friend Charles Diodati had died and perhaps his sister Anne (Phillips) Agar. Instead of returning to his father's home, where his brother Christopher and his family had been residing from around the end of 1637, he took lodgings in London, where he began schoolteaching with his sister Anne's sons, Edward and John Phillips, as his first pupils. John Phillips came to live with him in 1639 and Edward sometime later. Edward, the older, remained until around 1647 and visited periodically thereafter, remaining relatively close to his uncle. John remained until his majority in 1652, but thereafter appears to have had little contact with his uncle. Both served as amanuenses to Milton. Other pupils were added as day students through around 1647, although there were brief periods of tutoring of a few boys after that date as well. The nature of Milton's "private academy" can be inferred from *Educ* and Edward Phillip's *Life* of his uncle.

In 1642, perhaps in May, Milton married Mary Powell of Forest Hill, Oxon; much uncertainty surrounds the date and circumstances of the marriage, but at least it is evident that she was much younger than he (sixteen and thirty-three respectively) and that she was expected to serve as a kind of step-mother to the Phillips boys, aged twelve and eleven. Within a few months, Mary had returned to her parents' home and was not to return until the middle of 1645, the Civil War perhaps contributing to the delay. In the meantime Milton's father had moved in with him in April 1643 and his eyesight began to fail noticeably around autumn 1644. Mary and John's first child, Anne, who was retarded (?) or spastic (?), was born on July 29, 1646, and their second child, Mary, on October 25, 1648. Milton's in-laws moved in with him in 1645 and stayed through autumn 1647, and his father died probably on March 13, 1647. Domestically, therefore, Milton's life in the 1640s involved a series of changes and adjustments, difficulties and resolutions, and a not entirely stable household.

From autumn 1639 through the end of 1648 Milton continued his personal studies, making the majority of entries in *CB*, for example, and engaging in various prose and poetic writings. His private studies, though interrupted by public controversy, seem to have aimed at the production of a significant tragedy on one of several themes, the most detailed treatment and greatest amount of work being given to what became *PL*. Some minor poems were composed in these years, including his tribute to Diodati, *EpDam* (1639), *Sonn* 8–15, and *Rous*. The first edition of the minor poems in 1645 may owe something to Milton's annoyance with public reaction to his prose tracts and

may represent a different kind of activity in poetry rather than prose, which was more firmly resumed from 1645 through 1648. The contention that the two major poems published in 1671 may have been begun during this period is accepted by some scholars but rejected by most.

Into Milton's private life, studies, and poetic writings were thrust two groups of controversial tracts as well as his two most popular prose pieces. The first group—those five tracts dealing with the question of an episcopal system within the English Church, as fostered by Archbishop William Laud and championed by Bishop Joseph Hall—emerged in early 1641 and continued to engage Milton through April 1642. Possibly Milton was brought into the pamphlet war by Thomas Young and possibly his debut was "A Postscript" added to Smectymnuus's *An Answer to a Booke entituled, An Humble Remonstrance* (March 1641). It is conjectured also that the friend to whom Milton's first acknowledged effort in the controversy, *Ref* (May 1641), was addressed was Young. *PrelE* (June–July?) and *Animad* (July) followed swiftly, and then *RCG* (January ? 1642) and *Apol* (April 1642). Milton's arguments for the abolition of episcopacy, and in effect the establishment of presbytery, are historical, logical, and confutational of episcopacy's adherents. He is both vituperative against his opponents and somewhat confessional of his own life and hopes. The second group of controversial tracts, four (in a sense, five) dealing with advocacy of divorce, appeared from August 1643 through March 1645. Like the antiprelatical tracts, these argue their thesis through historical awareness as well as biblical interpretation, through logic, confutation, and in one case, vituperation. The divorce tracts are *DDD* (the second edition of 1644 so greatly expanding the first as to constitute a second tract), *Bucer, Tetra* and *Colas.* Neither group of writings seems to have had more than ephemeral impact and reaction, and the latter group placed a notorious reputation upon Milton as a "divorcer" or "fornicator." The two prose works of this period lying outside either group are *Educ* (June 1644) and *Areop* (November 1644). Neither seems to have created much stir in its own time, but both became significant by the end of the century, a significance that continues to the present day despite educational reforms and permissive attitudes toward censorship. Though published later, a few other prose works were written or begun during the 1640s: *Accedence Commenc't Grammar* (1669), *Brit* (1670), *Logic* (1672), *CharLP* (1681), *Mosc* (1682), and perhaps *CD* (1825).

In January 1649, during the trial of Charles I, Milton wrote his first anti-monarchical tract, one of his most philosophically important, *Tenure*. It aided in bringing him to the attention of the new government then being formed, and on March 15, 1649, he became Secretary for Foreign Tongues to the Council of State. He continued in a secretarial position until at least October 22, 1659, when a salary payment is recorded. Six months later the Restoration was to take place and Milton found himself in a precarious situation because of his work for the Cromwellian government. In 1650 he had lost much of the sight in his left eye and was totally blind by February 1652. His illness and reduced proficiency

brought him assistance in his office and during the later years of his tenure he was really a "Latin Secretary," the popular though not entirely accurate title by which many referred to him throughout his years of service. As Latin Secretary he was reduced to the rather perfunctory duty of translation of documents into or out of Latin, without leeway for originality and without other responsibilities or commissions he had enjoyed in the earlier years of the republic. Among such commissions were the charge to make clear the late king's and the Earl of Ormond's duplicity in the *Articles of Peace* (May 1649) and to refute the popular sentiment for the late king as martyr, raised by *Eikon Basilike. Eikon* (October ? 1649) became one of the two works detrimental to Milton's reputation in later years as a regicide and revolutionary. Another commission was to answer Salmasius's *Defensio regia pro Carolo I* (which appeared in England in November ? 1649), and of all Milton's works, prose or poetic, it was *1Def* (February 1651), which was best known in his day, most reprinted and read, and most notorious. *Eikon* and *1Def* were publicly banned and burned in France and, after the Restoration, in England, and they called forth the most numerous counterarguments of all the tracts. *1Def* was additionally the subject of three German dissertations within a few years' time. The controversy that developed out of Milton's work brought forth *Responsio Ad Apologiam Anonymi* (1651) from his nephew John Phillips, with his assistance in answer to John Rowland's *Pro Rege et Populo Anglicano Apologia;* Milton's *2Def* (May 1654) against Pierre du Moulin's *Regii Sanguinis Clamor ad Coelum;* and his *3Def* (August 1655), which opposed Alexander More's statements in *Fides Publica* and *Supplementum.* All of these works, in Latin to reach a continental audience, defend the Commonwealth or attempt to refute monarchic stands, and, like other of Milton's tracts, they often become vituperative and biographically personal.

Concluding Milton's attention to public controversy and life are a series of arguments against the Restoration or attempting to alter the monarchic settlement that was inevitably upon England in 1659–60: *CivP* (February 1659), *Hire* (August), *A Letter to a Friend, Concerning the Ruptures of the Commonwealth* (October 20; published in 1698), "Proposalls of certaine expedients for the preventing of a civill war now feard, & the settling of a firme government" (autumn; published 1938), *Way* (March 1660 and April 1660), *PresM* (March ?; published 1698), and *BN* (April). In spite of some full rebuttals, these tracts had no effect in deflecting the Restoration or influencing its form and settlement. The confusion of 1660 with its change of governments, punishment of parliamentarian leaders, and acts to propagandize the people saw Milton at first sought for punishment and in hiding, passed over by the Act of Oblivion (August 29), finally apprehended, perhaps on out-of-date orders, and imprisoned from around October through December 15. Milton's release would seem to have been effected by various friends, including Sir William Davenant and Andrew Marvell, upon payment of a fine. There is little to wonder at Milton's retirement from public life from 1661 until his death.

During the 1650s Milton's personal life was beset by illness and death, and his

personal studies and writing had but spasmodic attention. Milton's eyesight continued to fail during 1649–February 1652, when he became totally blind. Accompanying the troubles with his eyes was frequent general illness. His only son, John, was born on March 16, 1651, but was dead by June 16, 1652. His wife Mary gave birth to their fourth child, Deborah, on May 5, and died a few days later. On November 12, 1656, he married as his second wife Katherine Woodcock. She gave birth to a daughter Katherine on October 19, 1657, but both were soon dead—Milton's wife on February 3, 1658, his daughter on March 17, 1658. Understandably, the period of 1652–53 saw Milton recuperating from his losses and his ill health, and during this time, perhaps somewhat also through 1654 and 1655, he may have returned to personal studies and writing, though not exclusively. If so, there is no certainty as to what he was working on; suggestions have included a second edition of the minor poems, *PL, SA, PR*, and *CD*. From 1655 through 1658 he more certainly was working on such projects, and *PL* and *CD* must have received most attention, if not all. The remaining minor poems were composed between 1652 and 1658 (?)—*Sonn* 16–23 and *Ps* 1–8.

The last fourteen years of Milton's life were undoubtedly devoted to his writing, whether completion or revision of previously started works, or new compositions, or publication (some of which publication has already been noted). *PL* was completed by 1665 (published 1667) and revised around 1674, when the second edition appeared. *PR* and *SA* were composed, or completed, or revised for publication in 1671 (various theories have been proposed for the dates of composition). *Brit* was completed or readied for publication in 1670. *TR* (May ? 1673) became Milton's last original work published in his lifetime, for *A Declaration, or Letters Patents* (July ? 1674) is a translation. Moves were made to publish a second edition of the minor poems and *Educ* in November ? 1673; the State Papers, which did not appear, however, until 1676 in Amsterdam; and *Epistol*, which were published in May 1674 with seven college prolusions. Publication of *CD*, composed apparently around 1655–1660 and showing some revision thereafter, may have been contemplated, although it was not printed until 1825.

While Milton had employed scribes as early as 1637 and his nephews may have served in that capacity from 1642 onward, it was during his governmental employment and after his reduced eyesight that Milton worked through various amanuenses. Sometimes scribes were specially hired, sometimes they were friends. His scribes or servants, and his daughters Mary and Deborah, read to him; his daughters may also have written down notes and the like for him, but they did not handle full-scale scribal jobs. He taught a bit, for example, Thomas Ellwood, and such students might do a scribal chore now and then. He seems to have established a routine of work, Bible reading, general reading, and dictation in his later years. At times in the 1650s and less often in the 1660s and 70s he was visited by foreign dignitaries or by such well-known people as Marvell and John Dryden, and by close friends like Dr. Nathan Paget. The one

interruption from these years in London came during the visitation of the plague and subsequent fire in 1665–1666. Milton and his family escaped London from around June 1665 to around February 1666 through the help of Ellwood, who found a small house for him at Chalfont St. Giles, Bucks, the only Milton "residence" still standing.

Milton's household in 1661 consisted of his three daughters and whatever servants he was able to afford, but at least a housekeeper-governess was required. On February 24, 1663, he married Elizabeth Minshull, whom he met through her kinsman Dr. Paget. Stories of the relationship between the step-daughters and step-mother conflict, and the daughters' attitude toward their father are variously reported. It would seem, however, that the girls were not happy under their much-older father's strictness and demands, and they may simply have wished to assert themselves as individuals and as independent. Such attitudes, plus the not-uncommon frictions between step-relatives, may have caused upsets in the household during the 1660s. All three daughters seem to have left on their own before 1669 and not to have visited thereafter (at least not often). Most of the reports of family difficulties are given in the depositions concerned with Milton's nuncupative will. Deborah, though, in interviews during the eighteenth century, seems to have spoken well of her father; and her daughter, Elizabeth Foster, gives no indication of serious friction between father and daughter. We have no real evidence of other relatives' attitudes toward Milton or their frequency of visits, relatives like Thomas Agar, his brother-in-law, or Richard Powell, another brother-in-law, or his brother Christopher's children. Christopher did visit at times, and despite their political differences, they seem to have been on good terms.

In his last years Milton had recurrent attacks of gout, and in 1674, when his brother Christopher was visiting him, he expressed his wishes for the disposal of his possessions in case of his death. This so-called nuncupative will was examined in the Prerogative Court of Canterbury a month after Milton's death, but it was not probated. A settlement was reached leaving £100 to each of the daughters (plus some items of furniture and the like to Deborah) and the remainder of the estate to Elizabeth.

Milton died on Sunday, November 8, 1674, of the gout, and was buried on Thursday, November 12 in St. Giles, Cripplegate. Death was probably caused by heart failure due to illness, such as the gout, rather than by gout directly. The death date is an inference from 1) the record of burial and 2) the statement of his servant Elizabeth Fisher, made on December 15, that he had died on a Sunday about a month before. He apparently expired in his sleep sometime between retiring on Sunday and being found dead the next morning. [JTS]

ANOTHER ON THE SAME. The second of Milton's poems on the death of Thomas Hobson appeared in both the 1645 and 1673 editions of his poetry, in *Wit Restor'd*, in two editions of a similar collection, *A Banquet of Jests* (1640; 1657), and in some non-Miltonic manuscripts. The text in Milton's editions of

his *Poems* differs in a number of ways from the other copies of the poem, a fact that led W. R. Parker to conclude that these copies "probably reflect . . . a version of the poem earlier than the text which Milton printed. . . ." If this is so, it is significant in that it opens up the possibility that Milton did "last-minute revision of other poems in 1645" (*Milton*, 2:766).

Like the first of Milton's Hobson poems, it is written in rhyming couplets of iambic pentameter. Thirty-four lines long, it suggests, as does the first, that enforced idleness was the cause of Hobson's death; but it does so in a much wittier way, relying heavily upon pun, paradox, and wordplay. The wit, unfortunately, has not aged well. Lines such as "Too long vacation hastned on his term" are still faintly amusing, but the poem on the whole is a dated specimen of topical verse. Still, judging from the number of times that it appeared, it must have appealed to Milton's contemporaries; and it is pleasant to note that Milton could succeed, when he chose, in the writing of such verse. [ERG]

ARCADES. First published in 1645, this entertainment by Milton, which appears in *TM*, is a lyrical, 109-line theatrical work consisting of a song, then a single speech in pentameter couplets, and finally two more songs. The slight invention and incidental action of the entertainment concerns nymphs and shepherds of Arcady who, led by the "Genius of the Wood," approach and pay homage to an enthroned rural queen. Designed for outdoor performance on the grounds of Countess Alice Spencer's country estate in Middlesex. *Arc* is described in the 1645 edition as "Part of an Entertainment presented to the Countess Dowager of *Derby* at *Harefield,* by some Noble persons of her Family, who appear on the Scene in pastoral habit, moving toward the seat of State. . . ." Although the rest of the entertainment, whether written by Milton or another author, has been lost, the surviving work is complete in itself and has a clearly defined structure.

In the opening song the nymphs and shepherds express excitement and surprise as they make a sudden discovery of the rural queen on her "shining throne":

> This this is she
> To whom our vows and wishes bend,
> Heer our solemn search hath end.
>
> (5–7)

The main action of the entertainment is revealed in the central, 58-line speech by the Genius of the Wood, who appears before the nymphs and shepherds, halts their advance toward the seated Lady, and explains that he serves the queen by tending the plants in her domain. He then offers to conduct the noble performers to the rural queen, thus introducing the climactic presentation segment of the entertainment:

> I will assay, her worth to celebrate,
> And so attend ye toward her glittering state;
> Where ye may all that are of noble stemm
> Approach, and kiss her sacred vestures hemm.
>
> (80–83)

As the nymphs and shepherds move forward to kiss the garments of the rural queen, the Genius sings a presentation song:

> O'er the smooth enameld green
> Where no print of step hath been,
>   Follow me as I sing.
>
> (84–86)

Pastoral dances by the nymphs and shepherds evidently followed, for the final song by the Genius begins with the words "Nymphs and Shepherds dance no more" (96). The Genius concludes the performance by inviting his charges to remain on this "better soyl" (101) in a region where "greater grace" may be enjoyed:

> Here ye shall have greater grace,
> To serve the Lady of this place.
> Though *Syrinx* your *Pans* Mistres were,
> Yet *Syrinx* well might wait on her.
>   Such a rural Queen
> All *Arcadia* hath not seen.
>
> (104–9)

Internal references in the text, together with the limited external evidence available, suggest that *Arc* was performed after dark on the elm-lined green leading to the entrance of Harefield House, probably on May 3, 1634, in celebration of the Countess's seventy-fifth birthday. She was a distant relative of the poet Edmund Spenser. She would have played the rural queen simply by occupying a commanding position on the chair of state. The identities of the persons who approached her across the "smooth enameld green" are unknown, but included among the "noble persons of her family" were her stepson, John Egerton, Earl of Bridgewater, and his children, three of whom were later to appear in *Mask*. The court musician Henry Lawes, music teacher to the Egerton family and a collaborator with Milton on *Mask*, would have been well suited to the role of the Genius of the Wood; however, proof that he performed in the entertainment is lacking.

Scholars and critics have offered general praise of Milton's light and gracious creation; yet, in comparison with the poet's other writings, relatively few complexities in theme, imagery, symbolism, and thought have been uncovered.

Tension has been noted in the work between the forces of good and evil. The nymphs and shepherds observe that Envy can be found in the land undoing the praise of the rural queen offered by Fame (8–13), and the virtuous Genius must work to protect plants in the queen's wood from various "harms": the attacks of "noisom winds," "blasting vapours," and the "hurtfull Worm" (49–53). Moreover, Platonic elements are present in a statement by the Genius about the role of the Fates and the harmonious music of the spheres (61–73).

The few close critical readings available tend to focus upon what may be symbolized by the discovery of the rural queen. Cleanth Brooks and John Edward Hardy claim that the queen represents the spirit of English pastoral poetry. In their view the nymphs and shepherds are poets who are coming from Greece to England to create a new and better form of pastoral verse. J. M. Wallace, arguing that the symbolism of the work can be found in the dramatic event and in the social fame of the persons addressed, insists that the Countess in life was eulogized by poets for her wisdom. Sapience is then said to be the main theme of the work. J. G. Demaray centers attention upon traditional elements in Milton's entertainment, pointing out how the pagan disguising reflects an actual social event.

Entertainments such as *Arc* were presented in various indoor and outdoor locations and were given structure and content to accord with the requirements of a particular occasion: a banquet, visit, progress, or entrance into a city. Unlike the more elaborately staged court masques, these less ambitious works did not serve as an introduction to an indoor masked ball in which the audience participated. Entertainments, as a form of social art, were created with the aim of complimenting one or more noble guests through dialogue, song, and sometimes dance. The guests, and at times the aristocratic performers as well, were often depicted in a double-focus vision as figures whose influence brings harmony both to the pagan realm of the disguising and to the real social world. Thus passages in Milton's work deftly hint that the nymphs, shepherds, and rural queen, beneath their pagan trappings, are important members of an existing social establishment.

Arc in a general way resembles other entertainments, though no single work has been cited as its primary source. Lines praising Queen Anne in Ben Jonson's "An Entertainment at Althorpe" (1603) appear to be echoed in the opening song of Milton's work; character-types in *Arc* are comparable to those in Thomas Campion's "The Entertainment Given by Lord Knowles" (1613) and Ben Jonson's "The Entertainment at Highgate" (1604); and Milton's work was no doubt staged in a manner similar to that of the anonymous "The Entertainment of Queen Elizabeth at Harefield" (1602). [JGD]

AT A SOLEMN MUSICK. This 28-line poem appeared in both the 1645 and 1673 editions of Milton's poems. Three and a half drafts of it appear in *TM*, the indications being that Milton composed it there shortly after commencing the

manuscript itself. Its date of composition therefore depends upon when Milton began the manuscript, a date traditionally assigned to the early 1630s but more recently to 1637.

The three-and-a-half drafts tell us much about Milton's habits of composition. The first contains the essential outlines of the last, suggesting that Milton had the poem blocked out in his mind before ever setting it down on paper. Having blocked out the poem, he then subjected it to intense line-by-line criticism. P. L. Heyworth demonstrates that Milton's revisions show him keenly aware of euphony and of decorum, trying to make each phrase sound right while tailoring it to enhance the effect of dignity that he wanted the entire poem to achieve. Euphony, for example, dictated his changing the phrase, "sacred Psalmes / singing," which appears in the first and second drafts, to "holie Psalmes singing" in the second and succeeding drafts in order to avoid excessive alliteration, while decorum led him to omit the description in the first draft of "youthf[ul cher]ubim as "sweet-winged squires" from subsequent ones, "squires" seeming perhaps too earthbound for heavenly creatures. Having subjected each line to careful scrutiny, Milton once again considered the poem as a whole, excising a number of lines and significantly expanding the last part (lines 19–25 in the final draft) in order to strengthen the firm and subtle structure of the poem's final version.

In its final version, the poem divides into three parts. In lines 1–16, the poet hears solemn music, a blending of voice and verse. It is worth noting that "solemn" in the seventeenth century possessed none of the somber overtones it now has. Rather, it suggested festivity, albeit of a stately and formal nature, so that it is entirely appropriate that this music present to the poet's "high-rais'd phantasie" the heavenly music made when the angelic spirits join in song with the souls of the faithful "before the saphire-colour'd throne." In lines 17–24, the poet hopes that we may join in that music as we were able to do before sin destroyed the universal harmony of which we were once a part. In lines 25–28, he concludes with a brief supplication that it be not long until we renew that song, God uniting us to his celestial consort "To live with him, and sing in endles morn of light."

Metrically, SolMus is a rather free imitation of the Italian madrigal form. Most of its lines are pentameter, although there are three seven-syllable lines and a concluding Alexandrine. The first four lines rhyme *a b a b*. Thereafter, the poem disposes itself into couplets with the exception of lines 9 and 15, which rhyme with each other. It divides into only two sentences; and these are by no means of equal length, the first two parts combining into a sentence of 24 lines and the second into one of only 4 lines. The ingenuity with which the syntax is handled in the first sentence is remarkable, an early example of "the sense variously drawn out from one Verse into another" that was to be the metrical strategy employed by Milton to such marvelous effect in *PL*.

Long and complex traditions lie behind the ideas in the poem. That music

could induce ecstasy, that it had beneficent effects upon its auditors, that the world itself was constructed on musical lines—these ideas, which are as old as the Pythagoreans and Plato, had been enriched by many centuries of repetition and commentary when they reached Milton. Because of his musical bent, they were especially appealing to him, and it is interesting to note their appearance in his other poems, although as always, Milton is selective in utilizing tradition. Significantly, for example, the "solemn music" is not music alone, but a blending of music and poetry. The emphasis on the closeness of the arts is traditional, but it is also characteristically Miltonic. He referred to them in *AdP* as "arts of one blood and kindred studies" and especially praised his friend Henry Lawes for teaching English music how to fit itself to the sense and rhythm of the lyrics for which he wrote.

In keeping with the practices of his age, Milton adorned his poem with materials drawn from classical and pagan literature. The sirens whose powers he invokes in the opening lines, for example, derive from figures who appear in the *Odyssey* and in the *Argonautica* of Apollonius of Rhodes. Their ability to pierce "dead things with inbreath'd sense" suggests other classical legends— that of Orpheus, whose beautiful music attracted trees and rocks to him, and that of Amphion, whose music caused stones to move and build themselves into the walls of Thebes. Such materials, however, have been Christianized and coexist easily with the details of the heavenly music drawn from the Book of Ezekiel and from the Book of Revelation. [ERG]

AT A VACATION EXERCISE IN THE COLLEGE. First published in the 1673 *Poems* with a note indicating composition at age nineteen, *Vac* should be read in conjuction with Milton's *Prol* 6, of which it was a part. The prolusion was written to be delivered at the Vacation Exercise of July 2, 1628, which opened the long summer holiday. Most of our knowledge of the Exercise derives from Milton's performance. From it we learn that the Exercise was given "according to custom, with almost all of the young men of the institution assembled" and that it was "the almost annual observance of a very old custom." The master of ceremonies, in this case Milton, was known as "Father," while the other participants in the program were introduced as his "sons."

The portions of Milton's performance that have survived divide into three sections: (1) a Latin oration on the subject "That sometimes sportive exercises are not prejudicial to philosophic studies"; (2) a more informal address, still in Latin, filled with bawdy, topical humor; (3) a set of English verses. At the conclusion of the verses, a note observes that *"The rest was Prose"*; but whatever this may have been—perhaps Milton's introduction of his other "sons," perhaps some concluding remarks—it has been lost. Milton's switch from Latin prose to English poetry must have been surprising to his audience, for it was against university statutes. His rhetorical excuse, Parker notes,

"would be a preamble to introducing his 'sons' " (*Milton*, p. 45). More basic may have been a well-founded desire to show what he could do in English verse as opposed to Latin prose.

Written in couplets, the verse reveals a variety of influences—Jonson, Spenser, and Drayton; but it is not merely derivative. In the lines where Milton lists possible epic subjects, he speaks—perhaps for the first time—with his own unique accent. His list of epic subjects rounds out a number of interesting comments on poetry and language. Having stated that he has "packt the worst" into the Latin portions of his address, he admonishes the English language to bring from its wardrobe its "chiefest treasure":

> Not those new fangled toys, and triming slight
> Which takes our late fantasticks with delight.

The identity of these "late fantasticks" is debatable. W. J. Harvey has suggested that the fad indicated is the "cult of 'strong lines' " associated with the Metaphysicals (*Notes and Queries* 202:524). Perhaps, however, we should not look so far afield for an identification. Having noted that "the midsummer frolic for which these verses were written consisted of numerous skits and recitals," Shawcross tentatively suggests that "Milton's fellow performers were the 'late fantasticks' " (*The Complete English Poetry of John Milton* [1963], p. 33). Milton, at any rate, wished to give his audience more. For his "fair Assembly's ears," he wished to clothe his "naked thoughts" in the "richest Robes" that English could offer, but he frankly admitted that he would rather use English for "some graver subject." He then listed some topics that he regarded as appropriate for serious English poetry. The list is of great interest for Milton's future poetic ambitions, although one need not assume that Milton at this point was dedicating himself to epic poetry. At nineteen, he had a disposition toward the serious that the years were to confirm, but for the present he was content merely to glance at suitably epic subjects, then to proceed to the introduction of his "sons."

For the occasion, Milton had assumed the role of *Ens*, the Aristotelian principle of Absolute Being. His eldest son was Substance; his other sons, the accidents of Substance: Quantity, Quality, Relation, Place, Time, Posture, Possession, Action, and Passion. Milton's humor is topical throughout, its topicality being divisible into two kinds: (1) that devoted to the scholastic logic so familiar to his audience; (2) that devoted to the persons taking part in the celebration. An example of the first kind is his professing fear that Substance, according to a prophecy, "Shall subject be to many an Accident." This is amusing because in scholastic logic, Substance could be known only through its "accidents." An example of the second is his using the name of the boy who played Relation, Rivers, as the excuse for his working in a Spenserian catalogue of English rivers. Perhaps another example of this kind of humor is his telling Substance that "O'er all his Brethren he shall Reign as King," for it may be that

Edward King, whom Milton later commemorated in *Lyc*, took the part of Substance. [ERG]

EPITAPH ON THE MARCHIONESS OF WINCHESTER, AN. This 74-line poem appeared in both the 1645 and 1673 editions of Milton's poems. A seventeenth-century manuscript in the British Museum (Sloane MS 1446) probably represents an earlier version, which Milton revised for publication.

The occasion of the poem was the death on April 15, 1631, of Jane Paulet, the Marchioness of Winchester. Only twenty-three at the time of her death, she was noted for her loveliness and charm. When far advanced in pregnancy, she had an abscess on her cheek lanced and died of the infection, though not before she had borne a dead son. Since the Chancellor of Cambridge University was a kinsman of hers, it seemed likely that a memorial volume would be forthcoming, and Milton may have written his poem in anticipation of that volume, though if it was produced, it has subsequently disappeared without a trace. Poems on the Marchioness's death by Ben Jonson, William Davenant, and others also survive.

The opening line of Milton's poem—"This rich Marble doth enterr"—calls attention to the genre to which he assigned it, for the epitaph is a poem suitable for inscription upon a tombstone. Though longer and more elaborate than most epitaphs, *EpWin* retains the characteristics of the genre in that it identifies its subject, describes her station in life, and gives her age. In a larger sense, Milton's work belongs to the tradition of funerary poetry that was so popular in the seventeenth century. Milton himself had contributed to the tradition with a number of poems ranging from conventional Latin commemorations of university dignitaries to the English verses on the death of his niece, Anne Phillips.

EpWin represents a distinct advance over these earlier performances, but he continued to adorn his poetry with such classical and biblical allusions as reflect the background he shared with other well-educated men of his day. Beyond this, *EpWin* reveals an expanding literary awareness and sophistication in the use of sources. Lines 61–70, for example, suggest a Dantean influence. As Dante in his *Paradiso* had placed Beatrice and Rachel, both mothers who died in childbirth, together in the third rank of the celestial rose, so Milton in his work linked the Marchioness and Rachel together "Far within the boosom bright/Of blazing Majesty and Light. . . ." These lines do far more, however, than suggest that Milton had been reading Dante. The poem divides into two definitely contrasted parts. In the first forty-six lines, the Marchioness is referred to in the third person, and the pathos of her early death is emphasized; thereafter, she is directly addressed, and consolation is derived from her present happy state. The poem moves from past to present and, not surprisingly, from dark to light. Thus the lines quoted above take their place as a pendant to the earlier description of the Marchioness housed "with darkness, and with death."

Because *EpWin*, *L'Al*, and *IlP* are all written in octo- and heptasyllabic couplets (a meter sometimes employed by Ben Jonson), the three poems have

often been considered to constitute one distinct phase in Milton's metrical development. However, Michael Moloney (*Modern Language Notes* 72: 174–78) has shown that the couplets in *EpWin* differ from those in the companion poems in their greater reliance upon monosyllables and in their more heavily emphasized caesuras. In this, they reflect the influence of Jonson. Octo- and heptasyllabic couplets had more traditionally been used in English literature to create light effects, but Jonson, whose accomplishments in funerary poetry were considerable, had demonstrated that they could achieve a dignity commensurate with serious subjects. In *EpWin*, Milton followed his example with some success, creating couplets that are slow and stately in feeling. [ERG]

HORACE, THE FIFTH ODE OF. Milton's sixteen-line translation from Horace's first book of odes first appeared in *Poems, &c. upon Several Occasions* in 1673. Scholars disagree as to its date of composition with suggestions ranging between Milton's grammar-school period to after 1648. In his biography of Milton, William Riley Parker assigned it, albeit tentatively, to 1629 on the ground that its subject matter of unrequited love harmonized with other poems that Milton was writing at that time (*Milton*, 2:745–46). More convincing is John Shawcross's attempt at dating. The poem's omission from the 1645 edition of Milton's works; its Latin text, which does not seem to have appeared before 1636; and especially its place in the order of the poems in the 1673 edition—all suggest to Shawcross late composition, probably around 1646–1648 (*Studies in English Literature* 3:77–84). Parker objected to these dates on the ground that he could not imagine "the mature Milton, in his first years of parenthood, fascinated by Pyrrha and her fatal charms. If the translation was done by a man who in 1648 . . . was translating psalms for spiritual consolation, then perhaps some of the continental Miltonians have been right in considering him a good subject for psychoanalysis" (*Milton*, p. 745). Shawcross's explanation, however—that the poem represents the same kind of metrical rendering that Milton was doing in those translations of the psalms—is not unreasonable (p. 81). Quite simply, Milton may have undertaken the translation because of the technical problems involved rather than because of the subject matter of youthful love.

The poem examines the plight of a youth enamored of the lovely Pyrrha and unaware—as is the older, more experienced author—of the fickle nature of women and the stormy course of love. Its nature as a translation and the technical problems that Milton faced are indicated by the headnote that he appended to it: "*Rendered almost word for word without Rhyme according to the Latin Measure, as near as the Language will permit.*" He attempted, in other words, the extremely difficult task of writing English verse while using the rules of Latin prosody; and to a remarkable degree he succeeded, although in places he sacrificed sense to sound.

Critics in general have given the ode high praise. "Remarkably ingenious," "almost unbelievable perfection," "more Horatian . . . than Horace him-

self"—such phrases are representative of the critical reaction. Parker, on the other hand, considered it "a much overpraised poem" that "fails to catch the tone of the original and, worse, is poor poetry in its own right" (*Milton,* p. 57). On the contrary, others have recognized it as a rare example of a successful unrhymed lyric in English, which a number of poets imitated in the following century, the most successful being William Collins's *Ode to Evening.* David P. Harding examines both its fidelity as a translation and its foreshadowing of the metrical strategies of *PL.* In the ebb and flow of its verse, in its deliberate blurring of syntactical relationships, Harding finds clearly revealed "the degree of classical influence on Milton's mature style" (*The Club of Hercules* [1962], p. 128). [ERG]

L'ALLEGRO AND IL PENSEROSO. Milton's companion poems do not appear in *TM.* They were printed, undated, in both the 1645 and 1673 editions of *Poems,* where they follow the two short pieces on the death of Hobson the University Carrier (died January 1, 1631). Until our own time, the composition of *L'Al* and *IlP* was placed early in the so-called Horton period, 1632–1638 (actually, from 1632 to 1635 Milton was in residence at Hammersmith), on the basis of the many references to nature and descriptions of country scenery that were assumed to derive from direct observation. But it is now customary to date them in 1631 (see Tillyard, *The Miltonic Setting* [1938], pp. 1–28, which reprints views of the dating first set forth in 1932), because they seem intended for a university audience and bear close resemblance to the mood and rhythms of Milton's graceful Jonsonian performances in *May,* the Hobson poems, and *EpWin.* Though opinion has generally settled upon Milton's last Cambridge summer of 1631, other dates, earlier and later, continue to be advanced. F. W. Bateson (*Seventeenth-Century News Letter* 7:10) and Harris Fletcher (*Intellectual Development of John Milton* [1961], 2:479ff.) argue for the late summer of 1629 on the basis of *El* 6, addressed to Diodati, where Milton is supposed to speak of some poems he wishes to show his friend. Both insist that *cicutis* (line 89) must be translated as *pastorals* and therefore refers to *L'Al* and *IlP* rather than to *Nat.* This argument poses its own difficulties—that we accept the companion poems as less mature productions of Milton's art than *Nat,* a position that requires one to believe that after the extraordinary variety and suppleness of the tetrameter couplets of *L'Al* and *IlP,* Milton moved to the heavier rhythms of *Nat.*

The differences between the 1645 and 1673 editions are few and minor, confined chiefly to accidentals of orthography and punctuation. The only substantial variant occurs in *L'Al,* at line 33, where 1673 prints "trip it as you go," and 1645 prints "trip it as ye go." In 1673, an obvious misprint in 1645 at line 57 of *IlP* ("Id her sweetest" for "In") is corrected.

Compared to Milton's other poems, *L'Al* and *IlP* would appear to offer few obstacles to appreciation and comprehension. Even Dr. Johnson, who usually found as much to censure as to admire in Milton and condemned *Lyc* so

roundly, could find nothing but cause for praise in these twin poems. And if influence is an accurate guide to literary reputation, they bore an impress upon the poetic vocabulary and imagery of the following century that was a measure of their high esteem. Indeed, their very success in appealing to eighteenth-century taste has been in our own time reason enough to raise questions about their poetic vitality, because Dr. Johnson's preference for the generalized image, to name only one issue, is exactly at odds with the romantic and post-romantic demand for concrete particularization. So despite the fact that they are probably the most accessible of Milton's poems for the modern reader, they have been subject to divergent analyses that, while not really undermining their critical reputation, have certainly shaken any final view as to the nature of their success.

If we begin with the primary consideration of genre, we find no such clearcut relation as with *Lyc* (pastoral elegy), *Mask*, *PL* (classical epic), *SA* (classical tragedy), or *PR* (brief epic) that can guide our expectations as to the meanings and effects that come out of a proper response to genre. While pastoral setting and imagery are evident, especially in *L'Al*, and a pastoral choice is suggested, neither poem exploits primarily some distinction between urban and rural, elevated or low modes of existence, nor do they focus in any central way upon pastoral figures or activities. The hindsight of literary history encourages us to view *L'Al* and *IlP* as important progenitors of the descriptive-reflective poetry of the eighteenth century. However, within the context of Milton's milieu none of the literary genres, as ordinarily defined, makes for a very exact fit. It is usual to talk about the companionate relationship of the two poems as defining their genre, shifting the question to rhetorical and intellectual substance. Mirth and Melancholy may function as ideas, as embodied ideals, as goals of existence, or as protagonists.

Tillyard has found in *Prol* 1—"Whether Day or Night is the More Excellent"—the pattern and the substance after which the poems were modeled. He assigns them to the medieval and academic tradition of debate, which gave rise to so many poems debating the relative excellence of action and contemplation, the body and the soul, et cetera. The relevance is evident to both demonstrative rhetoric (the rhetoric of praise, which magnifies its subject in an encomium or diminishes it in a diatribe) and to deliberative rhetoric (which seeks to persuade to wise and worthy choices of action and to dissuade from those lacking in wisdom and moral worth). Tillyard suggested in *The Miltonic Setting* that each poem opens with bombast and intentional burlesque in the dismissal of its opponent by offering a gross and defamatory caricature. Later critics have emphasized that both the negative portrayal of Melancholy in *L'Al* and the praise of it in *IlP* refer to well-established concepts: the dreaded disease "loathed Melancholy" and the "divinest Melancholy" identified with contemplation and the intellectual endeavors of genius. No concomitant polarities have been advanced for Mirth, which is seen in *L'Al* as the innocent spirit of delight and in *IlP* as pleasure judged to be empty and frivolous. The way we

read the 10-line openings of each poem, with their elaborate stanzaic pattern (a3, b5, b3, a5, c3, d5, d3, e5, e3, c5), setting them off from the tetrameter couplets which make up the body of each poem, is of crucial importance. But whether we see them as burlesque, as a witty pointing to the negative underside of Mirth and Melancholy, or as both, these openings do establish the patterns of parallel and contrast that organize the images and demand a simultaneous reading. While the body of each poem is a self-contained praise, a distinctly deliberative edge emerges when we compare actions and images associated with Mirth and Melancholy. The three major trends in interpretation correspond to how the rhetoric is perceived. For critics who see the poems as debate in the strict sense, *L'Al* and *IlP* offer mutually exclusive choices, or, at a more inward and subtle level, represent the tug-of-war in a mind attracted to both Mirth and Melancholy. For critics who see the rhetorical direction as primarily demonstrative, the respective praises of Mirth and Melancholy issue in either a complementary relation of equal "goods" or in a hierarchical ascent from a lesser good to a higher.

We do best, however, to leave these final questions in abeyance until we have explored the poems' intellectual and artistic substance. In recent years, critics have turned increasingly to intellectual history as a starting point, focusing especially upon Melancholy. As early as 1940 Lawrence Babb (*Studies in Philology* 37:257–73) attempted to clarify the differences between the Melancholy that is the subject of praise in *IlP* and the Melancholy exorcised at the opening of *L'Al*. The latter is the disease of Galenic tradition, an affliction associated with depression and madness. The former is the enviable condition of the intellectually superior person according to Aristotle.

As we turn to the poems themselves, we find that their structure cannot be considered apart from their images. From the outset we can see imagery supporting rhetorical strategy and preparing us for the figurative actions of Mirth and Melancholy. Each poem opens with a dismissal followed by an invocation. Out of this is generated first a parallel of "loathed Melancholy" to "vain deluding joyes," and then a double contrast between the positive and negative versions of each. The exorcism of Melancholy in *L'Al* is an anti-encomium or diatribe that attributes parentage, "homeland," and mental and physical traits that are all reasons for dispraise, and in which images of blackness and hell predominate. Melancholy is assigned *Cerberus* (the three-headed dog that stands at the doorway of hell) and "blackest midnight" as parents, a "*Stygian* Cave forlorn" as birthplace, and is urged to banish herself to some "uncouth cell" presided over by "brooding darkness" and the song of the "night-Raven." The horror of this disease is properly confined "under *Ebon* shades" and in "dark *Cimmerian* desert." In contrast, the inviting invocation to Melancholy in *IlP* transforms the images of darkness into something altogether appealing. Since in Platonic and Christian thought light is traditionally associated with virtue, knowledge, and truth, darkness with evil, ignorance, and falsehood, a special extenuation is required to make blackness the more suitable

symbol for wisdom. In hermetic tradition and in various kinds of occultism, however, the profoundest knowledge is assumed to be obscure and hidden from ordinary view. Darkness becomes a material appearance concealing the spiritual truth that is too bright for the carnal eye:

> But hail thou Goddes, sage and holy,
> Hail divinest Melancholy,
> Whose Saintly visage is too bright
> To hit the Sense of human sight;
> And therfore to our weaker view,
> Ore laid with black staid Wisdoms hue.
>
> (11–16)

And to counter the scandalous parentage cited in *L'Al*, Melancholy here is the daughter of "bright-hair'd *Vesta*" and "solitary *Saturn*." Likewise, the Mirth invoked in *L'Al* as the "Goddes fair and free," *Euphrosyne* is the daughter (along with her "two sister Graces," Aglaia and Thalia) of Bacchus and Venus, not the "brood of folly without father bred," that the devotee of Melancholy would banish to "Dwell in som idle brain, / And fancies fond with gaudy shapes possess."

The assigning of noble and praiseworthy forebears is followed by a description of the gait of each. Mirth is invited to "trip it as ye go / On the light fantastick toe"; Melancholy to "keep thy wonted state, / With eev'n step, and musing gate." As her chief companion Mirth has "The Mountain Nymph, sweet Liberty," while Melancholy brings the "Cherub Contemplation." The liberty associated with Mirth is freedom from care, all the sorrow-denying, blameless pleasures; contemplation is the characteristic activity and goal of divinest Melancholy. The images of both poems substantiate figurative universals valued as modes of absorbing play or study that enable us to reach beyond the limits of routine existence. Through Mirth one enters into a direct sensuous and aesthetic response to experience "that wrincled Care derides"—that liberates from everyday concerns. And divinest Melancholy pierces beyond the common light of every day into "secret shades" of intellectual and religious experience. Their different substances embody differing forms of ideally complete and self-sufficient *pleasure*, the term that Milton explicitly ascribes to the experiences of both poems. Whatever relation "finally" obtains between these ideals—the conundrum to which so much criticism has been addressed—one must first recognize that both Mirth and Melancholy are ideals. As such, both stand apart from the ordinary. So far from comprehending the entire range of possible human pursuit (the implicit assumption of much criticism), they represent two emphatically ideal choices, about which, as with all ideals, the prime questions are likely to be, "How can they be realized? Can they be sustained?"

The foregoing seems indispensable in considering the imagery of the poems.

It is highly relevant, for example, to the issue raised by T. S. Eliot, who complained in *Essays and Studies* (1936; p. 34), that Milton's generalized images lacked Shakespearean particularity, that in *L'Al* one does not see a particular milkmaid. The most persuasive answer to this charge is provided by Rosemond Tuve, who insists that the images "are not 'individuals,' unique sights seen by one man's eye, but particulars, irradiated by the 'general' which they signify" (*Images and Themes in Five Poems by Milton* [1957], p. 22). Moreover, as Miss Tuve also pointed out, "the unindividualized character of the images is matched in the time-structure of the poems." As Milton conveys a sense of realized ideality by not portraying single objects, so the scenes of the poems are not represented with dramatic and temporal particularity. *L'Al* does not follow the dawn-to-sunset pattern of a single day, *IlP* a night to morning pattern. Instead, the scenes are drawn from various days and follow no strict time sequence. The temporal references are typical and unspecified, rather than particular and immediate. Some details are observed, others participated in directly, while still others are speculatively proposed by the imagination as typical activities outside any given time. The temporal setting of the poems is an eternal present of "Oft" and "Som times" in which present and future moments are hardly differentiated, since the action does not consist of a particular series of narration. To approach the imagery and the temporal organization with this awareness is to become skeptical about interpretations that assume and impose a narrative order that progresses from a beginning, through fixed stages, to a final destination. This quality of the images and of the time scheme also contributes to the self-contained completeness of each poem. The universality for which they have been so admired is convincing exactly because the details that convey that universality are memorably concrete without being narrowly particularized.

After its introductions, *L'Al* continues with an idyllic pastoral scene that incorporates responses to nature, human society, and the arts of poetry and music. The song of the lark signals "From his watch-towre in the skies" the course of l'Allegro's many refined pleasures. Then follows the "lively din" of the more mundane and domestic cock. An earthy English rusticity and an idealized hellenic pastoralism are introduced and mingle throughout the poem. The images of domestic agriculture—the Plowman, the Milkmaid, the Mower, and "every Shepherd tell[ing] his tale"—combine a generalized, yet solid, fecundity with an elegance, each of which strongly ballasts and leavens the other. Before seeking out the parallels these or other images have in *IlP*, the reader should perceive the wide spectrum of feeling the imagery of *L'Al* compasses. The eye moves to compose a series of contrasted landscapes, turning from nature awesome and remote in the "barren brest" of mountains to nature familiar and amiable in "Meadows trim with Daisies pide." Leaving nature for the works of man, the eye again ranges from romantic towers and battlements that stir the imagination to the chimney of a nearby cottage in which modest human contentment dwells—Corydon and Thyrsis partake of their "savory

dinner," dressed by "the neat-handed *Phillis.*" The rich promise seen in the fields and in country labor is fulfilled in plentiful "Country Messes." Instantly the scene shifts out-of-doors again, as Phillis joins Thestylis, another country girl, "to bind the Sheaves," but there is no determinable, literal movement of l'Allegro, whether as actual observer or participant, or as imaginary viewer or actor, from one scene to another or from one role to another. Scenes, activities, and images beget each other in his mind and are no less vivid to his imagination than to his actual presence.

From pastoral occupations the scene shifts to the musical and social entertainments of "up-land Hamlets." The daylight hours of the "Sunshine Holyday" are given over to "Dancing in the Chequer'd shade," to song, and to play. The pleasures of the evening are "the Spicy Nut-brown Ale" and "stories told of many a feat," tales of *Faery Mab* drawn from the native folklore, with their echoes of Mercutio in *Romeo and Juliet* and of *A Midsummer Night's Dream.* This evening of innocent country conviviality ends with the tellers of the tales and their audience all creeping to bed. "Towred Cities please us then," l'Allegro notes, but there is no reason to literalize the adverb. We do not proceed physically from the country to the town as an actual movement at a particular moment. Rather, the *image* of the participants in country pleasures all "lull'd asleep" begets associationally the *image* of the still ongoing and more sophisticated pleasures of the City. A world of courtly manners is summoned up— "throngs of Knights and Barons bold . . . with store of Ladies"—quite removed from the homespun of the pastoral world. The romantic sights of "pomp, and feast, and revelry, / With mask, and antique Pageantry" spiral away from the pleasures of pastoral everyday or pastoral holiday to a world of imagination exalted above previous experiences of the senses in nature and society. "Such sights as youthfull Poets dream / On Summer eeves by haunted stream" are no more visible to the merely physical eye than are the rapturous visions of Penseroso. The experience that l'Allegro here glimpses is not, however, mystical or even meditative, but aesthetic and humanistic, enhancing the senses rather than abandoning them. From this intense level of sensation l'Allegro relaxes, as he leaves the haunted stream for the "well-trod stage," the most social of all the arts. The plays he looks forward to viewing are appropriately enough comedies, both the classical "learned Sock" of Jonson and the "native Wood-notes wilde" of Shakespeare's romantic comedy.

Finally, all the activities of body and mind, sensuous and aesthetic, culminate in a great incantation to music—

> And ever against eating Cares,
> Lap me in soft *Lydian* Aires,
> Married to immoral verse
> Such as the meeting soul may pierce. . . .

(135–38)

The fact that Lydian music is unrelated to the sounds of universal harmony and order, to the Platonic music of the spheres that figures in *IlP* and elsewhere in

Milton's early poetry, does not mean that it should be judged as vitiating, as it was by Plato. Its peculiar power is truly to liberate us from care, and hence even from restless pursuit of further delight. So great is its re-creative power that it exceeds that of Orpheus and "would have won the ear / of *Pluto*."

Insofar as *L'Al* is related to Epicureanism at its philosophical best, to authentic liberation from care and pain because the pleasures pursued leave no bad aftertaste or reproof, the poem is also inevitably related to variety as distinct from the One, which is the goal of the religious contemplative. Accordingly, the music into which the action dissolves, though superior to that of Orpheus, is not a resolved harmony that composes the soul into a stasis. Under the aegis of Mirth, the highest good is fittingly heard as,

> many a winding bout
> Of lincked sweetnes long drawn out,
> With wanton heed, and giddy cunning,
> The melting voice through mazes running;
> Untwisting all the chains that ty
> The hidden soul of harmony.
>
> (139–44)

This volatility and emotional directness of the solo aria become ominous only when judged from the standpoint of the "pealing Organ" and "Anthems cleer" of *IlP;* however, within the frame of norms established in *L'Al* they are felt as altogether appropriate and desirable.

The mode of ideal concepts embodied in *L'Al* are not logical propositions. Its norms are unique and yet intelligible because they function through objects (the images) that have both a concrete and a generic identity. Of course, the special circumstance of twin poems complicates as well as enriches our response. Accordingly, a great danger in reading the beautifully paralleled and contrasted images of *L'Al* and *IlP* is that of isolating them from their respective poems and viewing them primarily within the context of intellectual presuppositions. Such a procedure more often leads to foregone conclusions than to an exploration of poetry. It is safe enough to assume that for Milton—the dedicated young student who argued the superiority of learning to ignorance in *Prol 7*—as well as in the cultural milieu of the Renaissance, contemplative Melancholy holds a higher place than does Mirth.

Discussion of *IlP,* like that of *L'Al,* proceeds from a starting point like that which Miss Tuve posited from a somewhat different perspective: "[Milton] portrays not pursuer or pursuit but that bodiless thing itself which the freely delighting mind or the meditative mind tirelessly seeks to ally itself with" (*Images and Themes,* p. 15).

Following the praise of Penseroso's noble ancestry and association with blackness, the goddess is invoked as a pensive Nun, "Sober, stedfast, and demure." The gravity of mien and fixity of mind evident in Penseroso's succeeding activities are established as the goddess's characteristic physical and mental posture. The pursuit of the One, though it ends in *exstasis*, must

proceed with deliberation: "keep thy wonted state, / With eev'n step, and musing gate." Images of discipline and detachment—"calm Peace, and Quiet, / Spare Fast, that oft with gods doth diet"—are decorous to Penseroso's quest of the pleasures of contemplation, just as spontaneity of movement and response decorously govern l'Allegro. As suggested earlier, both poems take pleasure as their value and destination; it is a simplistic distortion to confine the idea of pleasure to Mirth and to posit contemplative Melancholy as pleasure's opposite or even coordinate. Rather, Mirth and Melancholy are both subsumed under pleasure, but as different modes requiring differing patterns of decorum. This becomes explicit as Milton summons up the Horatian ideal of "retired leisure, / That in trim Gardens takes his pleasure." Withdrawal from the active world of affairs into the self-contained pleasures of the garden is a traditional emblem for both the Epicurean and Stoic-Platonic happy life. The kind of "busy-ness" that pursues what is external to man's inner contentment—erotic gratification, wealth, or power—and is therefore inimical to true delight, is alien to the norms of both poems. Scriptural, philosophical, and literary traditions reinforce the ideal of leisure in a pastoral world or in a formal garden as the appropriate setting for the highest, and least vulnerable, pleasures of body, mind, and soul. This broad range of experience is encompassed by the images of each of Milton's companion poems, making for the basis of their parallel relatedness, though with strikingly different emphasis, providing their patterns of massive contrast. The operative norms of *L'Al* and *IlP* accordingly do not collide as mighty ethical opposites, but are juxtaposed as contrasting perspectives.

To return to the images themselves, Philomel, "Sweet Bird that shunn'st the noise of folly," signals the start of Penseroso's activities—a nocturnal walk as he moves unseen through the landscape, gazes at the moon, and hears the far-off curfew sound. Whereas l'Allegro glances at towers from his position in intimate relation to the landscape, Penseroso is "in som high lonely Towr," his isolation from nature and society providing the vantage point for his pursuit of mysterious knowledge. The scenes of social intercourse in *L'Al* have no counterparts here. When the scholar seeks respite from his intellectual quest he turns not to light refreshment but to the highest humanistic pleasures of Greek tragedy, which he enjoys as a solitary reader rather than as a member of a theater audience. The diverting music of *L'Al* is holiday song and dance; here the speaker hopes for music of miraculous power—

> But, O sad Virgin, that thy power
> Might raise *Musaeus* from his bower,
> Or bid the soul of *Orpheus* sing
> Such notes as warbled to the string,
> Drew Iron tears down Pluto's cheek,
> And made Hell grant what Love did seek.
>
> (103–8)

Folktales recounted in *L'Al* over a cheerful mug of ale have in *IlP* a weightier counterpart in Chaucer's unfinished *Squire's Tale*, "The story of Cambuscan bold," continuing the theme of the quest for intellectual prowess. The arts convey in *L'Al* direct sensuous delight; the pleasures of poetry and music in *IlP* are oblique and have the appeal of "Where more is meant then meets the ear."

The glorification of darkness at the expense of light, so insistently argued in the opening, runs throughout the poem. In the first scene, Penseroso finds during his night walk refuge in a "removed place,"

> Where glowing Embers through the room
> Teach light to counterfeit a gloom. . . .
>
> (79–80)

And after the "pale career" of a night devoted to music and poetry, he sees "civil-suited Morn appeer, / Not trickt and frounc't as she was wont, / With the Attick Boy to hunt, / But Cherchef't in a comely Cloud . . ." (121–25). "When the Sun begins to fling / His flaring beams," Penseroso seeks out "twilight groves," unknown to the woodsman, where "in close covert by som Brook," and hidden "from Day's garish eie," he finds refreshment in sleep and dreams.

The consummating experience of Penseroso, like l'Allegro's, is couched in music. As he wakes from "som strange mysterious dream," he hears music sent perhaps by "th'unseen Genius of the Wood." His final vision, however, removes him from this natural setting to the "studious Cloysters pale." Dedicated study of nature's innermost secrets and man's highest wisdom issues ultimately, according to Christian and Platonic philosophy, in an absorbed contemplation of the Creator, in experience that approaches the mystical. The conclusion relates the intellectual endeavors of Penseroso to his religious dedication through music so exalted that it can dissolve him into ecstasies and "bring all Heav'n before [his] eyes." And such a contemplative existence, long enough pursued, may even enable the adept to "attain / To something like Prophetic strain."

These visionary final images are succeeded by the two low-keyed concluding lines adapted from Ralegh's "The Nymph's Reply to the Shepherd," which remind us that a choice of pleasures is being offered:

> These pleasures *Melancholy* give
> And I with thee will choose to live.
>
> (175–76)

As with the parallel conclusion of *L'Al*, the reader may well wonder: after so utterly convincing a realization of Melancholy why need such a question be even implied, as it is by the subjunctive of the verb "give." Surely the entire poem is the most vivid proof that Melancholy can and does give these pleasures. And the same, of course, applies to Mirth in *L'Al:*

These delights, if thou canst give,
Mirth with thee, I mean to live.

(151–52)

   The foregoing discussion has already suggested some of the major lines of interpretation. Earlier views of debate between opposed life-styles or values, and contrast between complementary moods, are currently giving way to more intellectually complex (but less emotionally subtle) interpretations. Of these the most influential is a hierarchical relation, first fully developed by Don Cameron Allen, for whom the poems "describe a progress from an enslaving dissatisfaction to an ultimate gratification" (*The Harmonious Vision* [1954], pp. 8ff.). For Allen the "dynamic symbol of the poem is the tower," which figures the ascent from the common experience of *L'Al* to the contemplative experience of *IlP*. Another account of the companion poems sees them as one poem, as a "vertical structure" that traces sequentially a progression of experience, indeed a progress of the soul (David M. Miller, *Publications of the Modern Language Association* 86: 32–37). In the remedies for diseased Melancholy prescribed in Burton's *Anatomy of Melancholy* (see W. J. Grace, *Studies in Philology* 52:579–91, for Milton's use of Burton in *L'Al* and *IlP*), Miller sees just those activities which make up the body of *L'Al*. From the superior height of divine contemplation, however, Mirth is dismissed as vain deluding joys and superseded by golden Melancholy, yielding a four-step progression of the soul from desperate Melancholy, to the "neutral middle ground achieved at the close of *L'Allegro*," which is then rejected as vain, and proceeding finally to "a more positive state: as near to the contemplation of God as man can achieve on earth." The difficulty with this attractive and convincingly argued thesis, as with the older thesis of Tillyard about a debate between day or night (extendable to other pairs of polarities), has already been set forth: it substitutes foregone conclusions—clearly predictable once the intellectual frame of reference is announced—for the process of poetic discovery. Moreover, with this same four-step progression in mind, one could replace the hierarchical assumption with a cyclical one by citing, for example, Rosemond Tuve's attractive and widely accepted idea that "We need make no trouble about a division, no fanfare about a unification, that every man daily makes, within the bounds of his own personality" (*Images and Themes*, p. 19).

   In conclusion, it is important to resist the tendency to seize upon a single pattern of imagistic or thematic explanation with a view toward breaking down the complex separateness-and-relatedness of the companion poems. The relation of balance and contrast between the two interacts with the self-coherence of each; the companion poems are precisely that—inseparable companions, not a single poem composed of two movements or divided into two parts. The richest thematic issues are probably not to be found in the contrast of images of Mirth and Melancholy and cannot be expressed in some abstractly defined relation between them. The more interesting tension seems to lie with the

question whether these companionate ideals can be possessed and sustained in all the perfection of their pleasures without deteriorating into something the mind must reject. Accordingly, it is best to consider the habits of formal discourse and thought that the poems clearly do employ—debate, encomium, progress of the mind or soul; Epicureanism, and Platonism—as materials employed in the making of a lyrical object whose forming principle cannot be accounted for by a thematic formula of any kind. [LN]

LYCIDAS. The basic texts of *Lyc* are to be found in *TM*, in *Justa Edovardo King* (1638), and in the 1645 and 1673 editions of the Poems. Though the text of *Lyc* is considerably revised in the manuscript, Grierson is of the opinion that it may not have been Milton's first draft. The verso of the last sheet of *Mask*, known familiarly as the "trial-sheet," contains four drafts (one struck out) of three portions of the poem.

The passages worked over most heavily in *TM* are the "Orpheus" passage, which is revised in the main text, rewritten in the margin, and rewritten again in the trial-sheet, and the "flower" passage, which is drafted, struck out, and rewritten in the trial-sheet, with the main text providing a marginal direction for its insertion. The Orpheus passage is expanded from four to seven lines; the menacing line "downe the swift Hebrus to the Lesbian Shore" is added to the marginal revision; its effect is intensified by the addition of "When by the rout that made the hideous roare" in the trialsheet; and the avalanche of horror is given further momentum as Orpheus's "divine head" becomes his "goarie visage." In the flower passages the number of lines is reduced from twelve to ten; a certain amount of exposition is discarded; and the passage takes on the quality of a procession, with each flower given a distinct and vividly focused presence. The movement in one case is toward angry elementality; in the other it is toward conventionality, the pastoral mood wrought to the height of its beauty. More than one view can be taken of these changes, which are examined in detail by J. B. Leishman (*Milton's Minor Poems* [1969], pp. 295–310). One possible view is that Milton recognized that the movement of his poem was shaped by certain basic oppositions and wished by his revisions to intensify rather than diminish those oppositions. Such a view would be borne out by the crucial replacement of "and crop yor young" by "shatter" in line 5, by the replacement of "sad thoughts" by "frail thoughts" in line 153, and by the restoration in 1645 of "nothing" which is replaced by "little" in the manuscript text of line 129. Later changes in the same direction are the restoration of "smite" in line 131 (1645; the 1638 version has "smites") and the replacement of "humming" by "whelming" in line 157, by Milton's hand in two copies of the 1638 text.

The King memorial volume consists of two parts, the first containing twenty Latin and three Greek poems and the second thirteen poems in English. Each part has a separate title page and is separately paginated. The book is rare, Parker recording no more than 31 copies, of which the one owned by the

Elizabethan Club of Yale University bears Izaak Walton's autograph. There is a facsimile edited by Ernest C. Mossner (1939). Milton's is the longest, last, and most elaborate of the English poems. The author is identified only by his initials. M. Lloyd in *Notes and Queries*, 5:432–34, suggests that the volume is designed as a unity and that *Lyc* is a summary and interpretation of themes already stated. The tone of the English poems is predominantly metaphysical and the verse predominantly in couplets, so that *Lyc* is set apart not merely by its excellences. Nevertheless references such as those in Isaac Olivier's poem to Arethusa and to St. Peter's treading of the waves are not without their bearing on Milton's poem.

The 1638 text, set throughout in italics, is not arranged with care. Milton's paragraphing in the manuscript is only partially followed, with paragraphs beginning at lines 15, 37, 132, 165, and 186. In line 9 "Young *Lycidas*" is put in parenthesis for the first and only time and an exclamation mark is added. Typical misprints are "lord" for "lov'd" in line 51 and "stridly" for "strictly" in line 66. The recollection of "don" in line 67 leads to the printing of "do" instead of "use" later in the same line. "Hid in" for "Or with" in line 69 is a celebrated variant. The manuscript has "Hid in" struck out and replaced in the margin by the familiar reading. The most striking misprint is the omission of line 177. In the Cambridge University and British Museum copies the line is marginally inserted in Milton's hand. The misprints in lines 51 and 67 are corrected in the same hand, "humming" is changed to "whelming" in line 157, and "he knew" in line 10 becomes "he well knew" as it is in *TM*. The texts of 1645 and 1673 both have "he knew." It is not clear whether Milton changed his mind or abandoned hope.

The 1645 and 1673 versions give us the text of the poem substantially as we know it. Patrides described 1673 as "merely a reproduction of the 1645 text with a few misprints" (*Milton's "Lycidas": the Tradition and the Poem*, ed. C. A. Patrides [1961], p. 233). One of these misprints is "To end" instead of "To tend" in line 65. For fuller apparatus see Patrides, *CM*, the editions of Milton's poetry by Helen Darbishire (1952), H. F. Fletcher (1943), and John T. Shawcross (1963), and for a study of the text, Shawcross, *Publications of the Bibliographical Society of America* 56:317–31.

The two-handed engine was merely at the door in 1638 but by 1645 Milton was able to enter in the manuscript and to reproduce in print his vindication of the poet's gift of prophecy: "In this Monody the Author bewails a learned Friend, unfortunately drown'd in his passage from *Chester* on the *Irish* Seas, 1637. And by occasion foretells the ruine of our corrupted clergie then in their height." Apart from the foretelling, the characterization of the poem as a monody is important. The important early poems are all suitably characterized. *Comus* is a "Mask," *Arc* is "Part of an Entertainment," and *Nat* is described in the text as both an "ode" and a "Hymn."

Both in 1645 and in 1673, *Lyc* is printed immediately after *Arc* and the juxtaposition cannot be accidental. The implied movement from Arcadia to

anguish is gently underlined by the setting of both poems within the pastoral frame. Both make use of the story of Alpheus with its implication of rebirth in another country; but the "renowned flood" of *Arc* 29, remembered in *Lyc* as the "honour'd floud," develops characteristically into the "perilous flood" (85, 185). The "Genius of the Wood" provides the principal statement in *Arc*. In *Lyc* 183 the dead shepherd becomes the "Genius of the Shore," on the far side of the "perilous flood." The plants in *Arc* (53) are preserved from the worm and the canker, which in *Lyc* 45–46 are the initial symbols of those destructive energies which the poem is forced to pass through. Even more instructively, the celestial sirens in *Arc* (61ff.) sing to those that "hold the vital shears / And turn the adamantine spindle round." The "sweet compulsion" of music keeps "unsteady Nature" to its law and ensures that the "low world" moves in concert to the "heavenly tune." In *Lyc* the shears are "abhorred" rather than "vital," the power that wields them is "blind," and Nature, far from moving in "measur'd motion," is radically challenged by the forces of chaos. Yet despite the depth of questioning in *Lyc*, the resolution is still able to bring us back to some of the images of the earlier poem. In *Arc* (96–101) the Nymphs and Shepherds are called on to "dance no more" so that they can be welcomed on "A better soil." In *Lyc* the shepherds are invited to "weep no more" since Lycidas is alive amidst "Other groves and other streams" (165, 174). The tune that the "gross unpurged" ears of morals are incapable of hearing (*Arc* 72–73) is reborn in *Lyc* as the "unexpressive nuptial Song." The pastoral world is restored in a Christian context.

Edward King, whom Milton's poem mourns, was born at Boyle in the county of Connaught, Ireland, in 1612. He was admitted to Christ's College, Cambridge in 1626, received his B.A. in 1630 and his M.A. in 1633. In 1630 he was awarded a vacant fellowship by royal mandate. King's feeling for his college is evident in his will of 1637. "First all my debts to be payd. And what remains entirely to be left to the use of Christe Coll." Nine days later King was drowned en route to Ireland. According to the Latin paragraph prefacing the commemorative volume, "the ship in which he was having struck a rock not far from the British shore and being ruptured by the shock, he, while the other passengers were fruitlessly busy about their mortal lives, having fallen forward on his knees, and breathing a life which was immortal, in the act of prayer going down with the vessel, rendered up his soul to God, Aug. 10, 1637, aged 25" [Masson's translation]. Milton did not mention the incident, notwithstanding what his nephew, Edward Phillips, terms his "particular Friendship and Imtimacy" with King. *Lyc* 96–99 may reflect the knowledge that it was not a storm that was responsible for King's death, but Henry King, Edward's brother, refers in his memorial poem to an "unluckie storm" and to the "treacherous waves and carelesse wind."

The commemorative preface mentions King's piety and erudition but says nothing about his poetic talent. However, Henry King claims immoderately that his brother's tempestuous eloquence was capable of Christianizing India!

King wrote several poems on what Le Comte terms obstetric occasions while Milton, according to Northrop Frye, had been practising on corpses ever since the death of the fair infant. Ben Jonson's death in the same month as King's and the death of Milton's mother in April of the same year may have wrought Milton's involvement in the shipwreck to the intensity of which *Lyc* is the witness. But when Diodati died in the year following (the month being once again August) the greater grief provoked the lesser poem.

Hanford's classic article on the tradition behind *Lyc* (*Publications of the Modern Language Association* 25: 403–47) remains required reading after more than sixty years. Theocritus and in particular his first Idyll (to which Milton refers twice in *EpDam*) constitute the "source" of the tradition and furnish precedents or beginnings for conventions such as a procession of mourners, the grief of nature at the death of the shepherd, and a reproach to the nymphs for not being present at the scene of the catastrophe. Bion's *Lament for Adonis*, which follows, is "one of the great classical models of the pastoral elegy," but its erotic—and decadent—tone, according to Hanford, was rejected by Milton's "sober and classic genius." *The Lament for Bion* (also referred to in *EpDam*) is a further milestone marking "the full development of the pastoral lament as an independent type." One of the more important conventions it establishes is the mourning of an actual person, a poet-colleague of the maker of the lament.

Virgil brings the lofty style into the pastoral (notably in the fourth eclogue). Since his concern is with the use of pastoral machinery rather than with rendering the immediacies of Sicilian life, he both establishes the pastoral as a style and opens out the style's possibilities, giving us a poetry that can be oblique as well as direct. In Puttenham's words it is sought "vnder the vaile of homely persons and in rude speeches to insinuate and glaunce at greater matters, and such as perchance had not bene safe to have been disclosed in any other sort, which may be perceived by the *Eglogues* of Virgill" (Scott Elledge, ed., *Milton's "Lycidas"* [1966], p. 113). Hanford sees the fifth and tenth eclogues as particularly relevant to Milton's poem. More specifically, the tenth eclogue has an invocation at the beginning, but no mention of the shepherd singer till the end; a procession of mourners; and an eight-line close referring to the end of day and the departure of the shepherd. The fifth eclogue establishes the convention of the apotheosis. Though Christianity gives the consolation in *Lyc* a different coloring, it is hard to believe, according to Hanford (Patrides, pp. 39–40), that Milton would have made his reference to the "Genius of the Shore" had not the idea held "an important place in this eclogue of Virgil." Milton's allusiveness is of course considerably more sophisticated than parallels like these might in themselves suggest. The multiple evocations of the Latin poetry are a fit preparation for the kind of literary performance that is called for by the pastoral elegy in its later stages. It is a world of poetry rather than individual poems that is summoned into being around the performance.

Virgil's fourth or Messianic Eclogue is easily seen as the obscure rehearsal of a

Christian truth to come. John 9:39–41 and 10:1–28, which Milton draws on in his denunciation of the clergy, are two among many biblical passages that encourage the conflation of the Christian and the pastoral. In Petrarch's sixth and seventh eclogues ecclesiastical satire is introduced, opening the way for Mantuan, Marot, and Spenser. "It is to the latter poet," says Hanford, "to whom we naturally look as the predecessor in this respect of Milton" (Patrides, p. 44). The May, July, and September Eclogues contain ecclesiastical satire, and May 38ff., according to Hanford, "bears a marked resemblance to the invective in *Lycidas*" (p. 51). In *Animad*, Milton quotes 103–31 of the May Eclogue. Such satire is expressive of the didactic strain initiated by Petrarch and Boccaccio and even more strongly by Mantuan in his ten eclogues. What Don Cameron Allen calls the "inherited right" of the pastoral poet "to be both satirist and allegorist" is confirmed and elaborated. "These Eclogues came after," Puttenham comments, "to containe and enforme morale discipline for the amendment of man's behauoir as be those of *Mantuan* and other moderne Poets" (Elledge, p. 113). Thus the introduction of alien material into the pastoral—personal, philosophic, or didactic—is legitimized. The digressions in *Lyc*, though without parallel, are not without precedent. It is also apparent that Johnson's complaint that Milton mingles "the most awful and sacred truths" with the "trifling fictions" of the pastoral and that these "irreverent combinations" are "indecent" and "at least approach to impiety" censures a Renaissance practice rather than Milton's alone. However, it is not enough to reply as Warton does that Milton sins in company. The "combinations" must be shown to be demanded by the logic and momentum of the poem.

Two Latin elegies of the Renaissance cited as bearing upon *Lyc* are Castiglione's *Alcon* and Sannazaro's first piscatory eclogue. The flower passage in *Alcon* is one of many that Milton may have remembered. Spenser's April Eclogue (136ff.) is often cited, Virgil's fourth and fifth eclogues have flower passages, though far less elaborate than Milton's, and *Winter's Tale* 4.4.113–32, is, according to H. H. Adams (*Modern Language Notes* 65:468–72), a source that Milton obscured in his revisions. James H. Sims (*Shakespeare Quarterly* 22:87–90) sees a parallel between *Winter's Tale* and *Lyc* in terms of the progression and not simply the inventory. Apart from his flower passage, Castiglione's description of the friendship between the dead shepherd and the singer of the lament reminds us of *Lyc* but perhaps no more than other such descriptions. Sannazaro's singer is Lycidas, his eclogue mentions Panope (a rare name among nymphs but used by Virgil in *Aeneid* 5.240), and lines in his poem may have suggested *Lyc* 183–85, and the arresting image of 158. The flower passage in Sannazaro is unusual in occurring in the apotheosis. Sir J. E. Sandys (*Transactions of the Royal Society of Literature* [1914], pp. 233–64) considers Amalteo's First Eclogue, which is entitled *Lyc*, a possible source. Dante's influence, while not lying within the "tradition" narrowly conceived, should not be discounted. Irene Samuel (*Dante and Milton* [1966], pp. 36–37), finds

Dante's impress "throughout the entire pattern" of *Lyc*. The "inner movement" of Milton's elegy asks the "great question" of the *Commedia* and reaches a similar understanding.

The pastoral lament in England was amplified by the several poems mourning the death of Sidney in 1586. William Browne's elegy on Thomas Manwood (the fourth eclogue in the collection entitled *The Shepherd's Pipe*) has been cited as a possible influence upon *Lyc*. W. B. Austin (*Studies in Philology* 44:41–55) detects similarities between passages in *Lyc* and two Latin elegies by Giles Fletcher, the Elder, on Clere and Walter Haddon. Phineas Fletcher's *Piscatorie Eclogues* published four years before *Lyc* may not have been out of Milton's mind. In general what Hanford terms "the vast and multifarious pastoral literature" written in England between *The Shepheardes Calendar* (1579) and *Lyc* can be accepted as a background that would have made a contemporary audience fully familiar with the gestures of Milton's poem.

Puttenham tells us that "Poeticall mournings in verse" were called "*Epicedia* if they were sung by many, and *Monodia* if they were uttered by one alone." Such lamentations had social status, since they were "vsed at the enterment of Princes and others of great accompt" (Elledge, p. 114). Scaliger (Elledge, pp. 107–11) divides the epicedium into the praise, the narration, the lamentation, the consolation, and the exhortation. The praise can be preceded by a calm proem "suitable for those who are sorrowful and even dazed with grief." The succeeding part must praise not only the man but also the manner of his death. The narration should describe the loss calmly and then with increasing excitement, as the amplification of the theme increases, the longing for the lost person. The lamentation follows naturally as the agitation of the narration reaches its climax. The consolation then begins—the death of a king, for example, can be alleviated by the virtues of his successor, whose qualities can be set forth in "an ardent and brief account." Finally comes the exhortation: the dead are to be emulated rather than mourned and to mourn them unduly would be to disparage their survivors.

It is apparent that Milton does not follow these requirements closely. The manner of King's death could have been but is not commended. It is on the meaning (or lack of meaning) of that death that the forces of the poem converge. The praise passes into the pastoral claim of kinship. Similarly, the narration blends with the lamentation and the movement from calm to excitement occurs not once but thrice in the ebb and flow of the poem. The consolation is in terms considerably less mundane than those envisaged by Scaliger. The exhortation (to which the closing *ottava rima* corresponds) does not exhort but presents the event as over in the sense that it is assimilated into the experience of the mourner. Milton's adherence to this structure is indeed so free that it may be wondered whether he is following it at all. Certainly the three-part structure (see below) provides a far more instructive understanding of the organizing movement of the poem.

King was a "learned friend" and is mourned appropriately in a learned elegy.

Milton's uses of the past in creating the literary present of the poem are apparent even in such details as the choice of the name Lycidas. Lycidas is a shepherd in Theocritus's seventh Idyll, faces death by drowning in Lucan (*Pharsalia* 3.638–39), complains against social injustice in Virgil's ninth eclogue, is a Protestant pastor in Bathurst's translation of Spenser's May Eclogue (see E. A. Straithwaite, *Modern Language Notes* 52:398–400) and brings gifts to Mary and her child in Sannazaro's *De Partu Virginis* (3.185–93). All these roles are relevant to Milton's poem. Yet an inventory of the past cannot pretend to provide an account of *Lyc.* The expectations that the tradition sets up are challenged as well as fulfilled. The inherited joins hands in the poem with the invented, but both the unattempted and that which is sung once more are stamped with the work's profound originality. "Where were ye nymphs" is a cry as old as Theocritus. The place names that follow take us into the world of Spenser and Drayton while preparing the way for that more majestic naming that surrounds the "great vision of the guarded mount." Milton's capacity to convey the elemental in the local is used here with a higher aim than virtuosity. The pastoral gesture is invested with momentousness and we are made receptive to the dramatic change of voice and proclamation of affinities as the Welsh landscape gives way to the Thracian, the Druid spells to the enchantments of Orpheus, and the spreading Dee is overwhelmed by the swift Hebrus. The "sudden blaze" into "Had ye bin there—for what could that have don?" (a question not asked by the pastoral tradition) is clearly called for by the forces of the poem. Similarly in line 99 ("Sleek *Panope* with all her sisters play'd") the name may not be Milton's but the characterization subtly bears his signature. The word *sleek*, fitted with fastidiousness into the pastoral diction, defines and vivifies the tactile quality of the line itself. Finally it suggests with deftness the comprehensive calm that prevailed, the multiple assurances of safety as the unruffled nymph played on the unruffled waters. The stock word *perfidious* gains in strength as we become aware of the dimensions of betrayal. We can even note that the question "Where were ye nymphs" has been answered in a manner that gives additional force to "what could that have don?" It is thus not simply in the higher mood that Milton is securely himself, and while competitive overgoing may take place (looking forward to the tactics of *PL*) the strings are not simply swept with greater brilliance. Modulation as well as surpassing, counterpoint as well as assertion, are part of the solemn music of *Lyc.*

Explorations such as those conducted above must be representative rather than exhaustive; but they should serve to indicate how fully *Lyc* exemplifies Eliot's conception of tradition and the individual talent. The poem makes us aware of the presence of the past rather than of its pastness. It holds and shapes the literature of Europe from Theocritus to Milton's day, in an order that is simultaneous rather than chronological. The ideal order that a tradition constitutes is changed by its creative extension into a work of art that is "really new" in Eliot's sense. The individual talent in its turn is excited into distinctiveness by the felt presence of literary history.

Despite its recondite attachment to its genre, *Lyc* remains a poem in a contemporary setting. That contemporaneity is not a matter of the identity of "Old Damoetas," who is in fact young in Theocritus 6 and Virgil's third eclogue, though he is a dying man in the second eclogue and a clown in Sidney's *Arcadia*. Chappell, Milton's tutor, and Joseph Mead, a popular Fellow of Christ's, are long-standing suggestions. Fletcher (*Journal of English and Germanic Philology* 60: 260–67) adds Michael Honeywood, a Fellow of Christ's from 1618, and Abraham Wheelock, first Professor of Arabic. Others feel that the question cannot or need not be settled. More important is the status of *Lyc* in the wars of truth. Haller considers (*The Rise of Puritanism* [1957], p. 317) that on the ideal plane "*Comus* and *Lycidas* are as authentic expressions of the Puritan spirit on the eve of revolution as anything that came from the hand of Prynne." The reference is the ideal plane is necessary. Corruption endures beyond a particular establishment, and revolutions, as Milton learned, are made to be betrayed. Finally there is the question of how *Lyc* expresses what might loosely be termed the literary spirit of its time. Roy Daniells (*Milton, Mannerism and Baroque* [1963], p. 45) considers the poem mannerist in its restlessness and in its "refusal to propagate a resounding resolution." For Wylie Sypher (*Four Stages of Renaissance Style* [1955], pp. 74–76) *Lyc* is "perhaps the greatest mannerist poem" marked by its "intervals and discontinuities," its "constantly shifted level of statement," and its "very personal, willful" use of the traditional elegy. For Lowry Nelson, on the other hand (*Baroque Lyric Poetry* [1961], pp. 64–76, 138–52), *Lyc* is "one of the most nearly complete fulfilments of peculiarly baroque tendencies in style," with the shifts in tense between the narrative past and the historic present enhancing one's impression of the poem as performance. Rosemond Tuve's cautions in "Baroque and Mannerist Milton" (*Journal of English and Germanic Philology* 60:209–25) need to be perused at this stage. Nevertheless it can be observed that what characterizes *Lyc* is not only the strong sense of literary performance but the eloquent involvement of the poet in the performance. Because the singer is caught in his song, not simply in its virtuosity but on the fundamental questions that it poses, his declamation can be successful only if it is also authentic as self-discovery. Given their distinct and powerful individualities, Milton at this point is not very distant from Donne.

With two books devoted entirely to *Lyc* and some hundreds of articles including over fifty on a single crux, the reader of Milton's pastoral does not lack advice on how to approach the poem or what to look for in it. Indeed, the problem of how to read the poem may soon become a subject apart from the poem. In the interpretation of interpretations five types of *Lyc* criticism have already been distinguished. With considerable simplification these can be classified as the approach via the genre; the poem as the expression of personality or of profoundly meaningful concerns, stated with the force of personal involvement; the poem as an escape from personality into the anonymity of the language-performance; the poem as archetype; and the poem as a pattern of

imagery in which its fundamental meanings are located. Meyer Abrams, who is responsible for distinguishing these five approaches, adds a sixth of his own, which is to read the poem with "dogged literalness, except when there is clear evidence that some part of it is to be read allegorically or symbolically" (Patrides, p. 221). The result of this exemplary caution is a reading in which the poem is approached through the interplay and development of its dramatic voices.

Of the "types" listed above, the approach via the genre has already been discussed. The poem as a declaration of personality goes back, though the practitioners of the approach may not realize this fully, to one of Johnson's more seminal intimidations: "Passion plucks no berries from the myrtle and ivy, nor calls upon Arethuse and Mincius, nor tells of rough *satyrs* and *fauns with cloven heel.* Where there is leisure for fiction there can be little grief." To those disturbed by this accusation or even to those who believe that conventional art is validated by something behind the convention, the natural reply is to suggest that the "real subject" of *Lyc* is not these pastoral gestures but the fundamental concerns that give meaning to the gestures. Thus for Tillyard (Patrides, pp. 59–60) the real subject is Milton himself and, more specifically, Milton's resolving of his fears of premature death "into an exalted state of mental calm." For Daiches (Patrides, p. 104) the subject is not "simply Milton himself" but "man in his creative capacity, as Christian humanist poet-priest." For Lawry (Arthur Barker, ed., *Milton: Modern Essays in Criticism* [1965], p. 114), *Lyc* is about "poetry and the poet, generally conceived, and of the conditions impelled by existence upon the poet and his works." Such distinctions anticipate the not-always-useful distinctions between conscious and unconscious meanings in *PL*. They also minimize the extent to which conventions themselves are the embodiments of universal and enduring concerns. There is a difference, of course, between embodiment and petrification, but Milton was clearly on the right side of this difference. The third approach, namely, to the poem as ritual performance, is open to the objection that ritual performances differ from each other by something more than the skill exhibited in the performance. It is also more than a verbal quibble to suggest that a poem can be impersonal without being anonymous. The archetypal approach begins at the other extreme, since its initial concern is not with the finished language-object, but with those basic rhythms and relationships through which experience is aesthetically received. The objection, however, is parallel to the one urged against the poem as performance. It is that archetypal statements in poetry differ from each other by something more than the authenticity with which the archetype is proclaimed. The poem found in its imagery may result, as Abrams not altogether frivolously suggests, in the conclusion that *Lyc* is really about water. At best it seeks the identity of the poem through only one of the poem's resources. We can argue that this identity should be declared in the imagery at least as clearly and probably more specifically than it is in the poem's other deployments. But the argument becomes less forceful when we admit that a

poem's special cohesiveness may be found not in anything that the poem does, but in the way it puts together everything that it does.

It is apparent that these approaches do not exclude each other and that few critics are fastidious enough or obstinate enough to live wholly within the purity of any single approach. The temptation "to combine all these critical modes into a single criticism" is therefore strong, but Abrams warns us that it will yield "not an integral poem but a ragout." To provide a coherent reading, he urges, "a critical procedure must itself be coherent; it cannot be divided against itself in its first principles." The warning would be irresistible were it not for one fact. *Lyc* is a poem divided against itself and the strength of its achievement may be built on that division. It is therefore possible to think of yet another type of *Lyc* criticism, which would examine the multifarious oppositions in the poem, the structure within which these oppositions are engaged, the style of engagement and of reconciliation, and the manner in which the poem's resources are brought together by its pattern and movement. Such an approach would not be contradictory in its assumptions; but it would seek to bring together understandings that are contrary because they build their houses on divisions established for the poem's purposes within the poem itself. Douglas Bush (*John Milton* [1964], p. 62) describes *Lyc* as "at once an agonized personal cry and a formal exercise, a search for order and a made object, an affirmation of faith in Providence and an exploitation of pastoral and archetypal myth." It is reasonable to approach the poem's wholeness through the manner in which these differing aspects of its existence are intensified and eventually reconciled.

Little is new under the sun of Milton criticism and the view of *Lyc* suggested above has already been urged. It originates perhaps in what are popularly known as the "digressions" in *Lyc,* which Warton apologized for (Elledge, p. 231) as the "gothic combinations of an uneducated age." Modern criticism begins with the conviction that the digressions have a profound propriety. In other words they do not digress at all and the justification for them goes considerably deeper than literary precedent. It is apparent of course that the digressions grow out of authorized pastoral concerns—untimely death and institutional corruption versus Arcadian innocence. But the change in literary manners from stylized lament to passionate vehemence confronts us with a conflict that we cannot evade and that we respond to as "belonging" in the poem. This awareness encourages the suggestion that the digressions are the heart of *Lyc* and that the poem best declares itself when it divests itself of its embroidered cloak. But if we are to avoid further distinctions between the poem's real and nominal subjects, or suggestions that the poem has run away with the poet (anticipating one school of *PL* critics), it would be best to regard the heart of the poem as lying in the relationship between the two literary manners and what they are made to embody. The musical metaphor implicit in the interplay between first and second subject is brought out in Barker's description of the poem as "three successive and perfectly controlled crescendos."

The first movement laments Lycidas the poet-shepherd; its problem, the possible frustration of disciplined poetic ambition by early death, is resolved by the assurance, "Of so much fame in heaven expect thy meed." The second laments Lycidas as priest-shepherd; its problem, the frustration of a sincere shepherd in a corrupt church, is resolved by St. Peter's reference to the "two-handed engine" of divine retribution. The third concludes with the apotheosis, a convention introduced by Virgil in *Eclogue* V but significantly handled by Milton. He sees the poet-priest-shepherd worshipping the Lamb with those saints "in solemn troops" who sing the "unexpressive nuptial song" of the fourteenth chapter of Revelation. The apotheosis thus not only provides the final reassurance but unites the themes of the preceding movements in the ultimate reward of the true poet-priest. (*Milton. Modern Judgements*, ed. Alan Rudrum [1968], p. 48).

This account of the poem's three-part structure is widely accepted. It will be noted that omitting the "sonnet" opening and the *ottava rima* close, the three parts consist of 70, 47, and 54 lines. It is familiar Miltonic practice that one part in a three-part structure should be carefully disproportionate. Indeed *Nat* draws attention (line 239) to the undue length of its third part. In *PR* and in *SA* the second temptation is considerably longer than the other two. The effect of irregularity within overall regularity is significant in *Lyc* for better reasons than the avoiding of boredom. It testifies to a vital quality of the poem itself and of the recognition it accommodates.

If we look more closely at the three parts we find that part one owes its length to its consisting of not one, but two crescendos—the Orpheus passage and the passage on fame. With the underlying rhythm of questioning established, the second part can have the impact of brevity and the apocalyptic consolation, in particular, gains in force from not being further developed. The third part, unlike the first two, has only a threatened digression, but its consolation-cum-apotheosis of twenty-one lines is by far the longest, as befits its finality. These variations might be sufficient to undermine the sense of symmetry if the three movements were not parallel in their development. Each begins with a traditional pastoral passage—the recollection of idyllic days spent in the fields, the procession of mourners, and the strewing of flowers. The assault of experience on the convention then develops, and the movement from decorum to disturbance gathers force until the restoration of an equilibrium that permits the pastoral mood to be resumed. The final "resumption" is of such a nature as to preclude the possibility of any further disturbance. To quote Woodhouse (*Essays in Honour of Gilbert Norwood* [1952], p. 273) the first two parts culminate in passages that "shatter the pastoral tone, while the third does not shatter but rather transcends it."

The repeated establishing of a decorum that is then repeatedly violated is apparent not only from the text as it stands, but from its evolution, as previously discussed. In particular, the alteration in line 5 indicates not only the vehemence of grief and the reluctance of a poet to write before his "season," but also suggests the manner in which the poem is to attack its own conventions.

The importance that Milton attached to this dominant characteristic of his three movements is also apparent when we notice that each of these movements is prefaced by a statement that the pastoral convention has been or is about to be violated. Two of these statements at lines 85–87 and 132–33 have been noted (J. Milton French, *Studies in Philology* 50:486, 489; Abrams, in Patrides, pp. 227ff.). The significance of the third at line 17 has been obscured because of the reminiscence of Virgil's fourth eclogue. But we have already been told of Lycidas's capacity to build the lofty rhyme (this in turn is a reminiscence of Spenser's October eclogue) and the invocation considered within the context of the poem puts us on notice that the pastoral convention is to be strained and surpassed. The lofty rhyme will give way, in a later poem, to the poetry that soars above the Aonian mount (*PL* 1.15) and one can even suggest that the Christian apotheosis of *Lyc* leads into the later invocation of a Christian muse that surpasses its classical counterpart.

It can therefore be said that there is involved in *Lyc* an assault upon the poem's own assumptions, which the poem in the act of making itself recognizes and progressively strengthens. The assault can be found to begin in the poem's play of language, in the contrast between stylized declamation and vehement, anguished questioning. It is also to be found in the larger tactical maneuver of the pastoral spectacle thrice set up to be undermined. The total attack, both formal and linguistic, can be thought of as the stylistic correlative to the deeper assault of experience upon the sense of order; and the restoration of equilibrium in convention and language corresponds to, validates, and intensifies the deeper restoration of a sense of design in reality. The poem, to quote Isabel Mac-Caffrey, involves "a growth simultaneously of the speaker's understanding and of the pastoral form itself," and Milton through the concluding vision "confirms the metamorphosis of his genre" (*"Samson Agonistes" and the Shorter Poems of Milton*, ed. MacCaffrey [1966], pp. xxviii–xxix).

It will be apparent that one of the crucial functions of the three movements is to engage repeatedly, and thereby assert with mounting force, the terms of a dialectic that is at first tentatively and then enduringly resolved. Varying descriptions of this dialectic are offered. For Brooks and Hardy (Patrides, pp. 136–52) the conflict is between Christian and pagan attitudes and the synthesis "finally accomplished" is a "typically baroque mingling" of both. It is an engagement exemplified in the imagery and particularly in the dual connotations of the word *Shepherd*. For Woodhouse (*Norwood*, pp. 261–78) the contrast is between the Arcadian world of the pastoral and the real world of extra-aesthetic life. Lloyd (*Essays in Criticism* II: 390–402), sees a contrast between the self-absorbed world and the world of the good shepherd with the pastoral imagery unifying the examination of both. Brett (*Milton's Lycidas* [1960], pp. 39–50) finds Renaissance humanism carried by the pastoral strain, in conflict with the Protestant convictions brought out by the digressions. Lawry (Barker, pp. 112–23) describes the "seeming opposites" as "pastoral *vs* local engagement, timeless poetry *vs* experience, art *vs* actuality." These produce a

"reconstituted possibility of poetry which in part grows out of the formerly opposed modes, *both* of which have seemed, whether by impotence or by antagonistic assault to signal the defeat of poetry." Finally Marjorie Nicolson (*John Milton: A Reader's Guide to His Poetry* [1963], pp. 87–111) sees the conflict emblematized in the contest between the myrtle standing for mourning and the laurel standing for the triumph of the victor, whether living or dead.

Some of *Lyc* can be found between any of these contraries, but it is doubtful if the poem is any of these oppositions alone or even any of them fully. The varying descriptions might rather be seen as testifying to the richness of the poem's life and the range of issues that it is able to bring together in creative confrontation. The result is to draw the reader's mind into the poem more fully and to make him more deeply responsive to its intensity of questioning and its power of reconciling. The "perception of identity and contrariety," the "ever varying balance of images, notions, or feelings, conceived as in opposition to each other" that Coleridge finds the shaping principle of *Lyc* (*The Romantics on Milton*, ed. Joseph A. Wittreich [1970], p. 179) may not be, as he claims, "the condition of all consciousness," but it does extend considerably the field of force of the poem. The principle that Coleridge invokes is not without foundation in seventeenth-century aesthetics. See H. V. S. Ogden, *Journal of the History of Ideas* 10: 159–82.

The two great classical myths the poem uses—that of Orpheus and that of Arethusa—can be seen as another manifestation of the poem's dialectic. Orpheus, born of Calliope, the muse of heroic poetry, represents the higher mood and the account of his death is in fact the poem's first ascent to that mood. Virgil's fourth eclogue, it might be added, specifically associates the loftier strain with Orpheus. Arethusa is the muse of pastoral poetry invoked, for example, in the tenth eclogue. Orpheus was interpreted as a type of Christ (Caroline Mayerson, *Publications of the Modern Language Association* 64: 189–207). In Fulgentius's allegorizing of the Alpheus-Arethusa myth (D. C. Allen, *Modern Language Notes* 71: 172–73), Arethusa represents the nobility of justice and Alpheus the light of truth. Alpheus's waters, by passing unpolluted through the ocean, demonstrate that truth is incorruptible. Carey and Fowler note (p. 246) that a similar view is taken by Sandys. It is significant that Arethusa is called upon after a reference to the purity and perfection of Jove's justice, while Alpheus is called upon after the two-handed engine delivers from a hostile world the shrinking stream of those who pursue the ideal. A slightly different interpretation is proposed by Peck (Elledge, pp. 297–99), according to whom the "mythologists suggest that as Alpheus (imperfection) follows Arethusa (virtue), so matter desires form as its proper good." Hughes cites Conti to similar effect. It might be added that the truth (Osiris, formerly Alpheus) suffers in *Areop* (4: 337–38) a fate similar to that of Orpheus, and the "empty dream" of the muse who could not protect Orpheus is abandoned in *PL* (7.1–39) for the heavenly guidance of Urania. Taken together, the two myths of *Lyc* that man's fate is to be destroyed and to survive, to keep alive what is

eternal in his identity, to pursue the harmony that has fled the world with what is lastingly creative in the self, to endure frustration and yet to find fulfillment. The upward metamorphosis already explored in *Mask*, the underground journey with its Christian overtones, and the reconciliation with the ideal in an order that transforms the terms of our reality are intertwined in a manner that once again bears witness to the integrative power of the poem.

The apotheosis in *Lyc* is a mingling of the Christian and the classical. It is reached, according to Abrams (Patrides, pp. 226–27), by "a gradual shift from the natural, pastoral, and pagan viewpoint to the viewpoint of Christian revelation." Nicolson, on the other hand (*Reader's Guide*, p. 96n.), considers the answers from above to be uniformly Christian. It is possible to regard the three consolations as built up by the three-part structure to provide an understanding that is cumulative and also progressive. Each part discloses a different face of God or, more precisely, a different form of man's recognition of God's nature. The God who calms the first wave of doubts is the God of justice, and emphasis is consequently laid on His impartiality, His "perfect witness," and on the "all-judging" power that weighs all things fully and impartially in its balance. The God of the second part is the apocalyptic God of retribution, whose single blow is sufficient to crush the armies of the godless. "Respiration to the just / And vengeance to the wicked" (*PL* 12.540–41) are the complementary consolations offered and the complementarityextends to the nuances of tone. The first consolation stills the malignant, monosyllabic march as the blind fury slits the thin-spun life, replacing it by the heartbeat of reassurance. Milton arranges the transition in mid-line with significant delicacy. The rhythm of awareness has different consequences when it is set in a different perspective. The movement is tranquil, as calm of mind must be in stilling the mind's outbursts. In contrast, the second consolation is unassailable in its finality, terminating a torrent of corruption that would otherwise rage unchecked. The "But" of line 130 suggests that in the nature of the case there can be no other termination, and the poem's pounding eloquence itself embodies the momentum of the force that is paralyzed. To make understanding doubly clear, Milton defines the specific quality of each reassurance immediately after the reassurance has been offered. Significantly, these definitions occur in those two crucial passages which admit the violation of the pastoral decorum. We return to normality from the "higher mood" of justice; we return to it again from the "dread voice" of retribution.

The third recognition of God is the one recognition that can truly answer man's questioning. It is the consciousness not of justice, but of the power beyond justice, not the might of him who wields the two-handed engine but instead "the dear might of him that walks the waves." The angel who guards England is invited to "melt with ruth." The dolphins "waft" a Lycidas whose bones only a few lines previously were being "hurl'd" beyond the "stormy Hebrides." As a creature both in and out of its element, the dolphin seems fitted to bear the questioning mind to a higher order, to the "blest kingdoms meek of joy and love." The language of the consolation, compassionate and

jubilant, is once again found in an accurately felt relationship to the previous consolations it both completes and supersedes. To quote *PL* (3.212) it is the "rigid satisfaction, death for death" that has dominated the first two "resolutions" in *Lyc.* The third resolution transcends the law and so reminds us that there are energies in the poem that even the law cannot silence. If peace is to be won, it can be won only through the higher satisfaction of redemptive love. Justice and Wrath—the quiet reassurance and the resounding intervention—must be seen within a larger context if they are to be seen properly as part of the providence of God.

The development of the poem can also be treated as relating and eventually integrating two different perspectives. The ground-level, existential progress toward understanding is associated with the decorum of the pastoral order and its increasingly inadequate consolations. The higher mood, representing a more inclusive understanding, enters the poem at its moments of crisis, guiding the protagonist to a comprehension that is demanded by his intensity of questioning but that is not available within the terms of his world. These entries are managed with characteristic care. In a reminiscence of Virgil's sixth eclogue, the higher mood *descends,* touching the trembling ears of what we can imagine as an averted face. The two-handed engine stands at the door. If justice is from above, retribution is from without. Both point to another realm of principles and forces from which what Reesing (*Milton's Poetic Art* [1968], pp. 123–25) calls the "divine rescue" of the protagonist must be effected.

The "great vision of the guarded mount" needs to be considered in this context. As "vision," it is made to stand apart from the pastoral world it is called on to redeem. The assurance it offers is guarded against those sounding seas of doubt that have raged through the poem with increasing ferocity. The mount itself is evocative of Paradise. The geographical sweep of the proper names suggests the widening horizon of understanding and the attainment of a perspective not possible at the level of this world or within the blindness to which that level consigns us. As we look out on the seas on which the Armada met its fate, the perilous flood comes to mean deliverance as well as destruction. The hill on which the angel stands takes its place in relation to the hill of virtue at the end of *Mask*, the hill of truth in *Sonn* 9, the hill on which Adam stands in the final books of *PL*, and the hill on which Christ stands in *PR*. Above them is the hill (*PL* 3. 56–59) on which God is seated "high thron'd above all highth." This is the infinite vision that human comprehension approaches through the limited vision offered by lesser hills. The collisions of decorum and language in *Lyc* thus provide the means for the higher mood to take over and reaffirm the pastoral convention that it initially challenges and eventually redeems.

The much-discussed water imagery of *Lyc* (see below) further defines some of the poem's characteristic collisions. The Dee contrasts with the Hebrus, the "honoured flood" of the "smooth-sliding Mincius" with the "perilous flood" over which Lycidas comes to preside, and the "level brine" on which Panope plays with her sisters with those "sounding seas" that are stilled by the "great

vision." Energy versus containment is the opposition immediately suggested, and if the forces of questioning rage with sufficient vehemence (as they undoubtedly do in this poem), they must undermine the possibility of meaning itself. The three movements confront us with the threatening likelihood that existence may be subject to no design except at best the design of malignancy. As Peck (Elledge, p. 273) and Nicolson in our time (*Reader's Guide*, p. 95) have noted, the Furies are not blind, and it is the Fates, not the Furies, who cut the thread of life. Milton's singular alliance is forged to suggest to us that persecution will be both arbitrary and relentless and that to stand apart is to invite being struck down. The second exposure of meaninglessness complements the first. If dedication is mocked, desecration must be rewarded. A corrupt priesthood is capable of higher irresponsibilities than the pastoral indulgence of sporting with Amaryllis, but the way of the world is inexorably "to good malignant, to bad men benigne" (*PL* 12.538). Injustice flourishes until it is "smitten" by a power beyond the world. The phrase looks forward to *PR* 4.561–62 and *SA* 1643–45. In this context the "monstrous world" of the third movement in which Lycidas's bones are "hurl'd" with familiar but intensified violence beyond the outer limits of the known becomes the objectification of the poem's rampant forces of disorder. As Reesing observes (*Milton's Poetic Art*, p. 22), we are swept to the conclusion that "the world is governed, not blindly, but not at all; that reality is, not merely irrational or deliberately malevolent, but totally mindless." The depths of the abyss must be seen more starkly than ever, before the turn takes place into the poem's peace and the affirmation of peace is validated by the chaos through which it has been repeatedly made to struggle.

The turning point of the poem can be a matter of dispute. D. C. Allen, contrasting the imagery of the flower passage with previous flower imagery (e.g., 45–48), finds the turning point in the flower passage. Others remembering the "false surmise" of line 152 and the menacing lines that follow would prefer to locate the turn at lines 159–64. The function of this image to which Eliot concedes unsurpassed "grandeur of sound" but is apparently prepared to concede little else (*On Poetry and Poets*, pp. 163–64) has already been partially discussed. The angel Michael is imagined as looking southwards to Bayona, a Spanish stronghold about fifty miles south of Cape Finisterre, near which stand the mountains of Namancos. All these places, Hughes notes, "are picturesquely prominent on Ortelius's maps." Apart from standing guard for England against her traditional enemies, the angel is also, Hughes observes, the patron of mariners "in Jewish and often in Christian tradition." Milton's emendation of Corineus to Bellerus in *TM* moves the poem into the mythological distance without divesting it of its political evocations. The legendary and the contemporary unite in the protective strength that is to surround the final understanding; the "guarded mount," with its intimations of Paradise, suggests the restoration not only of Lycidas but of the pattern of order in the scheme of

things; and the "great vision" prepares us for the concluding vision of the apotheosis.

In literary history and in legend, others beside Lycidas have been wafted ashore by dolphins. Arion, a Greek poet credited with inventing the dithyramb, saved himself from a crew of hostile sailors determined to kill him for his wealth by leaping into the sea and being carried ashore by a dolphin. Line 164 has usually been taken as alluding to Arion. Significantly Arion was born on Lesbos, where Orpheus was killed by frenzied Bacchantes (lines 58–63). However, Richardson and Newton, followed by Mabbott (*Explicator* 5, no. 26) and others, take it as alluding to Palaemon, who was drowned near Corinth and later honored as the protector of sailors in a temple built at the spot where a dolphin supposedly carried his body ashore. Michael Lloyd (*Essays in Criticism* [1961], 397–98) notes that in "Servius's version of the myth, Phoebus Apollo himself in the guise of a dolphin rescued his drowning son Icarius and carried him to Mount Parnassus." Perhaps this is the account that best fits the pattern of *Lyc*, but it is not inconceivable that Milton meant us to think of the tradition as a whole—a tradition of which Yeats's *Byzantium* can be regarded as the modern sequel—rather than of any specific "rescue." A feature of the deliverance that the language calls to our attention is its gentleness, a serenity that is in significant contrast to the stormy cycles of the poem's questioning.

D. C. Allen (*The Harmonious Vision*, pp. 41–50) has investigated the manner in which the pagan paramythia (the transformation of the man into the legend) becomes the Christian consolation. Apart from Virgil's fifth eclogue (see above) and Spenser's November eclogue with its deification of Dido, key texts in this progress are the concluding sections of Seneca's *Ad Marcian,* the funeral orations of Gregory Nazianzen, and Jerome's epistle to Heliodorus on the death of Nepolitan. This "*contaminatio* of pagan and Christian topoi" lies not behind *Lyc* alone, but behind all of Milton's elegies. While the tradition goes satisfyingly back, the texts from Revelation that the apotheosis invokes (7:17; 14:1–5; 19:6–9; 21:4; 22:2) carry the poem not only beyond time but into contemporaneity, since Revelation was so frequently used to expound the eschatological meaning of current events. Milton returns to allied texts from Revelation in the climax of *EpDam* and the nature of the "unexpressive nuptial song" is significantly glossed in a passage in *Apol* (3:306–7). We can also remember as we read lines 178–79 that in the battle in heaven in *PL* the loyal angels are repeatedly called saints and that the word in Puritan understanding signified the entire community of the elect. Everlasting blessedness in a kingdom that is at hand for all faithful herdsmen is an implication that may be strengthened if, as Madsen argues (*Studies in English Literature* 3:2–6), the speaker of the consolation is Michael. The general view, however, is that "the uncouth Swain" is the speaker.

Whatever its affiliations or whoever utters it, there can be no doubt of the security of the final affirmation. That security is also evident from the manner in which the closing lines detach the apotheosis from the persona whose

dramatized search for meaning it has climaxed. The opening quasi-sonnet and the closing *ottava rima* frame that can now be seen as the creative turbulence of the poem also define the advance to "eager thought" from the passion-driven shattering of the leaves. The shift from first to third person has been discreetly prepared for by the shift from second to third person in reporting that the shepherds no longer weep (165, 182). At this point Lycidas becomes the audience of the poem rather than its subject; the next step is to objectify him as the genius of the shore; the shepherds, too, are other people as much as the singer's colleagues; and the stage is now set for the singer himself to step out of his own experience. The "uncouth swain" is clearly not one of those whom John Donne dismisses as having "sucked on country pleasures, childishly." Instead, the heroic, in Landor's words (Wittreich, p. 35), has "burst forth from the pastoral" and bucolic innocence has been found capable of taking in all of experience. Notable also is the manner in which the swain begins his song at daybreak (recalling 25–26) and ends it as twilight falls (recalling 29–31). Apart from the artful reminder of the poem as *mimesis*, we are advised that the day of the song is a day in the life of a shepherd, to be left behind as other days have been, including those days of companionship with Lycidas that were earlier mourned as gone never to return. The rhythm of things calls for progress as well as recurrence. If the evening star (30) shone over the close of one day, the morning star (171) "flames" over the meaning of another. The "Doric lay" has induced what Aristotle (*Pol.* 8.5) calls a "moderate and settled temper," putting the affections "in right tune" by its music. As in *SA*, the catharsis is one of understanding as well as of emotion, though the end here is not "passion spent" but vigorous expectancy. As the sun stretches out the hills, the "eager thought" of the singer seems to survey a widening horizon. The sun drops and the curtain falls. The singer in front of it twitches his mantle, the blue of which signifies hope and, to some, the Presbyterian Covenanters. The fresh woods and new pastures advise us that a writer's covenant with his reader is that he shall not cease from exploration.

The "sources" of the "digressions" remain to be examined. Neaera's hair has entangled more than one commentator. Tibullus, Horace, Joannes Secundus, and Buchanan are among the poets who have referred to the subject. The poignant sensuality of the line is Milton's alone. For line 70 Todd cites Spenser's *Tears of the Muses,* line 404 ("Due praise that is the spur of doing well"). Bush calls the thought a commonplace going back at least to Ovid, *Ex Ponto* 4.2.36. The following line is referred by Newton to Tacitus, *Hist* 4.6 ("Even with wise men the desire for glory is last cut off") and by Bush to Boethius (*Consolatio Philosophiae* 11.7). In connection with Phoebus's consolation, Hanford cites Spenser's October Eclogue, lines 13ff., where Cuddie is told that the praise is better than the price and the glory greater than the gain. As has already been noted, Apollo in Virgil's sixth eclogue touches the poet's ear and warns him against ambition. Fame was everywhere the spur in the Renaissance, but as Allen points out (p. 66), Milton had well before *Lyc* "found a higher definition

of the word." This definition is in *Prol* 7 (12:279). *Lyc* at this point looks not only backward but forward to Christ's dismissal of glory in *PR* (3.25–144). Apart from what it puts together, the passage is remarkable for the manner in which the movement of the verse reflects the true voice of feeling. The buoyant consonants lend their sprightliness to sporting with Amaryllis; the conflagration of line 74 is assisted by the positioning of "blaze" and the alliterative link with "burst"; a second link, this time with "blind," undercuts the excitement of ambition by its delusiveness; and the stealthy progress of the monosyllables in line 75 seems to join calculation mordantly to blindness. At the same time the steps taken up the ladder—the loss of sensual happiness, the clearing of the spirit from the lower distraction, the dedication to a higher infirmity recognized and yet intensely coveted, the total frustration on the edge of achievement, make evident in their entanglement the nature of that purity which must attend the final reckoning. There is, we are made to understand, a difference between "pure" and "clear" as well as between "pure" and "blind"; and the obvious difference between "clear" and "blind" is less decisive than it seems at the first reading.

The Pilot of the Galilean Lake is usually taken to be St. Peter; Hone (*Studies in Philology* 56:55–61) argues that he is Christ. In 1 Peter 2:25 Christ is described as the Shepherd and Bishop of a straying flock. In John 6:15–21 and elsewhere he saves a boat carrying his disciples from shipwreck. In Revelation 1:18 he carries the keys of hell and death. The keys given to St. Peter (Matt. 16:19) seem to fit better into Milton's text. The denunciation of false teachers follows from 2 Peter 2 and decorum is less strained than it would be by Christ's presence in the procession. Two keys are allowed St. Peter by various poets; the golden and the iron clearly anticipate *PL* 2.327–28, and 5.886–87, and Psalm 2:9 may be invoked.

Apart from biblical origins, notably John 10:1–28 and Ezekiel 34, Bernard of Morlais's handling of the John parable in his *De Contemptu Mundi* is cited (G. R. Coffman, *ELH: A Journal of English Literary History* 3:101–13), and *Paradiso* 29.103–26, and 27.19–66, may have been in Milton's mind. Other possible allusions to Dante are listed by Irene Samuel (pp. 285–86). J. M. Steadman (*Notes and Queries*, n.s. 5:141–42) thinks that Milton may have been drawing upon a scene between St. Peter and the condemned clergy in *La rappresentazione del di del guidizio*. Line 115 may echo line 126 of Spenser's May Eclogue but *PL* 4.192–93 and 12.507ff. are anticipated. Those who dislike Ruskin's celebrated interpretation of "Blind mouths" (Elledge, p. 239), in which blindness and rapacity invert the pastoral functions of seeing and nourishing, can turn to Strabo (4.1.8), who applies the phrase to the choked estuary of a river. Shallowness and obstruction are the failing implied. Hunter (*Modern Language Notes* 65:544) considers that "rot inwardly" (127) comes from Aristotle's *Parts of Animals* 672 a–b, or a Renaissance adaptation thereof. Le Comte (69:403–4) argues that lines 125–27 are closely modeled on a passage in Petrarch's ninth eclogue where Petrarch is recalling the Black Death. The "grim

wolf" (128) is usually read as the Roman Catholic Church. Le Comte (*Studies in Philology* 47:606) notes that the arms of the founder of the Jesuits, St. Ignatius Loyola, included two gray wolves. The forward-looking reader will think of *PL* 4.182–92 and 12.507–14. Apart from indicating the range of Milton's reading, references to such details as the niceties of sheep-rot make clear the determination with which Milton keeps within the boundaries of the pastoral. The higher mood is established not by any change in the imagery or any deviation from the permitted topics, but by the vehement intensity of the utterance.

At this point the two-handed engine must be considered. Fortunately the prevailing interpretations are well summed up by Patrides (p. 240).

> Research has yielded parallels in the writings of such diverse figures as Gregory the Great, Dante, John of Salisbury, Savonarola, Du Bartas, Jehan Gerard, Phineas Fletcher, Donne, Thomas Adams and Robert Burton; while the riddle itself has been variously interpreted as the two Houses of Parliament, or liberty as wielded by them; the temporal and Spiritual authority of the Court of High Commission; the destructive power of the imminent civil war; "Puritan Zeal" in general; the combined forces of England and Scotland, or of France and Spain; the Catholic Church; the pastoral staff; the keys of Heaven and Hell given to St. Peter; the lock on St. Peter's door; St. Peter's sword (Matt. 20:51, John 18:10); the "Sharp two-edged Sword" of the Johannine vision (Rev. 1:16, 2:12); the Sword of Divine Justice (Ezekiel 21:9–17), particularly as wielded by Michael "with huge two-handed sway," (*Paradise Lost* VI, 251); the axe in general, or specifically, the axe that was "laid unto the root of the trees" (Matt. 3:10, Luke 3:9); the rod of Christ's anger; the Word of God; the Son of God; the scythe of Time; Man "in his dual capacity of labour and prayer"; the Sheep-hook; the iron flail of Talus (*Faerie Queen* V, i, 12; etc.); the temple of Janus; and so on and so forth.

Since Patrides wrote this note, commentary has been added by Thompson (*Studies in Philology* 59: 184–200), Rhodes (*Notes and Queries*, n.s. 13:24), Stempel (*English Language Notes* 3:259–63), Tuveson (*Journal of the History of Ideas* 27:447–58) and Reesing (*Milton's Poetic Art*, pp. 31–49). The "sword" class of interpretations is most popular and Reesing (p. 173n.) lists sixteen scholars who find the engine a sword in "one sense or another." Reesing himself argues for the engine as the rod of Christ's wrath, "which is the archetypal reality behind every bishop's staff." It would be no tragedy if the crux were not resolved; some element of mystery is necessary for the apocalyptic effect. Meanwhile the imminence of the deliverance, the power that is deployed in it, its swiftness, and its decisiveness are all made evident by the words on the page.

"Flowerets and Sounding Seas," the title of Wayne Shumaker's study of the affective imagery of *Lyc* (Patrides, pp. 125–35), may at first strike one as yet another formulation of the poem's dialectic. But Shumaker is concerned less

with the contrasts between the two classes of imagery than with the contrasts within each class. It is the use of these contrasts that enables *Lyc* to proceed from lamentation to triumph without shifting the terms of poetic discourse. The basic imagery remains consistent throughout, but its potentialities are used in different ways. Josephine Miles's examination of the primary language of *Lyc* (Patrides, pp. 95–100) discovers the integrity of the poem in its vocabulary, showing how the "essential motion from low to high, paralleled by that from past to future, takes place through the primary characteristic words of the poem." Apart from inherited pastoral diction, Milton brings certain words into strong use for the first time. Words such as *"fresh, new, pure, sacred, green, watry, flood, leaf, morn, hill, shade, shore, stream, star, wind, fame, ask, touch"* refer to the natural world "in more specific and sensory terms than were usual before Milton's time," but also transfigure that world through value-giving adjectives. Milton's language is strongly characterized by its "richness in adjectival quality." G. C. Taylor (*Notes and Queries* 178:56–57) finds the language less innovative. Of the 1,500 words in *Lyc*, only 46 entered the language after 1500. The Virgilian music is intriguingly achieved with a vocabulary that is 80 percent Anglo-Saxon in derivation. Carey and Fowler (p. 234) note that Milton's coinages include "inwrought" (105), "freaked" (144), and "scrannel" (124), that "rathe" (142) is used in the *Calendar*, that "daffadillies" (150) suggests the *Calendar's* "daffadowndillies," and that "Guerdon," which Milton uses in *Lyc* for the first and only time, is found no less than twenty-three times in Spenser.

Noting that "Grief is eloquent, but not formal," Newton found a "natural and agreeable wildness and irregularity" in *Lyc*. Hurd attributed the "very original air" of the poem to "the looseness and variety of the meter." Keightley observed that Milton adopted from Tasso and Guarini the "practice of mingling three-foot lines with the regular verses of five feet" (Elledge, pp. 227–28, 236). More categorically, W. P. Ker has advised us that "*Lycidas*, the *Ode to Anne Killigrew, Alexander's Feast*, the *Odes* of Gray and Keats and before them all, Spenser's *Prothalamion* and *Epithalamion* all belong to the order of the Italian canzone" (*Form and Style in Poetry*, p. 162). In his study of the Italian influence on the versification of *Lyc*, Prince (Patrides, p. 161) notes that two "technical experiments—the attempt to evolve a poetic diction equivalent to that of Virgil, and the attempt to combine the tradition of the *canzone* with that of the classical eclogue—marked Italian pastoral verse in the sixteenth century." Both these endeavors bear their fruit in *Lyc*. Prince shows how the key rhyme (*chiave*) that links the two sections of a *canzone* enables the rhyme schemes of *Lyc* to look both backward and forward, how six-syllable lines are placed "so as to give a sense of expectation," and how the couplet is used to achieve arrest: "the only true couplets in *Lycidas* are those which conclude verse-paragraphs." The result is a verse form that is "closely controlled" and yet not only allows but facilitates "freedom of improvisation." Milton's creative use of previous

rhyme schemes is not exhausted by his adaptation of the *canzone*. Oras (*Modern Philology* 52:12–22) finds precedents for *Lyc* in the madrigal, and Finney (*Huntington Library Quarterly* 15:325–50) in the *dramma per musica*.

Prince's remark that Milton had "sufficient Renaissance authority" for the unrhymed lines of *Lyc* should stand next to Ransom's view (*Patrides*, p. 68) that the lines "technically do not belong in . . . any stanza, nor in the poem" and represent an intrusion of individuality in a poem that is only "nearly anonymous." The rhymeless lines register the "ravage" of Milton's "modernity," and no other poem of the time is "so wilful and illegal in form as this one." Critics from Newton onward have been more receptive to what has been accepted as the poem's irregularity, but an article by Joseph Wittreich (*Publications of the Modern Language Association* 84:60–70) persuasively argues that the irregularities are designed to play against a "single, enveloping rhyme scheme" of remarkable complexity, within which the irregular is eventually regularized. *PL* 5.618–24 may well serve as an epigraph to Wittreich's article. Considered paragraph by paragraph, *Lyc* has ten unrhymed lines. Considered within the overall scheme, the ten lines reduce to three, "one in each of the *three* thematic units and always in the verse paragraph immediately preceding the consolation for that movement." The rhymes proceed through the alphabet and then repeat the process, but with the final consolation coming, with numerological aptness, in the tenth paragraph and taking us precisely ten rhymes into a third alphabet. The "chief control for the poem's pattern is the English madrigal," and the pattern itself is "built of a series of circles, inscribed by the rhyme, suggested and supported by the imagery."

The history of *Lyc* criticism has been intermittently dealt with in this article. Johnson's strictures, which dominate that history, have been contested from the beginning and can now be thought of as annulled. The nineteenth century is not prominent in bringing about this annulment. Criticism of *Lyc* by the Romantic poets as assembled by Wittreich is not very extensive and Stevens in the *Reference Guide to Milton* (1930) lists only nine items on the poem from 1800 to 1899. Ruskin's remarks (Elledge, pp. 237–44) stand apart and remain of much more than historical importance. Mark Pattison in *Milton* anticipates some future criticism when he finds the "fanaticism of the covenanter and the sad grace of Petrarch" meeting in Milton's monody. These opposites, "instead of neutralising each other, are blended into one harmonious whole." Of early twentieth-century appreciations, Bailey's (*Milton* [1915] pp. 123–31) is among the more perceptive.

Despite relics of Johnson's objection, such as the view that *Lyc* is a poem strangled by art (Robert Graves) or that it is no more than a collection of magnificent fragments (G. Wilson Knight), it has been the privilege of criticism of the last half-century to fully meet the accusations of empty conventionality and uncalled-for juxtapositions. In the process a detailed consensus has developed testifying to the intricate unity of the poem, the profound pertinence of its alleged digressions, the force of experience that the genre is made to

accommodate, and the highly charged meaningfulness of a creative performance that possesses the past in order to speak to all times. [BR]

MASK, A. Milton wrote his second dramatic entertainment for the Earl of Bridgewater and the Egerton family. Although the Earl had been made President of the Council of Wales in June 1631, and Lord Lieutenant of Wales and the Counties on the Welsh border in July 1631, he did not formally begin his duties until the fall of 1634. On Michaelmas, September 29, 1634, Milton's celebratory work was "presented" at the Earl's official residence, Ludlow Castle. The poem was recited, sung, and danced by the Earl's daughter, Alice Egerton, aged fifteen, who played the Lady; the Earl's two sons, John, aged eleven, and Thomas, aged nine, who played the Brothers; and the children's music master, Henry Lawes, who played the Attendant Spirit–Thyrsis, composed the music, staged the work, and had it anonymously published in 1637 as *A Maske Presented at Ludlow Castle, 1634.*

In his dedicatory letter to the elder son, John, Lord Viscount Brackley, Lawes explains that the poem "although not openly acknowledged by the author" is, nevertheless, "a legitimate offspring so lovely, and so much desired, that the often Copying of it hath tired my Pen to give my several friends satisfaction, and brought me to a necessity of producing it to the public view." There is, however, some uncertainty as to what Lawes "copied" to produce the text of 1637, and even more debate over what he copied or had copied for his friends, and, especially, for the Bridgewater family.

The two extant manuscripts of the poem differ considerably. *TM* (Milton's working copy) is not, as John Diekhoff has shown, in any of its forms the original draft of *Mask*, but a later transcript subjected to considerable revision before and after the 1634 production and the 1637 edition. It contains, among its many alterations and transpositions, a canceled version of the Epilogue as well as the full Epilogue with its references to Venus, Adonis, Cupid, and Psyche. *BrM* was once thought to be in Lawes's hand, but has been definitively identified as the work of a professional scribe. However, many commentators have accepted this manuscript as the version of the masque Lawes staged for the Egerton family in 1634, although the proof for this notion is entirely circumstantial. The *BrM* is shorter (908 lines) than the published versions (1023 lines) and the cuts seem to have been made primarily to accommodate the speeches as Milton originally wrote them to the acting capacities and memories of the Earl's children, to insure that no one in the first audience would be offended by extended discussions of the Lady's chastity, and to provide Lawes with an opening song instead of an inductive speech.

For those who date *BrM*'s transcription around 1634 it provides a neat evolutionary link between the early version of the poem (obscured behind the deletions and corrections in *TM*) and the printed version of the poem (revised *TM*). However, John Shawcross has challenged *BrM*'s date. He argues that it was probably not transcribed until 1637–38, that it "was transcribed from a

copy of the *Trinity MS* during its development into the version which survives," and that "the 1637 Edition was set from this same intermediate copy, revised by corrections and additions from the *Trinity MS*." He contends, therefore, that "the form of the mask which we know today as *Comus* could not possibly have been the form of the mask presented at Ludlow Castle." The debate is still open, although Carey in his edition and Parker in his biography have accepted Shawcross's view. However, whether or not *BrM* is *the* Ludlow version of *Mask*, it is still a valuable reminder that Milton's work was a theatrical familial enterprise as well as an intricately structured poem.

The later publishing history of *Mask* is less tortured than the state of its manuscripts. There is general agreement that the text for the 1645 edition of the poem, Milton's first printed acknowledgment of it, is based on the 1637 text with corrections, most of which are found in *TM*, and that the 1673 text is based, with slight changes, on the text of 1645. In the collected edition of his poems, 1645, Milton gave *Mask* the place of honor. It was, in Masson's phrase, "still in respect of length and merit his chief poetical achievement." It came last, with a separate title page, and was attended by Lawes's 1637 dedication as well as a letter from Sir Henry Wotton in high praise of the "dainty peece of entertainment's" "Dorique delicacy." By the time of Milton's second collected edition, *Mask* had lost its premier ranking and Milton printed it without the endorsements of Lawes and Wotton.

Although Lawes was responsible for the first publication of *Mask*, he most probably worked with Milton in establishing the text for 1637 and he almost certainly elicited from Milton the introductory motto from Virgil: *"Eheu quid volui misero mihi! floribus austrum / Perditus—"* ("Alas what harm did I mean to my wretched self when I let the south wind blow upon my flowers?"). The question remained entirely rhetorical during Milton's lifetime. The poem was highly regarded and, apparently, gave no trouble. However, early in the next century, *Mask* suffered the distinction of becoming the only poem Milton wrote that was retitled by his critics. When John Dalton "adapted" Milton's poem for a benefit performance in 1738 he called it (following Toland's biography) *Comus*, and revised it by deleting some passages and including others from several of Milton's shorter poems. Although he undoubtedly changed the title for theatrical convenience (as Masson said, approvingly, "it was really inconvenient that such a poem should be without a briefer and more specific name"), Dalton's liberties with the title and the text are, in an important sense, major acts of criticism. His arbitrary new title powerfully suggests the difference between the 1634 performance and all other performances of the poem, and it also suggests the transient history of the genre in which Milton chose to project his entertainment.

The original title conveys, as no other title could, the local insularity of the form as well as the particular pleasures it must have given when it was first produced, pleasures that can now be felt, at best, at two removes from their source. Despite its allusive range and serious treatment of serious themes,

Milton's poem was a libretto written for specific actors, a specific audience, and a specific place. The titular change from *A Maske Presented at Ludlow Castle* to *Comus* critically acknowledges the conversion of the unique performance of 1634 into a performable literary text, a process that had effectively begun with the edition of 1637. There is no evidence to indicate precisely how the Ludlow performance was managed, but it was certainly different from all subsequent performances of the poem in three crucial details: in the 1634 version, the actors (except for the performers, never identified, who played Comus and Sabrina) played themselves before an audience consisting of their family and friends. Lawes's dedicatory letter makes obvious reference to the masque's ceremonial linking of the imaginary and the real when he concludes, "Live sweet Lord to be the honour of your Name, and receive this as your own, from the hands of him, who hath by many favours been long oblig'd to your most honour'd Parents, and as in this representation your attendant *Thyrsis*, so now in all reall expression your faithfull, and most humble Servant *H. Lawes*."

Neither Milton nor Lawes left any record as to how the poem was mounted, how much music accompanied it (five songs by Lawes survive in manuscript), or how long it was danced, but its mingling of the real and fictive characters of its "presenters," its celebratory notes, its combination of verse, music, dancing, and spectacle clearly align it with other works of the period granted without argument the generic status of "masque." Milton's poem is certainly less open to spectacular effects than many masques of the period, but this is partly accounted for by the relatively domestic character of his audience and the subject of his celebration. Nevertheless, the poem has been turned into an aesthetic orphan, a work without a genre. It has been called among other things, a "dramatised debate" (Welsford), a "dramatic masque" (Haun), "an elaborated university disputation" (Tillyard), "a lyric poem in the form of a play" (Macaulay), "a musical drama" (Finney), "a pastoral drama" (Brooks and Hardy), "a dramatic composition" (Greg), "drama in the epick style" (Johnson), "a didactic poem or a dialogue in verse" (Hazlitt), "a Platonic dialogue in the guise of a masque" (Wright), "a Platonic pastoral drama" (Carey), "a debate in semidramatic form" (Muir), "a semi-dramatic poetical debate on a moral theme" (Leishman), "a philosophical ballet" (Charles Williams), and "a suite of speeches," "an epic drama," "a poem," or "a series of lines" (Thomas Warton). However, the absence of any single, defining, theoretical model of a masque, and the existence of many different, critically certifiable masques makes the task of those who would deny *Mask* its generic place (and its original title) very difficult.

By the time Milton took up the form it had radically grown from simple "disguisings" into elaborate pageants (almost always conveying a moral theme through simple, contrasting, frequently allegorical types) ending with a formal dance of considerable duration. In addition, both the City Masques and the Court Masques were inevitably complimentary in nature. The poet's main task was to create an exciting "device" or "invention" by which the compliment

could be grandly made in a mythological manner, while the designer's and director's job was to construct an ingenious "hinge" that would turn the "device" by completing the plot and releasing the masquers so that the formal dances could begin. Although the details obviously vary with individual masques, the key to the genre's "device" and "hinge" is a moment of striking transformation leading to dance.

The "entertainment" the masque provided derived in large measure from the wit and power of the "device"—in short, in the way the audience was drawn to the action and, ultimately, into it, and concomitantly, in the way the central masquers were concealed and then revealed. A masque is distinguishable from a play, then, not merely in its formal combination of diverse elements, but, more important, in the integration of the actors and the audience, the recognition of the audience (which does not want to remain and is not allowed to remain anonymous), and the incremental extension of the audience's participation as this is made possible by the form itself. There were no prescriptive proportions of music to dance to verse to spectacle, and no exact relationships of the serious to the comic or the ludicrous demanded of the poet. What seems to bother most critics of Milton who do not want to call the work a masque is that it is demonstrably better than any other masque, or as Leishman says, it is easier to "derive specifically literary pleasure" from it than from the others.

Milton's poem is unquestionably less spectacular than many other masques of the period (including Carew's and Lawes's *Coelum Britannicum*, in which the Earl's sons had recently participated), but it was not, perhaps, quite so spare as some of its critics suggest. Part of the problem here lies in the fact that when Jonson sought to save his masques for the future, he printed with his texts elaborate descriptions of the scenery, the changes of scene, the costumes, the *effects* of the transformations, and any other details he thought might help convert the transient into the permanent. In Milton's "literary text" (Tuve, Broadbent) the descriptions of scene and costume are held to a minimum, but there are clear enough indications that in the costuming and in the atmospheric effects, and, possibly, in the movements of the Attendant Spirit and Sabrina, Lawes was attempting the typically gorgeous and striking effects of the more opulent masques.

In brief, those who think the work is a masque and like it try to show (often with a polemical edge) how it succeeds where all the others fail; those who think it is not a masque and does not succeed try to show that it is too ambitious to be a masque but not ambitious enough to be a fully developed drama; and those who think it is not a masque and does succeed, try to show either that it is *sui generis* or that its successes lie in its themes rather than in its structure. Recently, B. Rajan set the dispute over *Mask's* generic status into the larger perspective of all Milton's poems when he observed that "the moral surely is that it is Milton's habit to strain at the form, to oblige it to surpass its own dimensions; yet the impression given is not of violation but of a highly

individual fulfilment, of something latent being raised into imaginative actuality."

Among those critics who consider the work sufficiently masquelike to discuss its structure in the context of the masque's decorum, the most serious divergences occur in the analysis of its "hinge," which has been variously named "a myth," "an act," "an emblem," and "an appearance," and in the identification of the principal masquers. There are some commentators who think there are no masquers in the conventional sense in the poem, some who think the children may be construed as masquers from the poem's beginning, and still others who consider the children as the principal masquers, but only in the last scene (when they do not speak). There has been more agreement about the wit of the "device." Milton's plot and the selection of the Earl's children as the principal actors have been attached, since Oldys, to a story (probably apocryphal) that the children "had been on a visit at a house of their relations, the Egerton family in Hertfordshire; and in passing through Haywood forest were benighted, and the Lady Alice was even lost for a short time." Barbara Breasted has restated evidence of rape and sodomy in a branch of the Bridgewater family that gives special point to the masque as a "cleansing family ritual" for that first audience "seeing Lady Alice Egerton act out her resistance to sexual temptation." However, independent of tale and scandal, the strength of the "device" lies essentially in its formalizing of the adventures of the Earl's children on their way to congratulate their father, a compliment increased by the fact that the children "present" themselves in elaborate and engaging poetry. (And Milton was probably not present at the original performance to claim immediate credit for his "invention" and spoil the illusion of the children's skills.)

The power of the "device" is evident as well in Milton's use of his "sources." Despite the Attendant Spirit's boast, "I will tell you now / What never yet was heard in Tale or Song / From old, or modern Bard in Hall, or Bowr," most critics of the poem have found an ample supply of "sources" related to the poem's structure and its putative themes.

One of the most recently discussed sources is a letter by a brother-in-law of Lady Alice, Robert Napier, who describes the fears of the Countess of Bridgewater that her daughter Alice had been bewitched. More distant but more literary bewitchments occur in most of "those lofty fables and romances" to which (in *Apol*) Milton says he "betook" himself. The defense of chastity dramatically rendered in the conflict between feminine virtue and malevolent magicians recalls Spenser while Ariosto and Tasso hover a bit more in the background. A frequently cited source for the poem is Peele's *Old Wive's Tale* (1595), in which two brothers seek their sister who has been enslaved by a magician. By a "commodious vicus of recirculation" most of the Renaissance versions of enchantment recall Circe's bewitchments in the *Odyssey* (10, 12) where the protective herb moly (unlike Milton's "haemony") is of sufficient

power to neutralize Circe's transforming poison. Rosemond Tuve has shown at great length how out of the "known connoted meanings" of the Circe-Comus myth "the pervading imagery of light and darkness springs quite naturally," and how "this is elaborated with the greatest originality by Milton, with conceptual refinements and extensions impossible to a lesser genius." Many other commentators on Milton have traced the permutations of the Circe myth through Ovid (*Metamorphoses* 14), Tasso's Armida episode (*Jerusalem Delivered* 14), Spenser's Acrasia (*Faerie Queene* 2.xii), and especially Spenser's story of Amoret and Busyrane in which the lady is freed from a male enchanter by Britomart (*Faerie Queene* 3.xii).

There have also been studies of the possible influence of the pastoral drama on *Mask*. At one time, the vogue was to cite Guarini's *Il Pastor Fido* and Tasso's *Aminta* as significant sources, but their places have been preempted by Fletcher's *The Faithful Sheperdess* (ca. 1610), which has received very careful attention from Carey and Leishman, among others.

The paradigmatic conflict of vice and virtue at the center of most masques' "devices" makes it difficult to locate individual masques that might have had a particular influence on *Mask*. Of the masques of the period, Jonson's *Pleasure Reconcil'd to Virtue* is probably the closest in design and does have a Comus as one of its characters (although he is much more of an obscene caricature than Milton's), but it is primarily helpful for showing how successfully Milton could use the essential components of the masque form for his own purposes. Other analogous masques include Browne's *Inner Temple Masque*, Shirley's *The Triumph of Peace*, and Townshend's *Tempe Restored* (for which John Demaray has made an extended case).

As William B. Hunter has pointed out, a major source immediate to the occasion is the set of biblical readings that were prescribed for worship by the Book of Common Prayer and in which Milton could anticipate his audience's participation on the evening of September 28 and the holy day of St. Michael and All the Angels, the 29th. Indeed, a reason to hold this inaugural celebration on this day was its evening text for the 29th, Ecclesiasticus 44: "Let us now praise famous men." In the communion service earlier the gospel reading, Matthew 18, damns those who incite children to do evil, even as Comus will attempt, and promises the assistance of angelic protection like that provided by Thyrsis if such happens. The collect for this service prays for just this help for those who need it. At that day's morning prayer service the priest read from Ecclesiasticus 39:16–29 the statement that the works of God are in themselves all good but they can be perverted from their intended ends by evil agents. As Comus urges,

> Beauty is natures coyn, must not be hoorded,
> But must be currant, and the good therof
> Consists in mutual and partak'n bliss,

(739–41)

but the Lady responds, as does Ecclesiasticus, Nature

> Means her provision only to the good
> That live according to her sober laws
> And holy dictate of spare temperance.

(765–67)

Finally, the often-decried alteration of the concluding words of 1 Corinthians 13 which Milton made, "Faith, Hope, and *Chastity*," finds an unexpected response in the fact that this chapter of Paul's letter had been read in the service the night before.

In general, studies of the sources for *Mask*'s plot and structure have been less definitive and compelling than studies of the masque's verbal and mythographic echoes, since these have been traced to Shakespeare, Sylvester, Jonson, Virgil, Horace, and especially Spenser (with regard to the images of paradise) by the poem's many editors from Warton and Todd to Carey and Hughes. And all of Milton's critics who have touched on the subject of sources have noted his imaginative liberties with the available material on the characters of Comus, who is, in the poem, a French and Italian import, not native to the Shropshire woods (out of Philostratus's *Imagines* and the Latin *Comus* of Hendrik van der Putten, 1608) and Sabrina (out of Geoffrey of Monmouth's *History of the British Kings*, Warner's *Albion's England*, Drayton's *Polyolbion*, and Spenser's *Faerie Queene*).

Mask's formal structure derives, however, not from any particular external source, but, rather, from two essential choices Milton made, one in keeping with the decorum of the masque, the other a variation on usual masque practice. Milton chose as his central figures lightly allegorical types—an Attentive Spiritual Messenger and Guide, an Unyielding, Virtuous Lady, two Brother-Heroes, a Vile, Sensual Enchanter, and a Restored, Virgin Sea-Goddess—and set them into a mildly plotted fable centered on loss, disability, resolution, and heroic recovery. He made no effort to develop his characters fully because he recognized that such development would put too much pressure on the delicate fabric of his stylized entertainment (and, possibly, too much strain on the young presenters). He did, however, decide to establish from the beginning of his masque the conflict between the forces of order and virtue and the forces of disorder and sensuality instead of (more typically of the genre) waiting to engage the opposing virtues and vices in a single climactic scene. By introducing the allegorical adversaries at the beginning of *Mask*, Milton freed himself from the usual severe restrictions on dialogue in the masque, enlarged the dramatic potential of the antimasque (which was essentially a divertissement in Jonson), and invested the relationship between the songs and dances demanded by the form and the energetic details of his story with an unusual degree of necessity and probability.

Milton organized his device *spatially* by dividing the action into a comple-

mentary series of vertical and horizontal movements. In this way, he gracefully developed a sense of the integral relationship between natural and supernatural events. The masque begins with the descent of the Spirit from "before the starry threshold of *Joves* Court," continues with the wanderings through the "drear wood" of Comus, the Lady, the Brothers, and the Attendant Spirit as Thyrsis, climactically images the ascent of Sabrina from "under the glassie, cool, translucent wave," the Lady's ascent out of Comus's "marble venom'd seat," and the descent of Sabrina "to wait in *Amphitrite's* bowr," journeys with the Lady, the Brothers, and Thyrsis to the palace of the President of Wales for the songs and dances of victory and celebration, and concludes with the ascent of the Spirit to the domain "far above" of Cupid and Psyche or "to the corners of the Moon."

The poem's opening speech is a good illustration of Milton's commanding use of the forms and *ficelles* typical of the genre. An induction is a common feature of many masques of the period, but in *Mask* the Attendant Spirit is both a dramatic character in the masque and the traditional "presenter" of the "device."

> Before the starry threshold of *Joves* Court
> My mansion is, where those immortal shapes
> Of bright aereal Spirits live insphear'd
> In Regions milde of calm and serene Air,
> Above the smoak and stirr of this dim spot,
> Which men call Earth, . . .
> . . . som there be that by due steps aspire
> To lay their just hands on that Golden Key
> That ope's the Palace of Eternity:
> To such my errand is.

The Spirit describes his role in the forthcoming action, and also presents in a concentrated form the framework within which all the characters in the masque will be placed. His "mansion" serves as the heavenly coulisse for all the other places—benevolent and malevolent—in the masque's physical and moral geography. His image of the earth as a "pinfold" where men are "confin'd" and "pester'd" establishes the masque's concern with the varieties of confinement that mark the natural and supernatural world—confinements by which men and women are tested and from which they may rise. The gloriously circumscribed life of the platonically "insphear'd" Spirits and "enthron'd gods on Sainted seats" provides counter-images to the distorted and corrupted life in Comus's palace of pleasure and to Comus's paralyzing, magic chair. This opening cluster of images is characteristic of the masque's complex verbal design. Through it Milton explores the essential distinctions between virtuous stability and monstrous fixity, between restraint and license, between the pure and the impure. The phrase "this mortal change" rings the first modulation on the masque's further concern with the existential process and spiritual meaning of transformation, and in his reference to "due steps" the Spirit introduces an

idea that will be dramatically and imagistically resolved only at the end of the masque when the Spirit's vision of a stellar paradise finally sets the wild and "tipsie" steps of the "solemn" dance of Comus and his rout of monsters into the clearest spiritual, psychological, and moral perspectives.

Many commentators on the masque have observed that the compliment is central to the form. As Northrop Frye says, "the masque is usually a compliment to the audience, or an important member of it, and leads up to an idealization of the society represented by the audience." In *Mask* Milton approached the conventional compliment with the same inventive boldness he approached the conventional prologue. The compliment to the President of Wales is preceded by the description of a world divided between Jove and Neptune. This is not a gratuitous mythological formulation. It narratively prepares for the dramatic moment when Neptune's surrogate, Sabrina, is raised by Jove's surrogate, the Attendant Spirit, in the masque's climactic scene. The Spirit's narration of Neptune's presentation of his domain to his "blu-hair'd deities" leads directly to the compliment:

> And all this tract that fronts the falling Sun
> A noble Peer of mickle trust, and power
> Has in his charge, with temper'd awe to guide
> An old, and haughty Nation proud in Arms:
> Where his fair off-spring nurs't in Princely lore,
> Are coming to attend their Fathers state.

Aside from its high praise for the attending Earl and his Welsh guests, the compliment sets the fable in motion, suggests the linear direction of the plot at its literal level, looks forward to the Brothers' philosophical debate, prepares for the introduction of Diana into the masque's categorical mythology, and describes a secular power that is virtuous because it is restrained. Furthermore, the Spirit's representation of a sacramental world in which the powers of good and evil are ranged against one another leads naturally to his discourse on Circe. She is described as the daughter of the sun, and the plot will engage her night-roving son, Comus, against the "sun-clad" chaste daughter of the secular regent of the land of the falling sun.

The final part of the Spirit's prologue establishes the masque's moral polarities in richer detail. The Spirit reinforces the radical disparity between Comus's dark domain and the "Regions milde of calm and serene Air" of the "bright aereal Spirits." This is an especially important comparison because Comus thinks of himself as an "imitator," yet his native haunts are, clearly, a grotesque distortion of those heavenly realms he seeks to imitate. In this poem only the court of the Earl of Bridgewater stands as an appropriate natural source of Jovial peace and harmony.

As the Spirit's narration ends and the dramatic action begins, the Spirit decides on a plan of attack. He will put off his "skie robes" "And take the Weeds and likeness of a Swain / That to the service of this house belongs / Who with

his soft Pipe, and smooth dittied Song / Well knows to still the wilde winds when they roar, / And hush the waving Woods." This is Milton's gracious compliment to Lawes and the house he serves, but it is also the first of the active transformations anticipated in the first lines of the prologue. Moreover, it signals the beginning of a series of emphatic reminders of the power of song, helps integrate the masque's plot and dialogue with its music, and anticipates the raising of Sabrina, the masque's incarnation of pure harmony.

When Comus enters, the Spirit hears "the tread / Of hateful steps." Comus's movements contrast, for all his mimetic skills, with the movements of those "that by due steps aspire." His position in the moral hierarchy of the masque is dramatically reinforced by the simultaneous appearance of the untempered anti-masquers: *"with him a rout of Monsters, headed like sundry sorts of wilde Beasts . . . they come in making a riotous and unruly noise."* Milton integrates the traditional masque dances into the overall movement of *Mask* in the same way that he makes the traditional songs structurally and thematically appropriate. Comus's first speech suggests that the movements in his world are imaginatively ordered, while the actual dances of his "rout" make it clear that in his world all movement is emphatically disordered. The rout's appearance destroys any illusion of dance as harmonic form that might be derived from Comus's description of the activities in his enchanted night-world. Despite his lilting language, Comus cannot conceal his true nature and the true nature of his rout. Despite his elaborately sustained images, the dramatic impression he makes is not of serene order but of frenzied disorder. His characteristic utterance mates a rhetorically gorgeous language to contradictory or paradoxical impulses. His images of fulfillment, containment, rest and recovery ("the gilded Car of Day, / His glowing Axle doth allay / In the steep *Atlantick* stream") are intercepted by the contrary rhythms of "midnight shout and revelry / Tipsie dance, and Jollity."

The self-expressive aspect of dance as gesture is heightened, conventionalized, and rendered morally significant by the masque. Anti-masquers have no choice: they must dance as a rout. Milton used the anti-masque as he inherited it from Jonson to reflect his themes formally. The appearance of the anti-masque is visual proof that life with Comus is a life of imprisonment. Despite their frenzied gestures, the anti-masquers are deeply constrained. They see increased beauty in their transformed heads but they constitute a herd. Although they appear to be physically free, they are morally paralyzed. Their dance is the dance of slaves. They dance only to Comus's lyric orchestrations.

Comus links himself with the monsters. After the invocation to the "Goddess of Nocturnal sport / Dark vail'd *Cotytto*" he "solemnly" declares his part in the anticommunity of the woods: "Com, knit hands, and beat the ground. / In a light fantastick round." And they all dance "the Measure." But their revels are interrupted by "the different pace, / Of som chast footing near about this ground." The Lady's "chast footing" holds the moral middle between Comus's "tread of hateful steps" and the "due steps" of those who aspire to the Palace of

Eternity, just as her later dances and the dances of her family will establish the proper earthly models of the starry round (as Comus's wavering motions cannot). Yet, although the Lady stops the rout she is in danger, not only because she is lost in a dark wood, but because she mistakes the source of the noises she hears:

> This way the noise was, if mine ear be true,
> My best guide now, me thought it was the sound
> Of Riot, and ill manag'd Merriment,
> Such as the jocond Flute, or gamesom Pipe
> Stirs up among the loose unletter'd Hinds.

The Lady will have to confront a devotee of *Cotytto* rather than Pan, but before she does, and to keep her spirits up, she first invokes her guardians and then sings a lyric to *Sweet Echo*. The song is filled with color and delicacy. The innocent and virtuous Lady knows of worlds less "drear" than Comús's, and her song with its romantic mythology, aerial perspectives, and fresh, flowering landscapes frees the action for a moment from the constrained closeness of the "blind mazes of a tangl'd Wood." The lyric is a reminder that song can be ordered and harmonious, and a reminder, too, of the close connection between music and transformation: "*So maist thou be translated to the skies, / And give resounding grace to all Heav'ns Harmonies.*"

The Lady's song, ironically, brings Comus (transformed into a "gentle Shepherd") out into the open and with him an oppression that will not be lifted until Sabrina is invoked through a song by the Attendant Spirit to save the paralyzed Lady. Between the Lady's song and Thyrsis's invocation, the world of the poem is bereft of music as the Lady is caught, trapped, and bound by an "imitator" of the starry quire. It is partly through song, then, that Milton establishes the children and court of the Earl as virtuous tribunes of harmonious order. Whether (as has been frequently debated) the presenters perform a Platonic or Christian vision of harmony, their music (and later their speeches and their dancing) range them clearly against the intrusive negative axis symbolized by Comus, Circe, Cotytto, and Hecate.

The contrasting chords of harmony and disorder struck in the opening scenes of the masque continue to sound as Comus and the Lady confront each other. He is affected by her song, and his response seems, at first, a momentary easing of the tension, but as he adds another singer and kind of song to the growing catalogue of singers and songs, he again demonstrates that he is the Lady's antitype:

> I have oft heard
> My Mother Circe with the Sirens three,
> Amidst the flowry-kirtl'd *Naiades*
> Culling their potent hearbs, and baleful drugs,
> Who as they sung, would take the prison'd soul,
> And lap it in Elysium.

As Comus leads the Lady off to his "low / But loyal cottage" the two Brothers make their first appearance in the masque. Although Johnson and Greg, and, more recently, Carey and Wilkinson (among others) have attacked this section of the poem, the speeches of the Brothers and their subsequent dialogue with Thyrsis serve as a commentary on the preceding scene between Comus and the Lady, imagistically forecast the Lady's career, and introduce "Divine Philosophy" into the masque. The Elder Brother, for example, introduces three new names into the masque's mythological register. First he puts the conflict between "Chastity" and "Vice" in terms of the story of Diana and Cupid, and then he thinks of Minerva:

> What was that snaky-headed Gorgon sheild
> That wise Minerva wore, unconquer'd Virgin,
> Wherwith she freez'd her foes to congeal'd stone?
> But rigid looks of Chast austerity,
> And noble grace that dash't brute violence
> With sudden adoration, and blank aw.

The Elder Brother's moral and spiritual reading of mythology dramatically sanctions a characteristic feature of masque mythography. He also verifies in an elegant way the Spirit's observation that he has been "nurs't in Princely lore." Yet Milton has also managed to wedge the speech into his fable. The Elder Brother does not know that he has ironically inverted the correct application of his "congeal'd stone" image. His sister is about to be tested by Comus and *congeal'd* and *rigid* are words that will better describe her condition than the condition of her enemy. It is Comus who (at least superficially) holds Minerva's power, not the Lady. However, the latter part of the Elder Brother's speech correctly prophesies the Lady's forthcoming response to Comus's blandishments, for she will be unmoved by the "unchast looks," the "loose gestures," and "foul talk" by which Comus hopes to "clot" and "imbrute" her soul.

After this philosophical dialogue, the Attendant Spirit as Thyrsis arrives and, in a pastoralized version of his earlier summary, alerts the brothers to their sister's predicament. Thyrsis's narrative substantiates the Second Brother's fears for his sister, but it also gives the Elder Brother another opportunity to expostulate on the defensive power of virtue as well as to declare his own heroic prowess. It is in answer to the brothers' declaration of heroic intent that the Attendant Spirit explains the affective powers of the "med'cinal" "*Haemony*," a restorative herb loosely related to but more powerful than the Odyssean "*Moly*." Charlotte Otten in *ELR* 5 (1975): 81–95, has shown that this plant, its meaning variously interpreted, was well known to herbalists as andros(h)aemon, so called because its juice is the color of man's blood. It belongs to the genus hypericum and is commonly called St. John's wort. Milton follows the herbalists in endowing it with magical properties.

After the various options for freeing the Lady are explored, the masque

moves directly to the climactic scene in which she is twice transformed. This change of scene incorporates the hinge of the masque: "*the Lady set in an inchanted Chair, to whom [Comus] offers his Glass, which she puts by, and goes about to rise.*" As he begins his temptation of the Lady, Comus intrudes into the masque's mythological world a new and far more serious equation than has yet appeared. *Minerva, Diana,* and *Echo* are now threateningly replaced by the rigid *Daphne:*

> Nay Lady sit; if I but wave his wand,
> Your nerves are all chain'd up in Alablaster,
> And you a statue, or as *Daphne* was
> Rootbound, that fled *Apollo.*

In her reply, the Lady establishes the effective power of chastity:

> Thou canst not touch the freedom of my minde
> With all thy charms, although this corporal rinde
> Thou haste immanacl'd, while Heav'n sees good.

Comus then offers "refreshment," "ease," and "timely rest." The Lady counters with a description of the restorative quality of spiritual goods. She has, unlike the monster rout, a "well-govern'd" appetite. Comus, in turn, then appeals to nature. Using his well-tried rhetoric of deceit, he tries to persuade the Lady with superficially splendid images, but his own material concerns are egregiously present in his speech. When he describes nature "strangl'd with her waste fertility," the principle of plenitude becomes a principle of license. He describes the "riches" of nature in such gross terms that his argument undercuts itself: "Beauty is natures coyn, must not be hoorded, / But must be currant." Furthermore, his explosive discussion of the nature, uses, and adversities of beauty takes place in the hostile context of the "grim-aspects" of his palace. The disjunction between the physical appearance of the palace and the grotesque configuration of its inhabitants (as the Lady very well perceives) is an emblematic reminder of the disparity between the richness of Comus's rhetorical display and the monstrous sense of his pronouncements. The Lady's response to Comus's set speech demonstrates her inviolate morality and her powers of analysis. Although some of Milton's critics consider the Lady's reply poetically inconsequential or philosophically evasive, she correctly identifies Comus's technique as "obtruding false rules pranckt in reasons garb," she does call for an "even proportion" of Nature's bounty, and she does establish a sense of context that makes her observations quietly exact:

> for swinish gluttony
> Ne'er looks to Heav'n amidst his gorgeous feast,
> But with besotted base ingratitude
> Cramms, and blasphemes his feeder.

And then she fully dismantles Comus's pretensions to participate in the starry choir:

> To him that dares
> Arm his profane tongue with contemptuous words
> Against the Sun-clad power of Chastity;
> Fain would I something say, yet to what end?
> Thou hast nor Ear, nor Soul to apprehend
> The sublime notion, and high mystery
> That must be utter'd to unfold the sage
> And serious doctrine of Virginity.

The power the Lady defines is stronger than the Elder Brother's "complete steel," and what she says proves dramatically true with Sabrina's appearance, for Sabrina's offensive weapons do not consist of material armament or logical argument, but the power and mystery of song.

The masque's "device" is now turning on its "hinge." After Comus is routed by the brothers, the Spirit enters but discovers that he cannot "free the Lady that sits here / In stony fetters fixt, and motionless." This is the emblematic climax of the masque. There is very little action in *Mask* before the turning of the device, but the masque remains vital and energetic in its first half precisely because Milton translates the *language* of the device in motion into the *actions* of the device turned.

In his opening speech, the Spirit described the conjunction of sea and sky power. This description is dramatically realized when Thyrsis, recognizing his own deficiencies in sympathetic magic, narrates the history of Sabrina. The story is brief. However, it fits naturally into the masque's design. Sabrina's "quick immortal change" recalls all the changes, real and hypothetical, that have been established through the language and action of the masque. Each of these tranformations provides perspective for, and is afforded perspective by, all the others. They include: the transformation experienced by those who after "this mortal change" are embraced by the "enthron'd gods" on "Sainted seats"; the transformation experienced by those who are foolish and weak enough to be tempted by Comus's words and who fall under the power of his julep or his wand; the transformation of *Echo;* the transformation of the Lady into a paralyzed mute; the transformation of Sabrina from a mortal into a surrogate of the gods; and the transformations of the Attendant Spirit into Thyrsis and Comus into a "harmless villager." And all these internal transformations are informed by the vehicular transformation effected by the masque itself as the audience—as a restored community complete in all its parts—is absorbed into the action through celebratory dance when the Lady and her two Brothers are presented to their parents by their Attending Spirit.

In the Sabrina episode, the relationship of song to the Lady's problem is finally made explicit: Sabrina can "unlock / The clasping charm" but she must be "right invok't in warbled song." As the Lady sang her song to *Echo* for help,

so here the power of song is enlisted in her behalf. The combination of verse and song is abstractly pleasing, but the combination of *these* verses and songs is also necessary and probable, given the dramatic situation as it has progressed to the climactic scene. The Spirit sings:

> Sabrina fair
>> Listen where thou art sitting
> Under the glassie, cool, translucent wave
>> In twisted braids of Lillies knitting
> The loose train of thy amber-dropping hair,
>> Listen for dear honours sake,
>> Goddess of the silver lake,
>>> Listen and save.

Sabrina is free. She has overcome the confinements of a negative force. She is the masque's mythological incarnation of freedom as well as a complimentary tutelary Welsh sea-spirit. She may, as some commentators have observed, represent the power of Grace, but she certainly represents graceful power. The free-flowing beauty of her hair is *ordered* beautifully. Comus wanted his nymphs to knit their hair as a prelude to his exotic night life. Sabrina's hair is free but also restrained. The Spirit calls on Sabrina to "Rise, rise." She does. In answer to the Spirit's summons she appears first as song; and in her song she sings of a scene and an atmosphere that with its blues and greens serves as an effective contrast to the artificiality of Comus's palace. The Lady's song to *Echo* has finally been answered. The free-moving Sabrina and the paralyzed Lady face each other:

> Brightest Lady look on me,
> Thus I sprinkle on thy brest
> Drops that from my fountain pure,
> I have kept of pretious cure,
> Thrice upon they fingers tips,
> Thrice upon thy rubied lip,
> Next this marble venom'd seat
> Smear'd with gumms of glutenous heat
> I touch with chaste palms moist and cold,
> Now the spell hath lost his hold;
> And I must hast ere morning hour
> To wait in *Amphitrite's* bowr.

The scene conveys a sense of power and serenity. "Sabrina *descends, and the Lady rises out of her seat.*" The device has turned. In a sacramental world, processes are complementary and interchangeable, and in Comus's palace the activities of the Lady (in speech) and Sabrina (in song) symbolically complement each other. The exact nature of the exchange is mysterious, but the results of Sabrina's ministrations are direct. With Sabrina's support, the Lady under-

goes a magical restoration. She has been touched by a mysterious feminine sea-power and can now proceed horizontally on her way home to her father's house, a seat of secular safety, the palace of the President of Wales.

With the change of scene to Ludlow town and the President's castle, the presentation of the children to their father, family, and friends becomes the center of the dramatic action, as the masque draws away from spiritual and psychological allegory and moves closer to the literal and domestic fact of their return home.

First, a group of rude "shepherds" dances. This is the literal analogue to the supernatural anti-masque performed by Comus and his monster rout. The revelry of these harvesters is not grim. It does not involve a perverse imitation of the starry choir. It represents, rather, the motion and music the Lady originally *expected* to encounter when she found herself lost in the drear wood, and it can be dispelled easily by the lyrics of the song now sung by the music-master-Thyrsis: "back Shepherds, back, anough your play." There is no moral drama here because magic and energy are unnecessary. Milton incorporated the familiar technique for banishing the anti-masque (most anti-masquers are sim-ply *told* to go away—and they do) into his dramatic fable to reemphasize the quality and degree of the magical dispensations that have freed the Lady from Comus's enchantments. The ease with which the Spirit dismisses the last group of anti-masquers (there is no need for either *Haemony* or Sabrina) introduces a note of seriousness into the several appearances and disappearances of the anti-masquers that is uncommon to the genre. The final anti-masquers can be disposed of through the power of song alone, and they will be replaced by the *"lighter toes, and such Court guise / As Mercury did first devise."*

The next song presents, with a "crown of deathless Praise," the three children who, having moved through *"hard assays,"* have *"so goodly grown."* The testing voyage is over and the dances that conclude it represent the *"triumph"* *"O're sensual Folly, and Intemperance."* The dance is ordered and restrained; it is the most overt gesture of the victory over sensual disorder. At this moment the audience joined the celebratory and ritualistic triumph of the Lady.

After the dances end, perhaps some hours later, the masque concludes, as it had begun, with a serious speech by the Spirit. (In Lawes's production, how-ever, it may have ended with a brief song rather than a long speech.) In his epilogue the Spirit recalls and reinforces all that has happened. He images a flight to the west and describes the Garden of Hesperus. He imaginatively soars above Comus's woods toward Paradise. Color returns with greater variety than ever before in the poem. The Spirit's autobiographical passage concludes with a visionary flight to complementary mythological pairs: Venus and Adonis (the forces of seasonal generation) and Cupid and Psyche. The paradisiac freedom of the wondering Psyche reinterprets and expands the significance of the wander-ing Lady's similar experience of freedom.

The masque ends with a final emphasis on restorative action: "Heav'n itself would stoop to [virtue]." The action of the poem has shown Heaven stooping

in the form of a rising Sabrina. Through the movements of his device, Milton shows that heaven's bourne includes not only the "Spheary chime" but the land below the translucent wave as well. The domains of Jove and Neptune are both homes for those guardian spirits who come to the aid of distressed virtue.

As Milton composed *Mask* the thematic emphasis seems clear. The masque begins with the Spirit's description of the "crown that Vertue gives" and it ends (as the directions reverse) with the Spirit's (sung or spoken) injunction: "Mortals that would follow me, / Love vertue, she alone is free, / She can teach ye how to clime / Higher than the Spheary chime." However, despite these guides, *Mask* has been subjected to an extraordinary variety of diagnostic allegorizations. The disputes over the poem's meaning frequently revert to the Lady's statement to Comus during their debate that she will not reveal to him the "sage and serious doctrine of Virginity." Many of Milton's critics suggest that even if the Lady retreats into silence the poem does not and that Milton revealed the doctrine symbolically rather than discursively. A distinct minority of contemporary critics is willing to let *Mask* off as a light allegorical invention. For the most part, the current reading of the poem's themes involves an elaborate exegesis centered on one or more of the following topics: the character of the Attendant Spirit, the speech of the Elder Brother on virtue, the description of *Haemony,* the debate between Comus and the Lady, the Sabrina episode, and, most especially, the relationship between the epilogue and the whole poem.

Three decades ago, A. S. P. Woodhouse attempted to apply the schematic ground plan of nature and grace to the development of *Mask*'s action. Woodhouse's central theorem is that "nothing less is symbolized in the Epilogue than life itself, as the Christian mind grounded in nature but illuminated by grace, alone can apprehend it." In the service of this proclamation, he tries to distinguish four different "virtues" in the Lady: temperance and continence (belonging to the order of nature), chastity, (belonging to the orders of nature and grace), and virginity (belonging to the order of grace alone). He attempts to resolve what he sees as an apparent confusion in the poem between the doctrine of virginity by arguing that the epilogue is the dialectical resolution of the two principal thematic ideas operating in the poem up to its conclusion. Woodhouse's insistence on the central importance of the epilogue to the masque's themes is supported by Tillyard, who argues on the basis of revisions in *TM* that Milton changed the epilogue in order to suggest allegorically that the Lady should enjoy spiritual chastity in marriage rather than remain a virgin. The crucial change occurred, Tillyard argues, because Milton himself underwent a radical transformation of sensibility when he gave up the idea of a creative celibacy. A. E. Dyson dismisses the emphasis on the epilogue as "altogether exaggerated." He finds in it "a significance which only a scholar who knows the text, almost literally, backwards, is likely to consider convincing." He, therefore, makes a primary philosophical substitution. For him "the great 'debate' is not between Chastity and Incontinence, and still less between Virginity and

Marriage, but between Reason and Passion as controlling factors in human conduct." In this reading the Lady is "Chastity (or Virtue) incarnate, and her purpose is to illustrate the immutable nature and wisdom of this virtue." For John Arthos, however, "Platonic and Neo-Platonic illustrations provide a self-consistent and comprehensive interpretation of the thought of the *Mask*." His major ally is Sears Jayne, who argues that "the subject of the Mask" is the four-step Platonic attainment of Virtue through passion (Comus), philosophy (Brothers), reason (Alice), to *Mens* (Sabrina). These views are put through the analytical wringer by Richard Neuse, who contends that to "read the poem as radical spiritual allegory of the Neoplatonic variety, does not seem to do justice to its particular mode of symbolization." Neuse strives to show that "the theme of *Mask* is close to 'pleasure reconciled to virtue' and involves the poet's traditional concern with the life of the senses rather than the exaltation of an ideal like virginity as a vehicle to the divine." In this reading the epilogue becomes "a great emblem of youth" that "stands in direct contrast to the make-believe world of seasonless 'waste fertility' into which Comus lures his followers." And whereas the Attendant Spirit—an early model of the Heavenly Messenger—generally resembles a guardian angel in the Christian dispensation for James Arnold, a typically Euripidean prologist for Welsford, a Platonic or Neoplatonic daemon for Arthos and Jayne (and is called, alternatively, a "daemon" in *BrM*), for Neuse he "comes to be seen as a representation, almost a definition of the functions and limits of poetry."

The most comprehensively balanced views of the masque's themes are those of Reesing, Demaray, and Rajan. Reesing observes that the two main categories of transformation (those determined by moral choice and those which involve the change into a beast or into a god) that underlie the anti-masque and masque sections may be identified as fundamental to an understanding of the poem. He sees these transformations as a fusion of Ovidian, Platonic, and Christian materials. He identifies the poem's theme as "the moral character of the timeless world of permanence and the moral conditions for membership in it." The masque is, therefore, "about the prospect of divinization open to all human beings who live virtuously." Reesing is one of the few modern critics of the poem who seem to be willing to accept the possibility that "it is sometimes hard to say where literal meaning ends and allegorical meaning begins." In this openness, he is close to Demaray, who writes that "if Milton, who was not generally disposed to allegorize, intended that the magic instruments and rituals in *Mask* have allegorical meanings, he did not make these meanings clear in the text." Demaray can find no common agreement on "what Milton's alleged allegory might have been," and thus concludes that "nothing in the text indicates that Comus's wand is meant to represent anything except a wand. The cup and potion of Comus also seem to be only magical objects. . . . The power of Sabrina is nowhere referred to in the text as anything except the power of a chaste, pagan Goddess of the Severn River." For Demaray, the masque's central theme is "the triumph of virtue, associated with rational restraint and order, over vice, associated with excessive passion and disorder." This view links him

with Rajan, who thinks that Milton criticism tends to regard the Nature-Grace, Reason-Passion thematic axes as "exclusive of each other," whereas "in fact their amalgamation is likely to be a primary objective in any poet determined to consummate the classical in the Christian." Rajan accepts the idea of Platonic purification as a helpful gloss on the poem, but he can accommodate it to Christian as well as Platonic leanings: "The soul's seeking of its form, its dedication to what is noblest in itself, is the true index of chastity." Rajan suggests that although "Sabrina may be an agent of grace," she is also "a water-spirit, a force in nature." He further argues that in the epilogue "youth and joy are shown as the outcome of the restraint that Comus scorned when he taxed the lady with letting youth slip by," and in this generation we are to understand that "a lower reality is not annulled in the acceptance of the higher." Rajan meets the poem on its own linguistic terrain when he observes that "the world of the senses is included and not annulled by the consecretation to the world of the spirit; discipline forms the basis for the liberation of creative energy rather than the means for its confinement."

Despite the variations, most of the critical allegorizers treat *Mask* seriously and as a thematic success. On the other side, writers such as Carey, Greg, and Wilkinson have attempted to demolish its pretensions to seriousness. Carey's is the most intensive attack: for him (following Muir), the poem is either ironic or hopelessly inadequate. Carey suggests that Milton actually wrote two poems in one masque. The outer shell of *Mask* gave the aristocratic Ludlow audience the opportunity to be self-congratulatory. The inner core of the masque allows for partial pleasures of a very different order: "There is no reason to suppose that [the Egerton children] would be sacrosanct to a high-minded middle-class intellectual. The first audience was complacent enough for any implied criticism to pass over its heads. But without turning *Comus* into a warren of 'ironies,' it is possible to ask some simple questions about what is said and done, and end up with the conviction that if the watchers on Michaelmas night 1634 scanned one facet of Milton's purpose with eager approval, another went, for that reason, uninspected." However, by the time Carey is finished asking his "simple questions" he leaves the poem a shambles. Although he begins his essay by observing that Johnson's realist strictures are not appropriate for a genre like the masque, he nevertheless resorts consistently to Johnson's approach to show how the poem demonstrates the moral, spiritual, social, and intellectual faults of its principal characters. And while Wilkinson considers the debate between Comus and the Lady a failure on aesthetic grounds because the combatants do not "engage poetically," Carey considers the debate a failure on ethical grounds: "it is not so much a matter of allegory being an inadequate mode as of Milton's being an inadequate allegory—dangerously so, by fostering belief in tempters who untemptingly mishandle their advantages." Greg surrounds these criticisms with his own. For him, all the speeches in the poem introduced "with a directly moral and philosophical rather than a dramatic end must be pronounced artistic solecisms."

The middle ground between attack and praise is held by the Bulloughs, who

identify the governing ideas in the poem as a mixture of Platonism and Christian asceticism, but who find a confusion between Milton's apprehension of purification through an ever-increasing spirituality (derived from Plato) leading to divine union and the worship of Temperance, "as if the act of self-denial were an end in itself and its result the Platonic vision of absolute joy." However, in their evaluative summation they become partisans: "the glow and ardour generated in the attempted union of Christian renunciation and Platonic sublimation suffuse the poem with a warmth and light and joy which Milton never recaptured." This is a view very close to Arthos's judgment that the masque "is everywhere written nobly, and the songs and the Epilogue, in their sense and above all in their music, communicate a kind of spiritual clarity that is the poem's most perfect achievement. This remains its final excellence, an accent and a music creating a clearer temper than we often imagine to be found in life."

The "accent" and "music," the strength and serenity of *Mask* derive, in part, from its style. Even Dr. Johnson (who had little else positive to say of the poem) recognized that in *Mask* Milton "formed very early that system of diction and mode of verse which his maturer judgement approved." The blank verse poetic paragraph holds an important structural place in the masque as Milton alternates it with rhymed, four-stressed lines, heroic couplets, and the more free-flowing lyrics of his songs. The blank verse is of the declamatory sort although, as the Bulloughs point out, "Milton allowed himself considerable freedom in the placing of stresses and in the number of unstressed syllables." They have also noted that "a fair proportion (about 1 in 12) of lines have feminine endings," and that "most clauses and sentences finish at the end of a line, but there are frequent medial periods." Nevertheless, Milton did not attempt to make his blank verse carry the subtle weights, pressures, and irregularities of individual character in action.

Milton did, however, support the dramatic *logic* of the masque with stylistic variety. The poem begins with the Spirit's blank verse prologue, which is followed, in Comus's first speech, by four-stressed couplets occasionally interspersed with five-stressed lines. When Comus must break off his "conceal'd Solemnity," he speaks in blank verse to describe the Lady's "different pace." The Lady enters speaking blank verse but then moves into her echo-song. Comus responds to her "enchanting ravishment" in a blank verse declamation that is quickly followed by the disjunctive *stichomythia*. When the Brothers enter they speak in blank verse, but Milton made some effort to distinguish them. The Elder Brother uses a more elaborately imagistic language than the Second Brother (although, as C. S. Lewis notes, Milton, in the successive versions of the poem in *TM*, carefully toned down some of the Elder Brother's more excessive phrasing), while the Second Brother tends to use a vigorously alliterative diction that reinforces his sense of his sister's distress.

Each of the sublunary characters uses a considerable number of semi-personified abstractions. Comus welcomes Joy and Feast and scorns Rigour, Advice, Strict Age, and Sour Severity; the Lady perceives Conscience, Faith, Hope, and

Chastity; the Elder Brother meditates on Virtue, Wisdom, and Contemplation; while the Second Brother fears the fate of Beauty in the grasp of Bold Impertinence, Danger, and Opportunity. Milton's use of these figures has been observed by Broadbent, who also describes other working elements of the verse: its colloquial idiom, its "extravagant naturalistic metaphors" (which were highly praised by Warton as "wild and romantick imagery") and its "idealistic images checked by a sense of the concrete." But, as Broadbent says, "the verse as a whole does not reconcile these varieties or commit itself to any one of them. It wings from one to the other, displaying its own astonishing virtuosity. The variations in tone and tempo are remarkable." Broadbent argues that there is a discrepancy between the masque's themes and its style: "the action and ideology of the masque suggest, rather than realize, ideals of harmony and fruition. In the same way the verse lacks an assured norm that would draw and shape its virtuosity into a recognizable individual act." Certainly, by the stylistic standards of Milton's epics and SA, this is an accurate judgment. But, in a way, it brings up, once again, the problem of the poem's genre. It might be argued that, in a stylized entertainment like Mask, the verse functions best when it does not overwhelm the music, dancing, and spectacle, as it surely would if it were able to measure up to the evaluative norms Broadbent sets for it. This is not to say that Milton, in 1634, could have produced a more integrative style. It is rather to note that, as in his treatment of the other elements that, compositely, make a masque, Milton forced a style with imaginative boldness but still allowed for the delicacy of his chosen form. He was, after all, the only writer of a masque who was able to produce a serious entertainment in which a "barbarous dissonance" is dramatically modified and subdued by a verse that could "still the wild winds when they roar / And hush the waving woods" as it converts itself into music and, finally, dance. [RBW]

ON SHAKESPEARE. Milton's first published English poem, entitled *An Epitaph on the admirable Dramaticke Poet, W. Shakespeare,* appeared anonymously among the commendatory verses prefixed to the Second Folio of Shakespeare's plays, 1632, sig. A5^r. There are three states of printing of this Folio page as a result of pirated reissues, perhaps in 1640–41, but the textual variation between them is slight. The poem was published also in Shakespeare's *Poems,* 1640, sig. K8, with the initials "I. M."; however, it was printed anonymously in the Third Folio (1663–64) and in the Fourth Folio (1685). Entitled *On Shakespeare* and dated 1630, presumably by its author, the poem was published in the 1645 and 1673 editions of Milton's *Poems* with slight variation from its versions in the Folios and in Shakespeare's *Poems.*

Shak was written while Milton was a student at Christ's College, Cambridge (he himself dated in 1630), but the circumstances of its composition and of its publication with the Second Folio are uncertain. Because Milton was then unknown as a poet, it seems unlikely that the publishers of the Second Folio would have invited him to write the epitaph; nor is it likely that he volunteered

the verses if they were unsolicited. Perhaps Henry Lawes, who composed the music for the songs in *Mask* and assisted Milton in gaining recognition, was the intermediary between the young poet and publishers of the Second Folio. Lawes would have made his connection with the Second Folio through his patron, William Herbert, Third Earl of Pembroke, to whom the First and Second Folios were dedicated.

Shak, a sixteen-line epigram in heroic couplets, resembles other epitaphs on Shakespeare that were published in the First and Second Folios; and it embodies the dominant theme, which was commonplace in Elizabethan literature, that an author achieves immortality through his work. Milton states in lines 9–16, for example, that Shakespeare's readers are his monuments. Other epitaphs on Shakespeare likewise develop this theme of immortality, though their treatment of it differs somewhat from Milton's. For example, the epitaphs by Ben Jonson and Leonard Digges, both of which were published in the First and Second Folios, state that Shakespeare's work, not every reader, is his monument and that he continues to live so long as he is read. *Shak* also alludes to the prevalent critical opinion, reflected in other commendatory verses, that Shakespeare was primarily a natural and spontaneous poet whose "easier numbers" contrasted with the laborious composition or "slow-endeavouring art" of others. This view is iterated in *L'Al* (133–34) in which Shakespeare is described as "fancies childe" producing "his native Wood-notes wilde."

Though numerous verbal and imagistic parallels have been adduced between *Shak* and other Elizabethan epitaphs and between *Shak* and Elizabethan literature generally, Milton's indebtedness to specific works cannot be determined. For instance, Milton's image that a reader becomes a marble monument seems to echo a similar conceit developed in William Browne's elegy on the Countess of Pembroke (1629). But other parallels for this same image may be cited not only from epitaphs but also from Elizabethan plays, including Massinger's *The Fatal Dowry* (2.1) and Tomkis's *Albumazar* (1.4.3–4). Another poem sometimes mentioned as a possible influence on *Shak* is *An Epitaph on Sir Edward Standly*, which was ascribed to Shakespeare. The image of "sky-aspiring Piramides" in this poem may be echoed in "Star-ypointing *Pyramid*" (line 4) in *Shak*. But this image is rather common in Elizabethan literature, so that specific influence on Milton cannot be acknowledged. Thus *Shak* is a conventional poem suggesting Milton's knowledge of epitaph literature and reflecting perhaps his awareness of other epitaphs on Shakespeare. [ACL]

ON THE DEATH OF A FAIR INFANT DYING OF A COUGH. Milton's earliest original poem in English appears only in the second edition (1673) of the minor poems. The reason for its omission from the 1645 *Poems* is uncertain. Line 53, "Or wert thou that sweet smiling youth," is short two syllables, which have been supplied since the 18th century as "Mercy": "Or wert thou Mercy. . . ." A couple of modern alternatives have been "Virtue" and "Peace."

The occasion for this elegy, according to Edward Phillips, was the death of

Milton's niece, Anne, the first daughter of the young poet's sister Anne and Edward Phillips. She was baptized on January 12, 1626, and buried on January 22, 1628. Line 76 implies the expected birth of another child, and Milton's niece Elizabeth was baptized on April 9, 1628. The date of composition, which according to these facts should be January–April 1628, has been questioned because a headnote in 1673 states, "Anno aetatis 17" (at the age of seventeen"). Milton was seventeen between December 1625 and December 1626, and this was a severe time of the plague, as lines 67–69 report, but no daughter of the Phillipses died during this period.

The death of the infant—a private event not lending itself to the rhetorical topics of the funeral oration—is at once accounted for by a "cause," as convention requires, and is magnified in significance through use of classical story and symbol. The initial lamentation is expressed in terms that elevate the infant to the level of the mythical figures whose fate of too early death she shares. Through simile Milton mythologizes and attempts to transform her into a figure capable of supporting meanings of crucial import to the universe. Such a symbolic transformation makes it possible for grief to give way to a consolation that is enlarged into a triumphant acceptance of the specifically Christian, as opposed to the natural, attitude toward death.

This progression provides the structural development of the elegy, which has been analyzed by Hugh MacLean (*ELH*, 24 [1957]: 296–305) into a three-fold movement. The ten stanzas constituting the body of the poem (that is, all but the final eleventh stanza, addressed to the infant's mother) may be partitioned into three groups of three, three, and four stanzas respectively. The poem opens by addressing the infant in terms of a familiar symbol for those who have died young, the primrose, sprung from the blood of the young Adonis (it appears again in *Lycidas*). Milton extends the significance by mythologizing the death of the infant as an unwitting destruction by a god enamored of her beauty. The physical circumstances are absorbed into the elegy's pattern of meaning by personifying Winter as elderly and childless.

The cause of the infant's death, as lamented in stanzas I–III, is an unconscious blunder on the part of nature. In IV, the tissue of mythological association, again by connecting a "dearly-loved mate" slain by an "unweeting hand," dignifies the fate of the infant by equating it circumstantially with that of Hyacinth, killed by Apollo. The denial of death's power asserted in stanza V marks a more decisive division in the elegy than does stanza IV, which in its allusion to Hyacinth, and differentiation of the infant's fate from his, only makes conclusive the futility of seeking recompense in some natural transformation, which, after all, has already made dry the blossom-infant. The announcement of faith in a better life that denies the final reality of "earths dark wombe" allows the speaker to address the infant as "Soul most surely blest" in stanza VI and to ask quite different questions from anything that could be posed within the mythologizing terms of I–IV.

Stanzas V and VI function transitionally as a pivot between the inadequate,

frustrating pagan view of death climaxed in IV with the infant *not* changed into a flower and the assurance of Christian consolation that the elegy finally reaches. The questions the speaker asks to have "resolved" in VI—whether the infant's soul now resides in a Christian or a classical heaven, whether the infant was mortal or divine, and why she took flight so soon from the world—are the substance of stanzas VII–X.

Stanza XI declines from the extravagant heights of rhetoric and symbol scaled in VII–X to the simpler plane of assuaging the grief of the infant's mother. The Christian consolation offered here is related, of course, to the exercise in faith that the main body of the poem has pursued, but transposed to a lower key and to a human level.

Milton's development of such profound meaning for the baby's death has led to a number of important critical commentaries about its significance, though one must observe at the outset the profound difference between what Milton was attempting and what he actually achieved. He did not produce a masterpiece in this, his first independent essay in an English medium. Indeed, most critics who even mention it judge it to be an unsuccessful example of forced poetic metaphors. As Don Cameron Allen observes (*Harmonious Vision*, p. 52), Milton "builds up to nothing. His own emotions were hardly involved and he ended the poem to be done with it." But in response, MacLean finds in the work "a meaningful poetical relation [between] classical and Christian image and idea" (p. 296), its central idea that the dead child "has become virtually a Redeemer" (p. 304).

Shawcross enlarges upon this interpretation (*English Miscellany*, 16 [1965]: 136–38). Having proved that nectar was a symbol of immortality for Milton throughout his life, he observes its association in line 49 with little Anne: Wert thou, Milton asks, "some goddess fled / Amongst us here below to hide thy nectar'd head?" Thus the child becomes a symbol of immortality and hence is a type of Christ, an idea continued in the next stanza where Milton would specifically think of her as Peace, sorely needed in England during her brief life because of the bitter struggle between the King and Parliament that climaxed in the impeachment of Buckingham.

Jackson Cope, who believes that everyone agrees that the poem "is resonant with indefinite overtones" (*JEGP*, 63 [1964]: 660), finds in it the seeds of *Paradise Lost* in that the loss of the baby equates with the loss of Eden; it even adumbrates Milton's belief in the fact that the Fall of Mankind was indeed fortunate for the human race; for only from the baby's death can come her resurrection. Thus again she is a type of Christ. For Cope, Milton's use of the myth of Astraea is the "pivotal center of the elegy," that goddess having fled from the wars of the gods in heaven (again a fortunate fall) but now returns there, specifically to the constellation of Virgo (i.e., the Virgin), befittingly identified with Milton's late niece. The identification of Astraea with Christ had been made by Lactantius; she also figures prominently in the "Pollio" prophecy of Virgil's *Eclogue 4*, traditionally interpreted as anticipating Christ's coming.

Thus from a variety of approaches one can see that Milton attempted to find in Anne's death the center of the Christian faith. But he himself seems untouched by personal bereavement such as Herrick, for instance, expresses so powerfully in some of his poems on the deaths of children.

Stylistically, Milton's earliest original attempt at English poetry indicates his allegiance to what in the 1620s counted as conservative Elizabethan models. The elaborate schemes of alliteration and assonance, the frequent archaisms both of diction and pronunciation, the strong congruency of syntactic junctures with the verse—all enhance the effect of decorative sweetness and fluidity of texture characteristic of Elizabethan verse in general and of Spenser and his followers in particular. The eleven stanzas are in rime royal with an alexandrine substituted in the final line (a_5, b_5, a_5, b_5, b_5, c_5, c_6). This final alexandrine is a key device of the Spenserian stanza, and Milton's form can also be viewed as an adaptation of the nine-line Spenserian stanza, with the sixth and seventh lines omitted. This same form was employed by Spenser's follower Phineas Fletcher in an elegy on Sir John Irby, titled *Elisa*, but not published until 1633, and Milton used it later in the introduction to the *Nativity Ode* and in the unfinished *Passion*. [LN]

ON THE MORNING OF CHRIST'S NATIVITY. Milton gave first place to *Nat* in the 1645 and 1673 editions of his poems. The phrase "Compos'd 1629" follows the title in the 1645 edition but is omitted in 1673. The 1645 edition has no Table of Contents; the 1673 edition places "The Hymn" separately in the Table of Contents. There is no manuscript for *Nat* and the variants between the earlier and later edition (with the exception of the clarification that changes "Truth, and justice . . . / Th'enameld Arras of the Rainbow wearing, / And Mercy set between" (XV) to "Truth, and Justice . . . / Orb'd in a Rain-bow; and like glories wearing / Mercy will sit between") are of little consequence.

The proem to *Nat* and *El* 6 both state that the poem was written as a "gift on the birthday of Christ" and was begun in the early hours of Christmas Day, 1629, when the stars "in squadrons bright" still shone in the sky. Milton composed *Nat* at an important point in his life, shortly after he celebrated his twenty-first birthday on December 9, and came of age. *El* 6 indicates the seriousness with which the young poet took *Nat*. In the elegy, written to his friend Charles Diodati, Milton speaks of the virtue needed by the epic poet. Unlike the writer of light elegiac poetry, inspired by love and the pleasures of wine and festivities, the writer of lofty verse (by implication the writer of *Nat* referred to in the elegy) must lead a disciplined life.

Nat strikes a new note in Milton's poetry and illustrates his belief in himself as a poet-prophet, inspired by God and committed to writing serious poetry. *Nat* signals the poet's turn to devotional poetry: serious, elevated verse befitting his coming of age poetically. Indeed, in 1629 Milton had not yet been "church-outed" by the prelates. Still studying for the ministry, he viewed poetry as a form of ministry and emphasized the close relationship between the art of

poetry and the art of pulpit oratory. Stanzas IX through XIV of *Nat,* which describe the angelic choir and the harmony of the angels, are, as Thomas Stroup observes, Milton's means of singing the joyous canticle *Gloria in excelsis.* Milton creates his own liturgy by drawing upon the words of the Herald Angels (Luke 2:14) or the elaboration of their pronouncements at the end of the Communion Service in Elizabeth's *Book of Common Prayer.* (See Thomas Stroup, *Religious Rite and Ceremony in Milton's Poetry* [1968], pp. 6–14.)

Nat, together with *Passion* and *Circum* may have been part of a plan to write elevated verses in commemoration of the events in the life of Christ and the Church calendar. All three are examples of the occasional verse that characterizes most of Milton's poetry prior to *PL.*

Nat, like the odes of Drayton and Jonson, owes much to the classical tradition of Pindar and his followers, Anacreon and Horace, as well as to the Psalms of David, and the ode tradition in both Renaissance Italy (established by Trissino, Alamanni, Minturno, and Tasso) and France (as exemplified by Ronsard and the Pléiade). Milton's comments in *RCG* show that he studied Pindar and had planned to write "magnifick Odes and Hymns wherein Pindarus and Callimachus [the Alexandrian poet] are in most things worthy." *Nat* follows the ode tradition because it is formal and public (not personal); it celebrates an occasion, and it relates the occasion to its cosmic meaning. The proem introduces the specific event—the birth of Christ—and establishes its larger Christian significance. Milton, like Pindar, speaks as poet-priest (invoking the Heavenly muse) and, like Pindar, returns to the opening scene (the manger at the close of the poem), to reinforce the momentous significance of the event.

Milton broadens the event's significance through a series of emotionally evocative pictures associated with the Nativity: the Pre-Fall existence, when Christ, "at Heav'ns high Councel-Table," volunteers to forsake "the Courts of everlasting Day"; the Fall of man and its "deadly forfeit"; and the everlasting future when man's redemption will be achieved. Topographically, the poem soars to heaven, with its magnificent angelic harmony, returns to earth, darkened by pagan deities and their false religion, descends to hell, the "infernal Jail" toward which the routed gods are fleeing, and back to earth where Christ is attended by angels. This use of suggestive detail recalls Pindar's method of glorifying a hero. Carol Maddison (*Apollo and the Nine,* pp. 318–30) notes of the Pindaric ode: "The myth assimilated the hero to the demi-gods, it idealized the present and transfigured the real, it made the temporal event timeless."

Pindar's extant lyrics are triumphal odes, which celebrate athletic victories. Milton appears to adapt this tradition to his depiction of the victory of Christ, who "Can in his swadling bands control the damned crew" of pagan gods. The emphasis in *Nat* is not on the peaceful Babe lying in His cradle, but on the transformation brought to this world by the enthroned Christ, surrounded by "Bright-harnest Angels," who "sit in order serviceable." An analogue for the Infant's performing prodigious feats is found in Pindar's first Nemean ode, in which the young Hercules strangles huge serpents.

Together with the tradition of Pindar, Anacreon, and Horace, psalmody (especially the Psalms of David) influenced the English ode. Like many other Renaissance poets (Sir Philip Sidney, George Wither, George Sandys), Milton translated Psalms. In the Renaissance the word *Psalm* was often interchanged with *Song*, which was further interchanged with the term *Ode*. The fact that Milton calls *Nat* both a "humble ode" and a "Hymn" indicates his awareness of the close connection between these forms and implies that he is reaching toward the inspired mood of David's Psalms. In *Nat* a joyful, reverent tone prevails, a tone that is later echoed in the morning hymn of praise in *PL* 5.153–208.

It is difficult to ascertain direct sources for *Nat*, a poem steeped in pagan and Christian tradition. James Holly Hanford notes the poem's similarity to Virgil's fourth eclogue, which describes the Golden Age that will follow the birth of a son to Pollio. Milton's belief that the oracles ceased at the birth of Christ can be traced to chapter 17 of Plutarch's "Of the Oracles that have ceased to give Answere" (a treatise commonly interpreted in Christian terms and quoted by Spenser in the *Shepheardes Calendar:* May, 1. 54), to Prudentius's fourth-century *Apotheosis*, to Tasso's *Rime Sacre* (which describes the overthrow of pagan deities in Greece and Egypt), and to Giles Fletcher's "Christ's Victory in Heaven":

> The angells caroll'd lowd their song of peace;
> The cursed oracles wear strucken dumb; . . .
>
> (st. 82)

Nat also resembles Prudentius's Nativity hymn "Kalends Ianuarius," Tasso's "Canzone sopra la Coppella del Presepio," and early sixteenth-century works by Mantuan and Sannazaro.

The presentation of the angels as stars derives from passages in Revelation (9:1, 2; 12:4), 1 Kings (22:19), and Judges (5:20). The connection between the angelic song of praise and the music of the spheres has its source in Job (38:7). The subject of the music of the spheres (also developed in his *Prol* 2) goes back both to Plato (*Republic* 10.617^B), where in the vision of Er, music is produced by the sirens "aloft upon each of the circles," and to Cicero (*De republica* 6.17, 18), who speaks of nine spheres.

In Renaissance England, the Nativity tradition was drawn upon by many poets prior to the publication of Milton's poem: Edmund Spenser ("Hymn of Heavenly Love"), Robert Southwell ("The Sequence on the Virgin Mary and Christ"), John Donne ("Nativity" in La Corona), Giles Fletcher ("Christ's Victory and Triumph"), Ben Jonson ("A Hymn on the Nativity of my Saviour"), William Drummond ("Hymn upon the Nativity"), Sir John Beaumont ("An Ode of the Blessed Trinity"), and George Herbert ("Christmas"). The subject also appears in other seventeenth-century poems by Richard Crashaw ("On the Holy Nativity"), Henry Vaughan ("Christ's Nativity"), Robert Herrick ("An Ode of the Birth of Our Saviour"), and Thomas Traherne ("On

Christmas Day"). Milton differs from his contemporaries by not concentrating on the manger scene with the shepherds and peaceful animals and by not dwelling extensively on Mary's motherhood. Instead, Milton symbolically amplifies the idea of Mary's purity by referring to her emphatically in the opening and concluding stanzas and by indirectly contrasting her truly immaculate state with Nature's attempted disguise of "innocent Snow," the "Saintly Veil of Maiden white."

Nothing was said about *Nat* by Milton's contemporaries. A century later, Samuel Johnson chose to ignore *Nat* in his discussion of Milton in *The Lives of the Poets,* and Thomas Warton, in *Poems upon Several Occasions* (1785), cursorily dismissed all but one or two stanzas of the poem for consisting of "a string of affected conceits, which early youth, and the fashion of the times, can only excuse." Nineteenth-century critics praised the Ode as being "perhaps the finest in the English language (Henry Hallam), as being "nearly all beauty" (Thomas Keightley), a "magnificent Ode" (David Masson). But it was not until the twentieth century, following A. S. Cook's scholarly "Notes on Milton's Nativity Ode" (1909), that extensive explication of the poem's thematic and structural patterns began. For the most part, modern critics view *Nat* as "the first of Milton's inspired poems" (Barker), his "Messianic eclogue" (Hanford), his "most perfect early work" (D. C. Allen).

Modern critics have focused on different themes in *Nat:* The "moral significance of Christ, who serves as a symbol of ethical and religious truth" (Hanford); the unity of religious and aesthetic experience, which is achieved only by those who have spotless hearts and which corresponds "in general to the effects of the Puritan conversion" (Barker); the austere movement toward Puritan victory, in which "harshness wars with, and in the end overcomes . . . peace and mercy" (T. K. Meier); the joyful acceptance of "the order of grace and its supremacy over nature itself . . . symbolized by the triumphant images of light, form, and harmony" (Woodhouse); "the effect of the Nativity, the routing of the heathen gods by Christ," which can be considered the "intellectual core" of the poem (Woodhouse); the profound celebration of peace, so integral to the Incarnation (Tuve); the harmony of the universe achieved by a series of balances leading to "timelessness," "Nature as immutable and untarnished," and the "harmony of God" (Allen); the interlocking of past, present, and future time, "the simultaneity of all moments under the aspect of eternity" (Lowry Nelson).

Structurally, the poem is divided into three movements. Apart from the four introductory stanzas, as Barker states, "the first eight stanzas . . . describe the setting of the Nativity, the next nine the angelic choir, the next nine the flight of the heathen gods. The . . . last stanza presents the scene in the stable." The three movements are held in relation to each other by various threads: imagery of "light and discord" counterbalance one another (Barker); patterns of heavenly light and harmony reinforce Milton's theme of peace, "God's reconciling of all things in earth and heaven to Himself" (Tuve); and "an undercurrent of

music" prevails throughout (Spaeth). The first movement is hushed: the night is "peacefull," the winds whisper, and "Birds of Calm sit brooding on the charmed wave" at the birth of the Savior; the second movement details the orchestral harmony of angelic song; the third movement reverberates with the discordant sounds of the fleeing pagan deities.

Milton, as Nelson observes, uses time as a structural device in *Nat* to move toward the timelessness of the everlasting future. The proem shows two time planes: before dawn, December 25, 1629, when "all the spangled host" are still in the sky and Milton is writing the ode; and the actual birth of Christ, indicated by the past tense: "Our great redemption from above *did bring*" (emphasis added). Milton puts himself into the poem and moves back in time to present the ode as a birthday gift to Christ. The timelessness of *Nat* attests to Christ's power as well as to the inspiration His love exerts on the birth of the poet's "humble ode." In stanzas III and IV of the proem the past and present merge as the narrator tells us that he aims to lay his poem at the "blessed feet" of the Infant God" *before* the "Star-led Wisards" arrive to welcome Him with their splendid gifts. Milton continues this alternation of tenses in the "Hymn":

> It *was* the Winter wilde,
> While the Heav'n-born-childe,
> All meanly wrapt in the rude manger *lies;* . . .
> (st. I [emphasis added])

Stanzas XII–XV bridge past, present, and future: the Creation, the golden age, the Nativity, and the Second Coming. Then, once the "Hymn" arrives at its final point in Divine history—the Last Judgment—the narrator stops alternating tenses and uses a heightened present tense to depict the fusion of time: "But now begins" intensifies the future bliss, which starts at the Nativity.

The narrator throughout *Nat* incorporates details from the broader context of Christian history to give meaning to the temporal event. Christ's birth is an event that occurs in a specific "Month" on a "happy morn," as well as an event that extends back to preexistent time and forward to the infinite future. The occasion heralds the birth of "Heav'ns eternal King," who was "wont at Heav'ns high Councel Table, / To sit the midst of trinal Unity" in "the Courts of everlasting Day." In our world, Jesus acts in time to release us from our "deadly forfeit"; in eternity, He will "work us a perpetual peace." Once Judgment Day arrives, the boundaries of space and time will be obliterated.

In the opening stanzas of the proem Milton provides factual information and establishes a narrative frame that guides the reader toward the eternal future, when redeemed man will live in "bliss / Full and perfet" (st. XVIII):

> This is the Month, and this the happy morn
> Wherein the Son of Heav'ns eternal King,

> Of wedded Maid, and Virgin Mother born,
> Our great Redemption from above did bring; . . .

The subject (redemption) and occasion (the Nativity) are introduced, and the speaker focuses on key words: *wedded Maid* and *Virgin Mother*. What should normally read "Virgin Maid" and "wedded Mother," the narrator changes by crossing the adjectives *(chiasmus)*. He thereby stresses the paradoxical nature of the event and thus implies the mystery of the Incarnation; the *chiasmus*, or X, achieved is a sign of Christ. He brings in the details of Christian history as a framing story (noted by Frank Kastor) with which to interpret the event: "That he our deadly forfeit should release, / And with his Father work us a perpetual peace." The "deadly forfeit" that man must pay for Adam and Eve's "First Disobedience" suggests man's Edenic perfection, the Fall, man's atonement, and his future salvation in Heaven, where peace will reign in a "Recover'd Paradise" *(PR*, 1.3).

The narrator also provides important information about himself; he is inspired by the "Heav'nly Muse" to speak in a "sacred vein" and to join the "Angel Quire / From out his secret Altar toucht with hallow'd fire." He, like the narrator of *PL* and *PR*, is speaking of the heroic achievement of Christ. He continues, in the proem, to prepare the reader for Christ's birth by contrasting the "Light," "far-beaming blaze," the "Courts of everlasting Day" with the fallen world that is to be changed by the Nativity.

Stanzas I–VIII, which describe the setting of the Nativity, begin with pagan Nature's reaction to the birth. She is the first worldly representative to be subdued by Christ. The narrator reinforces her submission by reducing light and sound and motion to a minimum. Nature doffs "her gaudy trim" and covers her face with a "Saintly Veil of Maiden white." Nature reaches toward the immaculate purity that is in contrast to her post-Fall state, where war and hate prevail. Milton repeats the word *peace*, as there is a suspension of all postlapsarian activities: the "Battels sound" of war, the trumpets, and the Kings' pronouncements. "The Winds with wonder whist, / Smoothly the waters kist"; the Ocean forgets to rave, and "Birds of Calm sit brooding on the charmed wave." Intensifying the scene, the stars "Stand fixt," their "glimmering Orbs" dimly lighting the morning, and the "inferiour" sun is ashamed to rise, for he sees "a greater Sun appear." Time is suspended while stars and sun halt their customary functions and Nature prepares to meet her master.

In stanza VIII the Shepherds, unlike Nature, are unconscious of the meaning of the Nativity. These innocent folk sit "chatting in a rustick row," their "silly" (naive and innocent) thoughts on "Perhaps their loves, or else their sheep." They are unaware that Christ, "the mighty Pan / Was kindly [gently and with kinship] come to live with them." On these simple folk the music of the spheres bursts. The new music astonishes them to such an extent that it takes "their souls in blissful rapture." Now man, too, is subdued by the great event.

In stanzas IX–XV light, sound, and motion intensify in order to portray the

eternal, cosmic music of the spheres. "A Globe of circular light" illuminates the "glittering ranks" of angels, who sing as harmoniously as they did at the creation of the world. Through light imagery the narrator conveys the effect of the harmony on man: "Time will run back, and fetch the age of gold"; Truth and Justice, "Orb'd in a Rain-bow," will "return to men" and Mercy, "Thron'd in Celestial sheen," is "set between" them. (The 1673 edition makes "And Mercy set between" more emphatic by using the active voice: "Mercy will sit between." It also specifically garbs Mercy in the "like glories" of Truth and Justice, who are "Orb'd in a Rain-bow").

The music of the spheres is reminiscent of the harmony that existed at the creation of the world (Job 38:7) when order was brought out of chaos by the Logos:

> Such Music (as 'tis said)
> Before was never made,
>   But when of old the sons of morning sung,
> While the Creator great
> His constellations set, . . .
>
> (st. XII)

The ordered beauty of musical concord reflects God's "well-ballanc't" master plan. Angelic reverberations resound in this central movement of the poem. Cherubim and Seraphim are heard singing "in loud and solemn quire." The "Crystall sphears," representing the ordered universe, "Ring out" their "silver chime" and "Move in melodious time," together with the "Base of Heav'ns deep Organ." The "ninefold harmony" of the spheres makes "full consort to th' Angelike symphony."

The heavenly orchestra brings about a sense of transport, bridging distinctions between past, present, and future. The narrator ponders the Golden Age, the Nativity, and the Second Coming. But then he abruptly turns to the Crucifixion and to the pain and woe of fallen man, accentuated by dissonant images of sight and sound: "bitter cross," "wakeful trump of doom," with its "horrid clang," "smouldring clouds," and "dreadful Judge." The narrator moves from the "bitter cross" back to the Fall of man, then to God's giving Moses the Ten Commandments, and finally to Last Judgment. "But now begins" heralds the alteration of the fallen world, which "from this happy day" has the promise of future perfection: "And then at last our bliss / Full and perfet is" (st. XVIII). Bliss is not yet achieved, but it is anticipated, particularly in the fleeing of the pagan deities at the birth of Christ.

The last movement (st. XVIII–XXVI) foreshadows the pagan gods' final departure to Hell at the Second Coming. The narrator selects gloomy images of sight and sound to convey the discord of the false gods and also to anticipate the turmoil of the "infernal Jail," which will ultimately house them. Grotesque forms and harsh sounds depict the false gods and their rout. Satan, the "old

Dragon," now powerlessly "Swindges the scaly Horrour of his foulded tail." There is a "hollow shreik," a "drear and dying sound," a "voice of weeping," "loud lament," "sighing," "lowings loud." The followers no longer can summon their gods: "In vain with Cymbals ring" and "In vain with Timbrel'd Anthems dark" they appeal to the deities, but their reign is over; the "hideous hum" of their rites has ended. The "Lars and Lemures moan with midnight plaint." "Peor, and Baalim, / Forsake their Temples dim," as do Dagon, "that twice batter'd god of *Palestine*," and "sullen *Moloch*," the "grisly King." This catalogue of false gods, with impressive sounding names, undergoes extensive development in *PL* 1.376-522. So, too, the dismal scene, with its images of darkness and smoldering fire, anticipates the fire, wind, "stench and smoke," and "mournful gloom" of Milton's Hell.

In stanza XX of this last section a sense of regret accompanies the banishment of the classical gods who haunt the "lonely mountains" and the "resounding shore":

> The lonely mountains o're,
> And the resounding shore,
>   A voice of weeping heard, and loud lament;
> From haunted spring, and dale
> Edg'd with poplar pale,
>   The parting Genius is with sighing sent,
> With flowre-inwov'n tresses torn
> The Nimphs in twilight shade of tangled thickets mourn.
>
> (st. XX)

Does the handling of the pagan "Nimphs in twilight shade of tangled thickets" and the "parting Genius [who] is with sighing sent" conflict with the point of view of the poem as a whole? Most critics say there is little conflict, as they attempt to explain the sense of regret for the loss of the classical deities in Milton's Christian poem. W. R. Parker says that Milton's childhood readings made him treat these pagan figures with fondness. Woodhouse observes that the poet banishes the deities (divinities in which he had rejoiced in *El* 5) because he is ready to accept "the order of grace and its supremacy over nature itself." Barker views the poem as "transcending the conflict between the two traditions" (pagan and Christian), as it develops a harmony symbolized by the music of the spheres. Brooks and Hardy believe that "the tone of the poem is too simple to admit of such tensions." The "aesthetic distance," the sense of "detachment," achieved by the "cosmic sweep of the Hymn" prevents a "contradiction between . . . regret [for the loss of the classical figures] and the greater joy caused by Christ's birth." Differing with these critics, Lawrence Hyman emphasizes that we do feel "a genuine regret" as the divinities depart and that this regret fits the pattern of the poem as a whole. The poem's ultimate harmony does "not erase the immediate sensation of darkness or of helplessness or of pain." This position is underscored by the fact that the "bitter grief which

we feel at the Crucifixion is part of the joy that we feel at the eventual triumph over death. The ecstasy of the Christian is made up of both the pain and the triumph."

It is also possible that the gentle handling of the pagan nymphs and Genius of the shore is Milton's decorous means of softening the harsh clang and moaning accompanying the retreat of the fallen Osiris, "sullen Moloch," and Dagon, "that twice batter'd god of Palestine." By this method, the pagan deities and their enchantment of evil are dispelled by Christ as smoothly as the shadows of the night are by the physical sun:

> . . . the yellow-skirted Fayes,
> Fly after the Night-steeds, leaving their Moon-lov'd maze.

The harshness of Christ's battle is thus ameliorated, allowing for a renewed emphasis on mercy, peace, and joy, which are traditionally associated with the Nativity.

In stanza XXVI, Milton uses the image of the sun's rising from bed to imply a similarity between the beginning of its day and the beginning of Christ's ministry as he lies in his cradle. This conceit, though clumsy, recalls the earlier section of the poem in which the sun, like the other temporal aspects of our world, is placed in submission and withholds "his wonted speed" at the birth of a greater Son. This image thus recaptures the mood of the earlier stanzas and prepares us for the conclusion, in which the stable is illuminated by the "Handmaid Lamp" of "heav'ns youngest teemed Star," which had guided the Wise Men. The star symbolizes the light Christ brings to the pagan world and the light of wisdom which shines within the Savior.

In the last stanza the star, at evening, is above the stable, where "Bright-harnest Angels ["helmed cherubim" and "sworded Seraphim"] sit in order serviceable," ceremoniously waiting on the Lord. Thus, at the close of the poem heavenly light and order return, and the pagan deities are now as submissive to Christ as are the sun, Nature, and man. The "rude manger" has been transfigured to a "Courtly Stable," where Christ is surrounded by a mighty army of angels who wait upon him and "at his bidding speed" (*Sonn* 19). They attend the cradle of the "Son of Heav'ns eternal King" (st. I). The splendor and glory at the close thus anticipates the Eternal Day, the Second Coming when Christ will once again be in the "Courts of everlasting Day," "midst of Trinal Unity."

In *Nat* Milton adapted and varied several literary traditions to create a form that is apparently his own invention. The stanzaic pattern of the proem is very close to rhyme royal, suggesting the lofty style of Chaucer (first appearing in "Complaint unto Pity"), Spenser ("The Ruines of Time" and "Fowre Hymnes"), and Shakespeare ("The Rape of Lucrece"). Instead of a final iambic pentameter line, Milton concludes each stanza with an alexandrine. It is the same form that he used in *FInf*. But the "Hymn" proper has a unique eight-line

stanza, radically different from the seven-line proem. As Røstvig (*The Hidden Sense*, pp. 54–58) and Butler (*Number Symbolism*, pp. 140–43) have noted, this difference suggests a movement from the worldly and transitory to the eternal. The number *8* in Christian numerology signifies the beginning of life with Christ and the end of mundane concerns. The number *7* marks the close of man's earthly pilgrimage. The seven-line stanza is thus appropriate for the proem to *Nat* and for the verses on the death of Milton's infant niece.

The "Hymn" has twenty-seven eight-line stanzas. It is a tour de force, metrically speaking, because four different kinds of lines are employed: a_6 a_6 b_{10} c_6 c_6 b_{10} d_8 d_{12}. Lines with three metrical feet alternate with five-foot lines, heralding, once again, the arrival of Christ. These first six lines, of alternating three-foot and five-foot combinations, are a construction that was common in fourteenth-century lyrics and in Elizabethan song and carol (in, for example, the canzonets and madrigals of Thomas Morley). By adding a final alexandrine, Milton achieves a stately sublimity for his "humble ode" (Martz). He also develops this effect by using strong monosyllables at the end of the first two lines in each stanza (except for "around," "amaze," and "Baalim").

The stately tone is also amplified by the roll call of the exotic, sonorous names of pagan deities whose powers have ceased at the Incarnation: Peor, Baalim, Ashtaroth, Hammon, Thamuz, Moloch, Isis, Orus, Anubis, Osiris. These names and the baroque description of the false gods contribute to the impressiveness and formality that we associate with odes.

Resounding names, and the baroque description accompanying them, are part of the combination of the simple and the complicated, so characteristic of the "humble ode." The alternate levels of complexity underline Milton's method of describing both the Christ-child's lying in a "rude manger" and the sublime subject of man's restoration. The blending of the unsophisticated and the intricate is apparent in the use of two traditions: the ballad tradition (observable in the first six lines of each stanza) and the literary tradition (observable in the alexandrine that concludes each stanza). A homely picture of "The Shepherds on the Lawn," who "Sate simply chatting in a rustick row" (VIII) accompanies the baroque details of Last Judgment, where "The wakeful trump of doom must thunder through the deep." The mixture of elaborate Elizabethan conceits with the plain descriptions that precede or follow them further demonstrates the poet's method. Nature is compared to a maiden covered with snow (II) and the sun to a man in bed who "Pillows his chin upon the Orient wave" (XXVI). The first conceit follows the image of the "rude manger" (I) and the second precedes the simple picture of the Virgin putting "her Babe to rest" (XXVII). E. M. W. Tillyard points to the "unique charm," the "clean exuberance" that these combinations provide:

A fifteenth-century Italian picture of the Nativity gives the simplest comparison. Here the absurdities—the rickety shelter, the far from new-born physique of the child, the cows peering with imbecile faces over a broken

wall, and the rest—unite with the simple brilliant colouring to create a most captivating sense of youthfulness and simplicity. The essence of the poem is not stateliness excusing conceit, but homeliness, quaintness, tenderness, extravagance, and sublimity, harmonised by a pervading youthful candour and ordered by a commanding architectonic grasp.

The poem moves, as Parker observes, from "strikingly simple" pictures to "crowded, almost baroque panels"; the different styles reflect the opposing elements within *Nat:* Christ and the pagan gods; peace and discord; harmony and chaos; Heaven and Hell. For some critics (e.g., Sypher and Hyman) the thematic clash remains unresolved. For others (e.g., Allen, Tillyard, and Barker) *Nat* builds toward a joyous acceptance of God's grace. *Nat* thus becomes almost unique in Milton's poetry because of its sheer joyousness, its enthusiasm and happiness, similar in tone to the hymn of praise in *PL* 5.154–208, and to the Psalms of David. [EBS]

ON THE NEW FORCERS OF CONSCIENCE UNDER THE LONG PARLIAMENT. Perhaps composed in the early months of 1647, *On the New Forcers of Conscience* appears in *TM* and in the 1673 edition of the poems. Although Milton's sonnet, written in the hand of an amanuensis (John Phillips), stands without number after the sonnet to Vane in the manuscript, there is some difficulty in determining where Milton originally intended *NewF* to be placed. Two notes, one by Milton and one by the scribe, both indicate that it should stand between the *Tetra* sonnet and the sonnet to Fairfax, a placement with possible chronological significance. In the 1673 edition of the poems, on the other hand, *NewF* is not only excluded from the sonnet sequence but separated from it by the translation from Horace and *Vac.* Such changes surely indicate that the problem of determining proper placement is at times vexed.

Based upon the various topical allusions, the precise occasion of the sonnet is similarly difficult to define. For example, the reference to "shallow *Edwards* and Scotch what d'ye call" (12), denoting Thomas Edwards, on the one hand, and probably Robert Baillie, on the other, suggests one possibility. Because of Milton's ideas concerning divorce, both men had attacked him in their respective tracts, Baillie in *Dissuasive from the Errours of the Times* (1645), and Edwards in *Gangraena* (1646). On the other hand, Milton's statement about the adjuring of the "Civill Sword / To force our Consciences that Christ set free" (5–6) might allude to the Presbyterian movement during the last months of 1646 and the early months of 1647 to demand immediate legislation for the repression of heresy and error. Despite the specific references in date and occasion suggested by these allusions, they do concur in providing a way to understand those underlying forces which prompted Milton to write his sonnet in the first place. The poem has been dated on such evidence from 1645 through 1647.

Having supported the Presbyterian form of church government in his antiprelatical tracts (1641–42), Milton grew disenchanted with what he considered

to be the Presbyterian intolerance of any ideas that might differ from their own. (The Presbyterian reaction to Milton's ideas concerning divorce is a case in point.) Appropriately, Milton directed his sympathies toward the more tolerant Parliamentary minority, the Independents. With them, he was critical of the power the Presbyterians were gaining in the Assembly of Divines, or the Westminster Assembly (1643–1649), commissioned by Parliament to deliberate on matters of church discipline and ceremony now that episcopacy had been formally abolished (1643) and the Anglican *Book of Common Prayer* renounced (1645). What resulted, particularly during the years 1644–1646, were the manifold contentions between the Independents and the Presbyterians, contentions signaled by a flood of pamphlets and treatises on both sides.

With the fervor of these pamphlets, Milton's sonnet succinctly expresses the Independent argument against the Presbyterians by emphasizing what it feels to be the two fundamental evils of the Presbyterian party: "force" and "hire." The precise character of those evils Milton was later to delineate in such tracts as *CivP:* "Two things there be which have bin ever found working much mischief to the church of God, and the advancement of truth; force on the one side restraining, and hire on the other side corrupting the teachers thereof. Few ages have bin since the ascension of our Saviour, wherein the one of these two, or both together have not prevaild . . ." (6:4). In *NewF,* "force" takes the form of the "Civill Sword" compelling our free consciences, and "hire" takes the form of the Presbyterian movement to return to the corruptions of episcopal pluralism, or the holding of multiple posts.

Corresponding with these criticisms are Milton's attacks on the desire of the Presbyterians to substitute their synodical hierarchy or "classis" for the episcopal form of church government and the Scottish support of the English Presbyterians with such men as Adam Stuart and Samuel Rutherford, both Scottish members of the Westminster Assembly. In contrast with the Scottish supporters, Milton invokes the Independents (such as Thomas Goodwin, Philip Hye, Jeremiah Burroughs, Sidrach Simpson, and William Bridge), "Men whose Life, Learning, Faith and pure intent / Would have been held in high esteem with *Paul*" (9–10). These men, branded heretics by the Scots, will uncover the Presbyterian deceptions, their "plots and packing wors then" those perpetrated by the Catholics at the Council of Trent (13–14).

As a result, Milton has faith that the Parliament will rectify the evils of the Presbyterians by "clip[ping]" their "Phylacteries" though "bauk[ing]" their "Ears" (17). The allusion to the phylacteries recalls Christ's charge that the Pharisees were displaying these insignia of devotion only in order to impress others (Matt. 23:5). Thus, Milton warns that the Presbyterians will suffer the removal of their hypocritical claims to piety, even though their ears are spared. In effect, the allusion threatens them, according to Mosaic law, with being rendered incapable of priesthood of any kind. (Significantly, lurking behind the reference to the severing of ears is the earlier *TM* version of the line, which alludes to the fact that William Prynne had been shorn of his ears in 1637.) This

castigation of Presbyterian hypocrisy culminates in the final line of the sonnet: "*New Presbyter* is but *Old Priest* writ Large" (20). The etymological identification of *priest* and *presbyter,* both deriving from the Greek *presbyteros,* completes a series of exposés that have shown the Presbyterians to be nothing more in their practices (and now in their very name) than another version of prelatical, popish, and pharisaical hypocrisy. Thereby, Milton has been able, in the final portion of his sonnet, to "find out all [their] tricks" (13).

What has aided him in his exposé is his use of the uncommon Italian form *sonetto caudato,* containing a stinging tail or *coda* to be used something like a whip. In *NewF* the device is appended to the body of what would otherwise be a conventional Petrarchan sonnet (abbaabbacdedec). As appended, the tail takes the form of two tercets, each consisting of a trimeter followed by a pentameter couplet (cfffgg). In that form, it becomes a very effective way of giving expression to Milton's satiric purposes. [ML]

ON THE UNIVERSITY CARRIER. This eighteen-line poem appeared in both the 1645 and 1673 editions of Milton's works and in a jestbook, *Wit Restor'd,* published in 1658. Early copies of it may also be found in non-Miltonic manuscripts. It is one of two, possibly three, poems that Milton wrote on Thomas Hobson, who died January 1, 1631, at the age of eighty-six.

In Cambridge, Hobson's longevity and picturesque ways had made him something of an institution. As the owner of a livery stable, he had been noted for always allowing his customers to "choose" the horse nearest the door, thus giving rise to the expression, "Hobson's choice," which means no choice at all. For over sixty-five years, too, he had driven a weekly coach between Cambridge and the Bull Tavern, London. Unfortunately, he had been forced to discontinue his trips in 1630 because of plague in Cambridge, and it may have been that the enforced idleness hastened his demise.

Such at least was the verdict of the students—Milton among them—who greeted his death with an outpouring of light verse. Milton's poem, which is written in rhyming couplets of iambic pentameter, opens with phrases that liken Death to an interruption of Hobson's long journey: it is as if Hobson had been "stuck in a slough, and overthrown." Lines 5–10 observe that Death would never have caught up with him at all had he not been forced to stay at home for a while. In the concluding lines, that home becomes the last inn at which Hobson stops and Death, the kindly chamberlain or attendant who shows Hobson to the room where he must spend the night, pulls off his boots, and takes away the light.

Milton's touch is gentle, his humor not at all unkind. By joining in an activity that was currently very popular at Cambridge, he clearly hoped to produce work that would appeal to his contemporaries; and it is gratifying to think that he succeeded. Indeed, given the context of Milton's career, *Carrier* may be most useful as a corrective to the view that his soul *always* "was like a Star, and dwelt apart." Because of its relative simplicity, *Carrier* has not been accorded detailed

critical analysis. The substantial commentary it has occasioned reflects rather difficulties that have occurred in establishing the text, in determining Milton's possible authorship of a third Hobson poem, and in presenting and analyzing the large family of Hobson poems. [ERG]

ON TIME. This poem appeared in both the 1645 and 1673 editions of Milton's poems. It also appears in *TM*, although it is only transcribed there and not, like *SolMus*, actually composed there. Its resemblances to *SolMus* suggest that the two poems were composed during the same period. Any attempt to date *Time* therefore depends upon the period when Milton began using *TM*, a matter admittedly conjectural, with estimates ranging from the early 1630s to 1637.

In *TM*, Milton originally entitled his poem, "[to be] set on a clock case," then later scratched through these words and wrote above them its present title, "On Time." The poem is a madrigal, a loose Italian form that Milton freely employed in English. The madrigal, F. T. Prince observes, had been much used by sixteenth-century Italian writers to reproduce the Greek epigram, a genre that originally consisted of poetry suitable for inscription. Milton's own poem, like *SolMus*, though longer and more ambitious than most poems of this type, nevertheless retains the essential features of "a triumphant epigrammatic close" and of "wit-writing." In addition to the sixteenth-century Italian writers, some scholars have seen a knowledge of the Beatific Vision in Dante's *Paradiso* reflected in the reference of line 18 to God's "happy-making sight."

The poem divides into two sentences that present an opposition between time and eternity. In the first sentence (1–8), time and that which it can consume are denigrated. In the second (9–22), Milton turns to the happiness that souls in heaven will enjoy for eternity when time comes to an end. O. B. Hardison, Jr., has argued that lines 11–12—

> Then long Eternity shall greet our bliss
> With an individual kiss—

show an awareness of Aristotle, particularly as he was interpreted by the Moslem philosopher Averroes (1126–98) and his medieval and Renaissance disciples. Taking their point of departure from a passage in Aristotle's *De Anima*, they had argued against personal immortality. According to Hardison, however, *Time* upholds the orthodox Christian position that each soul survives as a separate entity. The lines above then might be paraphrased for clarity as saying that Eternity will greet each soul "individually with a kiss."

Time is written in a basically iambic meter with line lengths varying from six to twelve syllables. The first sentence uses alternate rhyme (abab) in the first four lines, then switches to enclosed rhyme (cddc). Thereafter, succeeding lines rhyme with each other, except for the last four, which again use enclosed rhyme. Though based on an Italian form, the poem reveals Milton's growing sense of freedom in rendering such a form into English. This is particularly

obvious if we compare *Time* with his very careful imitation of the *canzone* in *Circum*. Probably growing out of Milton's well-controlled variations within the form is the syntactical complexity of the second sentence. It is noteworthy in that it helps to create dramatic intensity in the work and also in that it foreshadows his later use of syntax as a structural element in his poetry. [ERG]

PARADISE LOST. While in the nineteenth century some critics followed Blake and Shelley, the revolutionary crusaders, in glorifying Satan as Milton's real hero, the main tendency was to dismiss his religious theme and celebrate his grand style as the only salvation of *PL*. This tendency, exemplified even by the religiously and classically minded but strongly anti-Puritan Matthew Arnold, was summed up in Sir Walter Raleigh's remark that "The *Paradise Lost* is not the less an eternal monument because it is a monument to dead ideas" (*Milton* [1900], p. 88). In the earlier twentieth century such audible voices as Ezra Pound, T. S. Eliot, and F. R. Leavis damned the style and the man as well; more systematically, A. J. A. Waldock (*Paradise Lost and Its Critics* [1947]) applied to Milton's story the criteria appropriate to a realistic novel and also showed himself tone-deaf in regard to religious and moral values. Such uncritical criticism stimulated the flood of defensive and freshly expository studies which, since C. S. Lewis's *A Preface to Paradise Lost* (1942), have continued to multiply. But earlier, about 1917, several American scholars, Edwin Greenlaw, J. H. Hanford, and Allan Gilbert, had replaced the dichotomized Victorian image of the sublime stylist and repellent Puritan with the unified image of the Christian humanist of the Renaissance; and Denis Saurat (*Milton: Man and Thinker* [1925]), with aberrations, and E. M. W. Tillyard (*Milton*, [1930]), with fewer, developed that conception. During the last forty years dozens of books and countless articles have carried criticism to new levels by combining historical knowledge, sympathetic understanding of Milton's beliefs, ideas, and purposes, and sensitive aesthetic insight. It can safely be said that *PL* has come to be appreciated far more fully and intelligently than it ever was before. Although Leavis could assume that Milton had been finally dislodged from his bad eminence, so sophisticated a critic as Frank Kermode (who has not the vested interest of a "Miltonist") has prophesied that the time cannot be far off when *PL* "will be read once more as the most perfect achievement of English poetry, perhaps the richest and most intricately beautiful poem in the world (*Romantic Image* [1957], p. 165).

While an encyclopedia article, however limited in scope, must aim at orthodoxy, the many excellent modern critics have naturally not been a chorus of angelic unanimity on all points, so that many things said here, especially in the later sections, might be modified, and some perhaps denied, by others; and even the most orthodox ideas could be, and have been, much elaborated, refined, and illustrated. It has not been possible to give many bibliographical references or to give any of later date than 1970.

In the proem to Book 9 of *PL* Milton, repudiating the traditional heroic

poem in favor of his own higher theme, spoke of himself as "long choosing, and beginning late." Both phrases are borne out by his personal history. Whereas Aristotle had made tragedy the supreme poetic genre, Renaissance critical theory gave that place to the epic, and Milton, like many ambitious poets of the sixteenth and seventeenth centuries, dreamed of doing for his country what Homer, Virgil, and the rest had done for theirs. In his second original English poem, *Vac* (1628), the Cambridge undergraduate, now nineteen, confided to his college audience his desire to write heroic poetry that would take in both the physical universe and "Kings and Queens and *Hero's* old." His first great poem, *Nat* (1629), was at once religious and of epic range; it embraced all time, from the Creation to the Judgment Day and Eternity. In the Latin *El* 6, addressed in the same Christmas season to his friend Diodati, Milton contrasted the convivial maker of light verse with his implied ideal of the ascetic, priestlike poet of heroic themes. In the Latin *Mansus*, written in Italy in 1638–39, and, more explicitly, in *EpDam* (1639–40), the elegy on Diodati, Milton spoke of his plan for a heroic poem on King Arthur and his knights. This early choice of a hero of primitive national history was in accord with classical precedents and with Renaissance theory and practice. But we hear no more of Arthur. Milton abandoned the subject, partly, perhaps, because the research done for his *Brit* convinced him that Arthur was only a figure of monkish legend, and, more largely, because that story was an inadequate vehicle for what he now wished to say.

About 1640–1642 Milton compiled a list of nearly a hundred possible subjects for dramas drawn from early British history and from the Bible (if he made a similar list of epic subjects it has not survived). His inclination toward the dramatic form, probably stimulated by his Italian experience, and his choice of the Fall as his theme, are concretely illustrated by four early and increasingly full outlines for a dramatic treatment of that story. (These scenarios are conveniently accessible in J. H. Hanford's *A Milton Handbook*, 5th ed., revised by Hanford and J. G. Taaffe [1970], pp. 151–53, also in *CM* 18:228ff.) The numerous personifications, Ignorance, Fear, Death, Faith, and the like, suggest—apart from the use of a classical Chorus—a medieval morality play, but were presumably suggested to Milton by Italian religious dramas, which were one late manifestation of the medieval allegorical tradition. Moreover, Edward Phillips, Milton's nephew and biographer, told John Aubrey that, about fifteen or sixteen years before *PL* was thought of, he had seen a portion of Satan's apostrophe to the sun (*PL* 4.32–41) written as the opening speech of a tragedy (*Early Lives of Milton*, ed. Helen Darbishire [1932], pp. 13, 72).

We do not know what led Milton to return to his original plan for an epic. Perhaps the Renaissance veneration for the heroic poem reasserted itself. We may surmise a stronger reason: that, as the full scope and import of the theme developed in his mind, he felt cramped by the dramatic form and wanted the large temporal, spatial, and interpretative freedom of epic narrative—though *PL* was to be notably dramatic in structure and method. The actual beginning

was indeed "late." For nearly twenty years the Christian humanist had put his religious and civic duty before his poetic vocation—and we may think that the poem eventually gained in depth and timeless relevance from that self-denying ordinance and from its author's prolonged immersion in public affairs. He had also expended intermittent labor on his *Brit* and his huge Latin treatise, *CD*, which seems to have been finished by 1658–1660. Blindness, which became complete early in 1652 or at the end of 1651, when Milton was only forty-three or forty-two and the great poem was still unwritten, was a blow that the devout Christian needed all his faith and courage to sustain.

John Aubrey (*Early Lives*, p. 13) and much modern opinion place the actual beginning of composition in or about 1658; some scholars would put it two or three years earlier. One passage can certainly be dated after the Restoration, the passage in the invocation to Book 7 in which the poet speaks so movingly of his being "fall'n on evil dayes" and denounces "*Bacchus* and his revellers," who had destroyed the archetypal poet, Orpheus. We have Milton's own testimony in the poem to his composing much at night, so that in the morning he would need to be "milked," dictating to a paid amanuensis or to whoever happened to be handy, a relative or a caller. According to Phillips, Milton said that "his Vein never happily flow'd, but from the *Autumnal Equinoctial* to the *Vernal*, and that whatever he attempted [at other seasons] was never to his satisfaction, though he courted his fancy never so much; so that in all the years he was about this Poem, he may be said to have spent but half his time therein" (*Early Lives*, p. 73). We have no knowledge of how composition proceeded. It might have been in an approximately straight line from beginning to end—which Alastair Fowler calls "the common false assumption" (*Poems of John Milton*, ed. J. Carey and A. Fowler [1968]. p. 422)—though we do not *know* that it is false; and a poem often praised for its powerful forward march might have gained some of its momentum from such an effort. The obvious alternative is that the poem was composed in scattered blocks that were gradually worked into a coherent whole. Or Milton might have used both methods, as impulse moved him. In any case there must have been much recasting and revision on both a large and a small scale: one of the wonders of the poem, apprehended only by degrees with continual rereading, is the infinity of not only massive but minute links—parallels and contrasts in idea, image, phrase, word, and rhythm— which bind the poem together and greatly enrich its resonance.

According to Aubrey (*Early Lives*, p. 13), *PL* was finished by about 1663. It certainly must have been by the summer of 1665, when Milton gave the manuscript to his young Quaker friend, Thomas Ellwood, to read. It was not published until the late summer of 1667. Whatever other reasons may have contributed to delay, there was the general public disorder attending the Great Plague in London—during which Milton and his family lived in Chalfont St. Giles in Buckinghamshire (apparently from July 1665 till February 1666)—and the Great Fire of September 2–5, 1666. According to one early biographer, John Toland, publication was held up for a while by the clerical licenser, who smelled

treason in the simile of *PL* 1.594–99, in which "fear of change / Perplexes Monarchs." The poem was entered in the Stationers' Register on August 20, 1667, and published soon afterwards. By the terms of his contract Milton received £5 in April 1667, and a second £5 in April 1669, when the first impression of 1,300 copies was sold out (French, *Life Records*, 4: 429–31); Milton's widow got £8 more in 1680, when the printer acquired full title to the book. Of this first edition there were six issues, dated 1667, 1668, and 1669, and Milton took advantage of these to insert the brief preface in defense of blank verse, a prose Argument for the whole poem, and Errata. In this original form the poem had ten books. In the second edition (1674), which included the commendatory poems of Samuel Barrow and Andrew Marvell, the seventh and tenth books were each divided into two and some new lines were provided as beginnings for what were now the eighth and twelfth books; the Argument was split into twelve parts placed at the head of the respective books; and some small revisions were made. The initial sale of 1,300 copies in about a year and a half seems pretty good for a religious epic by a notorious "rebel" in the aftermath of the Plague and the Fire and in the London and England of Charles II and Restoration comedy and satire; and subsequent editions indicate the poem's rising prestige. The famous Jacob Tonson issued the fourth, fifth, and sixth editions of 1688, 1692, and 1695. That of 1688, which was illustrated, carried the names of over five hundred subscribers, a number of them persons of worldly or literary eminence. The poem's classical status may be said to have been established by the 1695 edition, which was very elaborately annotated by a schoolmaster, Patrick Hume, in the manner hitherto reserved for the sacrosanct Greek and Roman authors. The first century of Miltonic scholarship has been fully described and assessed by Ants Oras, *Milton's Editors and Commentators from Patrick Hume to Henry John Todd (1695–1801)* [1931; rev. ed., 1967]). The critical value of such eighteenth-century commentators as Jonathan Richardson and Thomas Newton has been stressed by Christopher Ricks (*Milton's Grand Style* [1963]); and the eccentric operations of the great classical scholar, Richard Bentley, in his edition of *PL* (1732), have been turned to critical account by William Empson (*Some Versions of Pastoral* [1935]) and by Ricks.

The second edition of 1674 is naturally the basic text for modern editions, although it has occasional errors that must be corrected from the first edition. The number of errors in both editions is surprisingly small when we consider the difficulties involved at two stages: first, the standardizing and correcting of the manuscript as written by various persons from Milton's dictation, often—as Edward Phillips said—with little regard for spelling and punctuation; and, second, a blind man's dependence upon other people's eyes and ears in the correcting of proofs. No manuscript of *PL* has survived except a fair copy of Book 1 that was used by the printer of the first edition; this manuscript, now in the Morgan Library in New York, was edited by Helen Darbishire in 1931. The full printed texts of 1667 and 1674 have been reproduced in the second and third volumes of Harris F. Fletcher's facsimile edition of the complete poetical works

(1943–1948); a facsimile of the 1667 edition has been issued by the Scolar Press (1968). Textual variations in the early editions are recorded in *CM* 2:487–540), in Fletcher's edition just cited, and in Darbishire's edition of the complete poems (1 [1952]).

One special question may be briefly noticed. In her editions of 1931 and 1952 Darbishire confidently argued that Milton had a system of spelling that provided for forms he favored (e.g., preterites ending in *d*, past participles in *t*) and for distinguishing emphatic from unemphatic pronouns (e.g., *wee, we, mee, me, their, thir*); cf. B. A. Wright, *Milton's Poems* (1956), xxi, xxiv–xxviii. This theory, which raised doubts in many minds, was well battered by R. M. Adams (*Modern Philology* 52 [1954–55]:84–91; *Ikon: John Milton and the Modern Critics* [1955]) and demolished by J. T. Shawcross (*Publications of the Modern Language Association* 78 [1963]:501–10; also in his essay in *Language and Style in Milton*, ed. R. D. Emma and Shawcross [1968]), who showed, by comparison with Milton's holograph spellings, that his supposed idiosyncrasies must be attributed to amanuenses or compositors. The debate is summarized in Carey and Fowler, pages xi–xii.

The problem of punctuation has been fully and expertly studied by Mindele Treip (*Milton's Punctuation and Changing English Usage 1582–1676* [1970]). She finds "the strongest arguments for the poet's control . . . in the impression of a strong poetic sensibility operating in the punctuation of the poem, especially that of the Manuscript [of Book 1], and in the fact that the printer so largely retained this pointing or respected its general style when correcting, although it was unrepresentative of the period" (pp. 6–7). Treip shows that, in his later autograph sonnets and in *PL*, Milton inclined (with his own refinements) to the older rhythmical and rhetorical principle of punctuation but made a partial compromise with the newer logical and grammatical method (pp. 68–69, etc.). Modern editors have recognized the general problem (e.g., Carey and Fowler, pp. x–xi, 427–28). For so subtle an artist as Milton, punctuation governs not only continuity and breaks in rhythm but the rate of speed, degrees of emphasis, shades of meaning, desired parallels and contrasts. Hence in modern editions that preserve the original punctuation, the sense may sometimes puzzle the reader (this Treip discounts); and modernized punctuation (which she outlaws), while clarifying the general sense, may blunt or destroy syntactical, rhythmical, and emotive relationships and nuances of meaning.

Milton's changing plans for an epic were touched upon above. The genre was so alluring to Renaissance ambition that the sixteenth, seventeenth, and even the eighteenth centuries were strewn with epics that would—as Richard Porson was to say of Southey's—be read when Homer and Virgil were forgotten. There were several basic assumptions. The material, as we have noted, should be drawn, like Homer's and Virgil's, from the early or legendary history of the poet's native land, and the action should be a subject of national magnitude. The heroic poet should be a universal scholar, should try to comprehend in his

work the whole range of life and knowledge and thought. Hence the epic must be the product of ripe maturity; and Virgil's career provided a canonical model of progression—the *Eclogues, Georgics,* and *Aeneid.* Such a poem should especially fulfill poetry's double aim of teaching and delighting, should set before the reader examples of virtue to be followed and of weakness and vice to be shunned.

Thus Spenser, in his letter to Sir Walter Ralegh attached to *The Faerie Queene,* summarized the didactic conception of the heroic poem, citing exemplars, from Homer and Virgil to Ariosto (whose moral teaching we may find scanty) and Tasso. Ariosto and Tasso had dealt with the conflicts of Christians and Saracens. The eclectic and more didactic Spenser had treated Arthur and imaginary knights under the religious and moral headings of his six completed books (Holiness, Temperance, Chastity, Friendship, Justice, Courtesy), all embraced in his general effort "to fashion a gentleman or noble person in vertuous and gentle discipline." Milton spoke in *Areop* of "our sage and serious" Spenser as "a better teacher than *Scotus* or *Aquinas,*" citing in particular the temptations Guyon met in the Cave of Mammon and the Bower of Bliss. He gave much fuller general testimony in *RCG.* Addressing Presbyterian readers of doubtful literary sensibility, and explaining—with a kind of sublime naiveté—why he felt compelled to set aside his poetic ambitions in order to champion the Puritan cause, Milton declared his fervent faith in the power of true poetry to nourish virtue and religion in a people (3:237–41). More specifically, along with Homer, Virgil, and Tasso, he spoke of the book of Job and the choice of some knight "before the conquest" as "the pattern of a Christian Heroe."

The classical doctrine of delightful teaching, revived by Renaissance humanists, received further impetus—as the names of Spenser, Milton, and Tasso remind us—from the Reformation and the Counter-Reformation. That impetus often included a revulsion against the paganism of the classics and a demand for biblical and Christian themes: examples range from Du Bartas's immense and immensely popular heroic poem (noticed below and elsewhere in this work) to Cowley's preface to his poems of 1656 and his unfinished epic on David. (See B. O. Kurth, *Milton and Christian Heroism: Biblical Epic Themes and Forms in Seventeenth-Century England* [1959]). Milton's early abandonment of the story of Arthur for the far greater theme of the Fall involved a drastic break with heroic tradition. In the proem to Book 9, with explicit reference to the *Iliad, Odyssey,* and *Aeneid,* he repudiated war, "hitherto the onely Argument / Heroic deem'd" in favor of the sad but "more Heroic" theme of sin and woe and death and, in the end, the way of salvation opened to erring man. That goes well beyond delightful teaching. Milton's characters became almost all supernatural (God, the Son, good and evil angels); the only earthly ones, Adam and Eve, were not ordinary human beings in a human society; and the essential action was now inward, its stage the souls of Satan and the Son, Adam, and Eve.

Such radical changes involved a radical change in the poet's conception of his own role. In *RCG*, Milton said—echoing Isaiah 1:5, which long before he had echoed in the prelude to *Nat*—that the poem he hoped to write would be

a work not to be rays'd from the heat of youth, or the vapours of wine, like that which flows at wast from the pen of some vulgar Amorist, or the trencher fury of a riming parasite, nor to be obtain'd by the invocation of Dame Memory and her Siren daughters, but by devout prayer to that eternall Spirit who can enrich with all utterance and knowledge, and sends out his Seraphim with the hallow'd fire of his Altar to touch and purify the lips of whom he pleases. (3:241)

Thus in the poem Milton repeatedly insists on the unique truth of Christian revelation and hence the superiority of his Christian theme. He will soar "Above th' *Aonian Mount*" (1.15); he sings "With other notes then to th' *Orphean* Lyre" (3.17); the Urania whose inspiration he implores is not the pagan Muse, "an empty dreame," but the Heavenly Muse who conversed "with Eternal wisdom . . . / . . . In presence of th'Almightie Father" (7.1–39). Milton thinks of himself as in the line of inspired prophets, the medium or voice of divine illumination, which will raise and support his human and personal insufficiency. In *RCG* the humanist had gone on to say that "to this must be added industrious and select reading, steddy observation, insight into all seemly and generous arts and affaires. . . ."

Like earlier Christian humanists, Milton, while profoundly assured of the uniqueness of Christian revelation, revered the art and the moral wisdom of the great ancients, and it was wholly natural that, as artist, the most scholarly classicist among Renaissance poets should bypass the more or less unclassical changes wrought in the heroic poem by Ariosto, Tasso, and Spenser and should, as far as his subject allowed, revert to the authentic classical structure and method—as *SA* was modeled on Greek, not Elizabethan, tragedy. In the first full critique of *PL*, Addison's eighteen papers in the *Spectator*, the poem was inevitably assessed in terms of the established set of epic conventions; Addison's contemporary, John Dennis, was much more independent and perceptive in his comments. (For both, see *Milton: The Critical Heritage*, ed. J. T. Shawcross [1970]).

Obviously Milton's central source was the Bible, not merely for the stories of Creation and the Fall, which he so greatly expanded, but for the Hebrew history presented to Adam in Books 11 and 12 and for a multitude of allusions, images, and phrases. (The standard survey of such materials is James H. Sim's *The Bible in Milton's Epics* [1962].) No less obvious is the biblical foundation of the theological scheme centering on the Fall and on redemption through the Christ foretold by the prophets. In an age of assiduous reading of the Bible, Milton's complete and intimate possession of the text was shared by many people; not so many shared the systematized and sophisticated knowledge displayed throughout his large Latin treatise *CD*. This work—which he called

"my best and riches possession"—cannot be called a "source," but (as Maurice Kelley showed in *This Great Argument* [1941]) it provides chapter and verse for most of the theological beliefs and ethical principles embodied in *PL*. The poem is not always in strict agreement with the treatise, and in any case the poetic and dramatic presentation of such beliefs and principles has for the most part a very different effect from that of expository prose. And epic latitude prescribed or allowed for large departures from theology proper: for example, Satan and his fellows received only a couple of pages in the *CD* (15: 107–11), compounded of biblical citations that include sparse and vague allusions to their being cast into hell. Moreover, in the poem Milton played down his personal "heresies": for example, the doctrine of "mortalism" (the death of the soul as well as the body until the general resurrection, which in the *CD* (15: 215ff.) is formally endorsed, becomes in *PL* only a dramatic utterance put into the mouth of the despairing Adam (10.782ff.). It would seem, from *CD* (e.g. 1, vii and x), that Milton, like most other educated people of his time (and indeed well into the nineteenth century), took the story of Adam and Eve as literal history, although he enlarged and reinterpreted it so freely.

Milton's fable brings in two related kinds of material (much of it discussed by Grant McColley, *Paradise Lost* [1940] and J. M. Evans, *Paradise Lost and the Genesis Tradition* [1968]). A great mass of biblical commentary, both Jewish and Christian, and many literary redactions had through the centuries enveloped the brief and simple stories of the Creation and the Fall with interpretive, speculative, and imaginative accretions. It is clear that Milton knew some part of these exegetical and imaginative materials, but we cannot tell how far his knowledge went. The story of the six days' work of Creation had become itself a poetic genre, the hexaemeral, which might remain separate or—as in *PL* 7— be united with the story of the Fall. Both themes, and much else, were elaborated in the most famous predecessor of *PL*, Du Bartas's *La Sepmaine* 1578ff.), which was translated, with an exuberance both flamboyant and flat, by Josuah Sylvester as *The Divine Weekes and Workes* (1591–92ff.). Du Bartas's grandiose poem owed its European fame to its subject, the picturesque energy of the writing, and the combination of religious and cosmic orthodoxy with a reassuring air of scientific authority. The young Milton (like the young Dryden later) was evidently attracted by Sylvester, and the elderly Milton may have sometimes echoed him: one line of *PL*, "Immutable, Immortal, Infinite" 3.373), was apparently recalled from *D. W. W.* 1.1.56. But we may discount the large claims—made chiefly by G. C. Taylor—for a large debt. External probabilities and points of internal resemblance have led modern scholars to take two dramas as less unlikely than other "sources" to have come under Milton's eye. These are *Adamus Exul* (1601), an early work of the great jurist Hugo Grotius, whom Milton met in Paris, and G. Andreini's *L'Adamo* (1613), which he might have seen in Italy. (Both works are translated, with other analogues, in Watson Kirkconnell's *The Celestial Cycle* [1952].) Such parallels as there are, are suc-

cinctly summarized in Hanford's *Milton Handbook* (pp. 210–14; on Grotius and *PL*, see also J. M. Evans, pp. 207ff.).

For us, two generalities may be enough. First, while no poet would tamper with the central truths of Christian faith (although, as we saw, Milton unobtrusively admitted some "heresies" he found in the Bible), tradition fully endorsed both poetic expositions of doctrine and, as we also saw, imaginative embellishment of characters and events. Second, since the huge body of exegetical and imaginative material was common property, it is mostly vain, and certainly tedious, to try to specify Milton's "sources." The most profitable result of reading earlier versions of his fable is the realization that in all essentials, in imaginative and artistic power, he was greatly original, and was indeed celebrating—to quote the line he borrowed from Ariosto—"Things unattempted yet in Prose or Rhime."

Parallel principles legitimized the use of classical materials in a Christian poem. If sanction was needed, beyond immemorial veneration for the classics, it was provided by two age-old doctrines, the allegorical reading of classical myth and the idea (a first approach to comparative mythology) that such myth was a refraction of the true history recorded in the Old Testament—as in the obvious likeness between Eden and the Golden Age or between the story of Noah and that of Deucalion and Pyrrha surviving a universal flood. Thus in his two accounts of Noah's flood (*PL* 11.719–901) Milton freely combined details from the Bible and Ovid (*Metam.* 1.253ff.) and perhaps Sylvester. With allegorical reading Milton (after *Mask*) had little to do; Orpheus, for instance, in *Lyc* and in *PL* (notably in 7.32–39) is not, as he was in Giles Fletcher's *Christs Victorie, and Triumph (3.7)*, a "type" of Christ, but simply the archetypal poet, done to death by a hostile mob. Nor—whatever he thought—does Milton take much account of "refraction": one reference of that kind is to "*Eurynome*, the wide-/Encroaching *Eve* perhaps" (10.581–82): the more memorable allusion to Mulciber is noticed below. (The latest, fullest, and most learned study of the whole subject is Don C. Allen's *Mysteriously Meant* [1970].) Milton did make use of the patristic tradition that the rebellious angels became the gods of heathenism. Behind the great figure of Satan we may see Prometheus, Odysseus, Achilles, Turnus, and others, but the important thing is that Milton contrasts the heroism of the classical warrior-chieftain (and even that perverted in Satan) with the true heroism fully possessed by the Son and finally understood by Adam. To some of the older—or unregenerate younger—critics, Milton's God had appeared unpleasantly close to Zeus or Jupiter, but any such resemblance was not, of course, intentional; so far as it goes, it is only an external result of the epic conception and structure.

The Milton of the earlier tracts had shown the religious, ethical, political, and social optimism of an idealist exulting in the aims and growing achievements of the Puritan revolution. The sustained eloquence—and incidental wit—of *Areop* had expressed high confidence in man's religious and rational capacity to

discern and to follow righteousness, to attain true virtue by facing the manifold temptations in the midst of which God had placed him:

> many there be that complain of divin Providence for suffering *Adam* to transgresse, foolish tongues! when God gave him reason, he gave him freedom to choose, for reason is but choosing; he had bin else a meer artificiall *Adam*, such an *Adam* as he is in the motions [puppet shows]. (4:319; cf. *PL* 3.98–128, etc.)

When Truth and Falsehood grapple, "who ever knew Truth put to the wors, in a free and open encounter"? (4:347).

Milton's first tract, *Ref* (1641), had ended with a fervent prayer in which he invoked Christ as "the Eternall and shortly-expected King" who would "put an end to all Earthly *Tyrannies*" and proclaim his "universal and milde *Monarchy* through Heaven and Earth" (3:78–79). In the same paragraph he had imagined a poet—such as himself, no doubt—"offering at high *strains* in new and lofty *Measures* to sing and celebrate thy divine *Mercies*, and *marvelous Judgements* in this Land throughout all Ages." But the tract boldly, indeed rashly, published on the very eve of the Restoration, *Way* (1660), was a cry of despair for "*the good Old Cause*" (6:148). During many years before that Milton had seen Truth often put to the worse, had grown more and more disillusioned with the mass of men and many of their leaders. The Restoration finally extinguished the vision that had long inspired and absorbed his energies (and had cost his eyesight as well)—the vision of a holy community, a Christian state governed by Puritan saints (as philosopher-kings), a sort of interregnum before Christ's second coming. Now, in 1660, the grand new reformation had become a mirage; and, especially in the latter half of *PL*, it is seen as fulfilled only after the Day of Judgment, when fire has made all things new.

Thus Milton's desire in *PL* to assert Eternal Providence,/And justifie the wayes of God to men" is not mere conventional piety; it is the effort of a devout Christian who, more than most men, had maintained and must maintain his faith in Prividence in the face of all the public and private shocks it had undergone. And wholehearted faith in Providence requires understanding, constancy, and divine help. In *Educ* (1644) Milton had, along with a secular definition of education, given a less familiar one that assumes man's responsibilities and religious striving:

> The end then of Learning is to repair the ruines of our first Parents by regaining to know God aright, and out of that knowledge to love him, to imitate him, to be like him, as we may the neerest by possessing our souls of true vertue, which being united to the heavenly grace of faith makes up the highest perfection. (4:277)

But the opening lines of *PL* dwell much less on salvation than on sin. The relative emphasis on "Mans First Disobedience" and on tragic loss is fully

borne out by the title and the poem as a whole, even though it is a "divine comedy." Thinking again of *Areop* and Milton's early confidence in man's rational dignity and power of choice (which, to be sure, are reasserted in *PL*), we can hardly help feeling that public and private experience has lessened his trust in reason and heightened his concern with humble faith and obedience. In *PL* (as in *PR* and *SA*) the poet's faith rests only on God and the capacity of individual souls, aided by grace, to achieve regeneration. *PL* was a personal testimony and a tract for the times as well as a beautiful work of art. We must consider, however briefly and baldly, some patterns of belief and thought that constitute the foundation or foreground or background of Milton's vision of human history and destiny. While it is axiomatic that a great artist's vision of life is timeless, it is no less axiomatic that it is conditioned by his own age and its inherited traditions. There is no short-cut to modern reinterpretation (as directors of Shakespearian plays so often assume there is), and we must read *PL* with bifocal lenses. Our first effort must be to understand what the author believed and thought and felt and said. If it is argued that such an effort is difficult or impossible for many or most modern readers, the obvious answer is that readers of any literature of the Christian past must bring unprejudiced historical, imaginative, and emotional sympathy to beliefs and ideas that they themselves may not hold; if they cannot do that, their stunted sensibility should turn elsewhere.

Further, we must not view *PL* as clouded by the old label, "the Puritan epic," a label unhappily not yet dead and buried although, in fact, Puritan elements in the poem are so few and small as to be almost invisible. C. S. Lewis pronounced the doctrine of *PL* "overwhelmingly Christian, . . . not even specifically Protestant or Puritan," except for a few isolated passages (*A Preface to Paradise Lost* [1942], p. 91). Going somewhat beyong Lewis, a Roman Catholic scholar, Sister Miriam Joseph, argued that *PL* is "capable of being read as a poem embodying theological doctrines in conformity with those of the Catholic Church" (p. 249 in *Laval théologique et philosophique* 8 [1952]:243–84). In the latest full study of Milton's beliefs, C. A. Patrides, quoting and opposing this conclusion, holds that *PL* "is not a Christian poem generally; it is, rather, a Christian *Protestant* poem. . . ." (*Milton and the Christian Tradition* [1966], p. 5). Modern readers, whether religious or secular in outlook, may be indifferent to such distinctions, but they can or must approach *PL* as a grand archetypal "myth" or paradigm of the human condition as it appeared to a poet of grand Christian imagination and much-tried faith.

Neither in his treatise nor in his poem does Milton offer what could be called a metaphysical explanation of that supreme crux of traditional religious thought, the existence of evil. Satan, the first rebel against divine order, whom Michael denounces as "Author of evil" (*PL* 6.262; cf. *CD* 1:ix), is a character in a poem, a superhuman dramatic embodiment of human pride. Milton's concern is with evil as a fact of life, a perpetual challenge to man's conscience, reason, and integrity; it exists, by God's permission, because man must possess free-

dom of will and choice. But if the true Christian faces perpetual temptation and hazard, at the same time he is assured that God will supply free grace and has provided for the ultimate defeat of evil. If the non-Christian's imagination cannot stretch to the final victory of good, he can at least accept the idea of everlasting war between good and evil in the individual soul and in the world at large.

Adam and Eve, united with each other and with God in love and joy, created perfect but not immutable, endowed with free will and reason and responsibility, and given a home of ideal beauty, disobey God's one prohibition, a test of their fidelity (*PL* 4.428; 8.325; *CD* 1:x). Eve is tempted by Satan, Adam by Eve. Their sin, as Milton says in *CD* (15:181–83), and says or implies in the poem,

> comprehended at once distrust in the divine veracity, and a proportionate credulity in the assurances of Satan; unbelief; ingratitude; disobedience; gluttony; in the man excessive uxoriousness, in the woman a want of proper regard for her husband, in both an insensibility to the welfare of their offspring, and that offspring the whole human race; parricide, theft, invasion of the rights of others, sacrilege, deceit, presumption in aspiring to divine attributes, fraud in the means employed to attain the object, pride, and arrogance.

This catalogue, however, seems to level all degrees of significance. In *PL* there are two main causes of the Fall, of disobedience: "presumption in aspiring to divine attributes," "pride" (in the religious sense), and Eve's weakness of reason along with Adam's weakness of will in abdicating his own responsibility and putting loyalty to Eve before loyalty to God and right.

Milton's subtle development of these themes will be outlined below and can here only be summarized in general terms. Pride was the traditional motive of Satan's revolt against God, and Eve, tempted by Satan to become a goddess, to seek superhuman knowledge and power, virtually reenacts his sin: "for inferior who is free?" (9.825). A hint of similar pride appears in Adam's colloquy with Raphael, when he is warned not to let astronomical curiosity displace his prime concern, the right conduct of life. This is not obscurantism on the part of the poet who, much more than most earlier humanists, had stressed the value of science in education, who had in *Areop* named Galileo as a martyr to astronomical truth, and who cites him more than once in *PL*. But, however limited Milton's reading in his later years, he could hardly be unaware of growing scientific and skeptical rationalism (he was certainly aware of Hobbes), since throughout his century many thoughtful Christians were troubled over excessive "curiosity" and pleaded for temperance in knowledge (see Howard Schultz, *Milton and Forbidden Knowledge* [1955]). To quote only one witness, Ralph Cudworth, the eminent Cambridge Platonist, in his famous sermon of 1647 to the House of Commons, had thus summed up the attitude we find in *PL:*

We think it a gallant thing to be fluttering up to Heaven with our wings of Knowledge and Speculation: whereas the highest mystery of a Divine Life here, and of perfect Happiness hereafter, consisteth in nothing but mere Obedience to the Divine Will.

Or, as Milton says, "obedience and love are always the best guides to knowledge" (CD 14:25; cf. PL 12.583–85). The central importance of the hierarchy of knowledge—of "priorities," as we say—is attested at the very end of PL, when Adam, now wiser, confesses his error in seeking to rise above human limits and declares his Christian faith and humility, and Michael replies:

> This having learnt, thou has attaind the summe
> Of wisdom; hope no higher, though all the Starrs
> Thou knewst by name, and all th'ethereal Powers,
> All secrets of the deep, all Natures works,
> Or works of God in Heav'n, Aire, Earth, or Sea
> And all the riches of this World enjoydst,
> And all the rule, one empire. . . .

If there is any theme in PL that should appeal directly to us, it is this, since our age has become so increasingly disturbed, indeed horrified, by the outward and inward sway of science and technology and—along with its immense benefactions—its anti-human power over life and death.

For a general statement covering the motives of Eve's and Adam's disobedience, a reminder of their traditional essence, there is Richard Hooker (Of the Laws of Ecclesiastical Polity, 1.7.6–7, in Works, ed. Keble, Church, and Paget, 7th ed. [1888], 1:224):

Reason therefore may rightly discern the thing which is good, and yet the Will of man not incline itself thereunto, as oft as the prejudice of sensible experience doth oversway.

   Nor let any man think that this doth make any thing for the just excuse of iniquity. For there was never sin committed, wherein a less good was not preferred before a greater, and that wilfully; which cannot be done without the singular disgrace of Nature, and the utter disturbance of that divine order, whereby the preeminence of chiefest acceptation is by the best things worthily challenged. . . . sometimes the subtilty of Satan inveigling us as it did Eve, sometimes the hastiness of our Wills preventing the more considerate advice of sound Reason.

What Hooker calls the disgrace of Nature and the disturbance of divine order Milton takes account of after each sinner has eaten the fruit (9.782–84, 1000–1004). His comments are not mere rhetoric, and the transformation of the ideal world of nature into ours (10.648–715) is not mere fancy; they reflect the unity and hierarchical order of the divine cosmos (see M. Y. Hughes, ELH: A

Journal of English Literary History 36 [1969]: 193–214). And man's hierarchy of faculties is likewise upset (9.1127ff., quoted below).

If the modern secular mind rebels against Milton's emphasis on the disobeying of God's command, we may remember—and perhaps even accept—the doctrine that he shared with other philosophic Christians, that true freedom can be enjoyed only by the good, that obedience to God—or love of goodness, if we prefer that phrase—is the natural choice of uncorrupted human reason. And that brings us to the traditional and cardinal principles of "Christian Liberty" and "Right Reason." The Reformation doctrine of Christian liberty was the charter and basis of the salvation open to fallen man, and Milton was one of its most earnest exponents. The Mosaic law, with its countless prescriptions and its animal sacrifices, was adequate for a people at the Hebrews' early stage of religious and moral development, but for the Christian Milton it is abolished (except insofar as elements in it accord with right reason). The finest passage in Book 12, apart from the conclusion, and a great example of the impassioned poetry of ideas, is the triumphant contrast drawn between the Old Testament and the New, the Covenant of Works and the Covenant of Grace (12.285ff.). Christian liberty means that the regenerate Christian, aided by grace, is an independent, self-governing being, freed from all subservience to external religious authority—a doctrine that did not need much extension to be revolutionary. And the inner voice of conscience is a higher authority than the Bible itself (*CD* 16:281).

Right reason is at once an ally and a curb of Christian liberty, As Michael tells Adam (12.83ff.),

> Since thy original lapse, true Libertie
> Is lost, which alwayes with right Reason dwells
> Twinn'd, and from her hath no dividual being.

Earlier, praising the faithful Abdiel, God in significant terms condemns the rebel angels

> who reason for thir Law refuse,
> Right reason for thir Law, and for thir King
> *Messiah*, who by right of merit Reigns.
>
> (6.41–43)

The concept of right reason, implicit at least in Plato and Aristotle, was fully formulated by Stoic moralists and was readily assimilated into Christian thought: it meant that all men, pagan and Christian alike, have a God-given apprehension of the basic moral principles, and the collective right reason of mankind issues in the binding doctrines of natural law. As Hooker said, in words that may sound startling from an Elizabethan divine,

> The general and perpetual voice of men is as the sentence of God himself. For that which all men have at all times learned, Nature herself must needs have

taught; and God being the author of Nature, her voice is but her instrument. (*Eccles. Pol.* 1.8.3; *Works* 1:227)

Or, to quote Milton, as distinguished from the written law of God,

> The unwritten law is no other than that law of nature given originally to Adam, and of which a certain remnant, or imperfect illumination, still dwells in the hearts of all mankind; which, in the regenerate, under the influence of the Holy spirit, is daily tending towards a renewal of its primitive brightness. CD 16:101)

But Christian liberty and right reason cannot prevent frail man from falling into sin, because true freedom must include freedom to err. Spiritual death

> consists, first, in the loss, or at least in the obscuration to a great extent of that right reason which enabled man to discern the chief good, and in which consisted as it were the life of the understanding. (*CD* 15:207)

Thus, in and after the Fall, the hierarchical order of faculties in Adam and Eve is turned upside down (*PL* 9.1127ff.):

> For Understanding rul'd not, and the Will
> Heard not her lore, both in subjection now
> To sensual Appetite, who from beneathe
> Usurping over sovran Reason claimd
> Superior sway.

To move from earth to heaven, in traditional orthodoxy the three persons of the Trinity are coessential and coequal. Milton had been a Trinitarian (witness the prayer at the end of his first tract, partly quoted earlier), but in the later strictly biblical theology of *CD* (1. ii–vi) God, the Son, and the Holy Spirit form a descending hierarchy. It is plain that in *PL* the Son is everywhere represented as inferior in authority to the Father, that—invested with the Father's power—he is the executive agent in the war in heaven, in the work of creation, in the colloquy with Adam on the latter's need of a companion, and in the passing of judgment on Adam and Eve; in the last three passages he is called "God" and "Universal Lord" and in 8.403ff., he speaks of himself as God. Such assignment or fusion of powers helps to explain why Milton's chief "heresy" awakened no or few misgivings in generations of pious readers, including the clerical editors Newton and Todd. Above all, however, the Son as mediator is the voice of love and mercy, and his supreme act is his voluntary sacrifice of himself as man's redeemer. Although at times the pamphleteer had perhaps seemed to approach Pelagian confidence in man, "There are few opinions that Milton held more sincerely or more consistently than his view of the Atonement" (Patrides, p. 141).

Up at least through *Areop* Milton had considered himself a Calvinist (there were kinds and degrees of Calvinism), but in *PL*, as in *CD* (1, iv), he explicitly

rejected arbitrary predestination and equated "the elect" with all true believers. In the heavenly council God foresees but in no way determines man's disobedience (a knotty theological point); he has made man "just and right, / Sufficient to have stood, though free to fall" (3.998–99). When the Son asks if mankind is then to be damned, God replies that he will freely grant grace to all those who are earnest in faith, repentance, and obedience. Yet the sin of disobedience and "Affecting God-head" must be atoned for (3.209–12):

> He with his whole posteritie must dye,
> Dye he or Justice must; unless for him
> Som other able, and as willing, pay
> The rigid satisfaction, death for death.

This pronouncement has especially alienated many readers, who have charged Milton with abhorrent Puritan legalism. But it is manifestly unfair to condemn him for sharing, in Protestant terms, a view of the Atonement held by many Christian spokesmen over many centuries (Patrides, pp. 130–42). Of such witnesses we can hear only one, the saintly Bishop Andrewes (whose death the young Milton had lamented in his third Latin elegy):

> Fond men! if He would quit his justice or waive His truth, He could; but His justice and truth are to Him as essential, as intrinsically essential, as His mercy; of equal regard, every way as dear to Him. Justice otherwise remains unsatisfied; and satisfied it must be either on Him or on us. (*Ninety-six Sermons* [Oxford, 1841] 1:784–85)

Some other questions concerning God and the Son will be considered later.

The doctrines so far noticed had more or less support in tradition, although Milton's degrees of emphasis were his own. He was much less traditional in his understanding of the grand concept historically expounded in Arthur O. Lovejoy's *The Great Chain of Being* (1936). When we think of the earlier Milton's Platonic dualism, particularly the ethical, we are hardly prepared for his metaphysical monism, his conception of matter as created "good" and not fundamentally different from spirit (*PL* 5.469ff.; *CD* 15:17ff.). It is highly significant that this is the first piece of instruction that Raphael imparts to Adam—significant too that the angel is here called "the winged Hierarch." A further distinctive feature of Milton's scale of nature is that it is not static (as it is in Pope's *Essay on Man* 1.233ff.) but dynamic, that the world is a world of becoming, matter perpetually passing upward into spirit (5.469–500). Whatever repeated shocks Milton's faith in men underwent, his monism is a form of metaphysical optimism. It is of course a part of his unshakable faith in God, and in *PL* he looks forward again and again to that eternity when "God shall be All in All" (3.341).

At the top of the hierarchy of being is the creator and sustainer of the world, the source of all life and good, of reason and law and love. God's most

metaphysical account of Himself is given as He sends forth the Son to create our world in the midst of Chaos, "the Deep" (7.168ff.):

> Boundless the Deep, because I am who fill
> Infinitude, nor vacuous the space.
> Though I uncircumscrib'd my self retire,
> And put not forth my goodness, which is free
> To act or not, Necessitie and Chance
> Approach not mee, and what I will is Fate.

This God is not the brute will seen by some critics from Sir Walter Raleigh to F. R. Leavis and William Empson; that idea, if usable at all, fits Calvin better than the anti-Calvinistic Milton. For Milton, as for his contemporary Henry More, the Cambridge Platonist, and for Newton also, God fills infinite space, although, in the lines quoted, He has not yet put forth His creative power upon Chaos. It is logical therefore that Milton denies the view that our world was created out of nothing and maintains that God created it out of his own substance (CD 15:17ff.). He is "uncircumscrib'd" (Non circonscritto, in Dante's less metaphysical phrase in Purgatorio 11.2) because he is free to act or not. Hence he is not to be confused with pagan or skeptical ideas of "Necessitie and Chance" and "Fate"; as a rational Deity, he creates a rational world.

The vast universe of Milton's imagining is both a spiritual and a spatial hierarchy, each reflecting the other. At the top is heaven, the perfect abode of God, the Son, and the angels; below is Chaos, the sea of raging elements, in the midst of which the newly created world (the Ptolemaic world of Spheres) hangs from heaven by a golden chain; at the bottom of the newly created hell, the fiery prison of Satan and his fellow rebels. These four regions are not completely separated; good and bad angels, and the Son and Sin and Death, move up and down from one to another, with some obvious restrictions. (The relations of the spiritual and spatial and the patterns of movement have been developed by Isabel G. MacCaffrey and J. I. Cope.) The supreme movement is that of God down to His creatures and of the creatures toward God (N. Frye, The Return of Eden [1964], p. 50). A miniature of the whole dynamic design is the morning canticle of Adam and Even (5.153–208)—based chiefly on Psalm 148—in which the sun, the stars, mists and showers and winds, beasts and birds and fish, all are rising or falling, walking, creeping, flying, gliding, all participating in and celebrating the divine universal harmony (J. H. Summers, The Muse's Method [1962], pp. 71–86). The same energy of movement and growth animates the pictures of the creation in Book 7. Milton fully shares the traditional belief, represented by Aquinas and Calvin alike, that "in contemplation of created things / By steps we may ascend to God" (5.511–12).

In answer to Adam's questioning, Raphael (8.66ff.) presents two theories of the physical world, the geocentric and the heliocentric (he omits the Tychonic compromise). Here as elsewhere Milton is noncommittal; but his use of the Ptolemaic scheme had the appearance of keeping "the sedentarie Earth" and its

human pair in the middle of both the spatial and the spiritual world. Moreover, Milton shows no trace of disquiet over the Copernican view; and he is not—as the religious and scientific Pascal was—appalled by the eternal silence of infinite space, because, as we have seen, God fills it. Nor is Milton in the least disturbed by the revival of an ancient idea that caused perhaps more religious concern than Copernican doctrine, the idea of a plurality of inhabited worlds (3.565–71; 8.140–58). He had always responded with fervor to thoughts of both plenitude and control. The ordinarily nonmystical poet is kindled into half-mystical ecstasy by contemplation of "Holy Light" and the "Starry dance" of the planets in their everlasting order—which he invokes as a parallel to the "Mystical dance" of the angels before God's throne (5.618–27). Thinking of the unity and harmony of this vast ordered universe, in which all creatures and things are related and interdependent, we understand why earth and nature groan when ideal order is disrupted by the sin of Adam and Eve.

Such elements of belief and thought as have been touched on here must be recognized by readers of PL (just as readers of Yeats and Eliot and Joyce do not grudge the necessity of homework). But the modern impact of the poem at once subsumes and transcends particulars. Modern readers, accustomed to an outer and inner world of confusion and disorder, are or should be well qualified to respond to Milton's presentation of confusion and disorder partly overcome, not without suffering and loss. However remote his beliefs and postulates may be from ours, he does not impose a factitious order upon human experience. His characters represent in various forms and degrees the weaknesses and the true or fallacious strengths that make up human beings in all ages. If for some readers Milton's archetypal myth of the human condition is disabled by its Christian frame, it may still be said that his vision remains potent in combining a passion for freedom with a passion for discipline, in proclaiming both the dignity and the responsibility of individual man. The religious conception of "pride," as treated in PL, needs no great extension to embrace the modern scientific hubris from which even scientists have been turning away (some time after other people). A number of modern writers and some events of modern history have brought back to life ideas of the Fall of man, of damnation and hell, not as an obsolete dogma but as as a fall continually reenacted, a hell continually re-created; and that is what Milton himself saw, in his way, a perpetual fall but also a possible recovery. Hell, Chaos, Eden, and Heaven are not merely places but states of mind, and hell can be felt in Eden. We may pass by here the old question of the hero of PL—whether the Son or Adam or both together; Milton's assertion of eternal Providence becomes a "mythic" parable of the nature and achievement of true heroism, and that keeps the poem, for all its vast range and apparent remoteness, at the center of human experience.

PL has such simplicity and complexity, such unity in multiplicity, that both the grand design and narrative details completely and minutely embody and express the controlling theme; it follows that various critics' diagrams of the structure have an inevitable basic agreement. Arthur Barker, invoking neo-

classical theory of the epic as drama, has seen the ten-book *PL* of 1667 falling logically into five acts of two books each. (We may remember that the third of Milton's early drafts for an allegorical drama was divided into five acts.) Barker suggests that the twelve-book structure gave more prominence to man's restoration and changed "a tragic pattern into the three-fold pattern of a divine comedy, underlining the intention expressed in the opening invocation by throwing into clearer relief the adaptation and modification of the Virgilian pattern," that is, "three movements of four books apiece," turning respectively on Satan, the Son, and Man (*Philological Quarterly* 28 [1949]: 17–30; repr. in *Milton: Modern Essays in Criticism*, ed. Barker [1965]). A. S. P. Woodhouse saw "the crisis of the human action, which is the subject of the poem, . . . framed by the narrative of the past and the narrative of the future," so that "we have the patterned series: Satan defeated in heaven by Christ, Satan victorious on earth over Adam, Satan defeated at last by Christ, who is the second Adam" (*University of Toronto Quarterly* 22 [1952–53]: 109–27). Isabel MacCaffrey sums up "the main configuration of the poem" as "from deep Hell up to the Mount of God, and down again to the 'subjected Plaine' of fallen earthly life" (*Paradise Lost as "Myth"* [1959], p. 59; cf. N. Frye,. *The Return of Eden 1965*, pp. 18–22]; *J. T. Shawcross, Studies in Philology* 62 [1965]: 696–718, and his essay in *New Essays on Paradise Lost*, ed. T. Kranidas [1969]; E. Sirluck, *Paradise Lost: A Deliberate Epic* [1967], pp;. 11–13).

The rapidly multiplying books of modern criticism have ample space for sophisticated discussion of the inexhaustible subtleties of *PL*, but here perhaps the best or the only course is the simplest: to follow the story as it unfolds, with occasional pauses over some main features. We may start, however, with what is chronologically the earliest event, as given in Raphael's recital to Adam: God's proclamation of His Son as His "great Vice-gerent" to whom "shall bow / All knees in Heav'n" (5.600–615). On the literal plane the proclamation is a dramatic device to inaugurate the epic action; metaphorically, it is a manifestation to the angels of their own creative principle, the Word (N. Frye, p. 33). It stirs envy and anger in the archangel Satan, who "thought himself impair'd" (like Macbeth at King Duncan's naming his son Malcolm as Prince of Cumberland). Pretending commands from God, Satan draws off "the third part of Heav'ns Host" to his seat in the north and rouses them (all but the faithful Abdiel) to rebellion. The ensuing three-day battle is ended by the Son, who, sent forth in "The Chariot of Paternal Deitie," embodies divine order and power. The rebel angels are driven through a gap made in the wall of heaven and fall through Chaos into the hell prepared for them. Milton's hell is far from its traditional place inside the earth.

Following the epic method of the plunge *in medias res*, the poem, after the invocation and exordium, begins when Satan and "his horrid crew" have for nine days and nights been "rowling in the fiery Gulfe / Confounded though immortal." Satan—fully pictured as he moves to the burning shore—rallies and reviews his legions, whose leaders are described in terms of their future roles as

heathen deities. "Thir Glory witherd," they are still loyal to "thir great Sultan" (a significant word), and he feels deep compassion for the fate he has brought upon them. But his speech to them, like his previous speeches, is a defiance of God and an exhortation to revenge. Mulciber (Hephaestus, Vulcan) directs the magical building of the palace of Pandemonium, an edifice which, with its artifice and glitter, is a meretricious imitation of heaven. The leaders' grand debate yields diverse proposals, from direct renewal of war to passive acceptance of their lot. The debate is wholly pragmatic; there is no recognition that evil has been overcome by good. Earlier, in his second speech to Beelzebub (1.162–65), Satan had acknowledged the true nature of the conflict and, in avowing his own aims, had indirectly declared God's, and also, in part, Milton's own view of his theme:

> If then his Providence
> Out of our evil seek to bring forth good,
> Our labor must be to pervert that end,
> And out of good still to find means of evil.

In the debate, the final proposal, put forth by Beelzebub but devised by Satan, is the most subtle kind of revenge, to corrupt the inhabitants of God's new creation, the earth. Satan alone is brave enough to volunteer for such a perilous expedition into the unknown; and he does not minimize its dangers.

His first stop is at the gates of hell, guarded by the foul monsters Sin and Death. Here begins the poem's one thread of allegory (as distinguished from symbolism). When Satan, in heaven, conceived of revolt, Sin had sprung from his head (obviously and ironically like the goddess of wisdom—and war—in Greek myth); and Death was the offspring of Satan's amorous dalliance with her (cf. James 1:15): "Then when lust hath conceived, it bringeth forth sin; and sin, when it is finished, bringeth forth death"). This allegory—to be continued later in the poem—was censured by such neoclassical critics as Addison, Voltaire, and Johnson, but for moderns it is a startling success: it shows the "heroic" Satan in his real setting and relations and, especially, it is a grisly counterpart to the Trinity and the generation and enthronement of the Son—as in Sin's triumphant anticipation, with its delayed and shocking adjective: "I shall reign / At thy right hand voluptuous." Meanwhile Satan's followers divert themselves with "epic games" or song or vain philosophic debate or exploration of hell; both their restless activities and the physical scenes reflect "A Universe of death," inward and outward. These first two books, in narrative, description, and dramatic speeches, are a magnificent display of the poet's sustained energy of imagination, language, and rhythm. And the preeminent figure is at once a grandly "heroic" leader and the embodiment of egoistic pride and passion, a spurious deity strong only in evil; the two books as a whole expose a false substitute for the harmony, joy, and true freedom of heaven.

The great invocation to Light (Bk. 3) establishes the blind poet's claim to tell

of things invisible, effects a transition from the lurid darkness of hell to the radiant purity of heaven, and creates an atmosphere of holy awe that prepares for the heavenly council, an obvious contrast to the council in hell. We have already taken some account of God's outline of man's situation and destiny, his freedom, his fall, and—through the self-sacrifice of the Son—his redemption. Milton's whole presentation of God has offended many of his readers—although the finest critic among them, Coleridge, thought his strong biblical anthropomorphism "very wise" (*Coleridge on the Seventeenth Century,* ed. R. F. Brinkley [1955], pp. 590–91; *The Romantics on Milton,* ed. J. A. Wittreich [1970], p. 278). Some critics, invoking Dante for contrast, have thought it a strategic blunder to make the Deity a speaking character at all, though God would seem to be, in a poem on the epic pattern, the inevitable expounder of His own authority and judgments. To the complaint that, in the midst of the poetic richness of *PL,* God's speeches are singularly flat and prosaic, the cogent answer is that Milton's reverence for God and Christian truth required the Deity's utterance to be bare, unadorned statement—a principle noted by Coleridge and developed by various modern critics, for example, Arnold Stein (*Answerable Style* [1953], pp. 127–29); Irene Samuel (*Publications of the Modern Language Association* 72 [1957]; repr. in *Milton,* ed. Barker); T. Kranidas (*The Fierce Equation* [1965], pp. 130ff.); Stanley E. Fish (*Surprised by Sin: the Reader in Paradise Lost* [1967], pp. 57ff.); I. G. MacCaffrey, on the theme of Book 3 (*New Essays on Paradise Lost,* ed. Kranidas [1969]). Yet Milton is quite able at times to suggest the mystery and majesty of God—"Dark with excessive bright thy skirts appear" (3.380). Evil characters, of course, are always much easier to draw than good ones, and it was still more difficult, even for a God-intoxicated poet, to render the dynamic perfection of heaven, although, along with the loving heroism of the Son, much is achieved through the use of light and movement and ecstatic song, the beauty of harmonious order.

Of God's legalism something was said above, but a little more is necessary here, at the point in the poem where it chiefly appears. We must remember that God is the source not only of life and good but of moral law, partly revealed, partly discovered by the right reason of man, and law has an inherent degree of rigor. As for Milton's method, he did some harm to his God by creating celestial drama, by dividing the attributes of Deity between the Father and the Son: God is the Absolute, the Unmoved Mover, while the Son—the dramatic antagonist of Satan—is the voice of love and mercy, and his speeches have a distinctive tone and rhythm (Summers, *Muse's Method;* cf. C. A. Patrides, *Journal of English and German Philology* 64 [1965]; H. MacCallum, on the role of the Son, in *Paradise Lost: A Tercentenary Tribute,* ed. B. Rajan [1969]). The effect of such a division, at least on minds averse to any notion of absolutes, is to make God seem merely harsh in contrast to the Son—and Milton takes pains to have God express agreement, prior agreement, with the Son's compassion for sinful man. To come back to the heavenly council and the satisfaction of justice, the Son alone volunteers to die for man's redemption, as Satan alone had

volunteered to compass man's ruin. "So Heav'nly love shall outdo Hellish hate." God glorifies His Son's self-sacrifice and looks forward to his ultimate reign as king, to his judging mankind at the last day; after that there will be no need of kingship.

From the heavenly council we turn back to the voyaging Satan. Landing on the outer shell of the newly created world, he flies down through spheres and stars to the sun and thence to the earth. There he bitterly apostrophizes the sun, whose light recalls the lost glory of heaven (and Milton's very different apostrophe to light in the opening of Bk. 3). Here, for once, Satan's character is given a tragic dimension. In contrast with his earlier "heroic" harangues to his followers, he is now, when alone, tortured by a conscience. In a soliloquy—which partly reminds us of Marlowe's Faustus—Satan condemns his revolt as severely as God himself could have done; and whereas he had earlier boasted of the freedom of hell and his sovereignty there, he now finds himself a prisoner: "Which way I flie is Hell; my self am Hell"—a pregnant reminder of Milton's supreme concern with states of mind and soul. However, pride forbids repentance, and, with the simple and terrible resolve, "Evil be thou my good," he makes his way into Eden. Although he has revealed tragic possibilities, they are to be dissolved by his further self-degradation; at most he may perhaps be called "a tragic villain" (Stein, p. 50).

It was a grand stroke of irony that Milton should delay his picture of the earthly paradise until we enter it with Satan and view it with his malevolent eyes and our own. The scene and symbol of man's happy innocence, which, in a "straight" presentation, might have been only a lush pastoral vision, lies from the start under the shadow of its destroyer. But this is only one attesting example of a comprehensive way in which Milton's epic goes beyond its predecessors: since—like Sophocles and others—he is telling a story universally known, he can envelop his two groups of opposed characters in dramatic irony on a grand scale (to be distinguished of course from the conscious ironies of various speakers; and heavenly beings remain above the author's irony). Thus, although Satan, chiefly in the soliloquy already noticed, can recognize the difference between good and evil, as a rule he and his fellows rebel and fight and plan revenge without any understanding that God and goodness are ultimately invincible—even though the corrupt Satan does succeed in corrupting man. If the poet's depiction of the doomed Satan in his heroic postures is harshly ironic, he is compassionate in his ironic depiction of Satan's victims; Adam and Eve likewise are ignorant of the future, and we register the various results of their failures of insight, constancy, and action, which multiply as they approach their Fall. A further idea, present to Addison and Johnson, has been strongly urged by Fish (*Surprised by Sin*): that Milton's irony takes in his readers too, that their spiritual and moral capacity is being tested at the same time as Adam's and Eve's, since they may reveal their fallen state by sharing impulses and ideas that they should reject. Certainly many of Milton's older critics, and a few modern ones, might stand as conspicuous examples.

To return to Satan's entry into Eden, the successive animal and other similes that attend his progress are not at all a new and deliberate debasement of a grand figure; they are, like his involvement with Sin and Death, reminders of his real self, now shorn of the half-spurious grandeur he had displayed in hell. All his base passions are kindled by the sight—which is also our first real sight—of Adam and Eve, and he turns into something between Richard III and Iago as, while pretending pity, he gloats over his prey and enjoys his own sardonic irony (4.375ff.):

> League with you I seek,
> And mutual amitie so streight, so close,
> That I with you must dwell, or you with me
> Henceforth . . . ; Hell shall unfold,
> To entertain you two, her widest Gates,
> And send forth all her Kings. . . .

The problem of preparation for the Fall is handled with great skill: Adam and Eve must preserve their ideal innocence and yet must be shown as vulnerable, so that the Fall, when it comes, will seem a logical climax, not a surprise. To that end Milton supplies hints of increasing significance. Eve in her first speech is the ideal wife, but, in recalling her first experience of living, she tells how she had (like Narcissus) admired her own beauty as reflected in a pool (4.460ff.). She recalls too—with another veiled echo of Ovid, this time of Apollo and Daphne—how Adam had pursued her. Both Eve's vanity and Adam's passion are quite natural and innocent, but the possibility of weakness is registered. Ideal love in an ideal world is celebrated in Eve's pastoral speech (4.635–58); and Milton goes out of his way to stress the purity and rightness of their physical relations in contrast with romantic and promiscuous lust. From over-hearing their talk of the forbidden tree Satan has already (4.512ff.) formed a plan of campaign: he will appeal to the desire for knowledge that will make the pair "Equal with Gods." And the poet's benediction on their nuptial sleep ends with a compassionate wish: "O yet happiest if ye seek / No happier state, and know to know no more"—an echo of Virgil's praise of humble Italian farmers who are content with their lot (*Georg.* 2.458). With all his upholding of conscious, rational righteousness, Milton reveals at times a nostalgic yearning for a world of unconscious, primitive innocence.

Beginning his campaign, Satan, "Squat like a Toad, close at the eare of Eve," sets about infecting her mind with ambition. In the morning she tells Adam of a disturbing dream (5.28ff.): obeying a voice she thought Adam's, she had gone forth, soon found herself at the forbidden tree, saw its fruit eaten by an angel-like figure who exhorted her to eat and become a goddess, and, doing so, she had soared aloft with him. Awake, she is relieved to find it a dream, and she is soothed by Adam's lecture on dream psychology. But the drama, apparently Milton's invention, is a significant step toward the Fall: it is or should be a

warning to both; it involves the main motive of ambition and the minor one of appetite and is an involuntary mental preenactment of the Fall; and, though Eve's waking reaction attests her present conscious innocence, in her uncensored dream her initial horror had given place to full enjoyment—without Adam—of her supposedly godlike exaltation.

At this point Milton combines two epic conventions best exemplified in the *Aeneid*: the retrospective account of events that preceded the opening of the poem and the divine admonition delivered to the protagonist. Raphael is sent from heaven expressly to warn Adam that continued happiness depends on obedience to God; his will, though free, is mutable and exposed to temptation. The naked, innocent pair rejoice in entertaining their celestial visitor at a picnic, and the question of angelic substance and digestion leads into the important metaphysical statement noticed above. Raphael's narrative of the past, in satisfaction of Adam's curiosity, opens with the first of several apologies—really the poet's—for the rendering of heavenly things in terms accommodated to human minds: in other words, the stories of the war in heaven and the creation are more mythic and symbolic than literal.

The cause and outcome of Satan's revolt we observed at the start. The war is described in concrete epic terms. Satan appears both as a wicked pretender to divine authority ("Th'Apostat in his Sun-bright Chariot sate / Idol of Majestie Divine"; 6.100–101) and, in his punning exchanges with Belial about the artillery he has invented, as a cynical professional soldier. Apart from its grand climax, the onset of the Son, the war has often been censured as too unrealistic for an epic and too realistic for a spiritual symbol. But in one persuasive interpretation the war is seen as a kind of monstrous burlesque in which realism or materialism plays a grotesque and ironic part (A. Stein); it has also been taken as a typological "shadow of things to come, and more particularly . . . of this last age of the world and of the Second Coming of Christ" (W. G. Madsen, *From Shadowy Types to Truth* [1968], p. 111). Certainly, for both Adam and the reader, the war is an object lesson on the violence unleashed by the egoistic lust for power that would overturn divine order, all order.

After heaven has been purged of destructive anarchy, Milton, at this central point in the poem, turns to the great work of peace, the creation of our world and man. Raphael again reminds Adam of the difficulty of describing divine acts and warns him against intemperance in the quest for knowledge. He then proceeds with his account of the six days' work. As Satan had created evil out of good, God creates good out of evil. The Son, as usual, is God's executive agent, though presented as the triune Godhead, "The King of Glorie in his powerful Word / And Spirit coming to create new Worlds." The description of order imposed upon Chaos is one of Milton's most impressive passages, and hardly less so is the quieter picture of the Son's triumphal return to heaven after he has accomplished his task "Answering his great Idea" (the Platonic word is significant). In his account of creation Milton takes in another epic or semi-epic genre, the hexaemeral, but his version stands alone. The theme of fecundity had

always stirred his imagination; he had already given it full expression in his description of Eden and distilled it in the exuberant lines on Raphael's arrival there (5.291ff.): "A Wilderness of sweets; . . . / Wilde above Rule or Art; enormous bliss." So the picture of creation, abundantly expanded from Genesis, is filled with the poet's sensuous excitement in the manifold burgeoning of life. Raphael ends with a repetition of his earlier warning: God's worshipers, created in his image, will be "thrice happie if they know/Thir happiness, and persevere upright."

Raphael's final phrase, as he invites further questioning—"not surpassing human measure"—is warranted by what follows in Book 8. The structure of the world leads Adam—with what may be called a touch of presumption, in comparison with his hitherto exemplary humility—to question the divine economy: would it not be better for the tiny earth, with its two inhabitants, to revolve instead of getting its light and darkness from the revolutions of the vast firmament? Raphael's scientific answer, while appropriate in an epic of cosmic scope, is much less important than his injunction about temperance in the quest of knowledge, the necessity of keeping first things first, that is, the conduct of life. Then Adam's story of his experience, while a natural sequel to Raphael's story of creation, reinforces, from a very different angle, the point that issued from astronomy and constitutes another stage in the preparation for the Fall. Adam ends with a eulogy of Eve which, in its mounting extravagance, must make any understanding reader anticipate Raphael's frown. Eve, says Adam, aroused new and overpowering passion: has Nature—that is, the Creator—failed in making him so subject to a being admittedly inferior, mentally and physically, to himself? In thus abdicating his higher responsibility ("Authority and Reason on her waite"), in putting a creature between himself and God, Adam is guilty, if not of idolatry, at least of intemperance. A man's love for his wife, much more than astronomical knowledge, is commendable in itself, but Adam has got his priorities confused; and his defensive response to the angel's rebuke does not annul the effect of his previous confession. He is right-minded, but his vulnerability is far more apparent than it was before.

In Book 9 Satan, who had been expelled from Eden by Gabriel, returns to carry out his plan. Just before he enters the serpent he has a midnight soliloquy that we link with his earlier address to the sun. Now, in self-pity, he finds ease only in evil, though he recoils from "foul descent" into a serpent, "This essence to incarnate and imbrute, / That to the hight of Deitie aspir'd" (the word "incarnate" recalls the Son, particularly 3.315). As for Adam and Eve, they develop the most sustained drama in a notably dramatic epic: in their mode of speech, as in their thoughts and feelings, they become less and less regal, more and more human, as their first disagreement warms up. Trouble begins with Eve's self-willed proposal that they work apart and accomplish more, without amorous interludes—a proposal not in accord with their appointed way of life and love. Adam's overprotectiveness rouses Eve to somewhat shrill insistence on her ability to look after herself. Adam, now more tactful, says that her

presence is a support to him. But Eve grows still more self-assertive; she misapplies the argument of *Areop*, which was written in and for a fallen world, and, as Adam tells her, she is disregarding God's will and warning. Indeed, Adam anticipates what is to happen, that reason may be deceived by "some faire appeering good." However, he surrenders and she goes off, "like a Wood-Nymph light" (the word "light" may be deliberately ambiguous), and the poet breaks out in pity for "much deceav'd, much failing, hapless *Eve*." Thus the serpent, luckily for him, finds her alone. In a beautiful variation on the earlier allusion to Proserpine (quoted below), she is described as upstaying the flowers. "Her self, though fairest unsupported Flour, / From her best prop so farr, and storm so nigh." Her beauty disarms even Satan, for the moment. Then, catching her attention, he addresses her with a sonneteer's flattery. Eve's astonishment at his ability to speak gives him his cue: from a wondrous fruit he has gained new powers. Led to the forbidden tree, Eve, "yet sinless," recoils, citing God's prohibition. Satan, "with shew of Zeale and Love / To Man," cunningly apostrophizes the "Sacred, Wise, and Wisdom-giving Plant," from which he has not suffered death but won new life: God only wants to keep his creatures low, when they might become "as Gods / Knowing both Good and Evil as they know."

The "credulous" Eve, soliloquizing, is completely taken in by Satan's arguments. She plucks and greedily gorges on the fruit, with "expectation high / Of knowledge, nor was God-head from her thought," "And knew not eating Death." (Celebrating God's exaltation of the Son, the angels had quaffed "immortalitie and joy": 5.638.) In this state of *hubris* and corruption, Eve goes on to practical reflection: perhaps "Our great Forbidder" has not seen her; shall she share her "change" with Adam or make herself his equal, or even superior, by keeping "the odds of Knowledge" to herself, "for inferior who is free?" (This was the motive of Satan's revolt.) But what if God ends her life and Adam lives on with another Eve? For wholly selfish reasons, she decides to have Adam share with her "in bliss or woe." So subtle is Milton's portrayal of Eve that we read her conclusion—"So dear I love him, that with him all deaths / I could endure, without him live no life"—with arresting uncertainty as to how far she is telling the truth, how far deceiving herself.

Paying to the tree the reverence she had denied to God, Eve returns with a bough of fruit to Adam (who has woven a garland of flowers to adorn her hair), and shows her acquisition of godlike knowledge by beginning with a lie: "Thee I have misst, and thought it long. . . ." She has, of course, been having the time of her life. As, "with Countnance blithe," she pours out her tale and, with false reasons, urges him to eat, Adam's garland "Down drop'd, and all the faded Roses shed." His first horror gives place, in his mind, to the resolve to die with her. All readers feel, as Milton felt, the anguish in Adam's imagining lovely Eden as, without Eve, "these wilde Woods forlorn." Then, addressing her, he argues, in her and Satan's way, that God may not punish them, that they may become gods; at any rate he will live or die with her. The declaration evokes

from Eve a fine stroke of the poet's irony, "O glorious trial of exceeding Love"—a line that, in itself, would at once suggest Christ's self-sacrificing love for man (indeed, Milton had so used "exceeding love" in his early *Circum*). Adam is easily persuaded to eat the fruit, "Against his better knowledge, not deceav'd, / But fondly overcome with Femal charm" (cf. 1 Tim. 2:14). Good liberals applaud Adam's human loyalty to Eve and condemn Milton (not to mention Milton's God) for implicitly condemning it; but such liberals would be the first to condemn the same lack of principle in the political sphere—"My country, right or wrong."

The "intoxicated pair now

> swim in mirth, and fansie that they feel
> Divinitie within them breeding wings
> Wherewith to scorne the Earth.

(The image of wings may parody the Platonic ascent of the virtuous soul: cf. *Mask* 374ff., *Phaedrus* 246ff.) But supposedly superhuman knowledge engenders only subhuman lust. Recalling the beauty of "Wedded Love" in their days of innocence, we can hardly repress a shudder at the levity with which Adam now sees Eve as only a sexual object—and she him likewise; and Milton ends Adam's speech (9.1029–33) with a conscious echo of the sensual invitations of Paris to Helen and Zeus to Hera in the *Iliad* (3 and 14).

Waking from gross sleep, the one-time "Lords of the World" move from shame and remorse to angry recriminations. There is sorrow in heaven for the fulfillment of what had been foretold, and the Son is sent down to pass judgment; here Milton somewhat expands Genesis with little change. Sin and Death, now freed from hell to prey on earth, build a causeway through Chaos to make passage henceforth easy for themselves and the fallen engels—a parody of Creation. Satan, entering the Pandemonium "In shew Plebeian Angel militant / Of lowest order" (the dictator's flair for the theatrical, as Tillyard said), gives a self-glorifying report of his success. There follows an anticlimactic and more than Ovidian metamorphosis: Satan, and then his followers, are transformed into hissing serpents, which feed on fruit that turns to ashes. In the universe above, the world of eternal spring, which had felt the wounds of the primal sin, is changed to our world of cold and heat and storm, of war and death among beasts, birds, and fish. Nature is fallen as well as man. This change, following the humanization—or degradation—of Adam and Eve, is a large step from the golden age into history.

In a long soliloquy (10.720–844) the despairing Adam, stretched on the cold ground, laments his lot, his alienation from God and the curses his posterity will heap upon him; he arraigns divine justice for imposing "terms too hard" and longs for immediate death. But finally, absolving God, he blames only himself and "that bad Woman." Being thus wrought up, when she appears he bitterly repels her first "Soft words." Milton had a problem in the presentation

of Eve: she must be the first sinner and the seducer of Adam, yet she must not fall too low to be restored to her dignity as mother of the human race. Much of that restoration is accomplished by her initiating reconciliation as she had initiated sin, by the penitent words and faltering rhythm of her first speech, the rhythm, as Joseph Summers says, of the Son, the voice of love. In tears she

> at his feet
> Fell humble, and imbracing them, besaught
> His peace, and thus proceeded in her plaint.
> Forsake me not thus, *Adam*, witness Heav'n
> What love sincere, and reverence in my heart
> I beare thee, and unweeting have offended,
> Unhappilie deceav'd. . . .
>
> (10.911–17)

She will appeal to God that His sentence may light on her alone.

Deeply touched, Adam is reconciled, and would, if he could, take all blame upon himself; they can only strive "In offices of Love, how we may light'n / Each others burden in our share of woe." Thus the pair, humanized and estranged by sin, are humanized and reunited by a love sadder but richer than their idyllic honeymoon had been; but full regeneration is still to come. Eve, "recovering heart," proposes two solutions for their plight: either to nullify their legacy of woe to posterity by abstaining from intercourse ("which would be miserie / And torment less then none of what we dread"—a remarkable testimony to Milton's understanding of the strength of desire), or to frustrate "A long days dying" by suicide. Adam, though struck by Eve's sublime "contempt of life and pleasure," shows, as always, more religious concern and insight than Eve, whose concern is always with him. Evasion, he says, will not serve; they must go back to the place where sentence was passed and offer penitential prayers. So, under the working of "Prevenient Grace" (11.3), they end Book 10 with a first upward step, an ending very different from the "mutual accusation" that ended Book 9. This lengthy outline of the Fall, however inadequate any outline is, may emphasize the fact that Milton did not spend his main interest or all his powers on the Satan of the early books.

God decrees (as in Genesis) that the remorseful but guilty and unreliable pair must be expelled from Eden, lest they eat of the Tree of Life and live forever in a fallen world (Frye, p. 81); and he despatches Michael to "send them forth, though sorrowing, yet in peace." Meanwhile Adam and Eve, as they go out to work, feel that their prayers have met with favor, but they see signs of an altered world, perhaps ill omens for them. Their reactions to Michael's message are typical: Eve is stricken by the loss of home and objects of her daily care, Adam by the loss of his accustomed communication with God. To Eve Michael says that she should think her native soil to be wherever her husband abides; to Adam he gives assurance that God is present not in one place but everywhere, "still compassing thee round / With goodness and paternal Love." To confirm

this, and to teach faith and patience, he has been sent to unfold the future: "good with bad / Expect to hear, supernal Grace contending / With sinfulness of Men." So, putting Eve to sleep, Michael takes Adam to the top of the highest hill in Paradise and presents things to come in a series of visions. This is the last large epic convention that Milton adapts to his special purposes, one that belongs to both the traditional heroic poem (as in the *Aeneid* 6 and 8 and *Gerusalemme Liberata* 17) and the hexaemeral genre. And it becomes a Christian parallel to the classical myth of decay after the golden age, though it does not end there.

The continuance of the original sin is shown in Cain's murder of Abel; in the pains and fatal diseases brought on by "ungovern'd appetite"; in the sensual allurements of a bevy of fair women who ensnare "the Sons of God"; in rapine and war and conquest, against which the righteous Enoch pleads in vain (11.665ff.); then in the licentious corruptions of peace, which Noah cannot curb; and finally the flood overwhelms the multitude of the wicked. (Milton recalls Heb. 11:1–7, on Abel, Enoch, and Noah—men of faith in the line of Abdiel.) But Book 11 ends with the rainbow, a perpetual reminder of God's covenant:

> Day and Night,
> Seed time and Harvest, Heat and hoary Frost
> Shall hold thir course, till fire purge all things new,
> Both Heav'n and Earth, wherein the just shall dwell.

In Book 12, pausing "Betwixt the world destroy'd and world restor'd," Michael shifts from vision to narrative, mainly no doubt because the saving illumination to come must be more directly impressed upon Adam. Some time after the flood the spirit of conquest and tyranny revives in Nimrod. But with Abraham Israel emerges as God's chosen people; and then God delivers the Law to Moses. Throughout, Adam's misjudgments have been corrected by Michael, and his linking of many laws with many sins brings the fervent exposition of the superseding of the Law by the Gospel (12.285ff.). The ultimate triumph of good in the birth, ministry, and death of Christ leads Adam to wonder—echoing a traditional paradox—if perhaps his Fall was fortunate in evoking this supreme manifestation of divine love.

Adam can now comprehend such love; but the idea of a fortunate fall as the climax of the epic argument gets more support from numerous recent critics than from Milton. Some other critics do not take Adam's exclamation—impulsive and oversimple, like his earlier judgments—as expressing the poet's view, which, as Books 11 and 12 amply show, is much more complex. In *PL* as in *Areop*, Adam fell into the "doom"—not the felicity—"of knowing good by evil" (*PL* 11.84ff.; 4:310–11). God will ultimately bring good out of the evil of the Fall, but man, the good man, however cheered by the promise of redemption, must face trial and tribulation with Christian fortitude before he "is raised to a far more excellent state of grace and glory than that from which he had

fallen" (*CD* 15:251). Even Christ's church will grow corrupt (12.507ff.). Lines 533ff. are a grim picture of life in the Christian era, of a world "To good malignant, to bad men benigne," a world to be changed only at Christ's second coming. Adam's response is a statement of the true and sufficient knowledge he has received, a statement quietly moving in its substance and rhythm, of faith in obedient love of God and trust in His providence, in the practice of righteousness, humility, and constancy. This, replies Michael, is "the summe / Of wisdom," far beyond knowledge of nature or wealth or political power: if he acts in accord with the Christian virtues, especially love, "the soul / Of all the rest," Adam, though leaving Paradise, will possess a paradise within him, "happier farr."

Michael's instruction to Adam has been found long, heavy, and dull by a number of critics, from C. S. Lewis to Louis Martz, but what Lewis called "an untransmuted lump of futurity" has also had many able defenders. (Lists are given by two recent ones: John Reesing, *Milton's Poetic Art* [1968], p. 184; B. Rajan, *The Lofty Rhyme* [1970], pp. 168–69. Two other recent defenses are by Mary A. Radzinowicz, in *Approaches to Paradise Lost*, ed. Patrides, and G. M. Muldrow, *Milton and the Drama of the Soul* [1970]). If Milton's narrative and descriptive method here owes something to the scenes on the shields of Achilles and Aeneas (*Iliad* 18.483–608; *Aeneid* 8.620–728: the latter are prophetical), the debt is small. His style for the most part is deliberately plain and bare, but his imaginative reason is deeply engaged; for these two books sum up all that the frustrated idealist had learned of the meaning of life and death, of the faith and fortitude and righteous happiness within the reach of fallen man. We have noted earlier that the view that the change from ten to twelve books had the effect of emphasizing the process of regeneration. Throughout the first ten books Milton had been able to relate his grand *exemplum* directly to the later life of man only through brief incidental allusions, similes, and comments. Now, the story becomes—apart from the survey of false religions in 1.376ff.—the first segment of human history, and the reader identifies his knowledge and experience with that of Adam and his posterity. Moreover, Michael's presentation and his correcting of Adam's many failures of understanding constitute Adam's spiritual, moral, and social education, the process of illumination that, as we see from his last speech, makes him the first Christian. But the reader is also, however unconsciously, made to share the poet's experience and vision, and without the historical survey he would not know and feel the profound pessimism that Milton's own faith in Providence had to conquer and did conquer. Finally and most immediately, the marvelous conclusion would fail of its effect if it had come, say, at the end of Book 10, without the picture of the world into which Adam and Eve are to go—a revelation very far from the glorious prophecy Anchises gave to Aeneas; and of course here the climactic figure is not Augustus—or Astraea—but Christ.

The ending of the poem is the finest achievement of the master of perfect endings. Michael brings Adam down from the hill and awakens Eve, in whom

his power had inspired comforting dreams: she can say to Adam "now lead on" in a spirit wholly different from the "Lead then" she had addressed to the serpent. The Cherubim, descending, glide over the plain as an evening mist "gathers ground fast at the Labourers heel / Homeward returning"—a homely, "un-Miltonic" simile that anticipates the daily toil of Adam and his sons. Led away by Michael, who disappears,

> They looking back, all th' Eastern side beheld
> Of Paradise, so late thir happie seat,
> Wav'd over by that flaming Brand, the Gate
> With dreadful Faces throng'd and fierie Armes:
> Som natural tears they drop'd, but wip'd them soon;
> The World was all before them, where to choose
> Thir place of rest, and Providence thir guide:
> They hand in hand with wandring steps and slow,
> Through *Eden* took thir solitarie way.

Without venturing upon vain analysis, one may say that these simple narrative and pictorial lines suggest through every word and phrase the most subtle and moving interplay of sorrow and fear, hope and love. Adam and Eve are again "hand in hand," as in the days of happy innocence. Providence is their guide, yet they are alone, dependent on each other, going into an unknown world, a humble pair who have, in some measure, defeated Satan. "*Eden*"—a paradise within—is to be "rais'd in the wast Wilderness" (*PR* 1.7). (The actual paradise will be swept away by the flood, to become "an Iland salt and bare, / The haunt of Seales and Orcs, and Sea-mews clang": *PL* 11.834–35.)

Even this bald outline of *PL* gives some notion of one prime and dynamic structural principle, the continual use of contrast, concrete or abstract, literal or symbolic: good and evil, light and darkness, the Son and Satan, love and hate, creation and destruction, eternity and human time, life and death, humility and pride, obedience and disobedience, order and anarchy, liberty and servitude, reason and passion, love and lust, grace and nature, nature and artifice. . . .

Although Milton's choice of the epic over the dramatic form gave him the full scope he needed, his subject involved difficulties that had not existed for Homer, that were somewhat troublesome for Virgil, and that became much more formidable for a biblical epic in the scientific and rationalistic climate of the later seventeenth century: that is, the use of the traditional mold of the heroic poem, concrete in its very nature, for themes of increasing abstraction. The everlasting war between good and evil, the Fall of Man and his means of redemption, and the significance of both for the temporal and eternal destiny of the human race, imposed new strains on the resources of the heroic poem, although for the most part Milton triumphantly surmounted them.

This epic development from Homer through Virgil to Milton brings up another but related kind of progressive change. Homer's narratives may be called impersonal and objective—in a relative degree of course, since complete

objectivity could not operate in poetry of any kind. But the *Aeneid,* as count-less readers and critics have felt, clearly reflects the temperament and philoso-phy of its author—"Thou that seëst Universal Nature moved by Universal Mind;/Thou majestic in thy sadness at the doubtful doom of human kind." And in *PL,* as Anne Ferry in particular has fully shown (*Milton's Epic Voice: The Narrator in Paradise Lost* [1963]), the masterful personality, the strongly held beliefs and values, the controlling voice, stern, compassionate, exultant, of the poet are everywhere apparent, from the total theme down to the smallest detail, are felt, indeed, in every word—notably in the repetition of such key words as *fruit, taste, woe, merit, seed.*

Recent criticism, while it has brought new insight to the substance and art of *PL,* seems to have largely taken for granted the basic adaptations of the classical pattern and conventions; but these adaptations, however commonplace, are too central to be passed over. Milton's whole poetic career demonstrates both his instinct for working within an established convention and his instinct and power to re-create it. In *PL* he may be most original when he may seem to be merely imitating Virgil or Homer. While the form of *PL* was governed by Milton's subject and avowed purpose, and while the poem has many incidental Homeric echoes, in structure it is much closer to the *Aeneid* than to any other epic. (Some references were given above. Many adaptations of Virgil are dis-cussed by D. P. Harding, *The Club of Hercules: Studies in the Classical Background of Paradise Lost* [1962]; cf. M. A. Di Cesare in *Milton Studies* 1 [1969].) *PL* is, even more than the *Aeneid,* a closely coherent story that never loses sight of its theme and its goal. One general parallel (whether or not Milton thought of it) is that, as the *Aeneid* depicts the fall of an old world in the east and the defeated hero's creation of a new world in the west, so in *PL* fallen man is enabled to rise again, to move toward salvation; "as in the *Aeneid,* the ending is the starting point renewed and transformed by the heroic quest of Christ." (N. Frye, p. 20).

The various structural conventions (partly noticed already) are also closest to those of the *Aeneid,* though some belong to epic tradition in general. All are given a new significance. Milton's Muse, Urania—the ancient Muse of astron-omy had been elevated, especially by Du Bartas, into the Muse of religious poetry—is "Heav'nly," and Milton's several invocations, far from being literary formalities, are earnest prayers for divine inspiration. (The "Spirit" of 1.17, etc., commentators have often taken as the Holy Spirit, the third Person of the Trinity, but Milton says—in *CD* 14:393–95—that the Holy Spirit may not be invoked. Unless he is violating his own doctrine, his "Spirit"—to bypass numerous discussions—would seem to be "a personification of the various attributes of God the Father," as M. Kelley says in *This Great Argument,* p. 117; cf. *CD,* 15:13.) Moreover, whereas Homer and Virgil had one major invocation at the beginning and occasional brief ones later, Milton's (except 1.376) are all elaborate and have varied thematic and structural functions. The opening one arouses portentous expectations in linking the story to be unfolded with the

creation of the world, and it links the poet with the author of Genesis. The invocation to Light (Bk. 3) heralds the change of scene from hell and the infernal debate to heaven and sets the tone for the heavenly council. Further, the idea of "Holy Light" elicits the poignantly personal lines on Milton's blindness, his continuing love of the classics and, above all, the Bible; but the personal is submerged in the impersonal, dramatic utterance of "the blind poet" who prays for the compensation of inward light. The prelude to Book 4, while not an appeal to the Heavenly Muse, is an anguished cry of horror and compassion evoked by Satan's approach to Eden. The invocation of Book 7, following the war in heaven, introduces the peaceful creation of the world, in particular the earth and man; and the poet, in the evil days of the Restoration, thinks of the fate of Orpheus. The invocation of Book 9, contemplating the Fall "and all our woe," contrasts that truly heroic theme with the martial and mundane themes of traditional epic and romance.

Plunging into the middle of things had of course been an epic device from Homer onward, but Milton's giving of his first two books to his cosmic villains, Satan and his fellows, was a highly original stroke. It was also, as critical history has shown, a hazardous one, although—not to mention Satan's age-old infamy—the poet had from the first moment presented his "heroism" as governed by evil pride and passion; he had no reason to anticipate the long sway of "Satanist" misinterpretation. It might not be overstrained to see a partial parallel (which Milton need not have had in mind) with the episode of Dido in Virgil's first and fourth books, since Dido is in some sense equivalent to Satan in leading the protagonist from the way of righteousness and providential design. At any rate, both poets have at times been charged with divided sympathies that have divided some readers' sympathies also.

Two large parts of the first two books illustrate Milton's enrichment of epic conventions. One is the roll-call of the fallen angels in 1.376–521. The catalogue of ships in the second book of the *Iliad* is commonly skipped by modern readers. In *Aeneid* 7.641ff. Virgil made such a roll-call more vivid through his embroidery of local associations, and more functional because his warriors are the followers of Turnus, the leader of resistance to Aeneas and to the divine plan; so Milton describes the chief devils, God's enemies, by anticipating their later roles as heathen deities, and his catalogue becomes a survey of the spread of idolatry through Palestine and the Middle East. As for the second convention, Milton's handling of the infernal debate has dwarfed the dozens of epic councils in the works of all his predecessors, including Virgil and Homer, thanks to his dramatic staging and the realistic and strongly differentiated characters revealed in the arguments, feelings, diction, syntax, and rhythm of his speakers. And since, apart from the superior though limited comprehension of Belial, they are all reasoning in ignorance of the real issue, the conflict between good and evil, the total effect of the debate is ironic.

We noticed before two other conventions, which have complementary functions and which, in Milton's treatment, occupy about a third of the poem. One

is the narrative of earlier events. Here again there is an obvious progression: Odysseus's relating of his personal adventures; Aeneas's account of the fall of Troy and his company's wanderings in search of their destined home, a national theme; and, in *PL*, the story of the war in heaven and the Creation, told by an angel—whose message of warning to Adam and Eve links him with the celestial messengers of Homer and Virgil, particularly Hermes (Mercury), to whom Milton alludes (5.285). The second convention, the prophetic survey of the future, is personal in the *Odyssey*, national and imperial in the *Aeneid* (6.756–853, 8.626–728), and, in *PL*, is the revelation to Adam of the course of Providence and the way of salvation.

One conspicuous element of the classical epic and of *PL* is the elaborate heroic simile. Similes in Homer, though they often picture violent actions, are perhaps most memorable when they give us vignettes of normal peaceful life as we read of war and death and perilous voyaging. Milton's similes are drawn from the most heterogeneous sources: his personal awareness of nocturnal hoodlumism and burglary in London and books of travel and history, nature and traditional folklore and the observations of Galileo. Such items are occasional but important links between the remote fable and the actual world. They may give semirealistic authenticity, or heightened mystery, to the unfamiliar or unknown, and they may carry or imply a moral judgment on character and action. And while Homeric similes may bear a loose general resemblance to whatever they are brought in to illustrate, Milton's commonly have an organic relevance, even in details, a relevance that may extend far beyond the immediate context.

We may note a few examples, simple and complex. In the pictures of Satan in the burning lake and moving toward the shore (1.192ff.), his huge stature and power are at once validated and ironically undercut by allusions to those enemies of divine order, the Titans and Giants, and to the biblical Leviathan or whale (in medieval fables the devil, mistaken by mariners for a safe island); and traditional general comparisons—a shield like the moon, a spear like a mast—have specific particulars added (1.286ff.). But these external similes, apart from latent irony, are much less imaginatively and emotionally charged than more original and dramatic ones that follow—as when the "Arch Angel ruind" is grand enough to be compared with the sun misted or partly eclipsed (1.589ff.). Earlier, enveloped in fiery heat, the dauntless leader

> stood and call'd
> His Legions, Angel Forms, who lay intran'st
> Thick as Autumnal Leaves that strow the Brooks
> In *Vallombrosa*, where th' *Etrurian* shades
> High overarch't imbowr.
>
> (1.300–304)

Milton's allusion to fallen leaves outdoes those of Homer, Virgil, and Dante, partly because the beauty of the "shady valley" Milton had seen in Italy,

intensified by visual and rhythmical effects, makes an ironical contrast with the burning lake and its shore. Then the idea of a weltering multitude of warriors is reinforced by a much more elaborate simile, which piles up images of destruction and confusion in a picture of the Egyptian pursuers of the Israelites—a forcible reminder of God's punishment of the wicked.

For a total contrast in substance and impact, there are the mythological allusions that alone can evoke the incomparable loveliness of the earthly paradise, of the first unspoiled innocence of nature and man. Yet, as we have seen, the whole description of the garden is poignantly ironic because Satan is already there, and irony is concentrated in the most famous of all Milton's similes (4.268–72):

> Not that faire field
> Of *Enna*, where *Proserpin* gathering flours
> Her self a fairer Floure by gloomie *Dis*
> Was gatherd, which cost *Ceres* all that pain
> To seek her through the world. . . .

Here an inspired conceit—Proserpine gathering flowers, herself a fairer flower gathered by the prince of darkness—becomes an unspoken anticipation of the fate of Eve; but no one can analyze the suggestions of beauty and frailty and loss and "all that pain."

For Milton, as for Shakespeare and countless others, classical mythology provided what no other source could provide, concrete images of superhuman power or evil or perfection or beauty, images rich in accumulated meaning and associations. In the Christian context of *PL* such allusions may appear, as in secular poetry, without comment, or may often be branded as pagan fiction—though Milton the artist remains uninhibited. One superb example is the fall of Mulciber (Hephaestus, Vulcan) in 1.738ff.:

> and how he fell
> From Heav'n, they fabl'd, thrown by angry *Jove*
> Sheer o're the Chrystal Battlements; from Morn
> To Noon he fell, from Noon to dewy Eve,
> A Summers day; and with the setting Sun
> Dropt from the Zenith like a falling Star,
> On *Lemnos* th' *Ægaean* Ile: thus they relate,
> Erring. . . .

The lines follow the pagan myth even while declaring its falsity, and they are a marvel—a gratuitous marvel—of pictorial art and still more of expressive changes in rhythm; the passage comes from the heart of a lover of beauty and it is quite remote from its half-comic source in Homer (*Il.* 1.590–94) in its romantic seriousness and idea of vast space. And "romantic" may be applied, along with "reductive" or "antiheroic," to the picture of the fallen angels

crowding into the newly built palace of Pandemonium (1.777ff.), where Milton blends reminiscences of classical myth, of the *Aeneid* (6.451–54), and of *A Midsummer Night's Dream*. Mythological allusion is a kind of imaginative and moral shorthand in which Milton surpassed all other English—perhaps all other—poets.

A few old and a few modern critics have damned Milton's "grand style" as if it were a kind of artificial and uniform brocade, mere magniloquence; and in or between the lines of the modern complaints lurks the assumption that all good poetry has been and should be colloquial in diction, syntax, and rhythm, an assumption that, of course, will not bear a moment's scrutiny. More perceptive critics, from C. S. Lewis to Christopher Ricks, have shown the real character of Milton's grand style. Obviously *PL* required—from a poet capable of achieving it—a style appropriate for a religious epic that embraced the whole history and destiny of man and a vast imagined universe, and whose characters were all divine and angelic except Adam and Eve. The texture of *PL* is stylized, as any long poem must be and as, in their different ways, the *Iliad, Odyssey,* and *Aeneid* are; but at the same time it is—often within a single passage—a mosaic of various styles, in keeping with the various characters and situations (including the comic). At its fullest and best, critical analysis cannot get very far into the essence of Milton's power, and here only a few headings can be set up; what matters is the sensitive reader's experience, however inarticulate.

To glance at a few obvious variations, the first book, dominated by Satan, is rich in vague images of lurid darkness and more precise images of martial and architectual splendor; in the second, the styles of the debaters range from the blunt forthrightness of Moloch the warrior to the sinuousness of Belial the intellectual. We noted above the contrast between the bare expository speeches of God, of Moral Law, and the compassionate tenderness of both language and rhythm in those of the Redeemer. In the sensuous descriptions of Eden and the process of Creation, of natural beauty and fecundity, pictorial energy partakes of religious delight in the divine handiwork. Adam and Eve at first address each other with a syntactical amplitude that betokens enjoyment of their power of speech and, above all, complete contentment and security—the ceremony of innocence. But when they begin to disagree, and when Eve, under the sway of the tempter, feels new desires for new experience, her exploratory debate with herself proceeds in short syntactical units and plain, direct language; her corruption can be measured by the distance between this mode of thought and her weaving and unweaving of an intricately ordered pastoral pattern in the asseveration of her love for Adam (4.639–56). And their quarreling after the Fall is far from majestic. Finally, plainness of narrative style is the staple of Books 11 and 12, the outline of human history, much of it condensed from the Bible. Thus "stylization," while it does describe the poem as a whole, loses half its meaning when it permits such diversities of functional level and tone.

The grand style and devices for attaining it had been discussed and practised by Italian poets and critics (F. T. Prince, *The Italian Element in Milton's Verse*),

and both in his sonnets, spread over some thirty years, and in his often impassioned and exalted prose Milton gave many signs of his mastery of such devices, of his approach to the style or styles perfected in *PL*. Perhaps the chief thing is the breaking up of the ordinary word order of prose, and this phrase, of course, covers an infinity of ways and degrees. Such deliberate "disorder" becomes, in Milton's hands, the most forceful and arresting kind of order. It includes the placing of words, phrases, and clauses for shades of emphasis, for parallelism or contrast, and such functional dislocation may be carried out with the freedom of an inflected language. (Janette Richardson has seen in such devices the strong influence of Virgil [*Comparative Literature* 14 (1962):321–31].) Along with this goes elliptical and muscular compression, which may disregard syntax for the sake of expressiveness. And there are other elements, such as allusive periphrasis, which is almost never mere inflation but rather is used to make a suggestive point, often one that adds an idea or a judgment. All these and other devices for achieving sublimity can succeed only when they become the natural mode of a supreme artist, and, as Dr. Johnson said, Milton's "natural port is gigantick loftiness." However, we must not forget that contrast is an instinctive principle of Milton's imagination and style, that much of his epic utterance is more or less straightforward, and that many of his most complex and sublime effects—as in the last lines of *PL*—are attained through the utmost simplicity of means.

The idea of hierarchy, of the great chain of being, which is so central in Milton's cosmic, religious, and ethical thought, works in his style also. Whereas poets in our time, in describing nature, strive for images and epithets never thought of before, Milton enjoys and seeks to share the high pleasure of recognition, of seeing every creature and thing performing its appointed function in the divine and universal order. Large examples are the pictures of Eden and the Creation, and smaller ones range from the morning canticle of Adam and Eve (5.153–208) to the ascending list of sights denied to the blind poet (3.40–44), which concentrates a total view of man and life in the culminating phrase, "human face divine." If in much neoclassical verse the principle of "general nature" yielded tame flatness, it does not in Milton, who, with or without added particulars, feels and communicates vitality. As F. T. Prince remarks (apropos of the swan in 7.433–40), Milton gives a "triumphant demonstration, a conscious exhibition of the true nature of things" (*Approaches to Paradise Lost*, ed. Patrides, p. 59). Or, as Anne Ferry puts it, "The language of Satan and of fallen man unnaturally disjoins the unities of God's creation, while the metaphors of the inspired narrator, so to speak supernaturally recreate those unities" (p. 121).

One impressionistic prejudice, repeated for generations, is that the diction of *PL* is so heavily Latinate that we sink under it. That is simply not true, as even the brief excerpts quoted here might serve to suggest. (E. M. Clark gave a precisely statistical refutation of the stubborn fallacy in *Studies in Philology* 53 [1956].) The occasional use of English derivatives in their original Latin sense

had been an element in the language of poetry since Spenser (to go no further back), and it appears in the supreme model of English English, Shakespeare—as in "Th' extravagant and erring spirit hies / To his confine." Moreover, Milton's Latinate words have various positive values. Thus "error," used of paradisal brooks (4.239), means not only "wandering" but the prelapsarian purity of "rightness in wandering" (A. Stein, p. 66; C. Ricks, pp. 110ff.). Abstract nouns may have far more power than concrete words: for example, "Magnificence" (2.273), or "the Tree / Of prohibition" (9.644–45: Ricks, p. 76). Such words range from the mock-heroic ("expatiate," 1.774) to the terms of Satanic or postlapsarian technology (6.512ff., 10.1070ff.). What gives Milton's English its supposedly un-English cast is rather, we have observed, his wresting of word order and syntax to manifold expressive purposes. Instead of administering dogmatic, schoolmasterish rebukes, hostile critics might better have been grateful that, as a stylist, Milton revealed a new world of resources in the language. And—as such critics do not recognize—in *PL* as in his other poems the meaning (whatever its latent subtleties) is almost never in doubt, whereas it very often is in Shakespeare.

The use of blank verse for a heroic poem was in itself a bold innovation (which Milton defended in his short preface), and the blank verse of *PL*, in keeping with the style, created a new world of expressive rhythm. One main characteristic was what Milton in his preface spoke of as "the sense variously drawn out from one Verse into another." Thus the opening sentence of *PL* is of sixteen lines, only a few of them end-stopped. Throughout the poem—except where the flow is deliberately disturbed—we feel what C. S. Lewis described as "the enormous onward pressure of the great stream on which you are embarked" (*Preface*, p. 45). It is quite idle to contrast—to Milton's disadvantage—the blank verse of an epic with the blank verse of Shakespearian dialogue. Milton's epic orchestration, like his verbal texture, is stylized, but with the same wide range of flexibility. Within the frame of the decasyllabic line Milton took every conceivable liberty. Except for the purpose of illustrating such liberty, we must not scan his lines in terms of conventional metrical feet. While the norm is iambic, words and syllables are stressed or slurred or elided, speeded or retarded, singly or in bunches, in accordance with the intended sense and feeling. Thus in the first line, "Of Mans First Disobedience, and the Fruit," the second, third, fourth, sixth, and tenth syllables carry the stresses that emphasize the theme; or syllabic stresses may be evened out to suggest steady flight: "All night the dreadless Angel unpursu'd" (6.1). The number of stresses is normally five but varies from three to the relentless eight of "Rocks, Caves, Lakes, Fens, Bogs, Dens, and shades of death" (2.621). Because stresses and pauses vary in number, weight, and position, the variations and the underlying norm provide a continual interplay of surprise and recognition. A caesura may occur anywhere, even after the first syllable: in the invocation to Light, after "Seasons return, but not to me returns" (3.41), the next line begins with "Day," poised by itself—a position and a pause that compel us to realize

its full meaning. (Further, as Donald Davie has remarked, the word comes as a surprise, since we expect a season to be named.) The lines on Mulciber quoted above are a great example of change of pace (and "Dropt" illustrates Milton's frequent use of a forceful monosyllabic verb as the first word of a line: cf. 1.45, etc.). Another superb example of change of pace is the passage in which the Son leaves heaven for the work of Creation: "They view'd" the turbulent sea of Chaos (an instance, by the way, of what Keats called Milton's "stationing" of figures) and after the turbulent lines the Son imposes order: "Silence, ye troubl'd waves, and thou Deep, peace" (7.216); and then a strong smooth flow of verse—not like the account of Satan's voyage—as the divine designer rides "Farr into *Chaos*, and the World unborn." Such manipulation of rhythm and examples can only begin to suggest the aural sensitivity a reader must cultivate, and the best thing he can do is to read *PL* aloud. In no poem in the world is rhythm a more active and essential element of meaning. [DB]

PARADISE REGAINED. In 1671 Milton's *PR* was published together with *SA* in a slim octavo volume of 220 pages, by the same publisher, John Starkey, who had brought out Milton's *Brit* the previous year. No manuscript of the poem survives, so that this first (and only) edition published in Milton's lifetime constitutes the authoritative text.

By 1671 Milton had had the satisfaction of knowing that his longer epic had found an audience, whether fit or unfit, numerous enough to buy up the full issue of 1300 copies. It is not recorded whether Milton received for his new volume of poems a sum of money approaching the £10 he was paid for *PL*, but his nephew Edward Phillips testifies (*Life of Mr. John Milton,* 1694) that then as now *PR* had difficulty finding its own fit audience, being "generally censur'd to be much inferiour to the other." Phillips also records Milton's irate repudiation of such judgments—"He could not hear with patience any such thing when related to him"—and offers his own opinion that "possibly the Subject may not afford such variety of Invention, but it is thought by the judicious to be little or nothing inferiour to the other for stile and decorum."

There is no firm evidence establishing the circumstances and date of composition of *PR*, though surviving contemporary records indicate a general belief that the poem was written just after *PL*. Edward Phillips assigns its composition to the period 1667–1670, though as a matter of inference rather than evidence: "*Paradise regain'd* . . . doubtless was begun and finisht and Printed after the other was publisht, and that in a wonderful short space considering the sublimeness of it." If we may believe the often-repeated tale of the inception of the poem recounted by Milton's friend Thomas Ellwood in his autobiography, *The History of the Life of Thomas Ellwood* (1714), the period of composition must fall between 1665 and 1670. Ellwood states that after reading the manuscript of *PL* late in 1665 he had observed to Milton, "Thou hast said much here of paradise lost; but what hast thou to say of paradise found?" To this statement Milton reportedly made no answer but "sat some time in a muse." Ellwood

further reports that at some unspecified time after he returned to London upon the cessation of the plague in 1666 Milton showed him *PR* (whether printed or in manuscript is not clear) and "in a pleasant tone" said to him, "This is owing to you; for you put it into my head by the question you put to me at Chalfont, which before I had not thought of." The story, with its dubious exaltation of Ellwood as surrogate for Milton's muse, has a somewhat apocryphal quality. Yet there is no reason to believe that the incident was invented out of whole cloth; at the very least it provides additional evidence of contemporary opinion as to the date of composition.

Most modern Milton scholars have accepted this dating and many of them (e.g., James Holly Hanford, *Studies in Philology* 15 [1918]:244–63; E. M. W. Tillyard, *Milton* [1930]; Douglas Bush, *English Literature in the Earlier Seventeenth Century, 1600–1660* [1962]) find that *PR* presents a culminating statement of the great themes and issues that exercised Milton for a lifetime—temptation, the true heroism, the paradise within. But the traditional dating has been challenged by some scholars. On the basis of certain statistically tabulated prosodic tests—for example, use of terminal and medial pauses, treatment of polysyllables, percentage of feminine or pyrrhic endings—John Shawcross has concluded (*Publications of the Modern Language Association* 76 [1961]:345–58) that the main speech sections of Books 1, 2, and 4 of *PR* were written before *PL*, and the induction to Book 1 and Book 3 added later, as the work was revised for publication. Without appealing to statistics but rather to the preponderance of dramatic speech in *PR* as compared to *PL*, as well as to some few inconsistencies in the text, Parker, *Milton*, has speculated that *PR* was first conceived as a drama and begun probably about 1656–1658 before Milton started to write *PL* as an epic, and that it was then revised as a narrative poem sometime within the period 1665–1670.

But arguments for chronological development based upon observed trends in prosodic and stylistic features without consideration of the demands of genre and theme have not met with widespread acceptance. Indeed, insisting that statistics on prosody must be read with attention to the interrelation of form and matter, Ants Oras has elaborated and extended his own seminal statistical study (*SAMLA Studies in Milton* [1953]) in a monograph that strongly reaffirms the traditional chronology, *Blank Verse and Chronology in Milton* (1966). He finds that Milton's use of adjectives and adjectival participles, syllabized and unsyllabized "-ed" endings, placement of monosyllabic and other adjectives before and after nouns, use of metrical pauses, and use of polysyllables all combine to reinforce a credible pattern of artistic evolution from largely Elizabethan beginnings in *Mask*, to Milton's creation of a distinctively magnificent epic style in *PL* 1–6, to the gradual emergence of a more austere, less ornamented style in the final books of *PL*, culminating in a further development and extension of this last style in *PR* and *SA*.

The only major source for *PR* is the biblical account of the Temptation of Christ in the wilderness, recounted in a few short verses in Matthew 4:1–11,

Mark 1:12–13, and Luke 4:1–13. Probably in part for dramatic effectiveness, Milton followed Luke's sequence of Christ's three major temptations (stones, kingdoms, tower) rather than the more often cited Matthew sequence (stones, tower, kingdoms). Moreover, Luke, and also Mark, provide some basis for the poem's nonbiblical temptations by intimating that Christ was tempted throughout the full forty days, an intimation that led Calvin and some other exegetes to the conclusion that Christ underwent many temptations, of which only the most important were recorded in the Gospels. On this slender basis Milton constructed an extended narrative account of Christ's temptation in four books, 2,070 blank verse lines.

In contrast to the abundance of poems and dramas about the Fall of Man, there were very few literary treatments of the temptations of Jesus that could provide Milton with suggestions or topics for elaborating the biblical story. The episode was treated in some mystery play cycles, most suggestively in the *Ludus Coventriae* in which a Council in Hell consisting of Satan, Belial, and Beelzebub discusses the problem of Christ's identity and determines upon a strategy of tempting him by means of the three root sins of mankind (as below); a soliloquy in which Christ complains of his severe hunger pangs; and an impressive panorama of the ancient and modern kingdoms offered to Christ in the kingdoms temptation. The temptation episode constitutes the third part of the Anglo-Saxon narrative *Christ and Satan* (9th century) attributed to Caedmon and just possibly known to Milton in the Junius manuscript; its three parts treated, respectively, Christ's battle with Satan in heaven, his harrowing of hell, and (in fragmentary form) his temptation by Satan in the wilderness. Christ's temptation also received brief and very summary treatment in biblical poems spanning several centuries, which treat the whole life of Christ or else focus specifically upon his passion and death—for example, Juvencus's *Evangeliorum libri quattuor* (ca. 330), Marcus Hieronymus Vida's *Christiad* (1535), Nicholas Frébnicle's *Jésus Crucifié* (1636). But in only two narrative poems did the incident receive extended literary development: Jacobus Strasburgus's *Oratio Prima* (1565, ca. 800 hexameters), the only "brief epic" that takes Christ's temptation as its subject, and the second book of Giles Fletcher's *Christ's Victorie, and Triumph* (1619), whose four books treat, respectively, the Parliament in Heaven adjudicating the Fall of Man, the Temptation of Christ, the Passion and Crucifixion, and the Harrowing, Ascension, and triumphal procession of the saved to heaven. In both works the temptation episode is presented in allegorical terms. Strasburgus (whose poem Milton can hardly have known, although some elements of it are suggestive for his conception) describes the episode as a "duel" waged in dialogue between the Satanic forces and Christ, a "young warrior" learning the rudiments *("rudimentum")* of the great warfare he is to wage at the Harrowing (cf. *PR* 1.155–62); the temptation itself is a psychomachia in which Christ is attacked by the furies of Hell and certain personified vices—Avarice, Glory, Ambition, etcetera, which his virtues resist and ultimately defeat. Fletcher's poem, which Milton probably did

know, presents Christ in the wilderness encountering along with Satan the allegorical figures of Famine, Despair, Presumption, and Pangloretta—this last presiding over a Spenserian "Bowre of Bliss" that incorporates all worldly pleasures and honors.

Although there are no obvious literary sources for Milton's poem, and very few analogues for it, one can identify "sources" of another kind in the materials that provided the basis for the conceptual framework and the interplay of ideas in the poem. Elizabeth Pope (*"Paradise Regained": The Tradition and the Poem* [1947]) was the first to call attention in this regard to the paramount importance of the biblical exegetical tradition, pointing to the identity which that tradition established between Christ's three temptations, the three temptations leading to Adam's fall, and the root temptations of mankind enumerated in 1 John 2:13; these primary temptations constituting the so-called Triple Equation are sensuality (in Protestant versions, distrust), avarice or ambition, and vainglory. In *Milton's Brief Epic* (1966), Barbara K. Lewalski has examined the source material in biblical commentary more fully, pointing to the basis it provides for Milton's treatment of the temptation as Christ's initiation into his threefold office as Prophet, King, and Priest, as well as for his poetic typological exploitation of various Old Testament types of those functions. Classical philosophy is also an important source of moral ideas and concepts in the poem—notably Plato, as Irene Samuel has established in *Plato and Milton* (1947), or Plato as modified by the Ciceronian emphasis upon the "cardinal" virtues of Justice, Fortitude, Temperance, and Wisdom, according to Arnold Stein's formulation (*Heroic Knowledge* [1957]).

The question of the genre of *PR* and the further question of the poem's relation to *PL* have been much disputed among modern Milton scholars. The matter seemed obvious enough, however, to eighteenth-century critics and editors of the poem, who took it to be an epic and an intended sequel to *PL*. In this vein the earliest essay on the poem, Richard Meadowcourt's *Critique on Milton's Paradise Regain'd* (1732) observes that the poem's exordium deliberately imitates the *Ille ego qui quondam* widely attributed to Virgil as the proem to the *Aeneid;* Meadowcourt's tract as well as Charles Dunster's 1795 annotated edition of *PR* are now available in Joseph Wittreich's facsimile edition (1971). Wittreich's preface analyzing trends in eighteenth- and nineteenth-century criticism points out that the general assumption of the poem's epic character often led to invidious censure of it in comparison with *PL* on such grounds as the narrowness of its plan, the paucity of its action, the lack of variety in its parts, and the slightness as well as theological inappropriateness of the temptation of Christ as an epic subject. In an effort to account for the disparity between the two epics and the incomplete or truncated epic apparatus of the second, Thomas Newton observed in his edition of 1752 that the poem must have been written in haste. At the end of the eighteenth century these observed differences were given a more positive emphasis, as in William Hayley's argument (*Life of Milton*, 1794) that *PR* created a new kind of epic embodying "the true heroism,

and the triumph of Christianity." The real breakthrough, however, occurred in Charles Dunster's edition which, although it described the poem as an intended and necessary sequel to *PL*, nevertheless used Milton's own distinctions in *RCG* to identify it as a brief epic distinct from the "diffuse epic" of *PL* and modeled "in great measure" upon the Book of Job.

Several modern critics, however, have found in the significant structural and stylistic differences between *PL* and *PR* grounds for assigning the latter poem to some other generic classification. E. M. W. Tillyard (*The English Epic and Its Background* [1954]) complains that the poem is "too short, confined, and simplified for the necessary epic variety and . . . quite lacks choric character"; elsewhere (*Milton*) he had observed that "it is not an epic, it does not try to be an epic, and it must not be judged by any kind of epic standard," being more appropriately seen as a moral allegory in the medieval mode. Howard Schultz (*Publications of the Modern Language Association* 67 [1952]: 790–808) approaches the poem primarily as an ecclesiastical allegory in which the words and actions of Christ stand for and refer to the situation of the Christian church *vis à vis* its historical and contemporary enemies. Some other critics (in addition to Shawcross and Parker) have described the poem as a drama: Douglas Bush (*English Literature in the Earlier Seventeenth Century*) refers to it as a "closet drama with a prologue and stage directions," and Arnold Stein (*Heroic Knowledge*) views it as a psychological drama staged in the hero's mind. Looking to yet another generic tradition Irene Samuel (*Plato and Milton*) has argued the work's mimesis of Platonic dialogue, and Kenneth Muir (*John Milton* [1955]) approaches it as theoretical argument, "nearer in genre to Dryden's *Religio Laici* than . . . to *Paradise Lost*." More recently Louis L. Martz (*ELH: A Journal of English Literary History* 27 [1960]: 224–25) presents the poem as a formal meditation on the Gospel account of Christ's temptation, which at the same time has strong affinities with Virgil's *Georgics* by reason of its bare, unadorned style and its ethical theme of the temperate, disciplined, frugal life.

Despite all this, a large number of modern critics still consider *PR* to be an epic according to some definition, and have addressed themselves to the discovery and clarification of that definition. In a seminal article (*Studies in Philology* 35 [1938]: 35–62), Merritt Y. Hughes described the impact of medieval and Renaissance romances and epics upon Milton's poem, indicating that their heroes paved the way for the allegorical Christ of *PR* by redefining heroic virtue or magnanimity in terms of the qualities of patience, endurance, and renunciation. Also assuming the poem's epic character, John Steadman (*Milton and the Renaissance Hero* [1967]) shows how Milton in both epics undertakes a critique and redefinition of the traditional epic values of fortitude, sapience, leadership, love, and magnanimity. More recently, Donald L. Guss (*Studies in Philology* 68 [1971]: 223–43) has defended the poem's epic purpose on the ground that it has the appropriate epic focus upon the historical situation of the hero and upon his extraordinary virtue in resisting Satan's plausible lure, and

that it creates thereby the appropriate epic effect, astonishment and wonder. He argues moreover that it is a brief epic in that it avoids the use of episodes, which Renaissance epic theory sanctioned in the "diffuse epic" as a means of producing variety. Ralph W. Condee (*Yale Review* 59 [1969–70]: 356–75) has discussed *PR* as the most complete realization of Milton's own epic theory, defined in *PL* 9.13–44 by means of a harsh critique of traditional epic données. *PR* is accordingly a poem in which traditional epic elements are included but turned to very different account: the great adventure here is not a heroic journey but a patient standing; here a great worldly kingdom is not founded but refused; here armies are displayed but no battles occur; here romance lords and ladies appear, but as waiters and waitresses at a Satanic banquet; here Christ achieves his final victory not by heroic combat but by simple restraint, standing still; here instead of the hero's emerging from obscure beginnings into glory he concludes his epic adventure still obscure, unknown, private.

Milton's Brief Epic, already mentioned, endeavors to establish a more precise generic identity for the poem by examining contemporary theory relating to the "brief epic" as a kind. The study begins by assuming, even as Charles Dunster had in 1795, that Milton's rather puzzling reference in *RCG* to "that Epick form whereof the two poems of *Homer*, and those other two of *Virgil* and *Tasso* are a diffuse, and the book of *Job* a brief model" is a serious statement of generic theory with direct applicability to *PR*. Investigation of the poem in terms of this statement has led to two literary traditions that furnished assumptions, materials, and methods for Milton's brief epic: (1) a tradition of biblical exegesis and literary treatment of the Job story as epic and epic model, which flourished from patristic times to Milton's own, and (2) a long tradition of theory and practice relating to the brief biblical epic as a special literary category with distinctive characteristics.

Some bases for the view of Job as epic have been studied by Charles M. Jones (*Studies in Philology* 44 [1947]: 209–27) and Israel M. Baroway (*ELH: A Journal of English Literary History* 2 [1935]: 66–91): (1) the idea of the great antiquity of the Book of Job, thought in the seventeenth century to be among the first literary productions of mankind; (2) the idea of its uncertain authorship and possible oral transmission, which links it to early folk epics of other nations; (3) the supposed hexameter verse form of the work, relating it to classical epic—an often-repeated error introduced into the mainstream of Jobean exegesis by St. Jerome. In addition to these links, Lewalski's investigation reveals a traditional conception of Job as an epic subject. Though many Reformation and modern exegetes tended to approach the book as drama or as philosophical discourse, the dominant patristic and medieval tradition of Origen, Chrysostom, and Gregory the Great—carried on by many Catholic and Protestant exegetes in the sixteenth and seventeenth centuries (Juan de Pineda, Balthazar Corderius, Joseph Caryl, John Diodati), and developed in such poetic versions as Henry Oxenden's *Jobus Triumphans* (1656) and Helie Le Cordier's *Job* (1667)—interprets the episode as a heroic combat of cosmic

significance between Satan, the Adversary of God and man, and Job, God's designated champion, warrior, athlete, and wrestler. The generic formula implicit in this reading provided a model for at least one other seventeenth-century brief epic on another subject, Robert Aylett's *Joseph, or Pharoah's* [*sic*] *Favourite* (1623) in five books (ca. 2,950 lines).

Milton's poem signals its relation to the Book of Job through a tissue of references and allusions: the character Job is named on six occasions (1.147, 369, 426; 3.64, 67, 95), the Book is quoted twice (1:33–34, 368), and either the Book itself or the tradition of commentary on it is alluded to on at least ten other occasions. The poem begins with Satan still in his Jobean character as Adversary continuing his Jobean wanderings to and fro upon the earth; he comes now to another "assembly," Christ's baptism, where he again hears God's high commendation of a superlative hero (Job 1:6–12; *PR* 1.30–39). In both cases God's acclaim provokes Satan's determination to tempt the hero, in both the hero is displayed as God's champion in the encounter, and in both the conditions of the combat are set forth in two supernatural councils—two councils in heaven in the Book of Job, and in *PR* Satan's council in mid-air followed immediately by God's heavenly council. Moreover, God's comment indicates that Christ's trial will be of the same order as Job's and will serve (in part) to display Christ's merit as an "abler" Job:

> he [Satan] might have learnt
> Less over-weening, since he fail'd in *Job*,
> Whose constant perseverance overcame
> Whate're his cruel malice could invent.
> He now shall know I can produce a man
> Of female Seed, far abler to resist
> All his sollicitations, and at length
> All his vast force. . . .
>
> (1.146–53)

The structure of Milton's poem is also modeled in part upon the "epic" conception of Job's trials and challenges—loss of goods and children, afflictions in his flesh, and then as his most arduous trial the steady, remorseless arguments of the three friends set on by Satan to lead him to false estimations of his own virtues and finally to despair. So in *PR*, Christ is first shorn of all material support, then assailed in his flesh by hunger, and then bombarded by Satan with a relentless stream of arguments intended to undermine his conception of himself and his mission. God's address to Job from the whirlwind, often interpreted as an apparent rather than a real rebuke intended as a further test of Job's faith and humility, has its counterpart in the storm scene of *PR*, which Satan interprets to Christ as a portent of God's displeasure. The ending of the Book of Job was construed by the commentators as setting forth God's proclamation of Job's complete triumph over all temptation, and Job's employment of the reward appropriate to a heroic victor—the twofold multiplication of all his

former goods. So, in *PR*, Christ's victory is proclaimed by the heavenly host, and all the goods he refused to receive at Satan's hands are given or promised to him in a more exalted form. (For a critique of this designation of the Book of Job as a generic model for *PR*, see Robert H. Stein's article in *Anglia* 88 [1970]: 323–33.)

Milton's Brief Epic also links *PR* generically to a European tradition of brief biblical epics—Neo-Latin, Italian, French, and English—extending over several centuries, thereby setting Milton's poem in a broader generic context than that supplied by the seventeenth-century English biblical poems studied by Burton O. Kurth (*Milton and Christian Heroism* [1959]). Poems comprising the brief epic category are about 1,500 to 4,000 lines, often in three or four books, and often on New Testament subjects. Among particularly influential examples are Juvencus's *Evangeliorum libri quattuor* (ca. A.D. 330, 3,226 hexameters); Sedulius's *Carmen Paschale* (ca A.D. 430, 4 books, 1,768 hexameters); the fragmentary Caedmonian *Christ and Satan* (ninth century, 733 lines); the *Mariana* of Giovanni Battista Spagnuoli, called Mantuan (1481, 3 books, ca. 1,500 hexameters); Jacopo Sannazaro's *De Partu Virginis* (1526, 3 books, ca. 1,450 hexameters), Marcus Hieronymus Vida's *Christiad* (1533, 6 books, ca. 6,000 hexameters), Du Bartas's *Judith* (1574, 6 books, ca. 2,000 lines); Robert Aylett's *Susanna* (1622, 4 books, ca. 1,470 lines) and *Joseph* (1623, 5 books, ca. 2,950 lines); Giovanni Battista Marino's *La Strage de gli Innocenti* (1610, 4 books, ca. 3,230 lines); Giles Fletcher's *Christ's Victorie, and Triumph* (1610, 4 books, ca. 2,120 lines); and Jacques de Coras, *Samson, Poëme Sacré* (1665, 5 books, ca. 2,470 alexandrines). Such poems customarily claimed epic status in proems or prefaces or critical treatises on the following bases: (1) the theory that parts of the Bible are already epic poetry and so can supply epic subject matter; (2) the definition of a hero as one whose virtues and spiritual conquests merit eternal fame in heaven; (3) the analogous virtues and actions of some biblical and classical heroes such as Samson and Hercules; and (4) the assertion that the true biblical subject has far greater nobility and excellence than have pagan fictions inspired by false muses.

PR uses the données of this generic tradition in an imaginative and highly original way: it is, not surprisingly, the crowning achievement of the kind. Of the three basic formulas devised for the biblical brief epic—the standard patristic format of a panoramic subject presented sequentially, the usual medieval model in which a sequence of episodes or scenes is linked together typologically, and the predominant Renaissance structure wherein a single action or episode is expanded and given broader epic dimension by the use of allusions, prophecies, recitals, and iconographical descriptions often based upon typological symbolism—Milton used the Renaissance formula. Though he does not employ the simplest and most common Renaissance strategy for giving an epic aura to the poem by thick-sowing it with Virgilian diction, epithets, and echoes, and he also eschews the often-imitated neoclassical structure of Vida's *Christiad*. But he does adapt a number of the expected generic topoi: an *in*

medias res beginning with Christ's baptism; two "infernal" councils now held in mid-air rather than in hell; a council in heaven wherein God addresses Gabriel and makes references to his earlier employment as angelic nuntius at the Annunciation (l.138–40); a prophecy of Christ's immediate and ultimate victory over Satan spoken by God before the encounter; two transformed epic recitals—Christ's meditation about his youthful experiences and aspirations, and Mary's reminiscences about the great prophecies and promises attending the hero's early life; an epic catalogue of the kingdoms of the world; a transformed prophetic vision in which the hero, instead of viewing his own destined kingdom, sees and rejects all those kingdoms which are not his; an epiclike, martial pageant of Parthian warriors; and a passage dealing with the education or learning of the hero (the learning temptation).

Within the brief epic tradition Milton's greatest conceptual debt may well be to Sannazaro's *De Partu Virginis*, in which the apparently unlikely "epic" subject of the incarnation and birth of Christ is not treated structurally as a truncated *Aeneid*, but (primarily through the use of typological symbolism) as the true nucleus or epitome of a vast epic action. For Milton the similarly unusual choice of the temptation episode as subject no doubt suggested itself as a complement to the temptation in *PL*, but beyond this, it is the one episode in Christ's life (except for the Harrowing of Hell which Milton's mortalism kept him from using) that is peculiarly suited to the format of the brief epic, in that it could be treated as a transmutation of the single combat of hero and antagonist—traditionally, the focal, climactic event of a long epic. Milton accordingly presents the temptation as an epitome of the perpetual battle of the Son and Satan throughout all time, and uses martial imagery to associate the permutations of the argument with the thrust and parry of a great duel. He does not present this dual as an allegorical *psychomachia* (as Giles Fletcher and Jacobus Strasburgus had done), but rather as an inordinately subtle and complex mental combat in which hellish wiles must be conquered by wisdom. Milton also took over the common brief-epic technique of using typological allusion to extend historical perspective and achieve epic dimension for the subject chosen, though by incorporating such reference into the debate between Christ and Satan he gave the technique unprecedented dramatic power. Through such allusions Milton presented the temptation episode against the panorama of all previous history, and displayed Christ as the epitome and fulfillment of all earlier patterns of heroism.

Accepting in part Louis Martz's account of the poem as an exercise in formal meditation, Stewart A. Baker (*Comparative Literature* 20 [1968]: 116–32) finds that Milton's poem transmutes the military themes of the classical epic to the spiritual values of Christianity primarily by means of an interplay of epic and pastoral motifs and vocabularies. He also finds Sannazaro's *De Partu Virginis* to be the most suggestive model for *PR*, noting that, like Sannazaro, Milton employs pastoral motifs to assimilate "the historical themes of epic into the consciousness of the individual," and that he does this primarily by establishing

the pastoral landscape as the symbolic setting for meditations upon the typological figures and events of Christian history. Pointing to the inverted pastoral landscape of the poem (a wilderness instead of the "happy Garden" of earlier epics) Baker notes the structural and thematic importance of several true and perverted pastoral elements in the poem: a wilderness "dusk with horrid shade" in which Jesus' presence creates something like the conventional pastoral landscape of hill and shady vale; true and false examples of the *locus amoenus;* the piscatory apostles with their complaint. Moreover, Jesus' rejection of the courtly glories of the world is an affirmation of the pastoral value of inner harmony over the epic values of material wealth, conquest, political power.

Such recognition that *PR* derives from a somewhat different generic tradition than *PL* invites the conclusion that it is a companion poem to the long epic rather than (as is often assumed) a sequel or postscript. *Milton's Brief Epic* urges that the focus of *PL* is upon the condition of mankind manifested in and extending from the story of Adam, and that the subject is the Fall and the redemption of man; whereas in *PR* the focus is upon Christ the hero, and the subject is his heroic achievement and mission in its deepest significance and broadest ramifications. The distinction seems mirrored in the stance of the epic narrator. In *PL* he presents himself as one of Adam's progeny, insisting in image and statement upon the inner darkness and spiritual blindness that dooms him to failure in his difficult task unless the Spirit will act upon him. In *PR* by contrast the narrative voice is easy and confident, since the narrator now sees himself not as fallen but as redeemed man, sharing in Christ's victory and therefore confidently expecting the Spirit's assistance in triumphing over the difficulties of his theme. The narrator's identification with Christ's perspective, and his constant activity in interpreting the poem for the reader and commenting upon the views expressed by the various characters is explored further by Roger H. Sundell (*Milton Studies* 2 [1970]: 83–101).

The chief reason why *PR* has not been a notable favorite with the critics is their dissatisfaction with the hero, Christ. Some have complained about the negative, restrictive values (Puritan or Stoic) that he seems to embody—in sharp contrast to the gentleness and love such readers expect to find associated with the Savior of mankind. So H. J. C. Grierson protested (*Criterion* 7 [1928]:254), "the restrictive virtues in themselves are somewhat cold and negative. . . . We miss in Milton's Christ the note of passionate, self-forgetting love. He is too serene and forbidding, if noble and imperturbable." In somewhat different terms, Tillyard *(Milton)* declared Milton's hero to be "in fact partly allegorical, partly Milton himself, imagined perfect." Northrop Frye (*Modern Philology* 53 [1956]:227–38) asserts that Christ becomes increasingly unsympathetic as the poem develops—"a pusillanimous quietist in the temptation of Parthia, an inhuman snob in the temptation of Rome, a peevish obscurantist in the temptation of Athens."

Another kind of complaint is directed to the static, undramatic character of

the hero, necessitated by the fact that he must perforce be presented as divine, or as perfect man unable to fall. Elizabeth Pope finds Milton conforming to the dominant interpretation of the temptation story throughout the centuries—the view that Jesus underwent the temptation as a man, with his divine power held in abeyance so as to teach mankind how to withstand temptation, but that he was nevertheless fully conscious of his divinity and even (some commentators held) that he deliberately mystified Satan about it through his ambiguous answers. Such a view is the basis for Allan Gilbert's comment (*Journal of English and Germanic Philology* 15 [1916]:606) that Christ, as the only-begotten of God, had no need for the human means offered by Satan, and of Douglas Bush's observation (*English Literature in the Earlier Seventeenth Century*, p. 412) that "the sinless divine protagonist of *Paradise Regained* cannot falter, much less fall." Other readings emphasize that the divine hero is also an allegorical representative of human perfection and on that score also an undramatic figure: in Hughes's conception (*Studies in Philology* 35 [1938]) he is an "exemplar Redeemer, the Word of St. John's Gospel, as it fused with the craving of critics and poets of the late Renaissance for a purely exemplary hero in epic poetry."

Other critics have recognized some genuine dramatic conflict and some real development of Christ's character in the poem, though they do not agree upon the course this development takes or upon the conception of Christ's nature that makes such development possible. Some see Milton's Christ as exercising only his human intellect and will throughout the temptation, and therefore as capable of dramatic conflict: M. M. Mahood (*Poetry and Humanism* [1950], p. 211) describes him as "the perfect man, as yet scarcely aware of His divine progeniture," and Northrop Frye (*Modern Philology* 53 [1956]) finds that he withstands the temptations as a human being until the tower episode, at which point the omnipotent divine power "takes over" the now fully proved human will. Arnold Stein (*Heroic Knowledge*) sees the work as a kind of drama of consciousness, finding that Christ's answers project a true action, a positive process of self-definition even as Satan also drives on to the ultimate self-definition he has chosen. Yet all these recognize the problem created for dramatic action by a perfect hero who cannot be moved, Stein arguing that Milton's chief solution for the difficulty was to shift much of the dramatic weight to Satan's temptation activity, his anguished consciousness, his desperate uncertainty about Christ's true identity.

Beyond this, however, several critics have discussed the identity motif as giving dramatic interest to the role of Christ as well as to that of Satan. Edward Cleveland (*Modern Language Quarterly* 16 [1955]:232–36) argues that Christ withstands all the temptations as exalted man until the tower assault, at which time he dramatically and gloriously reveals his divinity. A. S. P. Woodhouse (*University of Toronto Quarterly* 25 [1955–56]:173) declares that Christ gains from his experience in the wilderness "a progressively deeper insight into his own nature as well as into God's purpose," and actually advances from human

beginnings to a full realization of his divinity in the tower scene. John Steadman (*University of Toronto Quarterly* 31 [1962]:416–30) presses this insight further, to assert that Christ really does learn through the dialogue with the devil, beginning at a stage of limited knowledge and "gaining an ever-clearer and more comprehensive insight into God's will in the course of his wilderness ordeal." In *The Harmonious Vision* (chap. 6 [1954]) Don C. Allen finds still greater dramatic potential in a hero who fluctuates throughout the poem between the divine and human natures, giving evidence of this alternation by the striking tonal differences of his various speeches.

Milton's Brief Epic explores the identity motif in the poem more fully and examines the theological basis for it, attempting to show that Milton achieves genuine dramatic tension and movement by exploiting this motif. Obviously, as Satan later remarks, the divine title "bears no single sence" (4.517); Satan himself can claim with some justice, "The Son of God I also am, or was, / And if I was, I am; relation stands; / All men are Sons of God" (4.518–20). Milton works out the dramatic potentialities inherent in the conventional conception of a puzzled and self-deluded Satan seeking to determine throughout the temptation whether Christ is indeed divine, but he especially exploits his own Christology, according to which this incarnate Christ undergoes a kenosis that involves a true emptying out of his divine understanding and will, not merely an obscuring or covering over of his divinity. See in this regard Milton's discussion of the Incarnate Christ in his *CD*, Book 1, chapters 3, 5, 14, 15, 16. Such a Christology provides a basis for presenting Christ in the poem as a dramatic character undergoing a true test or temptation, in that he is (theoretically at least) able to fall, capable of growth, and genuinely (not just apparently) uncertain of himself. Having undergone such a kenosis, he meets the temptation as a man, gaining back only gradually and through God's progressive illumination as he merits it, his awareness of his Divine Nature.

Satan's address to his forces in the first Consult and Christ's meditation as he goes forth into the desert make clear that hero and antagonist begin their duel at approximately the same level of knowledge: both are cognizant of the prophecies, both saw the signs at the recent baptism, both are ignorant of the identity between this Son of God and the "first-Begot." Christ has learned what he knows of himself through his mother's tales of the miraculous prophecies attending his birth, and through the Scripture writings, which have convinced him that he is the promised Messiah. He is now led to the desert—"to what intent / I learn not yet"—obviously conscious of his limited human knowledge but conscious also of the guidance of the Spirit: "For what concerns my knowledge God reveals" (1.291–93). The debate-duel between Christ and Satan develops as a battle of wits in which both hero and tempter strive for the advantage which accompanies superior understanding. To succeed in perverting Christ Satan has to understand him perfectly, but he himself is the victim of imperfect knowledge and naiveté concerning Christ's nature and mission. To withstand Satan's temptations Christ must refuse all inadequate, partial, or

erroneous versions or parodies of himself and his mission, which Satan presents to him out of his vast store of firsthand experience with human weakness throughout all time. Though Christ knows such things only at second hand through his wide reading in Scripture and secular history, he has the special advantage of being able to merit the gift of divine illumination, which seems to be granted him after he has withstood each of the major temptations in terms of his own human powers. Their different modes of apprehension yield vastly different results as both Christ and Satan attempt to cope with the ambiguities of Christ's title, Son of God, and with the metaphorical prophecies about Christ's role. Christ comes to an imaginative realization of the full, spiritual meaning of such terms whereas Satan remains cunning, brilliant even, but ultimately literal-minded, unable to fathom God's metaphors.

Dramatic tension in the poem also develops in terms of one great central paradox that virtually transmutes activity and passivity into each other. Satan appears to do all the acting, dancing about Christ in a fever of motion and trying one scheme after another, one argument after another, whereas Christ seems to be impassive, immobile. Yet it is in Christ's consciousness, not Satan's, that true change and growth take place: Christ progresses through somewhat uneven stages and partial climaxes of understanding and revelation to full comprehension and definition of himself and the various aspects of his role in the grand climax on the tower. Satan, for all his feverish activity, cannot resolve the puzzle about Christ's identity and mission until that same climactic moment, which forces upon him the recognition of his long-time antagonist, and with that recognition, his own defeat and fall.

The fundamental themes of the poem have been variously defined, and the various definitions have implications for the way in which the poem's structure is understood. One approach finds the thematic center to be the presentation of some paradigm of heroic virtue by Christ the exemplary hero: such paradigms are commonly seen as revaluations in Christian terms of classical patterns of virtue and heroism. This reading usually takes the kingdoms temptation to be the essence of the poem, with the temptation of the stones treated as prologue and the tower temptation as climactic epilogue. Allan Gilbert (*Journal of English and Germanic Philology* 15 [1916]) laid the groundwork for this approach to the structure by sharply dissociating the stones-into-bread temptation from the banquet temptation despite their common concern with food, arguing that the Satanic banquet is the first of the glories of the world offered to Christ as gifts. From another point of view Roy Daniells (*Milton, Mannerism and Baroque* [1963], pp. 914–208) has described the structure of the poem in terms of late baroque architecture, with the first and last temptations subordinated as if they were small side passages flanking the expanded central element, the splendid and elaborate panoramas of the kingdoms.

Tillyard (*Milton*) understands the theme of the poem as the quasi-allegorical confrontation of reason (Christ) and passion (Satan). In terms of structure, he finds that the various Satanic offers that constitute the principal temptation of

the kingdoms are "carefully graded according to the subtlety and inwardness of their appeal," and are climaxed by the offer of philosophic learning; the tower scene he takes to be no temptation at all but the brief rout of Satan. Recognizing that Christ at one point (2.483) refers his renunciation of kingdoms to magnanimity, Merritt Y. Hughes (*Studies in Philology* 35 [1938]) discusses the poem's theme in relation to the redefinition and Christianization of that Aristotelian virtue in terms of constancy, patience, *contempus mundi*, and the fusion of the active and contemplative lives. From a somewhat different point of view Frank Kermode (*Review of English Studies* n.s. 4 [1953]:317–30) sees the theme of the poem as the definition of Christian heroism, which Christ exemplifies by confuting or transcending even the most exalted classical heroic ideals: an Ovidian banquet of sense, Scipio's embodiment of true earthly honor; Rome as the sum of pre-Christian civilization with its wealth, glory, and military power; Athens (Socrates) as the sum of natural wisdom. Though he does not address the question of structure, John Steadman (*Milton and the Renaissance Hero* [1967]) also sees Milton's primary theme in *PR* to be the definition of Christian heroism in its total perfection, which involves a critique and revaluation of the traditional epic values of fortitude, sapience, leadership, love, and magnanimity.

Also concentrating almost entirely upon the second temptation, Irene Samuel defines the theme of the poem as "the winning of happiness," achieved by progressive affirmation of and at length transcendence of Platonic ethical values. The temptations ascend according to the Platonic scale of the goods desired by various kinds of men and governments: pleasure, wealth, fame (true fame for Plato is defined as the praise of virtue by the judicious and by Milton as heavenly glory). Ethical knowledge or wisdom, the highest good for Plato, is transcended in *PR* by God's revelation of spiritual truth, and the place of wisdom at the pinnacle of Plato's scale of goods is taken by that loving trust in God which alone can regain human happiness and paradise. Arnold Stein (*Heroic Knowledge*) also finds that the Platonic scale of goods and the Platonic tripartite soul (appetitive, passional, rational) form the basis for the central theme of the poem, a dramatic definition of "heroic knowledge" that is a "preparation for acting transcendence in the world, by uniting intuitive knowledge with proved intellectual and moral discipline." But in his reading, this scale (and so also the structure of the poem) is modified by the hero's manifestation of the Platonic *unity* of the virtues, and by the antagonist's disposition to leapfrog forward and then retreat backward along the scale according to dramatic necessities and opportunities. This reading also enables Stein to take account thematically and structurally of the first and third temptations, interpreting the first as an initial "transcendence" that subsumes much that is to follow in the kingdoms temptation by its invitation to excessive trust in material goods, and the temptations of the storm and tower as the ultimate transcendence—a mythic enactment of the "way of death" that produces more abundant

life, and a climactic translation into action of the heroic knowledge that the hero has gained.

Emerging from this interpretive tradition, but with the significant difference of combining a structural emphasis upon Christ's exemplification of certain virtues with a dramatic reading of the poem's action, is Gary Hamilton's study (*Philological Quarterly* 50 [1971]:567–81). Hamilton sees the Christ of the poem regaining in the course of its action that Paradise Within promised to Adam and his progeny in *PL* 12.575–87, by exemplifying precisely those virtues denominated by Michael as the conditions for its attainment—in the first temptation (Book 1) Faith; in the banquet and riches temptations (Book 2) Temperance; in the offer of Parthia (Book 3) Patience; and in the offers of Rome and Athens (Book 4) that "sum / Of wisdom" which Michael proclaimed to be greater than all earthly riches or earthly knowledge. This schematic arrangement also functions dramatically, Hamilton argues, since what we see in *PR* is "a human Christ in the process of raising himself up 'under long obedience tri'd,' " and thus in some sense performing here his redemptive mission for Adam's sons; only after this achievement does he again assume on the tower his Divine nature and begin that redemption as a public mission.

A second major approach to the theme and structure of the poem accounts for the nature and sequence of the temptations in terms of the traditional identification of Christ as Second Adam. In her 1947 study Pope demonstrated Milton's significant use of the so-called Triple Equation, which has been mentioned. She also pointed out Milton's alteration of this traditional exegetical pattern in response to trends in contemporary Protestant exegesis, and also the demands of his own artistic conception. Thus he conceived the stones-into-bread temptation in Protestant terms as a temptation to distrust, and identified the temptation to appetite (the banquet) as Protestants did with the kingdoms temptation, though he incorporated in his banquet scene the full range of fleshly sins usually encompassed in the medieval reading of the first temptation. Moreover, for dramatic climax Milton reworked the tower temptation as a temptation by violence and an identity test, removing its usual associations with vainglorious presumption and assimilating these to the second temptation also. In Pope's reading Milton's poem is structured so as to set forth each day a different kind of temptation: temptation by necessity, based upon the Protestant version of the stones-into-bread; temptation by pleasures and gifts (the whole range of worldly goods, including carnal delights, vainglory, kingdoms and their glories); and temptation by violence, a special Miltonic conception not usual in treatments of the temptation, though susceptible of interpretation as the specific temptation of the Devil.

Woodhouse (*University of Toronto Quarterly* 25 [1955–56]) also finds that the primary theme of the poem concerns Christ as Second Adam and that a secondary identity theme is implied in the statement that the glorious Eremite will be brought forth from the desert "By proof th' undoubted Son of God." In

his view, Milton made some general use of the Triple Equation in developing the primary theme, but took special care to work out parallels with his own story of Adam: thus he invented the Belial proposition, "Set women in his eye," in order to provide a parallel for his own Adam "fondly overcome with Female charm," and he surrounded the kingdoms offer with two invented "contemplative" lures—the banquet temptation, which moves on the level of the senses to recall "the crude Apple that diverted Eve" (2.349), and the Temptation of Athens, which works on the level of the intellect to parallel the apple as the fruit of the Tree of Knowledge. Much more complexly, Burton J. Weber (*Philological Quarterly* 50 [1971]:553–66) argues that the patristic reading of the Triple Equation as involving temptations to sensuality, ambition, and vainglory defines the fundamental structure of the three days' trial; that these temptations relate to the parts of the Neoplatonic tripartite soul—sense, reason, and intellect (from which springs will); and that, moreover, "Milton turns each day's temptation, and each subsection of each day's temptation, into a test of the full neo-Platonic tripartite soul." Another study, Robert E. Reiter's University of Michigan dissertation, "In Adam's Room: A Study of the Adamic Typology of Christ in *Paradise Regained*" (1964), affirms that the Adam-Christ typological parallels and contrasts make up the principal thematic and structural elements of the poem. And as a minor aspect of the Second Adam theme H. H. Petit (*Papers of the Michigan Academy* 44 [1959]:365–69) points up Milton's suggestive treatment of Mary as Second Eve—nurturing Christ in his office whereas Eve enticed Adam to man's Fall and patiently enduring her uncertainties over Christ's absence whereas Eve, similarly puzzled by God's ways, rebelled. The link is reinforced in the ending of Milton's two epics: Adam and Eve go forth from Eden calmly together, and Christ returns home "private" to his mother's house.

Still another critical approach defines the theme of the poem in terms of Christ's redemptive office or mission, conceiving that role as both broader and more precisely related to Christ's own unique situation than either the Triple Equation or Second Adam motif admits of. Schultz has argued (*Publications of the Modern Language Association* 67 [1952] and *Milton and Forbidden Knowledge*, pp. 222–35) that Christ is not tempted in his private but in his official capacity (that is, as prophet, priest, and king of his Church) and that accordingly all of the temptations are ecclesiastic in their frame of reference, not moral: "Milton meant the Head of the Christian church to set a pattern not primarily for the Christian layman, but for the church and its ministers." Accordingly, Christ's refusals have relevance only to the special responsibilities laid upon the church as Christ's spiritual kingdom. Schultz takes the stones-into-bread temptation as an offer of false guidance to Christ the prophet of the Gospel; the banquet temptation as an offer of Popish idolatry, a pervasion of the Church's true worship; and all of the other temptations as worldly props and aids that Christ's wholly spiritual kingdom, the Church, may not use.

In a different vein Northrop Frye (*Modern Philology* 53 [1956]) takes the

thematic center of the poem to be the presentation of the temptation episode as Christ's second agon with Satan, looking back to the first, the Battle in Heaven, and forward to the final battle to come at the end of time. He argues that the episodes of the poem present Jesus not only as antitype of Adam, but also of Israel wandering in the wilderness en route to the Promised Land, so that some of the temptations concern the ways in which the Gospel is to annihilate and fulfill the Law—as in the abjuration of all force in Christ's Kingdom, and in the adumbration of the forthcoming destruction of the Temple in Satan's fall from its tower. Michael Fixler (*Milton and the Kingdoms of God* [1964]) also finds typology to be of primary importance in developing the fundamental themes of *PR*. Though he associates the temptations with the threefold office of Christ as prophet, priest and king, his primary focus is upon the ways in which Satan uses Jewish messianic speculation and especially contemporary echoes of it in Puritan millenarianism to promote a false chiliastic version of Christ's kingdom. He discusses, moreover, how various temptations subtly challenge Christ to distinguish precisely how and when the Law is to be replaced by the Gospel, notably the banquet scene wherein, as Fixler elsewhere shows (*Modern Language Notes* 70 [1955]:573–77), Satan disingenuously includes foods forbidden by the Law among the banquet's plenty, even while explicitly denying that he has done so.

In *Milton's Brief Epic* Lewalski has argued that the poem's theme and structure are ordered to display (through the three conventional temptations) a precise and progressive development and testing of the three functions of Christ's office—prophet, king, and priest. Many Protestants regarded Christ's baptism and temptation in the wilderness as his formal entry or initiation into his mediatorial office, and Milton incorporates this idea through two references in the poem's induction (1. 28, 189). Since these functions are assumed to continue forever in Christ's Church, Milton can permit reverberations of the future to be heard above the dramatic exchanges in the Christ-Satan encounter, and so can subsume within the temptation episode the entire course of Christ's life, the experience of his Church throughout Christian history, and even the anagogic fulfillment of these rules at the end of time. The poem also develops its theme through a pervasive typological perspective, by means of constant reference to Adam, Job, Moses, Elijah, David, Daniel, Judas Maccabeus, Hercules, Socrates, and many other recognized Old Testament (and even classical) types of Christ. Such typological references are made to function dramatically, in that Satan's constant temptation strategy is to invite Christ to accept inferior types of his redemptive action in place of those major Old Testament types whom he has seized upon as worthy models, or else to identify with these major types in their literal signification and thereby fail to fulfill them spiritually, as his mission demands. Christ must engage throughout with the difficult intellectual problem of how he ought to relate himself to history, how far the past is to provide a model for his actions, and wherein he must redefine its terms in order to become himself the model for the future. The typological allusions also

enhance the epic scope of the poem by projecting the episode of Christ's temptation against the panorama of history, with Christ becoming the summation, the compendium, the completion of all the earlier heroes. Through such use of typological reference and such projection into the future of Christ's office, this particular encounter between Christ and Satan is placed in the double perspective of the past and the future, as indeed the turning point between the past and the future: it is the center and epitome of all history.

As a test of the prophetic role, the first temptation sets in opposition truth and falsehood, using physical bread as metaphor. Christ identifies God's Word as his proper spiritual food (1.349–51) and declares of Satan, "lying is thy sustenance, thy food" (1.429). As founder of the new law, Christ associates himself on the basis of a common forty-day fast with two recognized types of his prophetic office—Moses and Elijah—while Satan in shepherd disguise offers Christ his own guidance, parodying Christ's role as Good Shepherd and making his own claim to oracular prophecy. Concluding this incident, Christ asserts unequivocally his claim to be the living oracle who will teach the final word of God, making all inferior prophecy cease. The motif of the prophetic role extends into Book 2, for the lavish banquet is in one dimension a diabolic parody of the heavenly manna and of the temperate repasts offered to Elijah. It is thus an invitation to Christ to identify himself literally with those prophetic types, Moses and Elijah, who were fed in the same desert by God: since God has not provided for Christ in the wilderness, the Devil will provide. In line with this, Satan's false claim that the banquet in no way violates the dietary provisions of the Law poses Christ the dilemma of whether in refusing it he would seem to subject himself (and his Church) to such ceremonies, but his authoritative affirmation of lordship over nature and Pauline "Christian Liberty" (2.379–84) asserts with new force his function as prophet of the New Testament, fulfilling and superseding the Law and the Prophets.

The banquet temptation also introduces the kingdoms sequence, which Satan undertakes in a new guise, "As one in City, or Court, or Palace bred" (1.300); that is, he now takes up his role as Prince of this world, condescending to a naive and inexperienced Christ. The banquet-wealth-glory sequence constitutes Milton's own special version and use of the Triple Equation: Christ overcomes here just those temptations which defeated Adam, and thereby displays that kingship over the self which Milton saw as the basis for any kind of public role or dominion. The banquet is an analogue of Eve's first temptation to carnal appetite and the parallel is further developed by the circumstance that some of the banquet foods are forbidden—unclean under the Law and forbidden to Christians insofar as the Devil's Table is always synonymous with idolatry. Eve's temptation to avarice and ambition has its parallel in Satan's effort to promote in Christ an inordinate desire for kingly dominion, with the offer of wealth as the only means to achieve it. And Eve's temptation to vainglory and pride in desiring to be "as Gods" is paralleled in Satan's offer of glory to Christ. In response to this offer Christ disparages the glory-seeking

world conquerors whom Satan has proposed to him as types—Alexander, Caesar, Scipio—affirming that glory "to God alone of right belongs" (3. 141). At the end of this sequence Christ names Socrates, the teacher of mankind and willing sufferer for truth's sake, as the noblest classical type of himself, identifying thereby the source of many of the ethical principles he has enunciated throughout this primarily ethical sequence. But he exalts Job even above Socrates as an exemplar of ethical wisdom and moral virtue.

By the statement, "But to a Kingdom thou art born, ordain'd / To sit upon thy Father *David's* Throne" (3.152–53), Satan shifts the terms of discourse from the kingdom within to the public realm, now challenging directly Christ's divinely ordained kingly role. In the first brief exchange Satan urges Christ to recapitulate the zeal and duty shown by his Old Testmanet type Judas Maccabaeus by taking up arms at once to seize his rightful kingdom, but Christ replies that zeal and duty consist first in waiting upon God's time. Presenting then a magnificent vision of Parthian armed might, Satan builds upon Christ's recognition of himself as heir to David's throne to suggest that Christ become literally a second David, seeking after David's physical kingdom, Israel, by David's means, armed might. Denouncing such means, Christ shows himself "*Israel's* true King," that is, the true, peaceful king of the new Israel, the invisible church. The Roman Empire next presented to him in glorious panorama is symbolically the great Antichrist—at once the Kingdom of this World and (as often in Protestant polemic and exegesis) the Roman Catholic church; it is thus a substitute kingdom—"all the world"—offered in place of Christ's own spiritual kingdom, and in renouncing it Christ refers to the metaphors of Daniel's tree and stone to indicate that his spiritual kingdom will at length conquer and subdue all worldly kingdoms whatsoever.

At this point, just when the reader is sure that Satan has exhausted all his skill in displaying Roman grandeur, Satan offers Athens to Christ in all of its fourth- and fifth-century glory as the compendium of classical learning. He equates this with wisdom, and presents it as precisely the nonmaterial good needed for Christ's accomplishment of all the lofty ideals and functions he has himself just defined—the kingly office of "ruling by persuasion," the prophetic role of teaching true wisdom, and the completion of the kingdom within the self. Christ's refusal of the offer identifies true wisdom as deriving only from above, and removes his church from any necessary reliance upon the world's wisdom.

In the final storm-tower sequence Christ endures with a patience surpassing that of Job the ultimate test of the kingdom within—violence and the threat of death. In addition, the false portents invoked to interpret the storm challenge Christ's prophetic role, and the prediction of difficulties to come for his kingdom threatens that function. But Milton especially contrived the storm-tower sequence to foreshadow and epitomize Christ's passion and death, the essence of his sacrificial priestly office, while at the same time, as has been noted, the tower episode functions as the ultimate identity test. Placing Christ upon the pinnacle of the tower where without miracle he cannot stand, Satan

supposes that he has allowed for all the possibilities: if Christ is a mere man he must fall from the spire; if he is divine he will save himself by a miracle; if he is uncertain he may cast himself down to test himself and God. But what happens is that Christ shows his divinity not by miraculous escape on Satan's terms but by calmly maintaining the impossible posture into which Satan has thrust him, imaging forth the passive endurance he will display at the Crucifixion. As he will then, Christ is now permitted to turn this very passion into a dramatic act of conquest over Satan, so that Satan "smitten with amazement" falls even as Christ receives and manifests full consciousness of his Divine Sonship.

Still other thematic and structural patterns have been discerned in the poem. Arthur Barker (in *Essays in English Literature from the Renaissance to the Victorian Age, Presented to A. S. P. Woodhouse*, ed. Millar McLure and F. W. Watt [1964]) has argued that the poem's structure does not depend upon balanced sequences of hierarchical temptations; indeed, that the temptations are hardly even of negative significance, so thoroughly confused is Satan about the Law, and even about pagan wisdom. He finds the essence of the poem to be its treatment of Christ's response to the true call sounded beneath the confused Satanic parodies of it, together with the treatment in each of the four books of some significant aspect of natural and supernatural renovation and of the resultant Christian liberty. Mason Tung (*Seventeenth Century News* 24 [1966]:58–59) discerns two interlocking patterns of temptation in the poem, involving the five main modes of temptation pointed to in the song of the Angelic choir (1.178–79): one pattern shows Satan attempting to "seduce," "allure," and "terrify" Jesus into revealing his mere humanity, and the other shows him endeavoring to "tempt" and "undermine" Christ into disclosing his divinity. These motives and methods are then related to the specific temptations. A structural division based upon the two fundamental biblical conceptions of sin—error, relating to the intellect (explored in the first two books), and rebellion, relating to the will (explored in the last two books), is advanced by Mother Mary Christopher Pecheux in *Calm of Mind: Tercentenary Essays on "Paradise Regained" and "Samson Agonistes,"* ed. J. A. Wittreich, Jr. [1971], pp. 49–65): she finds further that the themes of man's universal slavery to sin in both kinds, and Christ's total victory over both are emphasized in the tower scene and the concluding angelic hymn. A more formalistic structural study is that of Alexander H. Sackton (*University of Texas Studies in English* 33 [1954]: 33–45), which calls attention to elements of rhythmic repetition, balance, symmetry, and parallelism in Milton's poem, such as the three accounts of Christ's baptism presented from different perspectives, the variations on the theme of doubt and distrust throughout Book 1 and in the induction to Book 2, and the parallelism of the diabolical banquet and the angelic banquet.

The richness and the complexity of structure of *PR* are perhaps best seen in an overview. Basic of course is the tripartite structure provided by the three biblical temptations, in each of which Christ as private man withstands a characteristic human vice and exhibits its contrary virtue: in the first tempta-

tion, doubt and despair; in the second, the intemperance, avarice, and vainglory to which Adam and Eve succumbed; in the third, the fear and terror promoted by Satan's violence. Similarly, as public figure Christ in these three temptations learns about and is exercised in the three functions of his mediatorial Office and by that same token defeats Satan in the three aspects of *his* public role; the True Prophet overcomes the Father of Lies; the True King of the church and the world dethrones Satan, Prince of this World; the suffering Priest exposed in darkness and in air overthrows the Prince of Darkness and the Prince of the Air. In counterpoint to this, one may distinguish four rather than three basic structural components of the poem, since the private and public themes develop concomitantly in the first and third temptations but sequentially in the kingdoms temptation, with the shift to the concerns of the public office of kingship pointed by the words, "But to a Kingdom thou art born." Still another structural counterpoint within the kingdoms temptation is its organization according to the traditional tripartite scale of ethical goods— *voluptaria* (Belial's proposal of women and the banquet scene), *activa* (wealth, glory, kingship over Parthia and Rome), and *contemplativa* (classical learning and poetry)—as Howard Schultz notes in *Milton and Forbidden Knowledge* (pp. 224–27). Furthermore, the division into four books provides an additional counterpart, each book emphasizing its own thematic motif: Book 1 is wholly concerned with challenges to faith; Book 2 explores the motif of intemperance, either as related to bodily enjoyments or to external possessions and honors; Book 3 adumbrates the concepts of *time* and *force*, as related either to personal glory or to the public mediatorial kingdom; Book 4 presents a series of climaxes, each outdoing the last in scope and effect—Rome, Athens, and then the final victory and revelation on the tower. The tower scene shows Christ victorious in all three roles: as suffering Priest he sustains the violence of Satan, Sin and Death and overcomes all three; as True Prophet, Second Oedipus (as the epic simile suggests) he puts down the riddling tempter who would devour all mankind; as King he fulfills that aspect of his public kingly role which involves the destruction of Satan and all his works.

Stylistic commentary on *PR* has amounted chiefly to comparison, often invidious, between the dense, richly textured, evocative style of *PL* and the bare, unadorned, austere style of *PR*. As a concomitant of such comparison, critics often posit some falling off in Milton's poetic powers, or else apologize for his choice of an unfortunate subject for poetic treatment. These strictures have found restatement in W. W. Robson's article (*The Living Milton*, ed. Frank Kermode [1960]), which argues that the entire poem takes color from Christ's verbal style—strangely colorless and toneless, flat, laconic, terse, brusque, dry, and dull, though marked by gravity and formality. The result is an overall style that is inelastic and mannered, save where Satan's speeches evoke a broader range of feeling and deeper resonances.

The style, of course, has its defenders, who point out that its muted, chastened quality is entirely suited to its epic subject. David Daiches (*Milton*

[1957]) observes that Christ's simplicity of diction and quietly assured style contrasts with the almost parodic uses of grand rhetorical eloquence and ornament in Satan's speeches, especially in his presentation of Parthia and Rome. Martz (*ELH: A Journal of English Literary History* 27 [1960]) has identified the style as georgic—dignified, modest, somewhat latinate, reminding us of *PL* at a distance but deliberately muted; Martz calls attention also to the battle of rhetorical modes within the work, as this chastened style used by the narrator and the hero plays off against Satan's high oratorical style. Confirming these impressions, Ants Oras *(Blank Verse and Chronology in Milton)* has documented statistically Milton's use in *PR* of "a more austere style. Less orotund, less reverberant and ornamental, briefer in its rhythms, shorter in the words it used," reserving his earlier epic style of grandeur and magnificence only for special purposes—as in Book 3 when Satan attempts to convert Christ to worldliness through gorgeous pageants and magniloquent rhetoric. Donald L. Guss (*Studies in Philology* 68 [1971]) locates one source of *PR*'s modest style in Augustine's characterization of the style of the Bible as noble and grave, though not studiously ornamented, and Cassiodorus's description of it as "casta, fixa, verax," (chaste, piercing, truthful). Milton, Guss believes, undertook in this poem to imitate the style of Scripture through such devices as ellipses of verbs and subjects, use of parallelism and coordinate syntax, and epigrammatic texture created by sonorous short phrases, antithetical words, and verbal repetitions. A small dissenting voice to this general line of defense of the brief epic's style has been raised by Christopher Ricks (*Modern Language Notes* 76 [1961]: 701–4) who challenges the description of it as muted and chastened, pointing rather to several repetitions and weak periphrases suggestive of some flagging in Milton's usual taut stylistic control.

Detailed studies of various components of the style of *PR* have been undertaken in John Carey's introduction to *PR* in the Carey-Fowler edition of Milton's poems (1968), in several special articles, and also in *Milton's Brief Epic*, which argued that *PR* employs many of the same verbal, syntactical, and sound patterns characteristic of *PL*, although in lesser profusion and with a restraint dictated by the demands of the subject. For example, wordplay, evoking multiple meanings and resonances, is a prominent feature of the style of *PR* (even as of *PL*) and it is equally characteristic of Satan, the narrator, Christ, and the Father. Among the most common kinds are etymological metaphors, which call forth an older and more vividly pictorial sense of a word along with a modern sense (e.g., Satan described as being "Nigh Thunderstruck" by God's voice); puns, which also are often based upon etymology (Satan's description of Christ in the wilderness as "deserted"); and verbal reflections or echoes, often ironic, as in Satan's sardonic use of the term *rudiments* in reference to Christ's supposed rusticity, harking back to the Father's observation that the temptation will exercise Christ in the "rudiments" (first principles) of his great warfare against Satan, Sin, and Death. Satan's particular interest in ambiguity is man-

ifested throughout the poem in his questioning of and laying claim to the title Son of God.

Several studies have explored imagery and image patterns in the poem. Lee S. Cox (*ELH: A Journal of English Literary History* 28 [1961]: 225–43) has discussed in detail one such pattern, opposing Christ the Living Bread, the true food from heaven offering life, to Satan the false food, whose sustenance is lies; this pattern also opposes physical food supporting the life of the senses to the spiritual food that is God's Word. Identifying another significant range of imagery, Cooper R. Mackin (*Explorations of Literature*, ed. Rima D. Reck [1966]) argues that *PR*'s aural imagery—the harpies' wings, the vocality of Satan, the tempest—functions as a metaphor for the ultimate meaning of Satan's temptations as a disruption of harmony. *Milton's Brief Epic* calls attention to several other patterns: Christ as rock opposing Satan as Spirit of the Air; a pervasive light-darkness pattern identifying Christ as source of light in conflict with Satan as the power of darkness; and extensive martial imagery establishing the submerged metaphor of the temptation as a duel or single combat between the hero and his antagonist. Carey has discussed another feature of the imagery, the interesting permutations from remoteness and abstraction to concreteness in the descriptions of landscape and scene; he notes that the pageants of the banquet, the Parthian army, Rome, and Athens grow successively more specific, actual, and concrete, so that Athens, though least gorgeous, is most fully visualized. Carey calls attention also to specific Miltonic devices for creating remoteness—the concessiveness of the description of the banquet in which the repetitions "or . . . or" permit us to make up our minds rather than forming a defined image of what we have seen, and the total inclusiveness of phrases such as "All Fish from Sea or Shore," which promotes the generality of the generic. He notes also the interpenetration of desert and forest scenes, arising from Milton's attempt to amalgamate the allegorical "woody maze" and the bare, rocky desert—which later grows green as Christ seems in some measure to raise Eden "in the waste wilderness."

Poetic figures as such are not present in great abundance in the poem, though it is interesting to remark, as Carey has, that simple similes increase steadily in number as the poem proceeds. Christ's comparison of Satan to "a fawning parasite" is the only example in the first book, Books 2 and 3 have scarcely more, whereas in Book 4 there are many: Christ's comment on the pedants, "collecting toys, . . . / As Children gathering pibles on the shore" (328–30); his scornful characterization of an ornamented style when the matter is false, "swelling Epithetes thick laid / As varnish on a Harlots cheek" (343–44); the description of Satan's fall from heaven "like an Autumnal Star / Or Lightning" (619–20), and several others. There are several epic catalogues in *PR* as well—briefer than those in *PL* but achieving the same exaltation of language by massing together evocative and sonorous names: the catalogue of the places where the disciples sought Christ after his baptism; of the classical nymphs

seduced by Belial and the classical gods he impersonated in doing so; of the nymphs and knights attendant at the Satanic banquet; of the various ancient kingdoms subsumed in the Parthian empire; of the places from which the Parthian horsemen came; and of the places near and far now tributary to the Roman Empire.

The epic similes of the poem have also received some critical attention. Kingsley Widmer (*ELH: A Journal of English Literary History* 25 [1958]: 258–69) has argued that the similes in this poem as in *PL* function to point up the incommensurability of Christian and classical views of heroism and evil, that they generally compare "small things with greatest," and that they work together to suggest a "fascinating and shocking master simile," the world as evil and virtue as renunciation. *Milton's Brief Epic* notes that five of the six epic similes in *PR* occur in the last book and hence help to heighten the style of the poem as it rises to epic climax; moreover, this classical epic device helps develop the theme of the higher heroism, being wholly restricted to descriptions of Satan or of the Satanic values. The five similes in Book 4 all characterize Satan in defeat: three of them make up a finely graded sequence of comparisons for Satan's now compulsive temptation behavior, first a human analogue, then one in the animal kingdom, and finally one in inanimate nature, thereby imaging in the sequence itself Satan's steady disintegration and loss of control (4. 10–21). The two longer epic similes compare Satan's defeat by Christ to Antaeus's defeat by Hercules and to the Sphinx's destruction by Oedipus (4. 563–76).

Turning to syntactical and sound patterns as an aspect of style, we observe that these elements are less spectacular in the brief epic, yet produce a highly effective tenseness and terseness. The sentence length is decidedly abbreviated: the average in *PR* is seven lines, as Carey points out, with only two examples extending to 25 lines or over, a common enough unit in *PL*. Brevity of sense unit and laconic expression frequently characterize Christ's retorts: "Who brought me hither / Will bring me hence, no other Guide I seek" (1. 335–36); "Mee worse than wet thou find'st not" (4. 486). Monosyllabic lines, rare in *PL*, are relatively plentiful here, used for instance for Christ's parries but also in Satan's appeal for Christ's compassion (3.204–24). *Milton's Brief Epic* defends the decorum of such syntactical devices as follows: Christ uses the terse, pointed sentences to image the precision and rigor of his mind, and the narrator as redeemed man properly models his style upon Christ's. Satan also endeavors much of the time to imitate Christ's own reasonable, precise mode of speech so that his proposals will sound like the objectification of Christ's own thoughts, the discourse of his alter ego. Satan can of course use the long period for special effects, as when he presents the entire panorama of Athens as a single sentence of 48 lines.

PR also makes significant use of the fluid or liquid syntax that Christopher Ricks has found to be so characteristic of *PL*—constructions that introduce subtle nuances and ambiguities of meaning by admitting of more than one reading, as when verbs and adjectives connect with more than one object or

noun. For example, the description of famous world conquerors as "Rowling in brutish vices, and deform'd, / Violent or shameful death thir due reward" (3. 86–87) permits "deform'd" to adhere to "vices," suggesting perversion, and also to "death," suggesting physical misshapenness. A similar technique utilizes the slight hesitation of the voice at the end of the poetic line to convey a fleeting suggestion of a meaning other than that indicated by the completed syntactical unit. This device produces an ironic overtone in Satan's observation that the demons now "Must bide the stroak of that long threatn'd wound, / At least if so we can, and by the head / Broken be not intended all our power / To be infring'd" (1. 59–62). The slight hesitation after "power" invites first the reading that the metaphorical wound means destruction of all the devils' power but then Satan adds the verb "infring'd" to control "power," thereby blurring his momentarily accurate perception of his desperate situation. This device also reinforces the metaphor of John the Baptist as a herald with trumpet opening the lists between Satan and Christ: "Now had the great Proclaimer with a voice / More awful than the sound of Trumpet, cried / "Repentance" (1. 18–20); the brief withholding of the word *Repentance* by the line-ending enables the jousting metaphor to create its effect before we are brought to concentrate on the literal story.

Certain other syntactical devices, which create a sense of balance and stasis in the poem appropriate to the cerebral combat and the immobility of the hero, are enumerated by Carey. One such is the use of participles rather than other parts of the verb—often past participles that freeze action into posture, for example, "on him baptiz'd" (1. 20), "by the head / Broken" (1. 60–61), "whom he suspected rais'd" (1. 124); "Or torn up sheer" (4. 419), "With sound of Harpies' wings and Talons heard" (2. 403). This device often defines characters by reference to their more stable past conditions rather than to their present uncertain roles, for example, "King of *Israel* born" (1. 254), "the new-baptiz'd" (2. 1). The present participle is often used to reduce the swift or sudden to the continuous or gradual, for example, "on him rising / Out of water" (1. 80–81), "the Spirit leading" (1. 189), "Appearing, and beginning noble deeds" (4. 99), "men divinely taught, and better teaching" (4. 357). Another device establishing balance and stasis by suggesting leisure and expansiveness as opposed to brisk action is the almost pleonastic pairing of adjectives, nouns, and verbs: "defeated and repuls't," "agast and sad," "path or road," "obscure, / Unmarkt, unknown," "Unhumbl'd, unrepentant, unreform'd" "Cottage, Herd or Sheep-cote" (1. 6, 43, 322, 24–25; 3. 429; 2. 288).

Finally, both Carey's introduction and *Milton's Brief Epic* discuss the poem's important use of rhetorical schemes, especially iterative schemes—figures that derive their force from both sound repetition and word order, and that affect both sound and sense. Through structural balance and sound repetitions they elevate and stiffen the language, providing the impression of a patterned verbal duel analogous to a single combat. It is noteworthy that Satan's speeches are no more marked by such rhetorical figures than Christ's or the narrator's. *Ploce*

(repetition of the same word with some few words interspersed) is the most common figure and *traductio* (repetition of the same root work in various grammatical forms) comes next: both are habitual weapons in the Christ/Satan exhanges (e.g., 3. 44–120), where Christ picking up Satan's five uses of "glory" and "inglorious" in the previous speech, replies with "glory" or "glorious" eleven times, and Satan follows with "glory" or "glorious" eight times. Other constantly used figures are terminal or medial rhyme (true and slant), antithesis, *anaphora* (repetition of the same word or words at the beginning of successive poetic lines), *epizeuxis* (repetition of the same word immediately, with no intermission), and *epanalepsis* (repetition of the same word or words at the beginning and end of a line of verse).

Interestingly enough, however, these devices of sound patterning also contribute to the impression of spontaneous speech, a progressive and dramatic working out of meanings and understandings as Christ and Satan talk. More paradoxical still, those speeches which most critics have singled out as containing the greatest measure of emotional realism are among those contrived with the greatest rhetorical art, for example, Satan's despairing description of his own condition (3. 204–24). One of Milton's most remarkable achievements in the poem is precisely this, the creation of a patterned language that suggests a stylized verbal duel, but that is in no way antithetical to psychological realism or dramatic intensity.

Students of *PR* have also addressed a variety of special topics, too numerous to discuss here. The reader should consult Schultz's essay (*ELH: A Journal of English Literary History* 32 [1965]: 275–302) for an excellent survey and evaluation of scholarship on the poem. The following remarks focus upon topics of particular significance, either because they have attracted extensive critical comment or because they mark out important new directions in criticism.

The most puzzling, distressing, and for that reason most frequently discussed single episode in *PR* is the so-called learning temptation, in which Satan offers Athens to Christ as a kingdom embodying precisely that nonmaterial good—classical learning—which seems best suited to his nature and requisite for his office of teaching and ruling by persuasion. The difficulty is that Christ renounces so categorically all the realms of knowledge, sometimes in a tone of matter-of-fact analysis, often in a tone of harsh denunciation. Classical philosophy is "false, or little else but dreams / Conjectures, fancies, built on nothing firm" (4. 291–92); the classical poets are greatly inferior to the Hebrew poets since they sing "The vices of thir Deities, and thir own," and are, once one removes their "swelling Epithetes," found to be "Thin sown with aught of profit or delight" (4. 340–45); the classical orators are far below the Hebrew prophets in teaching "The solid rules of Civil Government" (4. 358). Such language has provoked some critics to rage against Christ's harsh repudiations, and others to condescending pity for what they take to be Milton's subconscious tensions about his earlier love of learning. R. M. Adams (*Ikon: John Milton and the Modern Critics* [1955]) sees in Christ's speech only a "provincial

contempt of the classics," and "a feeling for the Christian dispensation as not only supplementing but cancelling pagan reason." W. B. C. Watkins (*An Anatomy of Milton's Verse* [1955]) declares that Milton here "negates learning like an Alexandrian bonfire: and "rips to shreds the passion of fifty years." Douglas Bush (*The Renaissance and English Humanism* [1939]) finds it painful "to watch Milton turn and rend some main roots of his being." George Sensabaugh (*Studies in Philology* 43 [1946]:258–72) explains these "strange pronouncements" as stemming from a "deep Disillusion." And E. M. W. Tillyard (*Milton*) senses in the passage a mood of "mortification or masochism" in which Milton "goes out of his way to hurt the dearest and oldest inhabitants of his mind: the Greek philosophers—his early love Plato included—the disinterested thirst for knowledge, the poets and orators of Greece and Rome."

Defenses of the learning temptation and efforts to clarify Milton's intentions in it have been mounted from several bases. For one thing, several critics have observed that the offer of Greek learning is tainted by the terms in which Satan conceives and presents it. Irene Samuel has observed (*Publications of the Modern Language Association* 64 [1949]: 708–23; *Plato and Milton*, pp. 122–29) that Satan reveals himself in this temptation as an arch-sophist, offering Jesus universal knowledge as a means to universal power ("As the Empire must extend, / So let extend thy mind o'er all the world," 4. 222–23), and as an infallible weapon for universal persuasion. The claim that "Error by his own arms is best evinc't" (4. 235) is also sophistical; both Socrates and Jesus believe that only truth can conquer falsehood. Further, *Milton's Brief Epic* argues that by the terms of his offer Satan makes wisdom a wholly mundane thing, so that Athens, like Rome, becomes a compendium of the earlier worldly enticements—though highly refined. Here the ambition proposed is not for simple dominion over Athens but for such association with its intellectual richness as will lead to domination of the mind "o'er all the world'; the glory offered is the opportunity to "Be famous . . . / By Wisdom" (4. 221–22); and replacing the grove containing the Epicurean banquet is the "Olive Grove of *Academe*" (4. 244), filled with sensory delights directed to a much more judicious taste. Continuing this line of argument Phillip McCaffrey (*Milton Quarterly* 5 [1971]: 7–13) observes that Satan sees in Athens only another mode of power and fame, that he shows no appreciation of Athens' strictly intellectual and artistic accomplishments for their own sake—praising Plato chiefly for the attractiveness of his "retirement"; Aristotle as the "breeder" of world conquerors; Socrates for his great influence on later schools; Homer for the envy Apollo (really a devil) showed for his poem; Demosthenes for his ability to promote war. Satan thus does not offer learning, much less wisdom to Christ, having little appreciation himself for the best Athens can offer even in strictly humanistic terms.

Recognition of Satan's perversity does not, however, account fully for the completeness and vehemence of Christ's rejection of learning, and several other justifications of the episode have been developed in relation to various specific conceptions of the poem's hero and theme. In Samuel's reading the temptation

is addressed to Jesus as exemplar hero and model for every Christian, so that Jesus' reply is not to be explained by reference to his divine nature or his special role; rather, it only reaffirms Milton's consistent understanding of wisdom as deriving from Plato and Socrates, and modified by the Christian faith. The principles Jesus affirms are, Samuel asserts, the "adequacy of the human spirit, with or without particular books in the quest of all knowledge essential to the good life"; the denial of independent value either to learning as such or to any particular branch of it, save as it is used to help achieve the good life; the idea that learning is simply a tool for purging the sight whereas wisdom, the vision of truth, comes finally through faith that unites the spirit with its Maker. This last is a conversion of Plato's precept that when reason beholds the Good, every part of the soul finds its appropriate satisfaction. Arnold Stein is in essential agreement with this reading, but he focuses upon the dramatic acting out of this definition by Christ, who in the temptation itself is manifesting that useful knowledge and that inspiration and illumination of the "spirit and judgment" by which alone we may know the truth about God and man.

A radically different approach is that of Howard Schultz (*Milton and Forbidden Knowledge* [1955]), which resolves the problem of accounting for Jesus' harsh rejection of learning by denying the relevance or application of such rejection to the Christian everyman, referring it strictly to an ecclesiastical context in which Christ as head of the church enunciates counsels of perfection meant only "for the church and its ministers." In this interpretation, Christ's repudiation of learning means simply that he and the ministers of his church have no need of human learning to perform the offices of teaching and ruling the church, and the learning temptation is a precise analogue to the argument concerning the education of ministers outlined in Milton's antitithe tract, *Hire*.

The reading of this episode advanced in *Milton's Brief Epic* takes Jesus to be a dramatic character rather than an exemplary or allegorical model either for the Christian Everyman or for the Christian minister, and argues that the dramatic terms of Satan's offer precludes limitation of its reference either to the private moral realm or to that of Christ's kingdom, the Church. Satan indeed proposes classical learning as necessary to the accomplishment of Christ's kingly office of "ruling by persuasion," and to his prophetic (teaching) office of refuting the gentiles' "Idolisms, Traditions, Paradoxes." But he also offers it as requisite to achieve the wisdom appropriate to the life of contemplation for which Christ showed an early propensity, as well as the kingdom "Which every wise and vertuous man attains" with the self—"These rules will render thee a King compleat / Within thyself" (4. 283–84). What Satan is doing is offering Christ his own version of wisdom, which is knowledge of all things "in the world" and knowledge relating to moral virtue (ethics). This is a much too limited definition of wisdom even for the Stoics and Plato, and it is entirely foreign to Christians in the Augustinian tradition who, following Augustine, called the first sort of knowledge *scientia* rather than *sapientia*, labeled the second sort *prudentia* or else a variety of *scientia*, and held that true wisdom, *sapientia*,

comes only from above. Augustine's exegesis of Job 28:28, "Behold, piety, that is wisdom; but to depart from evil is knowledge," provided a basis for such distinctions by defending wisdom as discourse about divine things and knowledge as human ethical teaching. Augustinian Christians such as Filelfo, Nicholas of Lyra, John Colet, and a long line of commentators on the Book of Job enumerated the errors of the classical schools and contrasted Greek ethical knowledge with Job's wisdom in terms closely resembling Christ's language in *PR;* a particularly close analogue to the Miltonic passage has been traced by Edna Newmeyer (*Bulletin of the New York Public Library* 66 [1962]:485–98) to Theodore Beza's *Job Expounded.*

Dramatically, then, the episode develops in these terms: at the conclusion of the banquet-wealth-glory sequence Christ has appealed to both Socrates and Job as teachers and exemplars of the highest moral and ethical knowledge, proclaiming Job as the more nearly perfect. Later, in the learning temptation, Satan, using his accustomed strategy, invites Christ to identify himself with the lesser type, Socrates, and changes the terms of the discourse so as to equate the moral knowledge *(scientia)* for which Christ had earlier honored Socrates, with true wisdom from above *(sapientia),* which alone can achieve the life of contemplation, the perfection of the kingdom within, and the realization of the prophetic and kingly offices. In answer, Christ disparages as lacking in wisdom the same classical philosophers whose ethical knowledge he had before praised, associating himself rather with the more adequate Jobean conception of wisdom. He seems to allude also to that special status of which he himself is not yet fully aware—his own role as the true oracle, image of the Father's wisdom, unique recipient and exponent of the "Light from above, from the fountain of light" (4. 289).

With a fine sensitivity to dramatic nuance and interplay Balachandra Rajan (in *The Lofty Rhyme* [1970]) has provided a defense of the learning temptation in terms of Christ's emerging perception of his particular redemptive role in history. He sees the learning temptation as developing strictly out of the logic of combat rather than out of Milton's psyche, so that Satan at this point in the interchange cleverly offers Christ what heretofore he had seemed to be talking about, a kingdom not of this world. Christ refuses the offer, not in his capacity as perfect man but as the historic Christ whose destiny it is to bring down into history a power of grace beyond the light of nature. As Christ observes, in accents of compassion rather than scorn, the light of nature cannot show the truth about man's creation, Fall, and redemption by grace, and thus the philosophers must remain "Ignorant of themselves, of God much more" (4. 310) despite their pursuit of self-knowledge. The reader, also knowing these things, is expected to understand that Christ, who is to bring the higher wisdom into history and redeem nature by grace, cannot accept the lower knowledge as a substitute.

Another topic of particular interest to critics is the special significance of historical time in *Paradise Regained.* In *ELH:A Journal of English Literary*

History 26 (1959):297–513 Jackson I. Cope contrasts the dominant spatial orientation of *PL* with the flat, dimensionless world of *PR*. In his view the spatial visions of the kingdoms in the latter poem turn into evocations of history: space becomes time. He does not, however, conclude from this that the hero acts dramatically in the particular historical circumstances, but rather concludes that there is no real temptation in *PR*, only the "exfoliation of the eternally given into time." This last perception is pressed further in Cope's article (*Milton Studies* 1 [1969]:51–65), which argues that the time emphasized in the poem is ritual time, giving us no sense of drama but rather of a prediction fulfilling itself, a story that remembers its end in its beginning, an action that is in no place or time because in every place and time. By contrast, Laurie Zwicky (*ELH: A Journal of English Literary History* 31 [1964]:217–77) finds that the motif of the appointed time operates to heighten dramatic tension in the poem as the Christian sense of *kairos*, the divinely appointed moment of special revelation or action, plays off against Satan's concept of eternally recurrent cycles. Jesus' knowledge of the time prefixed is incomplete, yet he patiently waits upon it, whereas all Satan's temptations urge Christ to "seize the day" and act before his time. From a somewhat similar perspective Lewalski's article (in *The Prison and the Pinnacle*, ed. Balachandra Rajan [1973]) argues that the juxtaposition and confrontation of various perspectives—the Father's, Satan's, Christ's—on time and history is a dominant structural element in the poem and a source of its dramatic tension. Satan's cyclical concept of time and his fixed historical categories render him unable to conceive of anything he has not seen before: hence his insistence that Christ must repeat one or more of the historical patterns Satan proposes to him. Christ, however, with his stance of openness to divine revelation, can perceive and accommodate new departures, and so makes re-creation possible—new men, new lives, a new kingdom. As Christ works out his philosophy of history, what has been is the appropriate starting point but not the fixed definition of what will be. The historical process is seen to be linear, not cyclical, its course shaped by Divine Providence and human will. And Christian typology is shown to involve patterned repetitions that can at the same time accommodate progress, redefinition, and re-creation.

Finally, some efforts to treat *PR* in terms of affective criticism may be noted. One such study, a long chapter in Jon S. Lawry's *The Shadow of Heaven: Matter and Stance in Milton's Poetry* (1968), identifies two opposed stances in the poem: one at Jordan of annunciation and promise, where the persons of the drama gather to witness a seeming union of God and man; and the second in the sterile desert, where that promise is apparently lost but actually realized. Lowry finds that the reader's stance is established at Jordan with the chorus of Christ's followers who watch and wait, so that the reader participates in their discovery and enactment of patience. In relation to the desert stance, the reader shares the largely solitary, internal pressure of the dialectic, and must acknowledge his taste for "fallen" literary and intellectual heroics like those of Satan. The tower revelation shifts the stance to annunciation again, relieving the audience for its long patience at the edge of Jordan and permitting it to

experience in some degree the exaltation the Son now enjoys and the paradise he has regained. Analyzing reader response in rather different terms, Lawrence A. Hyman (*Publications of the Modern Language Association* 85 [1970]:496–508) argues that Milton, as a means of building dramatic interest and tension, deliberately evokes and uses the inevitable disagreement and lack of sympathy fallen readers must feel toward Christ. His point is that "the contrast between our feelings, our human desires for the glories of this world, and the rejection of these desires by Christ is the emotional center of the poem," leading us to apprehend imaginatively the terrible price that must be paid by Christ to accomplish his (and our) victory.

Also focusing sharply upon reader response but arguing that the poem works finally upon the reader in more positive ways, Stanley Fish (*Calm of Mind,* ed. Wittreich, pp. 25–47) invokes terms somewhat analogous to those he employed for *PL* in *Surprised by Sin.* Fish defines two basic patterns in *PR*—a dramatic pattern in which the sphere of activity of the hero is progressively narrowed until his will is wholly subsumed in God's, and a verbal pattern in which the complexity and volubility of language is progressively diminished in the hero until his individual voice is heard no more. Both of these movements reach their respective climaxes of inaction and silence on the tower. These two patterns generate in the reader expectation, disappointment, and perplexity, frustrating again and again his mounting desire for some kind of activity of at least full explanation on the hero's part. However, if the reader can learn to subordinate his own will to the terms of the poem in a manner analogous to the hero's subordination of all assertive action and self-expression to his obedience to God, the reader can be led from impatience and frustration to understanding and approval of the Son's stance and of the poem's values.

Though *PR* has received much less critical attention than *PL,* the dimensions uncovered by those who have studied the work are already sufficient to support Coleridge's tribute to its consummate art when he described the poem as "in its kind . . . the most perfect poem extant." The perfection is not merely formal: perhaps the greatest distinction of *PR* is the large measure of success it achieves in incorporating, evaluating, and ordering the complex of classical-Judeo-Christian values, which constitute the heritage of Western man. The particular ordering vision, like all human things, is partial. But the poem's dramatic situation—Christ's search in the wilderness to comprehend his nature and discover his mission; his subsumption of the past but rejection of its dead literalisms; his abjuration of the many evil or ignoble or imperfect or less perfect modes of action, which would preclude attainment of the highest concept of personal excellence and mission—presents a myth of human striving toward ideals of comprehension and order, of wisdom and noble action, that must remain relevant and powerful as long as such ideals hold any meaning whatever for us. [BKL]

PASSION, THE. A fifty-six line fragment, *Passion* appeared in both the 1645 and 1673 editions of Milton's poems. In its opening lines, Milton alludes to *Nat,*

which he had written in December 1629. Possibly he planned to write a series of poems around the major feast days of the Christian calendar, and his success with the ode encouraged him to compose *Passion* the following March. A note that he appended to it tells us, however, that he found the subject "to be above the yeers he had, when he wrote it, and nothing satisfi'd with what was begun, left it unfinisht."

Milton's lack of satisfaction with his work was justified. His failure was not due to lack of technical proficiency, for the stanzaic form he used was the same one that he had successfully employed in the proem of *Nat*—six lines of iambic pentameter plus an Alexandrine, with a rhyme scheme of ababbcc. Utilizing this form, he created competent verse despite some minor imperfections, for example, employing the same rhyme sounds in the concluding couplets of his first, second, and fifth stanzas. His real failure lies at a deeper level: the stanzas, quite simply, do not go anywhere.

They tell us what he has been writing *(Nat)*, what he has been reading (the *Christiad* of the Italian poet Vida), and what he intends to write (an elegy on Christ's death in contrast to Vida's epic treatment of his life). They do not in any sense fulfill that intention. Neither an appeal to "night best Patroness of grief" nor a journey in Ezekiel's chariot to "where the Towers of *Salem* stood" enables the poet to come to terms with his proposed subject. Extravagant descriptions of his grief suffice only to carry him through two more stanzas before he breaks off, temperamentally incapable perhaps of writing on Christ's Passion. Indeed, the extant stanzas constitute only a proem to a poem, whose envisioned form we can not guess.

Temperamental incapacity at least is the explanation of James Holly Hanford for the poem's failure: "The truth is that the crucifixion was not a congenial theme to him at any time. Even this early he seems to have felt instinctively that man's salvation depends upon himself and that he needs Christ as a guide and model perhaps more than as a redeemer" (*A Milton Handbook*, 5th ed., p. 115). More moderate is William Riley Parker's view that the young Milton "lacked the experience of life to make a poem upon so tragic and triumphant a theme" (*Milton*, p. 72). However one explains it, the poem is a failure, though not perhaps without its significance. From it, Milton may well have realized the danger of overextending himself in tackling subjects for which he was not yet emotionally and artistically ready. [ERG]

PSALMS, MILTON'S TRANSLATIONS FROM THE. For the compositions of the nineteen psalms translated or paraphrased by Milton, we have very clear dating. The paraphrases of Psalms 114 and 136 were printed in *Poems* of 1645 with the note that they were "don by the Author at fifteen years old," that is, in the year before Milton went up to Cambridge. The Greek version of Psalm 114, also printed in the 1645 volume, is almost certainly the poem in Greek hexameters enclosed in Milton's letter of December 4, 1634, to Alexander Gill the younger. The version of Psalms 80–88 printed in *Poems*, 1673, is

dated April 1648; and Psalms 1–8 are dated 1653, with all but Psalm 1 given specific dates from August 8 to August 14. All of these later psalms were apparently first printed in 1673, though Bishop Henry King's translation of the Psalms in 1651 has parallels with the italicized (added) words and phrases of Milton's 1648 psalms, which suggests that Milton's psalms received some kind of circulation, perhaps in broadside, at about the time of composition. Milton's note for these psalms—"wherein all but what is in a different Character, are the very words of the Text, translated from the Original"—emphasizes a literalness of his translation perhaps for some particular reason. Yet they are not really literal translations from the Hebrew, but rather, like other Puritan psalters, amplifications of the texts. The choice of a group of psalms including 82 may suggest a political application. Its verse 6, or the first half of it, was a popular text for those arguing the divine right of kings: "I have said ye are gods." It was the text for Henry King's sermon in 1640 on the anniversary of the coronation of Charles I and was quoted in "The King" in Thomas Fuller's *Holy State*. Milton had some reason in April of 1648 to point out that verse 7 reads "But ye shall die like men, and fall like one of the princes," since the debate about whether or not a king could be brought to trial was then going on. Indeed, until the Army decided to face the combination of the defeated Royalists and the Presbyterians who were negotiating with Charles for the setting up of Presbyterian church government in England, Milton was in some personal danger, which may have given particular fervor to the translation of David's pleas for help when surrounded by enemies. If these psalms were intended to serve in some way in a propaganda war, it was important that they be noted as strictly literal translation from the Hebrew.

Translation literally from the Hebrew was complicated, since the Masoretic text of the Old Testament presented problems in identification of individual words and in correct separation of words and sentences; therefore Milton was involved in textual criticism like that applied to the classics. A chief source of light on textual matters was the Greek Septuagint, based on a lost Hebrew text antedating the Masoretic text. In addition, what we know of Milton's teaching Edward Phillips and others "Hebrew, Chaldee, and Syriac" makes it clear that Milton took the textual problems seriously, the discovery of a Syriac text, first printed in 1553, being attended by much the same sort of interest that has developed in our day around the Dead Sea scrolls. Perhaps for some of his translations, perhaps for all of them, Milton consulted the Hebrew, Aramaic, and Syriac versions, a Latin Bible, probably that of Tremellius, who had been Regius Professor of Hebrew at Cambridge, though he may also have considered the Clementine (Roman Catholic) Bible, and certainly several standard English prose versions. Among the prose versions of the Psalms, he would be most familiar with that of the Authorized Version of 1611 and the earlier version found in the Prayer Book. During his time as a student he would have attended daily services in which he would have read all the Psalms through monthly in this latter version. He also had seen many of the metrical versions in English

and would be familiar with the versions commonly sung, particularly *The Whole Book of Psalmes*, commonly called Sternhold and Hopkins, as well as the little volume of 1632 called *All the French Psalm Tunes with English Words* and George Sandys's *Paraphrase Upon the Psalmes of David*, which was set to music by Henry Lawes in 1638. He displays an indebtedness to George Buchanan's Latin paraphrase of the Psalms in one of his earliest compositions, line 65 of Psalm 136 (line 51 as the Psalm is printed in *CM*) being a literal translation of Buchanan's *Quique Amorrhœis Seon regnavit in oris* for Psalm 135:11, as David Masson pointed out. There are also phrases in Milton's later translations that seem to be derived from Buchanan.

During the sixteenth and seventeenth centuries the translation of the Psalms or of selected psalms into meter occupied the energies of a number of English writers. Poets like Wyatt, Sidney and his sister, or Sandys approached the Psalms much as Gawin Douglas and Surrey approached the *Aeneid:* as great matter that called forth the best artistry they had. Others aimed at little more than reducing the words of the accepted prose translation like Coverdale's Bible or the Authorized Version to rhymed fourteeners or ballad stanzas suitable for congregational singing, no matter what the wrenching of syntax the enterprise involved. Almost innumerable editions of Sternhold and Hopkins were bound with the Bible or with the Prayer Book. This version continued as the standard for English churches until it was superseded in 1696 by the version of Tate and Brady. The simple tunes to which these psalms were adapted were arranged for four parts as early as 1563 and were elaborated in the late sixteenth and early seventeenth century by such musicians as Campion, Dowland, and Milton's father. Although misconceptions of the Puritan and Presbyterian position on church music are still current, the contemporary evidence indicates that the severest of churchgoers criticized musical settings of the Psalms only if the music overpowered and interfered with the understanding of the psalm itself. For such critics obviously the best metrical translation would be that which presented the accepted meaning without variation or addition, in a form called metaphrase. There are a number of versions that are very close to the words of the Prayer Book or of the 1611 Bible, though problems of rhyme and scansion and occasionally of doctrinal emphasis may produce variations.

The versions called paraphrases are usually much freer than those called translations or metaphrases, with a good deal of amplification of figurative language. Some of the poems of this period called paraphrases of a psalm are really original poems suggested by some part of a psalm. *PL* 7.565–68 directly reflects part of Psalm 24. Even when the paraphrases stay within the range allowed free translation, they are often experimental in metrical pattern and elaborate in diction and figurative language. Milton's paraphrases of Psalm 114 and Psalm 136 show him trying his hand on the styles popular in his youth. When in 1653 Milton translated Psalms 1–8 he used eight different metrical forms almost as if he were exercising to work off some stiffness induced by his enforced concentration on his prose. Particularly noticeable in these psalms is

his varying the caesura in the lines and producing "the sense variously drawn out from one verse into another," so that even short lines are tied into verse paragraphs or long periodic sentences.

Milton may have been drawn to translating the psalms at this time when he had leisure for his own affairs after being relieved of some of his official duties because of his blindness, which was now complete. Accounts of Milton's habits of study at this period mention his beginning the day early with some reading from the Psalms, which he had always, apparently, preferred to all other poetry, as he tells us in various passages in prose or in verse like the following:

> Yet not the more
> Cease I to wander where the Muses haunt
> Cleer Spring, or shadie Grove, or Sunnie Hill,
> Smit with the love of sacred Song; but chief
> Thee *Sion* and the flowrie Brooks beneath
> That wash thy hallowd feet, and warbling flow,
> Nightly I visit:
> (*PL* 3:26–32; cf. *PL* 1.6–10 and *PR* 4.331–50)

In general, Milton's method of translation seems to parallel Dryden's method with Virgil, which often produced a mosaic of phrases from previous translations. For the psalms of 1653, however, Milton's method involved having to work from hearing and recall only.

Ps 1 (month and day of 1653 not given). The verse is rhymed iambic pentameter couplet with the sense run on from line to line and the position of the caesura varied. This couplet was already the preferred form for translating poets like Ovid and Virgil. It is the meter that Sidney used for this psalm.

Ps 2 (August 8). The verse is *terza rima,* the verse form of Dante's *Divine Comedy.* Sidney had used this form in Psalm 7, and other translators of psalms had used it, usually with end-stopped lines and with the end of a stanza coinciding with the end of the sentence. Milton treats the form arbitrarily, sometimes using the end of a line to separate a subject and verb or substantive and modifier. At the end of verse 2 in this psalm occurs the word that can be transliterated *Messiah* or translated *Christ* or *the anointed.* Milton chose *Messiah,* although both the Prayer Book and the Authorized Version read *anointed,* perhaps because of the special meaning given by the Royalists to "the Lord's anointed." For a connection between Milton's study of the Psalms and *PL,* compare this psalm with *PL* 2.326–28; 5.602–8; 6.703–18, 886–87.

Ps 3 (August 9). The stanza in six iambic lines of varied length rhyming aabccb is an experimental lyric form similar to many invented in this period. In this poem Milton arranged to have the end of his sentences coincide with the end of the stanza, except for line 15, where the end of the sentence creates a striking

caesura. It has been suggested that in these translations Milton usually prefers a general word to a specific one; but in line 7, where Milton has a choice between the Prayer Book "my defender" and the Authorized Version "a shield for me," he chooses the latter.

Ps 4 (August 10). The stanza of five iambic trimeter lines and one pentameter rhyming abbacc seems to be experimental. It may be characteristic of Milton that at lines 23 and 24 he adds the idea of justice to the phrase "the sacrifice of righteousness," but he could have found *iustitiæ* as the word for righteousness in the Latin texts and some similar expansion in Buchanan's paraphrase and in Sidney's translation of this verse (verse 5): "The sacrifices sacrifie / Of just desires, on justice staid."

Ps 5 (August 12. August 11 was a Sunday). The verse consists of eight quatrains of alternating trimeter and pentameter couplets rhyming abab. In this translation there are clear echoes of earlier metrical translations. The Scottish version authorized in 1650 begins: "Give ear unto my words, O Lord / My meditation weigh," and later, in a passage corresponding to Milton's lines 9–12, has the following:

> For thou art not a God that doth
> In wickedness delight
> Neither shall evil dwelle with thee!
> Nor fools stand in thy sight.

In other places Milton uses rhymes like *fall, quell'd, all, rebell'd* in lines 29–32, which he could have found in a number of his predecessors. Milton may have found in this psalm and in Psalm 8 a source for his explanation of the fact that Satan was allowed some success: "That with reiterated crimes he might / Heap on himself damnation while he sought / Evil to others," and so forth (*PL* 1.214–20).

Ps 6 (August 13) consists of iambic pentameter quatrains rhyming abba. Much of the language of this version is suggested by the standard prose translations, but in line 5 Milton seems indebted to Sandys's line 5: "O heal! My bones with anguish ache." Lines 13–15, which describe how the psalmist's sight is going because of grief, are elaborated, as M. H. Studley (*Philological Quarterly* 4 [1925]:364–71) has pointed out, so that the reader is reminded forcibly of Milton's own blindness:

> mine Eie
> Through grief consumes, is waxen old and dark
> Ith' mid'st of all mine enemies that mark.

Neither the darkness nor the idea of the enemies' marking is in the original. Marginal references for this psalm, however, might direct Milton to Psalm 88 or

to Job 17:7 where similar verses about the eye consumed by grief also mention being laid *in darkness;* in several psalms David seems as conscious of the derision of his enemies as Milton could ever be.

Ps 7 (August 14) consists of ten stanzas of iambic tetrameter rhyming ababba and a quatrain rhyming aabb. There is no striking evidence in language or in rhyme to indicate borrowing from some earlier metrical version. This psalm, like Psalm 2, suggests the irony involved in Satan's efforts, which serve only "to bring forth / Infinite goodness, grace and mercy shewn / On Man by him seduc't, but on himself / Treble confusion, wrath and vengeance pour'd" (*PL* 1.217–20).

Ps 8 (August 14) consists of six quatrains of iambic pentameter rhyming abab. Only *Ps* 7 and 8 of this set of psalms were divided into stanzas in the printing. In *Ps* 8 particularly, however, Milton runs over the ends of stanzas as well as of lines, making the whole into one verse paragrah. He expands the text by repetition and by the addition of fairly conventional modifiers so that in the first two lines *excellent* becomes *wondrous great and glorious.* Milton apparently draws on Psalm 8 in *PL* for his picture of creation and of the subjection of nature to Man.

Ps 80–88 (April 1648). Milton translated these psalms into the simplest of meters used in hymnals, the equivalent of the ballad stanza. These psalms were printed originally without division into stanzas, with marginal numbers indicating the verse of the psalm translated. Possibly for reasons suggested above in the general statement on the psalms, Milton in *Ps* 80–88 comes closer than elsewhere to a literal treatment. In the italicized words or phrases, where Milton adds to "the very words of the text, translated from the original," he gives little that was not expansion of ideas already expressed. In the third quatrain of Milton's *Ps* 80, for example, the italicized *be seen* is implied by "In Ephraims view" and *by thy might* by "Awake thy strength." Similarly, the "going back from thee" of line 73 implies the italicized *To wayes of sin and shame* of line 74. In these italicized phrases, however, we do find words, usually rhyming words, not found in the Authorized Version or the Prayer Book and so rare in other metrical versions that they are good evidence of borrowing where they occur. In Milton's *Ps* 80 the italicized line 52, *With rudest violence,* is echoed in Bishop Henry King's translation of the same passage and a few lines further on Milton mentions grapes in an italicized line and apparently suggests King's "Pluck off hir grapes" since no other contemporary version mentions grapes. Other italicized words of Milton can be found in King so consistently that they suggest that King must have seen these psalms of Milton before he published his translation in 1651.

In *Ps* 85 Milton apparently borrows an italicized phrase from his own *Nat,* which of course depends in part on this psalm. In stanza 3 of the Hymn, Peace is "His ready Harbinger." In Milton's translation of Psalm 85:13:

> Before him Righteousness shall go
> *His Royal Harbinger.*

We may compare also stanza 15 of the Hymn with lines 45–48 of the psalm:

> Yea Truth, and Justice then
> Will down return to men.

[*Nat* 141–42]

> Truth from the earth *like to a flowr*
> Shall bud and blossom *then,*
> And Justice from her heavenly bowr
> Look down *on mortal men.*

(45–48)

In *Ps* 87 perhaps the most interesting additing is the inclusion of a gloss in lines 11 and 12: "I mention Egypt, *where proud Kings/Did our forefathers yoke,*" which explains the reason for glorying over Egypt. The Latin version of Tremellius gives for verse 7, *canunt aeque ac exsultant,* which explains why Milton's line 25, "Both they who sing and they who dance," varies from the 1611 prose version. Milton's version is supported by the Revised Standard translation of 1952. In *Ps* 88 most of Milton's additions emphasize the horror of death. Some of the words are suggested by the Latin text of Tremellius, such as *perdition* in verse 11 and *oblivion* in verse 12, rather than by words in the English prose versions. It is possible that Buchanan's phrase "*sub mole sepulchri*" in his paraphrase of verse 5 suggested Milton's "*Deaths hideous house*" in line 24.

It is not surprising that Milton borrowed from several English and Latin versions even when, as he says, he is translating from the original. There were textual problems and the inadequacies of dictionaries to create problems. That Milton was neither careless nor perfunctory can be seen from the evidence that he considered different translations—sometimes giving both, as in lines 31 and 32 of *Ps* 88, where Milton's marginal note reads "*The* Hebr. *bears both.*"—and that he checked glosses that sent him to other parts of the Bible for information that he incorporates. In his theory of the function of the translator, he clearly gave first place to making the meaning clear when this involved expansion of the text.

Ps 114. Milton's paraphrase of this psalm, written when he was in his last year at St. Paul's, was printed in *Poems* of 1645. The version is in iambic pentameter couplets slightly more run-on than the standard heroic couplet of contemporary writers and translators like George Sandys. Milton's paraphrase allows him to expand and to add figurative language. "The blest seed of *Terah's* faithful

Son" provides an example of periphrasis. Here Milton is in effect incorporating a marginal loss giving the ancestry of Jacob. In line 3, in translating *Out of Egypt* as "from Pharian fields," Milton makes use of an Anglicized form of one of the standard Latin names for Egypt. He might also here be following George Buchanan, whose Latin paraphrase of Psalm 114 uses the expression *arva Phari.* In lines 7–9, which translated "The sea saw *it* and fled," Milton's additions include epithets like "froth becurled" describing the appearance of the sea and expansion of the idea of flight in "And sought to hide his froth becurled head/ Low in the earth." The "froth becurled head" and the "high, huge-bellied Mountains" of line 11 are examples of the somewhat fantastic language that the young Milton could have found to admire in the writers popular as he was growing up: Joshua Sylvester, the translator of DuBartas, Giles and Phineas Fletcher, or perhaps Francis Quarles.

Milton in these early poems seems to be reflecting the traditional academic love of *copia,* which produced notebooks full of synonyms for one level of composition and commonplace books and *florilegia* for another. Such collections of "copy" were more necessary in an age when a good scholar was expected to write Latin and Greek verse in a variety of meters and even to compose extempore speeches in classical languages.

Ps 114, in Greek hexameters. As has been mentioned, it is most likely that this paraphrase in Greek is the poem mentioned in Milton's letter to Alexander Gill of December 4, 1634. Greek scholars of the eighteenth and nineteenth century were severe about its errors in idiom and even in quantities, but some classical scholars have found some merit in the composition. Variations between the version printed in *Poemata* of 1645 and of 1673 suggest that many of the errors were printer's errors.

Ps 136 (composed, like *Ps* 114, in 1624, and printed in *Poems,* 1645). The quatrains are basically (but not rigidly) iambic tetrameter couplets, a common service meter, with a couplet refrain. It is the only one of Milton's psalms still regularly found in hymnals (perhaps because it employs a refrain) and it is also one of the few seventeenth-century translations of a psalm still in common use (see adaptations). There is considerable expansion, but Milton characteristically adds significant material and not just padding. His equivalent of verse three in the Authorized Version, "O give thanks unto the Lord of Lords," is "O let us his praises tell,/Who doth the wrathfull tyrants quell," which gives an ingenious explanation for the term *Lord of Lords,* an explanation he could have found in George Buchanan's Latin paraphrase of this verse: *Cui Domini rerum submittunt sceptra tyranni,* and one that appears in 1636 in Sandys's translation:

> The bountie of Jehovah praise
> This God of gods all Scepters swaies.
> Thanks to the Lord of Lords afford
> And his amazing wonders blaze.

In his later stanzas Milton makes the moon and stars into "the horned moon" and "her spangled sisters," and the sun into "the Golden-tressed Sun," a phrase that may derive from Buchanan, though in classical Latin *auri-comam* was an epithet for the sun. "The *Erythraean* main" for the Red Sea in line 36 may seem far-fetched to the modern reader, but it was in classical Latin a name for that body of water. Milton might have seen the name and also the *glass-pass* rhyme of the next stanza in several places in Sylvester's DuBartas where DuBartas is recalling Psalm 136, such as

> that meek Man,
> Who dry-shod guides through Seas Erythrean
> Old Jacob's fry: and Jordan's liquid glass
> Makes all his Hoast dry (without boat) to pass
> (The 4th Part of the Second Day of the II Week)

In translating verses 19 and 20, Milton incorporates what might be a marginal gloss. Milton's Bible might have referred him here to Joshua 12, where Sihon is identified as ruling over several shores, and Og King of Bashan is identified: "which was of the remnant of the giant." When Buchanan in the earliest editions of his Latin paraphrase describes Seon (Psalm 135:23) "*Quique Amorrheis Seon regnavit in oris*" and Og (Psalm 136:37) "*Stravit Ogum magno fidentem corpore frustra*," he is also incorporating these glosses. [MPB]

SAMSON AGONISTES. The dating of *SA* has provoked some of the sharpest controversy in Milton scholarship. In 1949, Allan H. Gilbert proposed an early date for the drama on the grounds of disparity between the Preface and the body of the play, a disparity due, Gilbert conjectured, to Milton's hastily preparing an unfinished manuscript to be published along with *PR*. Gilbert's dating in the early 1640s, has had little support, in part because his evaluation of the play is patently inaccurate. It is difficult to agree with Gilbert that the iteration of words, images, ideas is scattered so as "not to produce rhetorical effect" (*Philological Quarterly* [1949]: 103–4).

In the same special Milton issue of *Philological Quarterly* appeared W. R. Parker's far more influential essay, "The Date of *Samson Agonistes*." This was followed by "The Date of Samson Agonistes: A Postscript," *Notes and Queries* 203 (1958): 201–202; a longish section in the biography (*Milton*, 2:903ff.) headed "On the Date of *Samson Agonistes*," and a posthumous essay, edited by John T. Shawcross, called "The Date of *Samson Agonistes* Again" in *Calm of Mind*, edited by Joseph Anthony Wittreich (1971). Although Parker continued to refine his arguments from paper to paper, it is fair to present them here together since substantially the essay published in 1971 sets forth the same major reasons for a composition date of 1647–48. The major arguments are these: (1) There is no solid basis for the traditional late date for the poem, only the publication date and the Anonymous Biographer's "finished after the Res-

text with "A blind author and an indifferent printer proved a combination that resulted in printed texts which are uncertain in too many instances, and certainly wrong in too many others" (4:39).

The major source of the plot and characters of Milton's drama is chapters 13 to 16 of the Book of Judges of the Old Testament in the Authorized Version. (Milton knew the Hebrew and Septuagint versions; and George W. Whiting argues that he drew upon the Geneva Bible for *Samson (Milton and This Pendant World* [1958], pp. 201–222). The Samson story is widely considered to have existed in oral and written form in widely separated cultures and "elements of the story are scattered throughout Hebraic legend" (Michael Krouse, *Milton's Samson and the Christian Tradition* [1949], p. 22). It is assumed that the Deuteronomic reforms rigorously edited the Samson story, adding most of Judges 13 and a number of minor interpolations in chapters 14, 15, and 16 in order to link the story with Israel's other judges and to elevate the story "to the level of a religious document" (Krouse p. 24). The prosody indicates that Milton prounounced the names of his characters with stress on the first sylla- ble: Mánoa, Dálila, Hárapha.

The Samson story is set during a time when God was punishing the Israelites by giving them in bondage to the Philistines. Chapter 13 describes the annun- ciation and birth of Samson to Manoa and his wife, long barren. An angel of the Lord appears, tells Manoa's wife she shall conceive, and commands her to raise the child as a Nazarite unto God. Among the ancient Hebrews the Nazarite was marked as "separate unto God" by not cutting his hair, by abstaining from wine, and by not touching a dead body (Numbers 6). The Nazarite often displayed charismatic gifts of spontaneity, energy, insight. He had much in common with the earlier prophets, as suggested by Amos (Amos 2: 11–12). The events of this chapter are quite thoroughly interwoven into the play; for example, the fact of the Nazaritehood not only further dramatizes the fall from high estate in the play, but also becomes the starting point for the choral excursus on temperance. The two visits of the angel inaugurate a pattern of twice-repeated actions that operates throughout the drama. The imagery of fire, which is of some importance in the poem, begins in the fiery ascension of the angel. Clearly too, some of the interesting variety of tone in Manoa's speeches has its source in the human comedy of man, wife, angel-visitor, expected child (perhaps as developed particularly by Josephus).

There is no biblical account of the child's education, only in the last two verses of chapter 13, "and the child grew . . . and the Lord blessed him, and the spirit of the Lord began to move him at times . . . " (v. 24–25). Chapter 14 proceeds to the episode of the woman of Timnath, the ugly story of the riddle and the killing and stripping of the thirty men. Here understandably Milton has been less emphatic, though all the major episodes of the chapter, including the disapproval of the marriage by his parents and the killings are mentioned.

Chapter 15 of Judges continues the story of Timnath. Samson avenges the giving of his wife to another man by tying 300 foxes in pairs, setting them on

fire and turning them loose in the Philistine fields. The Philistines respond by burning Samson's wife and father-in-law to death. Curiously, Milton makes no use of these six verses, though he uses the giving of Timnath to the paranymph (the cause of the episode with the foxes), and he mentions Samson's dwelling in the rock of Etam after smiting his enemies hip and thigh (in revenge for the death of his wife and father-in-law). The biblical account then tells of the Israelites' surrendering Samson to the Philistines, his bursting the bonds and the killing of the thousand men with the jaw-bone of an ass, whence comes the miraculous spring of verse 19. All of this difficult material is used in the play. The second major omission of biblical episode is of verse 20 of chapter 15: "and he judged Israel in the days of the Philistine twenty years." This omission is more understandable; it allows us to consider Samson as falling at the height of his mature powers. The concision of the play may be due not only to the brief span of time represented, but also to the relatively brief if spectacular career of Samson before his fall.

Chapter 16 of Judges opens with the episode with the harlot at Gaza, Samson's encirclement, and his bearing away of the gates of Gaza. Milton has omitted mention of the harlot but refers to the "the Gates of Azza post and massy bar" in the parodos (line 147), which would necessarily have called the harlot to mind. At verse 4 begins the episode with Dalila, described only as "a woman in the valley of Sorek" whom "he loved." The Philistines bribe Dalila to see "wherein his great strength lieth"—the first mention of the key to his strength being secret. Dalila asks Samson on three separate occasions the secret of his strength and "wherewith thou mightest be bound to afflict thee." In verses 6 to 14 Samson gives Dalila three rather peculiar procedures for binding him. She tries all three and they fail. Why Samson should continue to consider her questions harmless after her three attempts to bind him is never made clear. She "pressed him daily with her words, and urged him, so that his soul was vexed unto death." At verse 17 "he told her all his heart . . . if I be shaven then my strength will go from me, and I shall become weak, and be like any other man." The rest of chapter 16 moves quickly through Samson's entrapment, blinding, his grinding at the mill, the growth of his hair again, and the performance at the feast of Dagon. Samson asks to be led to the pillars that support the stadium in which are seated three thousand men and women. He prays, "O Lord God, remember me, I pray thee, and strengthen me, I pray thee, only this once, O God, that I may be avenged of the Philistines for my two eyes" (v. 28). As he grasps the pillars he says, "Let me die with the Philistines" (v. 30). The dead "were more than they which he slew in his life." In the last verse, Samson is buried by "his brethren and all the house of his father" between Zorah and Eshtaol in the burying place of Manoa, his father.

Milton has included almost all the episodes and a good deal of the imagery of the four chapters. He includes some rather intractable material like the riddle and the killing and stripping of the thirty men. It is easy to see why he leaves out the episode of the foxes, the harlot, and the three preliminary (and rather

ludicrous) exchanges with Dalila. In terms of the potential and the tragic waste of his hero, the omission of his twenty years of judgeship prior to the Dalila episode seems useful and right. Why he omits the murder of Timnath is less clear. Milton throve on real conundrums: the vengefulness of the Philistines would seem to provide a fine comparison and contrast with Samson's, but Milton chooses to ignore it.

There is clearly respect for and skillful use of the material of the biblical source. There is a good bit of that Miltonic stubbornness in including, and trying to make work, chunks of material that would seem unusable to the maker of well-made plays. But there is no slavish adherence to the text, the best example being Samson's last words, which in the play are very different, far superior ethically and dramatically, to the personal revenge for eyes of the story of Judges. And Milton makes Dalila Samson's wife.

The only other mention of Samson in the Bible is in Hebrews 11:32–35, whose author lists him with Gideon, Barak, Jephtha, David, Samuel, and the prophets "Who through faith subdued kingdoms, wrought righteousness, obtained promises, stopped the mouths of lions, Quenched the violence of fire, escaped the edge of the sword, out of weakness were made strong, waxed valiant in fight, turned to flight the armies of the aliens."

These passages lead us to the extensive Samson literature of the medieval and Renaissance period. If Milton received his basic material from the Old Testament source, it was the brief mention in the New Testament that inaugurated the tradition of Samson's importance as an individual. In Jewish tradition Samson is a boisterous, nonintellectual sport whose weaknesses were usefully studied by the devout, but whose strengths were considered dissipated. It is a Samson "authenticated" by the Christian tradition who is placed in the midst of a Hebraic plot outline. It is for a Christianized figure that Milton created the three intellectual episodes with Manoa, Dalila and Harapha, as well as the exchanges with the Chorus and the officer.

A heroic play about Samson could not have been written, at least by Milton, within the Jewish tradition alone. Despite an interesting claim by Josephus in *Antiquities* for Samson's magnanimity at his death, most Jewish commentators treat him as less than worthy of emulation. Josephus adds some interesting comic elements on Manoa (his jealousy of the angel of annunciation); he deemphasizes the murder of the thirty and he suggests that Timnath divorced Samson; he eliminates the harlot of Gaza and specifies Dalila as harlot; he also makes Samson "disordered in drink" in his relations with Dalila. Josephus points toward a heroic figure of Samson, but he does not present such a figure purely enough to provide a model for Milton's hero.

The Christian tradition of Samson that Krouse first examined in detail gives us a Samson who was a type of Christ, one of a series of Old Testament figures whose careers prefigured the career of the Savior. Each event in Samson's life, from the foretelling of his birth by an angel to the destruction of the temple of Dagon, had been interpreted as pointing toward a similar event in the life of

Christ; in Christ all the preceding prophecies and prefigurations found fulfillment and resolution. Krouse's brilliantly executed study has recently been supplemented by specialists in Hebrew influence (Stollman). The authority of his chapters (3, 4, 5) on the Patristic, Scholastic, and Renaissance periods has not been seriously challenged, though Barbara Lewalski has added a new dimension to the treatment of typology. Beginning with Josephus's attempt to make Samson respectable, Krouse proceeds to show the early, literal forms of the story of Saint Samson in the *Chronicon Paschale* (5th century), Isidore of Seville, Clement of Rome, Ambrose, Prudentius, Origen, Theodoret, and Procopius. The difficulties of treating Samson's story as both saintly and literal led to glosses by Origen and Augustine. Allegorical interpretations, adapted from the Greek Homeric criticism by rabbinical theologians like Philo of Alexandria in the first century, came to the rescue of the Samson story as early as the fourth century in the writings of Ambrose (Krouse, p. 40). In his *Sermo de Samsone* Augustine elaborated the allegorical interpretation most fully, establishing numerous parallels between Samson and Christ. Even the difficult episode with the harlot of Gaza is construed as "a figure of Christ lying in the bonds of death" and his bearing away the gates, as the harrowing of Hell (Krouse, p. 41).

While Krouse's argument for a pervasive Christian tradition on Samson has been widely accepted, his claim for the influence of that tradition on Milton's play has not. Krouse himself was aware of the difficulties in making his case: "one looks in vain for more tangible evidence of allegorical interpretation in *Samson Agonistes* although there are passages in which one whose ear is attuned to the tradition can hear echoes of the many allegorical analogies between Samson and Christ" (p. 122). Lewalski puts the problem bluntly: "since there is no explicit reference to the crucifixion in *Samson Agonistes* there is no clear evidence that Milton intended to invoke the antitype of Christ's sacrificial death in the drama" (p. 1054). Other critics and scholars, as widely separated in method as Arnold Stein and John M. Steadman, have rejected the Krouse claim for influence. In any case, Samson's stature as a figure fit for tragedy in the seventeenth century depends a good deal upon the tradition of Christian exegesis, which evolved into a view of him as a type of Christ.

If Krouse has best presented the Christian tradition of Samson as hero-saint, Watson Kirkconnell, in *That Invincible Samson* (1964), has presented the fullest set of analogues to the drama. He translates five Continental works that predate Milton's, and prints a "Descriptive Catalogue" of over one hundred items, fifty-five of which predate *SA*. Among the works in the first group the most interesting is still Joost Van den Vondel's Samson of *Heilige Wraeck, Treuspel* (Amsterdam 1660). The work had been cited as a possible source of Milton's play as early as 1825; the argument was most fully developed by George Edmundson. The Vondel play stands out from the analogues for its seriousness and for a number of structural resemblances, but Kirkconnell (pp. 178–180) and Verity in his edition *Milton's Samson Agonistes* (1932) clearly demonstrate the

untenability of the argument. Also untenable is the claim by Whiting that Milton is "slightly indebted" to Francis Quarles's *Historie of Samson* (1632), (*Milton's Literary Milieu* [1939], p. 253). Kirkconnell shows that Milton's choice of the "Dagonalia" episode for his drama is not unique; indeed, among the elements of plot and character that Milton chooses, only the Harapha episode is unique. Kirkconnell himself vigorously states the originality of Milton's drama, and nowhere does he claim direct influence of any of the works he considers.

Numerous brief articles argue specific sources for images and passages in the drama. Jonson, Sidney, Euripides, Sophocles, Horace, Ovid, Virgil, Boccacio, Vida, and G. Fletcher are among those mentioned by commentators. Useful annotated editions are those of Todd, *The Poetical Works of John Milton*, vol. 4 (1809; reprinted 1970); Verity's edition; M. Y. Hughes, *Milton: Complete Poems and Major Prose* (1957); F. T. Prince, *Samson Agonistes* (1957); G. & M. Bullough, *Milton's Dramatic Poems* (1958); and Carey and Fowler's edition.

The debt to Euripides was explored by P. W. Timberlake in "Milton and Euripides" in *The Parrott Presentation Volume* (1935). Timberlake suggests that Milton found a number of artistic and dramatic devices in Euripides that served him well: Prologue, messenger, the formal rhetoric and debate, as well as specific lines. In addition, Euripides' idealism and nonconformity are seen as appealing to Milton and influencing him. Timberlake's claims (ignored by Parker in his booklength study) end with this distinction: "So if the theme and structure of the tragedy owe nothing to Euripides, in language and treatment, he is indeed present on every page" (p. 338). The opposite kind of demonstration is made by J. C. Maxwell in *Review of English Studies* n.s.3 (1952:366–71), where he carefully corrects claims of verbal echoes from Aeschylus, while admitting possible Aeschylean influence on the structure of *SA*.

The texture of *SA* is so complex, the dramatic density so allusive, and the erudition of its author so broad and deep that source studies are likely to continue. If we remember that Milton honored the Bible and his own experience as reader-thinker beyond any traditional influence, we will be able to accept and evaluate correctly his use of the materials that fed, and were digested by, his imagination.

It is appropriate here to enquire into the "spirit" of *SA*, insofar as it is derived from Greek or Hebrew or Christian sources. In his famous address to the British Academy, "*Samson Agonistes* and the Hellenic Drama" (1908) Sir R. C. Jebb found the classicism of language and structure in *SA* to be Greek, but its spirit Hebraic. Citing Arnold's "The Hebrew has force, the Hellene has light," Jebb asserted that *Samson* set God against gods, not man against fate. Comparing Samson and Herakles as heroes, he saw Samson as God's champion, while Herakles was "a lonely instance of superhuman strength towering above the rugged, low range of human history, and confronting, though not vanquishing, except by the death which led to immortality, the awful malignity of fate." Jebb's address has stimulated almost as much commentary as Johnson's com-

ment on the lack of a "middle"; and that commentary is relevant in discussing theme and structure as well as "source." Here it is simply noted that Jebb found *SA* Greek in structure and style (except for the thorny choruses), but Hebraic in feeling.

The major response to Jebb was W. R. Parker's *Milton's Debt to Greek Tragedy in "Samson Agonistes"* (1937). Parker systematically and painstakingly reviewed the structural parallels between Greek drama and *SA* and confirmed earlier claims for similarity. In addition, he added a significant interpretation of the play in defense of its middle. At the end he addressed himself to the problem of "spirit." He first pointed out the dangers of defining the Greek spirit too narrowly. Aeschylus, Sophocles, and Euripides differed radically in their various opinions. "Who, then, was 'Greek' and who was not?" (p. 193). Then he suggested that the "indefinable something" (Verity's phrase) that makes *SA* Greek was "Milton's fine understanding of the tone, of the end, which the Attic dramatists attained by the expression of their various principles and beliefs. . . . Milton would not identify 'rules' with 'spirit.' And no more, I think, would he feel it necessary to identify the spiritual tone, the 'intellectual' impression left by Greek tragedy, with the specific ideas which, in their day, produced that impression" (p. 197). Greek spirit, continued Parker, is a blend of the serious, thoughtful, didactic, sublime, and religious aspects of Greek tragedy (pp. 198–99). "Milton was one of the last men whose intellect comprehended all the aspects of the Greek spirit and whose genius caught that spirit in a piece of living art" (p. 210).

Though Parker exaggerated the exclusiveness of Greek influences (cf. Whiting's and Krouse's vigorous claims for the Christian tradition in response to Parker's overstatement), within his discussion of those influences he is eclectic, flexible, and convincing. Last, he presents definitive proof of structural and stylistic influences; and he makes a sophisticated and believable claim for the influence of the Greek spirit on Milton. But the argument on "spirit" affected much of the ensuing discussion of what kind of play *SA* really is. The investigation of sources and influence leads to the still unsettled question of genre.

Unless Milton's Preface is ironic to the point of perverseness, *SA* is a tragedy. Even without the Preface, the reader is likely to deduce that this is a tragedy based on Greek models, a play utilizing the Chorus and austere dispositions ("economy" is a good word) of characters, including the messenger, of Greek drama; a play furthermore self-consciously echoing the definitions of Aristotelian catharsis at its very close and insisting again and again in its body on referring to that fall from high estate which was identified with medieval as well as Greek concepts of tragedy. One could expand his expectations for tragedy even without a Preface or a title page from Milton's high regard for that genre, from his early, careful comment on "Public Shows" in *CB* and the passionate cadences of *RCG*. And throughout his career, though he might disparage theatricality in his opponents (largely Anglican), he keeps distinct in his analysis the posings of theatricality and the integrity of real drama. Should the title

page and Preface of *SA* be lost, it would still quite likely be called a tragedy, and one based on Greek models.

But there is the Preface, perhaps unfortunately; and it has served for many years by its apparent explicitness to suggest to certain readers that Milton had provided his audience with a quite precise poetics for the reading of the play. Yet the explicitness in the Preface does not provide a poetics; as John M. Steadman has demonstrated in *Calm of Mind*, edited by Joseph Anthony Wittreich (1971): "The preface is not a systematic treatise on tragic theory, but an apologia or defense of the genre as *anciently* composed—and of Milton's practice in following the ancients. . . . Milton's remarks on tragedy are too fragmentary, and perhaps too oblique, to enable us to deduce a complete and coherent dramatic theory from them" (p. 200). We will not discover the blue-print for the drama by identifying which version of Aristotle Milton was reading, though we need to know the sources of Milton's borrowings, however carefully he contains them. Steadman finds that Milton's principal source is "Aristotle as seen and interpreted through Renaissance eyes" (p. 201). Also it is clear that "Milton's remarks on tragic purgation seem, on the whole, to repre-sent a conflation of Aristotle's definition of tragedy with opinions on catharsis advanced in the *Politics*. These he amplified and explained, in turn, with doctrines likewise derived from Aristotelian sources—the moderations of the passions, from the *Ethics;* imitations of the passions, from the *Poetics* and the *Politics* alike; mimesis as the source of pleasure, from the *Poetics*. The medical analogy, explicit but still undeveloped in the *Politics,* he elaborated as other critics had done before him" (p. 191).

A number of scholarly arguments have attempted to establish the meaning of the Preface and particularly of the term *catharsis* as the definitive way into the play. Among these are the old, still interesting essay by Ingram Bywater (*Journal of Philology* 27 [1899–1901]:267–75); Bywater traces the sources of Milton's pathological interpretation of catharsis back to sixteenth-century Ital-ian criticism and concludes that Milton's "words in the preface to *Samson Agonistes* are no proof of his having broken ground for himself, or excogitated a new interpretation of the Aristotelian text" (p. 275). In *JEGP* 9 (1961):712–30 Paul R. Sellin attacks the views by Bywater, Spingarn, and Gilbert and suggests Daniel Heinsius as the source of Milton's reading of *lustratio*. Sellin writes, "Since ancient tragedy, Milton thinks, was designed to effect an ethical end, the poets can do no better than follow classical rules and imitate classical models" (p. 717). The potential for critical Procrusteanism is obvious. Martin Mueller's counterattack in *Studies in English Literature* (1966):139–50, denies "the slightest trace of contemporary influence" (p. 143) and suggests that Milton "became familiar with these theories at first hand during his Italian journey, and not through the medium of other scholars, e.g. Heinsius" (p. 150). John Arthos considers the possible influence of Monteverdi's subtle theory of catharsis in Part 2 of *Milton and the Italian Cities* (1968). Stimulating and scholarly though these investigations have been, they have sometimes appeared to underestimate

the reality and complexity of the play in pursuit of a definitive reading of the preface. The Preface has a real but limited relevance to the play. It is not the key to understanding the play, though it certainly contributes to that understanding.

Three essays, exemplary in their modesty as well as their scholarship, have made this point. The first is John Steadman's, already discussed, whose analysis of the Preface as a rhetorical document is at least as important as his analysis of the Aristotelianism in the piece. The second is Annette C. Flower's statement in *SEL* 10 (1970):409–23. Flower sensibly, and for perhaps the first time in three hundred years, analyzes the Preface line by line and finds that it is in two parts: sentences 1–10, which are a defense of tragedy; and sentences 11–17, which are an introduction to *SA*. Her analysis of the first part complements Steadman's emphasis on the apologia elements. The main thrust of her article, however, is to examine the contemporaneity of Milton's piece. She concludes that "Milton was far more in the main current of critical opinion of his time than many commentators have been willing to admit." Though the roots of the Preface are in Aristotle, Horace, and the Italians, "the poetic theory of the Preface has also affinities with the moral and justificatory *Defence* of Sidney, with the quarrel of the ancients and moderns set forth in Dryden's *Essay*, and with the controversy between Dryden and Howard over mixed genres and the unities" (p. 423). Though others had studied Milton's possible relation to his contemporaries in *SA*, no one had so sensibly read the Preface as a piece of prose written circa 1670–71. It is a corrective to strong claims for *the* reading of *SA* based on *the* version of Aristotle referred to in the Preface. Another useful investigation into the meaning and worth of the Preface is Barbara K. Lewalski's in *Publications of the Modern Language Association* 85 (1970):1050–62. Lewalski investigates the reference to Pareus's *A Commentary upon . . . the Apocalypse* (trans. Elias Arnold [1644]), a reference doubly important because it repeats Milton's statement in *RCG* (1642) that describes the Apocalypse as "the majestick image of a high and stately Tragedy, shutting up and intermingling her solemn Scenes and Acts with a sevenfold *Chorus* of halleluja's and harping symphonies: and this my opinion the grave authority of *Pareus* commenting that booke is sufficient to confirm." Lewalski's version of the typology offers a major new reading of the play (see below), but the claim for the reading comes from the play, not from imposition of a pattern from the Preface. Irene Samuel's urbane essay in *Calm of Mind* is less convincing. Dispatching those critics who see Samson as a martyr, she tries to establish the Green-ness of the play, the validity of Aeschylus, Sophocles, and Euripides as models, by showing Dalila as a witless and unworthy antagonist, Samson as a brute who is tragic in his wrongness.

While most commentators agree that *SA* is a tragedy, there is significant disagreement on the kind of tragedy it is. The disagreement affects every area of discussion of the drama. It is appropriate here to consider several of the claims for Samson within the genre of Christian tragedy. In the face of Puritan attacks on the theater, seventeenth-century dramatists and critics self-consciously dis-

tinguished between good and bad drama. Milton's prose, as has been shown, does this. So does Sir Richard Baker in *Theatricum Redivivum* (written in 1648, published in 1662) which is a point-by-point refutation (but briefer) of William Prynne's hysterical but effective attack on the theatres, *Histrio-mastix* (1633). Despite the closing of the theaters in 1642, both drama and dramatic theory continued to be written. Almost certainly Milton would have known Sandys's translation (1640) of *Christs Passion* by Hugo Grotius, the great Dutch scholar whom Milton had met in Paris, and Francis Goldsmith's translation of *Hugo Grotius His Sophomponeas or Joseph* (1652). Both pieces contained commentaries on the uses of tragedy. One would expect him to know Sir William Lower's translations of Corneille's *Polyeuctes or the Martyr: A Christian Tragedy* (1655), perhaps even Richard Flecknoe's unctuous *Love's Dominion, A Dramatic Piece, Full of Excellent Moralitie, written as a pattern for the Reformed Stage* (1654). The point is that though the theaters were closed, the idea of a theater was not dead; Milton lived in the midst of a considerable discussion as to what a tragedy was and what a Christian tragedy was. The fact is that he does not, for all his flourish of nomenclature, call *SA* a Christian tragedy, despite his citations of Christian exponents of the genre.

Cogent attempts to distinguish the play as Christian tragedy have been made. In *The Frontiers of Drama* (1945), Una Ellis-Fermor assigns Samson "to the rare category of religious drama, a kind which, by the nature of some of its basic assumptions, cannot be tragic" (p. 17). Her essay is one of the first to present the "profound and dramatic psychological contrast" in the play as "action" (p. 30); her treatment of the prosody is extraordinary (p. 31). But her major argument does not hold. "Few of us . . . are content to call Samson's triumphant death a tragic catastrophe. How could we, when 'nothing is here for tears'?" (p. 17). In an essay brimming with insights, the reading here of "triumph" and of "tears" seems simplistic. Surely Samson's triumphant death is suffused with some sense of sorrow; surely "nothing is here for tears" is appropriate for the closing of any good tragedy, the tragic experience being above and beyond the histrionics of easy empathy. T. S. K. Scott-Craig, (*Renaissance News* 5 [1952]:42–53) sees the play as "substitute for liturgy; the celebration of the agony of Samson is a surrogate for the unbloody sacrifice of the Mass. It is a lustration of fear" (p. 47). These two essays, often cited, have seldom satisfied the basic question: How can a drama of regeneration be a tragedy? If God's will be done willingly by the "hero," can the play be anything but a divine comedy? The answers include some of the best criticism in English, and can be best treated under the discussion of theme. But several comments that pertain immediately to genre can be made here.

First, Milton's use of the critical penumbra of classical tragedy must indicate that he was serious in calling his play a tragedy. Second, the sense of religious resolution, whether in the service of Christ, as in typological readings, or in the Hebraic strength of God Almighty, does not obviate the concern for Samson the man. It is the interplay between free-will and providence that makes the

play a tragedy, not a tract. It is the fact that Samson suffers and learns as a man before he can fulfill God's will. The whole play is suffused with God's presence but it is also suffused with human stubbornness, ignorance, weakness, and pride—and human worth. These sins are worked out in human terms as well as in divine. If the working-out is largely a spiritual and inward process, as John Steadman has pointed out (in *Milton: Modern Essays in Criticism,* ed. Arthur Barker [1965]), it is nonetheless human. We are left with a double movement—one toward fulfillment, one toward death. As A. S. P. Woodhouse argues, "That [Samson's] repentance is achieved under the impulsion of divine grace does not alter the fact that it is Samson's own." And "The reconciliation, the mitigating of the sense of disaster, is worked out in purely human terms before the larger rhythm of the divine comedy is invoked, lest that rhythm should not only resolve the tragic irony of the actions, but dissolve the whole tragic effect" (ibid., pp. 464–65). There is neither religious ecstasy nor renunciation enough to burn up the humanity of Samson. In this insistence on the human value of his hero, in his insistence on Samson's signifying *himself*—his chastened, obedient, heroic *self*—Milton has given us a tragedy, unhyphenated. For tragedy presents man as man, moving always to defeat, but seriously, even in a sense triumphantly, expressing his sense of identity as man. "Wonders are many on earth, and the greatest of these / Is man. . . ." "What a piece of work is man!" "God of our Fathers, what is man!" These are bitter, proud exhortations—questions turned into exclamations: that is, "catharsis." The bitter knowledge of such a play's reality cannot still the extraordinary wonder at man's having signified. Not much more than that can be said of *Prometheus Bound, Oedipus at Colonnus,* and *Herakles,* plays that clearly influenced *SA* and that are very different from one another. In presenting a man about whose selfhood we care, even in the face of overwhelming evidence against him, Milton has written a tragedy.

The most often quoted critical statement about *SA* is Johnson's comment in *The Rambler* (no. 139, 16 July, 1751): the poem "has a beginning and an end which Aristotle himself could not have disapproved; but it must be allowed to want a middle, since nothing passes between the first act and the last, that either hastens or delays the death of Sampson." The statement continues to stimulate criticism, especially with relation to the play's theme and structure. It is generally agreed that the play has the formal structure of a Greek play as described in Aristotle, with an opening Prologue—Parodos, Scenes, and an Exodos–Kommos. Or to put it into acts: the play is highly symmetrical with five acts, each followed by a chorus. J. B. Broadbent (*Comus and Samson Agonistes* [1961]) is in close agreement with Parker when he blocks out the play into Prologue and Parados, lines 1–175; First Episode: Samson and Chorus, lines 176–292, followed by the First Stasimon, lines 293–325; Second Episode, Samson and Manoa, lines 326–651, followed by the Second Stasimon, lines 652–709; Third Episode, Samson and Dalila, lines 710–1009, followed by Third

Stasimon, lines 1010–1060; Fourth Episode, Samson and Harapha, lines 1061–1267, followed by Fourth Stasimon, lines 1268–1296; Fifth Episode, Samson and Officer, lines 1427–1440; Exodus and Kommos, lines 1441–1758. Jebb includes the Prologue and Exodos with the first and fifth acts respectively, but the shapeliness of the drama, the strongly segmented and symmetrical structure, is widely accepted. *SA* is a tightly knit "Greek" tragedy, with little of the physical action of the sort common in English drama but rather a series of intense comings and goings similar to those in *Prometheus Bound,* in *Medea,* and in both the Oedipus plays. These physical juxtapositions represent conflicts in which intense emotional languages subsumes physical violence. Simple juxtaposition of physical bodies does not mean simplicity of relationship; nor does it mean non-dramatic relationship.

There is a tensile structure of oppositions to be noted in the drama. The title represents this well: *Samson,* the Hebraic, religious, primitive, uncontrollable matter; *Agonistes,* the Greek and hence "secular," civilized, controlled by art—in a sense, form. Yet, of course, both parts of the opposition are not simply the poles of that opposition. Samson was a type of Christ, Hebrew verse is higher than Greek, *Agonistes* implies the suffering for religion. Each part of the antithesis illuminates and is illuminated by the other. Each part emphasizes the "otherness" of the other and partakes of the other. This is literally a structural principle in the play. Hebrew/Greek, Christian/secular, Hebrew/Christian, Hebrew/Protestant, Nature/Art are ideas opposing and reinforcing each other in the play. Individual scenes are shaped by this opposition; for example, Samson and Dalila are brilliantly contrasted precisely by being brilliantly compared in Dalila's series of sophistries. The series of oppositions in Dalila's arguments shapes the scene into a defeat for her, growth for Samson, and further understanding for the Chorus and audience. It is not a question of separating black and white but of observing and learning from their interaction. Several essays have viewed this as an operation of homeopathic catharsis (Georgia Christopher, *ELH: A Journal of English Literary History* 37 [1970]:361–73; Lee Sheridan Cox, *ELH* 35[1968:51–74; and Sherman Hawkins, *Milton Studies* 2 [1970]).

Not restricted to considering catharsis, but clearly seeing antithesis or opposition as a crucial structural element, are Thomas Kranidas, *SEL* 6 (1966):125–37; Anthony Low, *PMLA* 84 (1969):514–20; and Stanley Fish, *Critical Quarterly* 11 (1969):237–64. Low reminds us that one of Milton's "deepest habits of mind was to divide, oppose and reconcile contraries, and that reading and training only sharpened this natural tendency" (p. 515).

A simpler structure of repeated pairs can also be identified. The mention of the two visits of the angel (lines 23–129) initiates a series of pairs that help tie the drama together—two wives and two "inspirations," two visits of Manoa and the Officer, two ships, two official graves. This use of pairs creates an expectation of the second chance, and nourishes our knowledge of the Dagonalia even

as we are being faced with the dire facts of Samson's imprisonment and immobility. And, of course, in every episode character against character creates a structure upon which our knowledge of Samson's growth is built.

Another structural principle is the imagery of selfood. Samson's movement from fragmentation to wholeness, from imprisonment to liberation, from exploitation by the Philistines to exploitation by his God—which latter is full usefulness—is marked by a steady opening out of the imagery. This is one of the surest things in the drama, a structural device of steady measurement with which the dramatic and psychological movements of the play interact. There are moments of psychological and ideational darkness in the play—for example, at the end of Manoa's first scene and as late as Harapha's departure—when the structural principle of a steadily cohering unity keeps the play from flying apart.

Arnold Stein has most fully demonstrated the way images and phrases function as in music to point the way for the drama and to make the drama cohere. In *Heroic Knowledge* (1957) he has taken as chapter headings four phrases from the first five lines of the play. It is perhaps the most compelling demonstration there is of the complex unity in *SA*. Other images that unify the play are those of fire-angel-bird-phoenix, of grave-sepulchre-monument, of physical and spiritual armor, of ships-tempest-pilot (see Barbara K. Lewalski, *Notes and Queries*, n.s. 6 [1959]:372–73), of speech and hearing (see Marcia K. Landy, *Milton Studies*, vol. 3 [1971], and Anne Ferry, *Milton and the Miltonic Dryden* [1968]), and of course of light-dark-sight-blindness. Without doubt, Samson is one of the great examples in any literature of that "almost inconceivably close and delicate organic wholeness" which F. R. Leavis found lacking in Milton's major poems (*Revaluation* [1972], p. 62).

SA unfolds its story as a drama that utilizes all structural devices of lyric poetry to reinforce and to complicate the severe dramatic unity of Greek tragedy. Milton's choice of word for plot seems deliberately modest: oeconomy. It is not quite an eccentric word in this context: he had used it in the same way in *TM*. Ascham had used it similarly (*Works* [1904], p. 276) and Dryden and Edward Phillips would use it later. But it does imply an understatement of the Aristotelian emphasis on plot (cf. Martin Mueller, *ELH* 31 [1964]:156–74).

As a narrative the play unfolds quickly. Samson's opening monologue tells us of his plight and his past and suggests, at least lightly, his future. The congestion of feelings is set out in detail. The hero, fallen and suffering and yet suggesting a bare possibility of redress, establishes a wide range of possibilities in the imagery of his first speech. The Chorus visits him and presents its temptation to become a scapegoat, to become unrigorous in self-analysis. Samson begins to pen up, to respond to the stimuli of the outside world. Very soon in this first encounter we know Samson's superiority to the Chorus. The visit of Manoa renews and refines the assault on Samson's self-image, and again Samson opens up more; he defends himself and God in ways that tell us not only what a hero he was but what a man he is becoming. Dalila's encounter

presents inversions of the arguments for justice, patriotism, religious devotion, and love and tests Samson's (and the reader's) knowledge of these things as well as his ability to withstand the still very real temptation of Dalila's flesh. Samson clearly wins the debate and withstands the temptation; Dalila's poise is shattered and the Chorus verifies her exposure: "She's gone, a manifest Serpent by her sting / Discover'd in the end." Samson emerges from the episode again more open to stimuli and better able to answer to them; he is further purged of the surface rancor that was represented in the images of constriction. He is better able both to wait and to act.

Harapha appears, reminding us of the old Samson (though even in the past Samson's heroism was naked, as it were, compared to the flashy "heroism" of the Philistines); here too Milton brings in some of the legal questions about Samson's rebellion, difficult unfinished business. The effect of Harapha's appearance is to stimulate Samson into an aggressive posture, one made possible by the earlier encounters. Samson's language is sardonic and clear; he recognizes definitively the limitations of the old heroism, and in his insistence on separating surface qualities from real strength, strength of the whole man, he shows that physical knowledge is conditional, that it must be used in the service of God. But it is not to be disparaged, it is not trivial to the good man. Samson's response to Harapha's stimulus to self-abasement is to challenge Harapha in the name of God. Here the narrative consistency is violated. Samson rejects the offers of Manoa and Dalila, while here he presses his offer on Harapha. The shapeliness of diagram is slightly disturbed, but the thematic and psychological consistency is maintained. Harapha's shallowness seems appropriate to the introduction of the difficult legal question of allegiance. And it is interesting that Milton should choose to discuss those matters here, in the scene with the only character totally original with Milton. Harapha leaves "somewhat crestfallen," the Chorus worries a bit, and Samson indicates that he is ready to die; he also indicates, for the first time, that his death might be of some good use: "Yet so it may fall out, because their end/Is hate, not help to me, it may with mine/Draw their own ruin who attempt the deed." The Chorus signalizes Samson's victory over Harapha with the stasimon celebrating heroes and saints. From here to the end of the play the reader is continuously reminded of Samson's coming triumph and death in the arena. Despite the deliberate slowness of the exchanges between Samson and the Officer, between Manoa and the Chorus, and between Manoa and the Messenger, there is felt a precipitous rush to the climax; the effect is achieved through reiterated images of ironic encounter and disaster for the Philistines, of arrival, triumph, and death for Samson.

The climax of the play comes between the two visits of the Officer. This is the *peripetia* and the *anagnorisis*. As Samson sets forth this reason for not going to the arena, he is setting forth the reasons for going, and the ironic use of "Command" at either end of this decision process frames the great decision. When Samson says: "venturing to displease/God for the fear of Man, and Man prefer,/Set God behind," he makes the great equation of the drama. It is clear

that as he speaks "Man" means Philistines; by the time he has finished it means Samson. It is the final movement from the old conception of heroism, but it is not "letting go"; he leaves the stage committed to action not "unworthy/Our God, our Law, my Nation, or myself." Samson leaves the stage, an action as decisive, and as elaborately built up to, as Agamemnon's stepping onto the carpet, Aegisthus's going through the door, or Oedipus's refusing to leave Colonnus.

Manoa comes and a lower level of irony develops. Against the old father's useless, loving plans for ransom, one feels Samson's rushing to his death. The ransoming speeches, this-worldly and political, move slowly while God's providence, and the Samson heroism, which now recognizes and operates within that providence, swiftly, almost simultaneously, unfold. The Messenger's speeches use both kinds of time, political and providential, a narrative, horizontal, sequential unfolding and a "lyric" vertical simultaneity.

The play ends with a Threnody ("kommos"), part barbaric chant of triumph, part rationalistic attempt to elevate the event, part paternal pride, sorrow, and resolve. The whole is greater than the sum of its narrative parts. It is not merely that tribal and paternal consciousness strikes a mean with the eternal. It is rather that much of the imagery and action resolve into a larger context, consciousness of the play itself. The ending of the play signalizes the fully meaningful and celebrated death of a man who was born again. A *tragic* death is one that testifies to the significance of the life that was lived as well as of the death that was died. "*Samson* hath quit himself / Like *Samson*." The ending of the play ties all the motifs—personal, social, and religious—together.

Critics agree that Samson leaves the stage and pulls down the temple of Dagon on the Philistines and himself. But the meaning of the act continues to be disputed. Most readers are agreed that Samson is regenerated, psychologically and practically, made whole so that he can once again serve his God. Samson in his opening monologue is blind, defeated, raw with awareness of his sins, and useless except for earning his bread. In those extraordinary first 114 lines Milton presents a man conscious of sin and yet not master of that consciousness. In a sense the pain has not reached him, he clocks full awareness, full feeling, as the blocked metaphor of the hornets' stings suggests (line 19–22). Samson knows but does not know feelingly, he can intellectualize his acceptance of God's punishment and yet not accept totally, that is with his feelings as well as mind, as a total human being. So in the great address to light, "O first created Beam," when Samson attempts to analyze his blindness, to understand with the mind in deliberate, painfully controlled rhythm, the rhythm and the imagery escape his control, largely through compulsive emphasis on the word *light*, and the rationalist slips into the lament "Myself my sepulchre, a moving Grave" (lines 101–2). Samson's opening speech is one of Milton's greatest achievements. It suggests a fragmented, suffering, and highly intelligent man analyzing his condition. The channels of feeling are blocked; relations between inner and outer man are painfully obstructed. The clearing of

these channels, the making whole of this fragmented, vulnerable man, is the theme of *SA*.

For Milton, as clearly for Samson, "making whole" means making useful to God and always in some practical way to man. So Samson will move from "Eyeless in *Gaza* at the Mill with slaves" to the horrendous slaughter in the temple where he killed (and here the tradition is unerringly insistent) "in number more / Than all thy life had slain before" (lines 1667–68). This social role is carefully developed. From the beginning, Samson knows things about his role as deliverer that others—all others—in the play do not know. He knows that his first marriage was "motion'd of God" (line 222); he knows too that Israel's bondage is not his fault (lines 241–276). Very clearly, he refuses the role of scapegoat—an easier penitence, surely, than the one he undergoes in this play, and a false role for him. He was *not* responsible for Israel's bondage. (Cf. Anthony Low, *Texas Studies in Literature and Language* 11 [1969] 915–30). In the exchange with Manoa, Samson with considerable dignity tempers his father's complaint against God, and in the tempering moves toward a calmer attitude toward self. Movement, of course, is not perfectly steady. And if in Samson's first speech to Manoa the didactic opening has dignity and control, "Appoint not heavenly disposition, Father," the end of the speech is clotted with self-loathing: "These rags, this grinding, is not yet so base / As was my former servitude, ignoble/Unmanly, ignominious, infamous" (lines 415–17). And at the end of the scene, Samson's despair is at its deepest. "My hopes all flat, nature within me seems / In all her functions weary of herself; / My race of glory run, and race of shame, / And I shall shortly be with them that rest." Manoa leaves to "prosecute the means" of deliverance, and Samson's great monody on pain follows. This is traditionally seen as the low point of the play. Samson's description of his pains, physical and spiritual, is unparalleled in English literature. It is with these two passages that D. C. Allen can best support his widely accepted argument that Samson is in a state of despair, technically identifiable, and that the Christianity of the play depends largely on this identification. (*The Harmonious Vision* [1954]. See also William O. Harris, *ELH* 30 [1963]:107–20).

Surely the pain and the petition for death indicate the psychological low point of the play. But in another sense, this is the *verbalization* of the psychological low point, and that ability to verbalize is a sign of the way up. In short, the pain here is *achieved*, unlike the first speech: the guilt is fully articulated and hence on the way to being controlled. All of this has been stimulated by the Chorus (cf. John Huntley, *Modern Philology* 64 [1966]:132–45), and by Manoa. Throughout the play the statement of a position means in some sense a conquering of that position:

> My griefs not only pain me
> As a ling'ring disease,
> But finding no redress, ferment and rage,

> Nor less than wounds immedicable
> Ranckle, and fester, and gangrene,
> To black mortification.

By the end of the speech, his griefs have found "redress," an exit in words, at least in part. At the end of the scene with Dalila there is a similar effect:

> *Dalila* Let me approach at least, and touch thy hand.
> *Samson* Not for thy life, lest fierce remembrance wake . . .

Yet, at the end of the Dalila scene, Samson has controlled "fierce remembrance." The climactic example of this kind of processive irony, Samson's *anagnorisis*, has already been commented on.

Samson grows in self-knowledge throughout the play; even as he slips back there are signs of progress toward unity and usefulness, in the imagery, in the loosening of rhythms, in the brilliantly lucid signal-ideas that Arnold Stein has pointed out. The private and social being grow together. And finally the privately collected man moves off-stage to perform his public and religious duty. His last words suggest the heirarchy of his values:

> of me expect to hear
> Nothing dishonourable, impure, unworthy
> Our God, our Law, my Nation, or myself;
> The last of me or no I cannot warrant.
>
> (lines 1423–26)

The process briefly sketched here has been described by James Holly Hanford (in *Studies in Shakespeare, Milton and Donne* [1925]) and by Parker, Ellis-Fermor, Woodhouse, Steadman in essays already cited, and by Joseph H. Summers in *The Lyric and Dramatic Milton* (1965), as well as by numerous others. It can be called the orthodox reading of the play. Its richest and subtlest statement is in Arnold Stein's *Heroic Knowledge*, where the encounters with Manoa, Dalila, and Harapha are described with fullest attention to their dramatic function. Stein best describes "the long turning of the tide, sustained in a fascinating tension of doubt" (p. 183); and he gives the best analysis of Samson himself. He sees Milton "allowing, as it were, a digestible ration of despair, as he allows him a kind of nuclear sensibility of the essential self which is able to feel the agony of ridicule as a 'vanity' that does not avoid the natural course of his spiritual sickness, but advances to meet the advancing disease; is inoculated, as it were, and achieves immunity making despair convert itself into a necessary transition to humility" (p. 210).

More recently, however, there has been a concerted effort to disprove the comprehensiveness of the regeneration theory. Problems in accepting the play as tragic appear earlier in sympathetic essays by Ellis-Fermor (*Frontiers*), David Daiches (*Milton* [1957]), and C. M. Bowra (*Inspiration and Poetry* [1955]), who

writes, "we may suspect that Milton was temperamentally incapable of writing a truly tragic play. He liked to have everything explained and justified, and authentic tragedy neither explains nor justifies but creates a condition of mind in which grief transcends its own nature by its very extravagance" (p. 128). Samson's triumph in the temple becomes a means of splitting human and theological concerns, or rather of trivializing the human in the catastrophe. William G. Madsen (*From Shadowy Types to Truth* [1968], pp. 181–202) sophisticates the Krouse argument from typology: "it is essential to the whole system of typology that the type be different from as well as similar to the antitype" (p. 187). Samson is the active hero incapable of the higher fortitude of Jesus in *PR*, with which *SA* was intended to be read. Samson shows his limits in the physical bluster of the Harapha scene. "The two major motives of blindness and delivery from bondage receive only a limited metaphorical extension that falls far short of Christ's achievement" (p. 195).

Madsen's essay is the most influential of those which argue for various kinds of anti-heroism among the good characters in the play. Madsen presents Samson himself as anti-hero, one whose limitations illuminate the perfections of Jesus. Irene Samuel *(Calm of Mind)* presents Samson as a Greek hero by reason of his marked limitations. Franklin M. Baruch (*ELH* 36 [1969]:319–39) subtly analyzes the language of Manoa and the Chorus at the end of the play. He sees Manoa and the Chorus as revealing their common distortion of spiritual truth—indeed, even in blindness to it (p. 328). Lawrence Hyman *(Tennessee Studies in Literature* 12 [1968]:91–98) splits the human and religious decisively: "The greatness of this play does not consist in its reconciling either the hero or the audience to the ways of God, but bringing to the highest pitch the contradiction between the human desire to find our triumph in this world and God's will that His champion must prove God's power through suffering" (p. 67). An earlier version of this was Charles Thomas Samuel's essay in *Dalhousie Review* 43 (1963–64):495–505 in which we read that "The God of Milton's last poem is a God above the laws, and the poet . . . [is] no longer interested in making God seem humanly, rationally correct" (p. 501). In his essay already cited, Stanley Fish begins by asking the question "what is the relationship between the recovery of Samson's faith and the act of pulling down the temple; and the answer, 'none, necessarily' " (p. 210). Fish concludes: "the choice is not between informed action and precipitate action, but between action taken on the basis of inadequate information—faith professing action—and paralysis" (p. 263).

The main thrust of much criticism then has been to challenge the "orthodox" view, represented by Stein, that regeneration takes place on the human and on the theological level. George Wilkes makes the frontal attack in the *Huntington Library Quarterly* 26 (1963):363–79. Wilkes finds an "unmistakable discontinuity" between Samson's decision to accompany the officer and the action preceding (p. 377). "What makes it all cohere is the sense of providence undeflected by anything in its path, making use of Samson's betrayal, his blind-

ness, and his chains in its uncontrollable intent" (p. 379). French Fogle builds from this argument in seeing Samson's "regeneration" in terms derived from *CD* (in *Essays in American and English Literature Presented to Bruce Robert McElderry, Jr.*, ed. Max F. Schultz [1967] pp. 177-96).

The persuasiveness of these attacks on the cohesiveness and comprehensiveness of regeneration in the drama is considerable. It would appear that the only way to dispute these arguments is to press for more and more complete positioning of the argument in the total context of the play. So Wilkes's claim that Samson needs to be totally despairing at the beginning of the play to make the regeneration argument work is dramatically impossible for a play about a *man*. Again and again the argument used for separating the planes of "human" and "religious" action is built upon a too-thin reading of the human part of the action, a failure to recognize the complexity of the "merely human" condition before it is related to the otherworldly.

The most interesting essay on this separation of the understandably human from the godly is Ann Davidson Ferry's statement in *Milton and the Miltonic Dryden* (1968). Ferry sees Samson's progress as progress toward "heroic silence . . . increasing imperviousness, increasing reticence" (p. 165). In the temple Samson stands "inviolate to the human world outside himself . . ."; when he brings down the temple he "passes beyond the visible world, beyond society, ultimately beyond definition even by the metaphorical meanings of language," and "Samson's rest is a kind of negation of human experience, an obliteration of the self." (pp. 172–74). The essay ends with a difficult vision: "The poem itself therefore paradoxically denies the power of eloquence, of literature, which must inevitably be bound by the limits of language and of all things human, at the same time that it creates a vision of those limits heroically transcended" (p. 177). The argument falters when the humanity of Samson is minimized and when the representation of isolation is made to seem a denial of society.

The isolation of Samson, the exemplary withdrawal from false social values (i.e., *most* social values), does not isolate him from his people as his final words quoted above show. And if he stands alone and prays silently in the temple, he stands at the center of meaning for his society, touches the pillar of the temple of Dagon, and brings his people some years of freedom. Truly, Samson is "a realization that it is the individual who must succeed," though not, as John Shawcross continues, "in his own little world, in his own little way" (in *Calm of Mind*, p. 304.) Samson's loneliness is not an argument against usefulness; it is rather an argument for the kind of intense and painful discriminating that Samson has been engaged in throughout the play.

The question of Samson's isolation leads to the last group of interpretations to be considered here: *SA* as a political play, one emerging perhaps from the intense personal disappointment of John Milton after the failure of the great revolution. The autobiographical reading of the play, with Milton-Samson, Dalila-Mary Powell, and Harapha-Salmasius has long been discredited. For one thing, it distorted the misogyny and the violence into personal expressions;

both can be seen more accurately as givens of the subject matter as it was understood in the seventeenth century. But Woodhouse ("*Samson Agonistes and Milton's Experience*") suggests some connection between biography and art that are intriguing.

Treatments of the play as political are to be found in William Haller's discussion in *Reason and the Imagination*, edited by Joseph Mazzeo (1962), pp. 201–11, and in M. A. N. Radzinowicz, *PQ* 44 (1965): 454–71. Haller analyzes the growth of *SA* from "Milton's early interest in writing a poem for his fellow-countrymen on a heroic theme drawn from their own history. The fable came to be sure from the Scriptures, but is was a fable which came closer to the Englishmen of his time than anything he might have drawn from Geoffrey of Monmouth or the Chronicles" (p. 211). Radzinowicz brilliantly analyzes the relation of Milton's prose, and the audience created, to *SA*. She describes Milton, after the Puritan defeat, "faced with the judgement of reason and conscience on God's Englishmen and the most concrete need to justify God's ways to men" (p. 459). Her reading "shifts emphasis . . . to a moral analysis of political failure with the possibility of personal deliverance contained in it" (p. 464). Baldly stated here, the thesis seems arbitrary; seen in relation to the prose richly understood within the article, the argument is important and convincing. In a sense Barbara Lewalski's already cited essay has real political implications. Lewalski shifts the typological emphasis from Samson's resemblance to Christ to Samson's relation to the "the sufferings and agony of the Church under Antichrist" (p. 1051). From Pareus and other commentators on the Apocalypse, Lewalski defines a Protestant tradition of typology different from that documented by Krouse (*Milton's Samson*). *SA* calls upon another typological association—developed especially in Protestant exegesis—which presents Samson and the other Judges "as types of the Christian Elect" (p. 1054). This interesting reading emphasizes Samson's judgeship (but why does Milton omit those twenty years in Samson's career?) and calls attention to Protestant, especially Puritan, identification with the Book of Judges (p. 1057). Samson fulfills his "vocation" in killing the Philistines and the Chorus celebrates his victory as such a fulfillment. As an interpretation, Lewalski's reading is more satisfying than either Krouse's or Madsen's typological readings. There is no need to bring an extraneous "triple equation" into the play, nor is there need to completely redefine the meaning and weight of characters and lines for the sake of a hypothesis externally deduced.

It is the application of the external hypothesis, often glittering in its comprehensiveness and elegant in pedigree, that most often distorts the play. Setting out to prove that *SA* is Greek, Hebrew, Catholic, Puritan, typological, Aristotelian, political, autobiographical, or anti-human, the critic or scholar can illuminate details; sometimes the pattern wrecks whole sections of the sensibility, the feeling, the meaning of the play.

Perhaps some attention to the Harapha scene will demonstrate this. Harapha the giant, father of Goliath, comes on stage to look at Samson, and regrets not

having met him in the field. Samson responds to his condescension by challenging him to a duel. Harapha refuses, claiming it is beneath his dignity to combat an unwashed blind man. He accuses Samson of breaking the law and of using black magic. Samson responds with vigor and clarity and repeats his challenge. Harapha slinks off, "somewhat crestfall'n." There have been useful discussions of the sources for Harapha's character. Daniel C. Boughner (and earlier Allan Gilbert) makes a good case for his descent from the braggart soldier of Italian Renaissance comedy (*ELH* 11 [1944]:297–306). John Steadman makes an even better one in *JEGP* 60 (1961):786–95, in which he claims that "though classical tragedy and Renaissance comedy may have been contributing influences, [Harapha's] character and significance derive largely from I Samuel 17, and his name from II Samuel 21. . . . In the encounter between a physically handicapped 'hero of faith' and a Philistine giant in full armor, Milton found an ideal vehicle for the ethical opposition between *fiducia in Deo* and *fiducia carnalis*" (pp. 794–95). In *PQ* 39 (1960):82–92, George R. Waggoner explores the considerable tradition of justification by single combat, deriving from commentary on David and Goliath. All three of these essays contribute to our understanding of the encounter between giant and blind man. None of them can, nor does any one of them claim to, supplant a reading of the scene as drama. And here one of the most serious problems of interpretation crystallizes. Because of the long, clearly overemphasized tradition that the play is a closet drama not to be acted, in a sense *not dramatic*, external patterns have been imposed without the sense of a dramatic scene opposing, testing, orchestrating, or rejecting, as it were, the imposed pattern. When Madsen, Samuel, and Samuels impose their interpretations upon the Harapha scene, do they envision the gorgeously clad Harapha, strong, healthy, seeing, "secure," circling the blinded ruined man and talking about what might have been? Do they recognize the extraordinary interplay of the imagery of inner and outer man, of superficial values versus inner values? In the face of the *scene* can they dismiss Samson as showing us *his* shallowness, not Harapha's? Is that not to impose an *untragic* severity of abstract idea upon a human and dramatic situation?

The play is a play. Austere, monumental, severely limited in motion, it is like *Agamemnon, Oedipus Rex, Medea*, a play with intense dramatic values. George Steiner has written of it: "Performance holds one spellbound, and the merest intelligent reading conveys the formidable excitement of the play. Only an ear deaf to drama could fail to experience . . . the hurt and tension of the successive assaults on Samson's bruised integrity" (*The Death of Tragedy*, p. 32). There has been some cultivation of the deaf ear in Samson criticism. Those readings which have stayed closet to John Milton's words—in context—have been the most satisfying and the most illuminating.

Critics of the style of *SA* tend to divide into two camps—those who find, with Samuel Johnson and J. A. Symonds, the verse full of "dryness, ruggedness, and uncomprising severity" (Symonds quoted in Edward Weismiller, in

The Lyric and Dramatic Milton, ed. Summers, p. 115), and those who find under the problematic severity "achievements . . . quite beyond any other English poet's, perhaps any modern poet's" (Gerard Manley Hopkins, Letter to Robert Bridges, 3 April 1877," in *The Letters of Gerard Manley Hopkins to Robert Bridges* [1935], p. 38). The men of letters have sometimes been puzzled by the austerity and irregularity, and the poets have come forward to explain the difficult art. The distaste of Johnson, Newman, Symonds, and Leavis is overbalanced by the scrupulous admiration of Coleridge, Hopkins, Bridges, F. T. Prince, and Weismiller.

Johnson (*Rambler* 140, 20 July 1751) spoke with mixed admiration and condemnation of the style, which he found "through the whole dialogue remarkably simple and unadorned, seldom heightened by epithets, or varied by figures, yet sometimes metaphors find admission, even where their consistency is not accurately preserved." A modern critic like Christopher Ricks will pick up this claim of the blocked metaphor for disapproval (*Milton's Grand Style* [1963], p. 50). But Johnson's comment over the Choruses is more clearly disapproving, though obviously puzzled. The parts of the Chorus, he writes, "are often so harsh and dissonant, as scarce to preserve, whether the lines end with or without rhymes, any appearance of metrical regularity." There has, since the beginning of criticism of the Choruses, been an uneasy feeling that something was going on under all that harshness. Coleridge experiments with parsing the lines, yet even he seems a little uneasy with them, though he speaks with insight of the language of the whole play: "Colloquial language is left at the greatest distance, yet something of it is perserved to render the dialogue probable" (*Coleridge on the Seventeenth Century,* ed. Roberta F. Brinkley [1955], p. 607). But it was Hopkins who first made cogent analysis of the prosody of the Choruses: "The choruses in *Samson Agonistes* are intermediate between counterpointed and sprung rhythm. In reality they are sprung, but Milton keeps up the fiction of counterpointing the heard rhythm (which is the same as the mounted rhythm) upon a standard rhythm which is never heard but only counted and therefore really does not exist. The want of a metrical notation and the fear of being thought to write mere rhythmic or . . . un-rhythmic prose drove him to his. . . . Milton's mounted rhythm is a real poetical rhythm, having its own laws and recurrence, but further embarrassed by having to count" (*Letters to Bridges,* pp. 44–45). The complexity and excitement of the *Samson* choruses is a recurring subject in Hopkin's correspondence: "the choruses of *Samson Agonistes* are in my judgment counter-pointed throughout; that is, each line (or nearly so) has two different coexisting scansions. But when you reach that point the secondary or 'mounted rhythm,' which is necessarily a sprung rhythm, overpowers the original or convential one and then this becomes superfluous and may be got rid of; by taking that last step you reach simple sprung rhythm. Milton must have known this but had reasons for not taking it" (*The Letters of Gerard Manley Hopkins and R. W.*

Dixon [1935], p. 15). This testimony from a major poet (and indeed one hostile to Milton the man) served, and should continue to serve, as a major stimulus to enquiry into, and pleasure in, the Choruses of SA.

Robert Bridges (Milton's Prosody, rev. ed. [1921]) elaborates and slightly coarsens Hopkins's insights, finding inversions, elisions, etcetera, "responsible for the dactylic and trochaic effect," and the "iambic" system even where it seems to disappear, "maintained as a fictitious structure and scansion, not intended to be read, but to be imagined as a time-beat on which the free rhythm is, so to speak, syncopated, as a melody" (p. 55). SA, according to Bridges, "contains Milton's most elaborate and artificial versification" (p. 46) and Milton was "not inventing anything new or unheard but seeking rather to make a good use of natural stress rhythms, without falling into their singsong, or setting all his verse to dance" (p. 66).

S. Ernest Sprott (Milton's Art of Prosody [1953]) agrees that SA is metrically the pinnacle of its author's achievement" (p. 131). He finds in the blank-verse sections "iambic pentameter quite like Paradise Lost—but a stronger impression of trochaic" (p. 130). Of the Choruses, he writes: "the whole secret of the rhythms is comprehended in the understanding that the so-called lyric choruses are essentially heroic blank verse which has thrown off the bondage of preserving a uniform length of line" (p. 130). Like Sprott, Frank Kermode turns away from Greek models for Milton's verse; in an important article in the Durham University Journal 14 (1953):59–63, he finds significant parallels between Samson's choruses and Hebrew lyric measures and rhymes.

But the most impressive statements on Milton's versification are those by F. T. Prince and Edward Weismiller. Prince traces possible models for the language of SA in the "lyrical rhetoric" of Tasso's Aminta, Guarini's Pastor Fido, and Andreini's L'Adamo (1617). He finds transition lines from chanted verse to spoken (as at lines 326–29, 710–15, and 1060) or from speech to chant (as at lines 80–83). The essay (in The Italian Element in Milton's Verse [1954], pp. 145–68) is useful throughout, but concentrates, of course, on the Chorus. Prince shows that Milton's choruses rhyme less often than we think, that "Milton varies the incidence of rhyme to suit the mood and structure of each passage" (p. 158). but he is even freer in his use of rhythms. As an equivalent for Italian freedom of hendecasyllabic rhythms, Milton settled on the use of a variety of lengths of line. This recalled his early experiments in Time and SolMus but, Prince argues, also benefited from the immense expansion of scope that PL had provided him (pp. 160–61). "The almost wanton variety of rhythms in the choruses of Samson is his expression of these accumulated impulses" (p. 161). Prince makes most suggestive comments on the place of rhyme in Italian prosody, which, he shows, is based on rhyme even when rhyme disappears (p. 165) and which provides "in the last place of the line . . . a word which is as weighty as a rhyme-word" (p. 166). "One might say, then, that the secret of the music of this verse (i.e., Samson's choruses) is that it is rhymed verse which does not rhyme,

or unrhymed verse which seems to do so: whichever description we prefer, the intermittent occurrence of full rhyme is essential to the total effect" (p. 167).

Weismiller's essay (in *The Lyric and Dramatic Milton*) argues that Milton "seems to have become unwilling, in his later years, to do without any possible resource that would lend variety of movement to his syllabic line—even where that variety threatened for a moment his basic meter" (p. 119). The first pages of analysis consider problems of the blank verse, offering some new solutions to several difficult lines, but Weismiller suggests that the problems of *SA*'s blank verse are fundamentally similar to those raised by *PL*, and they are soluble problems. It is the choral verse that is difficult, "and . . . its structure has never yet, so far as I know, been satisfactorily explained" (p. 119). Weismiller finds "nearly absolute uncertainty" about such lines, and assumes that Milton intended the "metrically ambiguous" lines (pp. 121, 125). But we are not absolved by being told that a form is "free" or "open" (in Milton's Preface) from trying "to define the nature of its freedom" and fixing "the limits within which, still, its effects are communicated." We must continue to search for illuminating parallels (p. 128). Weismiller finds that "apart from actual ambiguity of structure . . . the strangeness of rhythmical effect . . . arises principally from the fact that . . . lines of differing length occur together in combinations to which the ear trained in the rhythms of English stanzaic poetry is little accustomed" (p. 134). He then establishes that, though Milton's technique in the choruses is a "sum of elements of a vast poetic experience . . . , the *Pindarique Odes* [in Cowley's *Poems*, publ. 1656] influenced Milton strongly" (p. 144). The range and depth of Weismiller's argument has only been suggested here; his essay brings the study of style in *SA* to the same high level as the study of theme.

For clearly, until quite recently the study of style in *SA* has been one of the lacunae in Milton scholarship. In *Samson Agonistes: A Study in Contrast* (1964) Sister Miriam Clare pursued exhaustively the figures of contrast and particularly the "imaginative but controlled use of antithesis" (p. 150), but she too modestly refrained from applying the findings. Una Ellis-Fermor *(Frontiers)* has made some fine but few comments on style, as have Arnold Stein and Joseph Summers. Among studies of the imagery are those by Duncan Robertson *UTQ* 38 (1969):319–38; Roger Wilkenfeld, *ELH* 32 (1965):160–68; Albert Cirillo, in *Calm of Mind*, pp. 208–33; as well as the essays by Ferry and Landy cited above. John Carey, *MLR* 62 (1966):395–99, uses the Dalila parallels to Samson to denigrate the hero and in his edition of the *Poems* to find the ending of the play "morally disgusting." Albert Cook makes some suggestive comments on "the several accentual patterns . . . felt as coiling ahead and backwards" in *UTQ* 29 (1960):385.

The richness of the style of *SA* is still to be explored. This "poem of the minimum theatre," as B. Rajan has called it *(The Lofty Rhyme* [1970], p. 129), insists on confronting us with a style and a structure bristling with problems and ambiguities. And the first of these problems is the obviousness of genre,

the obviousness of harshness, the obviousness of rhyme. Style is used obviously to confuse the reactions of the reader, to make more cunning the complexity of the piece, to dramatize the difficulty and grandeur of choice. Sophocles, Shakespeare, and Donne moved to that same kind of use of the obvious for complexity. Thomas Mann has described it brilliantly in the eccentric Kretschmar's words on Beethoven's Opus 111:

> convention often appeared in the late works, in a boldness, one might say an exhaustiveness, and abandonment of self, with an effect more majestic and awful than any reckless plunge into the personal. (*Dr. Faustus* 1948, p. 53)

The style and structure of *SA* experiment with conventions in a way that makes the more shocking the violation of those conventions. And the style and structure of the play thus reinforce, with a cohesiveness and a density virtually unsurpassed in English literature, the "controlled turbulence in which an equilibrium is deliberately imperilled so that a richer, more inclusive equilibrium can be achieved through the process of disorientation" (Rajan, p. 143). The turbulence, so apparent in structural, stylistic, psychological, and religious terms, is allayed in the larger equilibrium of the poem—a significant act of faith in the importance of man in the face of God—"*Samson* hath quit himself like *Samson*." [TK]

SONG: ON MAY MORNING. This poem appeared in both the 1645 and 1673 editions of Milton's poems. Its date is conjectural, but it probably belongs to the poet's Cambridge period. In conception and mood, it strongly resembles *El* 5, a much longer and more elaborate celebration of the coming of spring. The resemblances led A. S. P. Woodhouse to conclude that the two poems must have been written at the same time, that is, in 1629, for Milton indicated that the elegy was composed at age twenty (*University of Toronto Quarterly* 13 [1943]: 73). Parker, however, argued for a slightly later date because of its position in the early editions of Milton's poems and because of its metrics. Believing that the order in which the poems originally appeared was significant, Parker observed that *May* was placed between *EpWin*, dated around April 15, 1631, and *Shak*, which is dated 1630. The metrical similarities of *May* to *EpWin* further convinced him that *May* could be assigned with some confidence to May 1631 (*Milton*, pp. 768–69). Others have dated it as early as 1628 and as late as 1632.

In both early editions, the word *song* in the title was conspicuously spelled with capital letters; and a sentence on the title page of the 1645 edition stated that the songs in the collection had been set to music by Henry Lawes. It cannot be stated with certainty that *May* was set by Lawes, since no further evidence survives, or that it was intended for singing. But its artistic affinities, at any rate, are with the work of the Elizabethan song-writers and their seventeenth-century successors, Jonson and Herrick.

For all that, *May* is characteristically Miltonic in its simple language and generalized imagery. It is true that Milton is often accused of employing an eccentric, Latinate vocabulary, but analysis of his individual poems usually reveals otherwise. In *May*, certainly, his preference is for one- and two-syllable words out of which he creates the generalized imagery that is more aptly associated with him. His adjectives, for example, usually identify an attribute either implicit in the noun or closely associated with it—"the Flowry May," "the yellow Cowslip," "the pale Primrose." Such adjectives do not accord well with the modern taste for particularity in poetry, but they are justified by Milton's success in universalizing the experience he treats. The flowers, which do not succeed as individualized cowslips or primroses, nevertheless function well as elements in a pattern that reveals the essential qualities of the May morning—its freshness and fertility.

Variations in line length emphasize the divisions into which the poem falls: a four-line introduction, in which the morning star and May are personified as girls participating in a May dance; a four-line salutation to "bounteous May," which is the song itself; and a two-line conclusion, in which the poet and nature reiterate their greeting. In keeping with these divisions, lines 1–4 are pentameter; lines 5–8, tetrameter; and lines 9–10, pentameter and tetrameter, respectively. [ERG]

SONNETS, MILTON'S. Milton wrote twenty-three standard Petrarchan sonnets, five of which, 2–6, are in Italian, and a "tailed" sonnet (sonnetto caudato), "On the Forcers of Conscience," in twenty lines. *Canzone* is also part of the Italian sonnet sequence. Numbers 7–23 and "On the Forcers of Conscience" were recorded in the Trinity MS, although 18–20 and part of 21 are now missing; 1–10 were published in the 1645 *Poems* and reprinted in the 1673 edition, which adds 11–14, 18–21, 23. The remaining four sonnets (15–17, 22), apparently omitted for political reasons, are given in Edward Phillips's *Letters of State* (1694) in corrupt texts. (The numbering is that of *TM* and 1645, and employed by Smart.) While the sonnets are generally considered as separate poems, some critics have argued that they can be viewed as sequential or, even apart from the Italian sequence, as constituting subgroups, although they were written from around 1629 (?) to 1658 (?).

The sonnet was a very popular form of poetic expression in the English Renaissance, but Milton, writing after its vogue had passed in England, went back to the Italian originals of the form for his pattern. The octave in Milton's sonnets invariably rhymes abba, abba, after the Petrarchan model, but he allows himself considerable variety in the sestet, a variety justified by his Italian sixteenth-century models, Bembo, Tasso, and—particularly—Della Casa. His favorite rhyme scheme for the sestet is cdcdcd, which occurs in six sonnets (8, 12, 14, 18, 22, 23), but this is closely followed by the normative, regularly patterned, repeated tercet cdecde, used five times (9, 10, 17, 19, 21). Other sestet

schemes are: cdedce (2, 6, 7, 13); cdcdee (3, 4, 5); cddcdc (11, 15); cdedec (1); cddcee (16); cdceed (20).

F. T. Prince has objected that in the Italian sonnets Milton does not show adequate understanding of the implications of the octave-sestet division in the structure, but, as Honigmann points out in his edition, the mature English sonnets demonstrate that Milton came to know very well what was required in the transition from octave to sestet. He frequently used a pause or turn (volta), of the kind used by many Italian sonneteers, at the precise start of the sestet (e.g., 7, 10, 13, 15, 20). Elsewhere (11, 16, 19, 22), a distinct turn is also apparent, though it occurs in the eighth, ninth, or tenth lines rather than at the exact beginning of the sestet. It is quite clear that from 7 onwards Milton is in command of the form, and uses it with remarkable flexibility and skill.

The earliest sonnets follow the mainstream of the convention; they are poems of erotic longing, four of them being addressed directly to the "donna leggiadra" (beauteous lady) of 2. After the Italian poems, however, Milton broadens the scope of the sonnet to include his personal aspirations, tributes to friends, acquaintances, and public figures, and commentary on affairs of church and state. There was ample precedent for this enlargement of subject matter in Della Casa and other Italians, and Prince (pp. 25–30) has a helpful discussion of "the more moving poetry" written by Della Casa "when he withdraws a certain distance from the object of his emotions and makes his poem a moral reflection on his own state of mind and way of life." For limited examples of departure from convention, however, Milton need only have looked to his English predecessors in the sixteenth century. The Commendatory Sonnets by Spenser are an example of the nonamatory use of the form, and the one addressed to Gabriel Harvey suggests, in its opening and development, the sonnet of compliment, which Milton would later address to such figures as Lawes, Cromwell, or Vane. Each sonnet will now be considered separately, apart from the Italian poems, which lend themselves to treatment as a group.

Sonn 1. It is generally assumed that this was written in the spring of 1629 (perhaps 1630). The Latin *El* 5, which includes in its title the information that it was written in the poet's twentieth year (or when he was aged twenty), and can therefore be dated 1629, contains two lines (25–26) that are virtually translated to provide the opening lines for this sonnet. The conventional eroticism of this poem is so vague that one need not assume any very strong personal involvement on the part of the poet; *May*, which was probably written at about the same time, contains very similar sentiments. The sense of youthful amorous expectation here is paralleled in *El* 5 and 7.

It is hard to quarrel with Parker when he says, "Milton's first attempt at the sonnet form is more interesting as an illustration of his state of mind than as a poem" (*Milton*, p. 58), yet this does have considerable attraction as an example of the young poet's feeling his way with some success into an unfamiliar form. It has been pointed out that the opening lines recall Bembo's "O rosignuol, che 'n queste verdi fronde / Sovra 'l fugace rio fermar ti suoli" (from *Rime*, 1564),

but there seems to be no transition from octave to sestet, a feature to be found also in some of his later English sonnets.

The theme is straightforward enough, though some commentators have discovered unsuspected subtleties and even humor in the poem. The nightingale, traditionally associated with true love (as compared to the cuckoo, whose "shallow" note indicates mere lechery, cuckoldry, and jealousy), inspires the speaker to hope for success in love, if only its song will precede that of the "rude Bird of Hate." The poet has some claim upon the good offices of the nightingale, whether the bird is thought of as linked to "the Muse" (poetry) or to Cupid, the god of love, since he serves them both. The nightingale seems to have had a particular appeal for Milton; see *IlP*, lines 55–64, *Mask*, lines 233–34, 565, *PL* 3.38–40, and *El* 5, already referred to. It has been argued that Milton came to see the bird, with its associations of purity, opposition to brute force, loneliness, and nocturnal song, as a symbol of his own poetic voice. (See Ovid, *Metamorphoses* 6, for the story of Philomel.) However, this is an early Miltonic use of the nightingale, and it would be difficult to argue that the bird had at this juncture acquired any great personal symbolic importance for Milton.

Sonn 2–6 and *Canzone*. It used to be thought that the Italian poems were written during Milton's visit to Italy in 1638–39, but Smart argued convincingly for a much earlier date. It is now generally thought that composition took place between 1628 and 1630; Parker (*Milton*, p. 755) puts it tentatively in 1630. However, Honigmann (pp. 76–80) remains unconvinced by the many arguments for an early date that have been put forward and favors the hypothesis that the Italian poems were written during Milton's visit. Sergio Baldi proposes the span of 1626–1630 for the original composition of the poems, but puts forward the notion that they might well have been revised and polished in 1638–39 when Milton's knowledge of Italian was much improved. (Incidentally, Baldi does not accept the low view of Milton's use of Italian that is held by a good many Italian critics; Baldi asserts that the critics are condemning the Petrarchan manner ["il petrarchismo"] rather than Milton's handling of Petrarchan themes. What one finds in the Italian poems is a skillful and effective imitation of sixteenth-century sonneteers—Bembo, Tasso, and Della Casa.)

Sonn 2–6 and the *Canzone* are usually seen as a sequence in praise of a lady to whom Milton was attracted, a lady who bade him write in Italian because "this is the language Love boasteth as his own!" (*Canzone* line 15). The identity of the lady (assuming she really existed) was a mystery until Smart put forward the hypothesis that there was a riddling clue to her name in the first two lines of 2. He saw these lines as referring to the region of Italy known as Emilia, and made the inference that the lady's name was Emilia. Smart's text and translation of the lines are as follows:

> Donna leggiadra, il cui bel nome onora
> L'erbosa val di Reno e il nobil varco.
> (Bright lady, whose fair name honours the
> flowery vale of Reno and the famous ford.)

The Reno is a river that flows through Emilia, and the "famous ford" can be that of the Rubicon, celebrated for its crossing by Julius Caesar in 49 B.C. as he advanced into Italy proper from what was then Cisalpine Gaul.

Smart's case is very well argued, and his hypothesis has been generally accepted. However, Honigmann points out that a great deal rests upon Smart's textual emendation of the original "Rheno" (unchanged in 1673) to "Reno." "Rheno" could be "the Rhine rather than the insignificant Reno" (pp. 80–81). This changes the import of the allusion. To this may be added that "the famous ford" is not necessarily the only satisfactory translation of "il nobil varco." Baldi cites Florio's *Queen Annas New World of Words* (1611), the enlarged edition of *A Worlde of Wordes, or Dictionarie in Italian and English*: "*Varco*, any foard, ferrie, passage, or wading ouer a riuer. Also any narrow passage, as a stile ouer a hedge." (Smart uses Florio's definition, but he does not include the "narrow passage" connotation in his quotation.) "Il nobil varco" has in fact been translated "the noble pass" *(The Student's Milton)*, and "noble gorge" *(CM)* and "the noble gorge" would suit some sections of the Rhine.

Despite Honigmann's challenging of the Emilia hypothesis, it is taken for granted in the fifth edition (1970) of Hanford's *A Milton Handbook*, and Parker *(Milton*, p. 78) accepts and uses it. Starting with the Emilia identification, Parker elaborates a whole episode of young love (pp. 78–80) which is certainly attractive, however conjectural: the young Milton meets and is immediately attracted to Emilia, a girl of Italian origin; encouraged by her, he writes a sonnet in praise of her in Italian, the language she has praised as a true vehicle for love poetry; the other poems come in natural sequence, concluding with the fifth sonnet, "the most confident, the most direct and personal of the series." For Parker as for Smart, one of the most striking things about these Italian poems is that, despite their Petrarchan idiom, they are fresh and original, and do not follow any conventional Petrarchan situation. Parker concludes that Milton was genuinely in love, and that the Italian sonnets are an unaffected manifestation of that love.

Honigmann is unable to be so definite at this. While he agrees that it is very probable that "Milton commemorated a real lady's real command," the fact remains that "the 'tradition' had famliarised similar situations—the lady who orders her lover to write in her praise, and the lover who attempts poetry for the first time to please his lady (as Milton attempted *Italian* poetry)" (p. 81). Whether or not one accepts the notion that the sequence is autobiographical, J. T. Shawcross adds another dimension to its understanding, arguing that the Italian poems should be read on two levels, and be seen as speaking of divine as well as human love: "The opposition between human and divine love, in the first sonnet [i.e., 2], has moved to achievement in the language of human love and hope for expression of divine love, in the second [3], to the resolution that the language chosen for achievement carries approbation, in the third poem [*Canzone*]" (p. 29). Clearly, within the framework of this interpretation, the concept of the "immortal guerdon of never-withering green" (*Canzone*, line

11), which is the reward of the truly dedicated poet, is of great importance. (Cf. *Lyc*, line 73; and with lines 7–8—"Other shores, other waters, the banks of another stream,"—cf. *Lyc*, line 174. The similarity in terminology is surely not accidental, and supports Shawcross's argument.) Inferences that can be drawn from the remaining poems in the sequence, especially 4, with its Platonic treatment of "Beauty exemplifying an Idea unknown, which filleth the heart with beatitude," help to sustain the notion of a spiritualized level of meaning. However, not all will agree with Shawcross when he concludes that the lady of the Italian poems is a "personification representing the inspiration through which man can raise earthly beauty and love to emulate heavenly beauty and love" (p. 33), so that attempts to determine her family name and her relationships with Milton and others become idle.

Sonn 7. The ambiguity of the phrase *my three and twentieth year* has occasioned controversy about the date. On or about December 9, 1632, Milton's twenty-fourth birthday, was advanced by Parker, but Hunter has more recently argued for the twenty-third birthday in 1631 or soon thereafter. In *TM*, 7 is transcribed at the bottom of one of the two drafts of a letter to a friend in which Milton defends his love of learning and his reluctance to take holy orders. The sonnet is included there as an additional justification and explanation of his position.

The octave laments the poet's lack of visible poetic achievement, and he compares himself with others, "som more timely-happy spirits," who are already making a name for themselves. It hardly seems necessary to hunt down specific examples of such "spirits," but for a summary of suggestions that have been made see Honigmann, pp. 96–97. The sestet demonstrates a willingness on Milton's part to submit himself to "Time" and "the will of Heav'n," but the last two lines, especially the concluding phrase, "my great task Masters eye," have caused some difficulty because of the view of God as a censorious overseer that they seem to present. The meaning of the phrase may be elucidated by turning to the letter that precedes 7 in *TM*, where there are references to the parable of the talents (Matt. 25:14–30) and the parable of the laborers in the vineyard (Matt. 20:1–16). The marginal comment on the parable of the talents in the Geneva Bible, with which Milton would have been familiar from his boyhood, says, "This similitude teacheth how we ought to continue in the knowledge of God, and do good with those graces that God hath given us." "If I have grace to use it so" is not too remote an echo of "those graces that God hath given us," and in the parable the word Maker is repeatedly used of the figure who stands for God. (The connection with *Sonn* 19 is of course also apparent.) In the parable of the laborers in the vineyard, the "maker of the vineyard" rewards those who worked for him not according to what they thought they deserved but according to his own will and pleasure; even those who came late to the work earned the same pay as the one who started early. One can see how this would appeal to a young poet, full of high aspirations, who felt himself to be a slow starter. God is the master and judge, and since the

reward is given by Him according to His own values, all that is required of him is to serve God as best he can. The eye of the divine master watches over His servants to guide and direct, but it also watches in loving concern. The sestet may thus properly be called a resolution of the conflict and distress manifested in the octave, since it concludes with reference to a Deity Who is loving as well as watchful.

Sonn 8. This has two titles in *TM*, neither of which was used in 1645 or 1673. In *TM*, 8 is in the hand of a copyist, who gave it the title, "On his dore when ye Citty expected an assault," but this is crossed out and the title, in Milton's own hand, is changed to: "When the assault was intended to ye Citty." It is customary to date this sonnet in the autumn of 1642, when the Royalist army was advancing on London after the inconclusive battle of Edgehill on October 23. Confronted by a determined army at Turnham Green, the Royalists retreated on November 13, but not before the Londoners had become aware of their danger; a victorious Royalist army might well have sacked the city and carried out its own form of rough justice if it encountered notorious rebels. If one makes the reasonable supposition that Milton's tone is mocking and ironic rather than cringing, November 1642 is a likely date. However, Honigmann points out that the date 1642 written beside the sonnet in the margin of *TM* has been deleted, which is admittedly odd, and he does his best to arrive at a date of May 1641. Nevertheless, 1642 still seems the most likely date.

A situation is imagined in which the Royalist troops are already advancing into London; the poem is thought of as affixed to the door of the poet's house. But, Smart observes (p. 49), "The suggestion that the sonnet was actually placed on the door of his dwelling, to placate some Royalist commander, need not be taken seriously: we are in presence of a poetical situation, not of a practical expedient." In the octave, poetic fame is promised to the poet's protector, but the extent of Milton's irony is seen in the sestet, where he not only compares himself implicitly with Pindar and Euripides ("sad *Electra's* poet")—too extreme a comparison at this stage of Milton's career for it to be taken seriously—but also likens an imagined Royalist officer of no very great status to Alexander the Great ("The great *Emathian* Conqueror"). It is good to be reminded that Milton had a sense of humor, though Shawcross is probably right when he comments: "Despite the mocking tone . . . Milton is seriously comparing the far-reaching powers of poetry with the inglorious limitations of war" (*Complete Poetry of John Milton*, p. 197).

Sonn 9. The date of this sonnet is uncertain, but it seems to belong in the period 1642–1645. If, as Honigmann and Parker suggest, the unidentified "Lady" is Mary Powell, then the poem could have been written during Milton's courtship of her around May 1642 (Parker, *Milton*, p. 875). But Parker thinks that Lady Alice Egerton, "twenty-three in 1642 and still unmarried," would be the most likely "Lady."

This comparatively undistinguished poem of commendation is laden with biblical allusions, which are annotated in most editions.

Sonn 10. *TM* has as title: "To yᵉ Lady Margaret Ley." Parker points out that this title could not have been used in the 1645 *Poems* because it "would have been a discourtesy to John Hobson, whom Lady Margaret married on 30 December 1641." He considers the MS title a good reason for assuming that composition took place before the end of 1641, and would not in any case put it any later than 1642 (*Milton*, p. 876). Honigmann (pp. 49, 112) suggests that the sonnet may well have been intended as a commendatory poem to the posthumously published *A Learned Treatise concerning Wards*, by Lady Margaret's father, James Ley, Earl of Marlborough, which was first issued in 1641. Certainly more is said about the Earl than his daughter. The graceful words of praise in the sestet remind us, however, of Edward Phillips's remarks: "This Lady being a Woman of great Wit and ingenuity, had a particular Honour for him, and took much delight in his Company . . . and what Esteem he at the same time had for Her, appears by a sonnet he made in praise of her . . . " (Darbishire, *The Early Lives of Milton*, p. 64).

Sonn 11. ("I did but prompt the age to quit their cloggs.") The consensus of the best modern editors places this sonnet before, not after, "A Book was writ of late call'd *Tetrachordon*," though this reverses the numbering in *CM*. There are two versions in *TM* of "I did but prompt the age," one in Milton's own hand and one in a scribal hand; both are numbered "11" in a scheme that indicates the intended order. The autograph MS title, followed, with spelling variations, in the scribal MS, is: "On the detraction wᶜʰ follow'd upon my writing certain treatises." This does not appear in the printed version of 1673, possibly because in the autograph MS there is a mark directing deletion. There are some variants of accidentals as well between the final form of the MSS and the printed version, and there is an engaging variant in line 4 of the autograph MS, where instead of the eventual "Owles and Cuckoes" Milton has "Owls & buzzards."

The date is uncertain, but it presumably followed by some months the publication of the divorce tracts *Tetra* and *Colas*, ("twin-born progenie" to which allusive reference is made in line 6), on March 4, 1645. Autumn 1645 is a reasonable date.

A great deal of information is provided in Honigmann (pp. 114–19) about probable and possible topical allusions in the poem, but the main point is that it was a prompt response to attacks that had been made on Milton because of the extreme views he expressed in the divorce tracts. It is commonly assumed that the "detraction" Milton mentions is a reference to the Presbyterian attacks, from a theologically conservative standpoint, on his treaties; Honigmann disposes of the suggestion that, in line 11 particularly, the radical sectaries are alluded to (p. 120). All modern editions provide adequate annotation of the classical (lines 5–7) and biblical (lines 8, 10) allusions, but Smart is particularly helpful on the symbolism of line 4 ("Owles and Cuckoes, Asses, Apes and Doggs") where, as one might expect, all the creatures named symbolize such unpleasant characteristics as ignorance, quarrelsomeness, and ingratitude. He

also has a valuable note on line 11 ("Licence they mean when they cry libertie"), where he traces the distinction between license and liberty back to Roman political thought. (A pun is also clearly intended on the word *license*). The final line, with its intention of "wast of wealth, and loss of blood," has been taken as an indication that the First Civil War (1642–1646) was still going on when the poem was composed, but this is hardly the point, since after the decisive Parliamentary victory at Naseby in June 1645 there were only a few sieges and skirmishes until the King's surrender in May 1646. Milton is looking back at the course of the war and lamenting its mismanagement by those who failed in the prime requisites of wisdom and goodness, even though they claimed that they were fighting for liberty.

Sonn 11 is distinguished from the sonnets that precede it by its idiomatic vigor and its vehemence. The precise forcefulness of its diction is exemplified by the phrase in line 3, "barbarous noise," where Milton is going back to the Greek origins of the word "barbarous" with its connotations of unintelligible gibberish spoken by uncivilized foreigners. (Cf. *Mask*, line 550; *PL* 7.32.)

Sonn 12. ("A Book was writ of late call'd *Tetrachordon*.") (Numbered 11 in *CM*.) In the 1673 *Poems* this preceded "I did but prompt the age to quit their cloggs" (discussed above as 11), despite the order indicated in *TM*. "It is rather obvious that the printed order was an effort to make the subject of *I did but prompt* (titled [in the 1673 *Poems*] 'On the same') clear to readers almost thirty years later" (Parker, *Milton*, p. 897). The date generally agreed on is 1647, and there are no textual problems, though in view of the phrase *barbarous noise* in 11 (see above) it is interesting that according to *TM* Milton's first rendering of line 10 began, "those barbarous names"; this was later transmuted to the milder "rugged names."

Like 11, there is a response to public reaction to the divorce tracts—in this case just one, *Tetrachordon*—but it is more lighthearted in tone and satirical in manner. The abridged octave (seven and one-third lines) provides a delightful sketch of the bookstall browser trying in his ignorance to spell out the title of the tract with painful slowness. The extended sestet points out that though the public may have difficulty with names taken from Greek, it copes readily enough with the outlandish names of Scottish generals and divines, grown familiar from war reports and accounts of the meetings of the Westminster Assembly of Divines. In the last three lines, Milton interprets the supposed "stall-reader's" problems with a Greek title as a mark of general detestation of learning. (Though the interpretation of the names in lines 8–9 as well-known Scottish ones given by Smart is generally accepted, Shawcross, following Masson's biography of Milton, asserts that the three names in line 9 all refer to the same person, "Alexander MacDonnell, known as MacColkitto and MacGillespie, Montrose's major-general.")

This sonnet shares a good deal of the vitality of 11, and its vigor and flexibility are emphasized by the deliberately ludicrous nature of some of the rhymes.

"On the Forcers of Conscience." Because of its date and theme, this "tailed"

sonnet properly belongs in close proximity to 11 and 12. Honigmann (p. 198) and Parker (p. 928) assign it to early 1646, and Shawcross (p. 638) dates it a year later, but both dates place it close to 12 in time of composition. The title is expanded in the 1673 *Poems* to read, "On the new forcers of Conscience under the / Long PARLIAMENT," apparently for reasons of clarity after a considerable lapse of time. The original form of the scribal MS in *TM* has some interesting canceled readings, notably line 17, "Clip your Phylacteries, though bauk your Ears," which originally was, "Cropp yee as close as marginall P[rynne']s eares."

The sonnet is essentially an attack on the Presbyterian majority in the Westminster Assembly of Divines, who wished to impose the Presbyterian system of church government (called in line 7 "a classic [i.e., synodical] Hierarchy") upon England, with no allowance for freedom of worship and liberty of conscience. The form serves the ends of the poem very effectively; up to line 14, where the regular sonnet scheme comes to its end, for all the denunciation there is nothing more than a vague threat—"We do hope to find out all your tricks"— but the "tail" introduces the notion of Parliament's turning the tables on those who would use civil power in ecclesiastical causes and arraigning the Presbyterians on the charge of seeking to restablish the old Episcopal power in another guise.

Most of the allusions are satisfactorily dealt with in the annotated standard editions, but it should be pointed out that "our Consciences that Christ set free" (line 6) refers to Galatians 5:l: "Stand fast therefore in the liberty wherewith Christ hath made us free, and be not entangled again with the yoke of bondage."

Sonn 13. "To Mr. H. Lawes, on his Aires." This is the title given in the third draft of the sonnet in *TM*; this draft, in a scribal hand, appears to date from the year 1653, when Lawes's *Ayres and Dialogues* began to appear. The original title for Milton's first draft, dated February 9, 1646, in *TM*, was "To my freind Mr Hen. Laws," and this was the title used when the poem was printed in the *Choice Psalms* of 1648, by Henry Lawes and his brother William, whose death was more or less commemorated by the volume. Milton's second draft in *TM* was entitled "To Mr Hen: Laws on the publishing of his Aires," and this was originally used in the scribal transcription; it was subsequently modified to "Mr H. Lawes on his Aires," the title used in 1673.

This graceful and perceptive poem of compliment gains in interest when one realizes that Lawes, Milton's former collaborator in *Mask*, had Royalist sympathies, and that his brother died fighting on the King's side.

Sonn 14. There are three drafts of this in *TM*, two by Milton and the third in the hand of the scribe who copied *Sonn* 13. (For a discussion of the various amanuenses, see Kelley, *Modern Philology*, 54, [1956]): 20–25 and Shawcross, *Journal of English and Germanic Philology* 58 [1959]: 29–38.) The first draft has the title: "On ye religious memorie of Mrs Catharine Thomason my Christian freind deceas'd 6 [canceled] Decem. 1646" The other drafts are untitled.

Little is known about the subject of this sonnet, who was the wife of the bookseller George Thomason, celebrated for his collection of pamphlets, but she was apparently widely read and admired for her character (Smart, p. 69). It has been asserted that Sonnet 14 reads almost like a condensed version of *Everyman*, particularly in the first draft, because of the extensive use of personification; there is certainly a good deal of biblical allusion.

Sonn 15. The original title in *TM*, afterwards deleted, was: "On yᵉ Lord Gen. Fairfax at yᵉ seige of Colchester." This points to a date of about the middle of 1648, since the seventy-five-day siege of Colchester by Fairfax ended on August 27. Judging by "O yet a nobler task awaites thy hand" (line 9), Milton wrote when the siege had just ended or was coming to an end. The text is normally based on *TM* rather than the 1694 edition *(Letters of State)*. There are significant differences in lines, 5, 8, 10, 11, and 12, but *TM* readings are preferable in every case except line 8, where "her Serpent Wings" (1694) makes more sense than "their serpent wings" (the usual reading of *TM*). Shawcross (*Notes and Queries* 2 [1955]: 195–96) argues cogently that the original MS reading was "her," which was later changed to "their"—a non-Miltonic spelling. If this reading is adopted, "the fals North displaies / Her brok'n league, to impe her serpent wings" can be taken to mean that the invasion of England by the Scots, in contravention of the Solemn League and Covenant of 1643, was a display or public demonstration of Scottish treachery "thus repairing, that is, engrafting new acts to [imping], Scotland's serpentine perfidiousness, which was well attested in Milton's study of history" as Shawcross concludes. The "North" has further overtones of bad faith and rebellion; see *PL* 5.689, 726, 755, where Satan is referred to as lord of the north.

Sir Thomas Fairfax (1612–1671), who became Lord Fairfax on the death of his father in March 1648, was commander-in-chief of the New Model Army, created by Parliament when it decided to put the conduct of the war on a proper footing. He led the New Model Army to a resounding victory over the Royalists at Naseby in 1645, and continued to display outstanding qualities of military leadership during the remainder of the First Civil War and during the brief Second Civil War, in which the siege of Colchester was an important episode. The implications of the sestet, turning skillfully and naturally to aspirations for the future after the praise of Fairfax's achievements in the octave, are that the Army under Fairfax should bring an end to the mismanagement of affairs by the Long Parliament and establish order and security in a distracted society. Milton's feelings about the Long Parliament at this stage may well be reflected in the "Digression" in *Brit* concerning the Long Parliament (10:317–25; 18:247–55). Fairfax did not provide the hoped-for leadership; he retired into private life, and Cromwell, who had defeated the invading Scots at Preston (August 17–20, 1648), took his place.

Sonn 16. The original *TM* title, afterwards deleted, was: "To the Lord General Cromwell May 1652 / On the proposalls of certaine ministers at yᵉ Comm[it]tee for Propagation of the Gospell."

Cromwell did not become Lord Protector until December 1653, but as the successor to Fairfax (see 15, above) as commander-in-chief of the New Model Army, he was the *de facto* ruler of the British Isles and deserved the title given him in the opening line of this sonnet. The "proposalls" that alarmed Milton and caused the writing of this appeal were ones "made by certain Independent ministers with a design to perpetuating an Established Church with a state-paid and state-controlled clergy" (Parker, *Milton*, p. 413). The main issue for him was that of religious freedom—liberty of conscience. Thus, although the pattern of the poem is similar to that of 15, the urging of the sestet (a somewhat truncated one here) is more specific; the Lord General is reminded that there are victories of peace awaiting him if he will sustain his reputation as a defender of religious toleration and independency of outlook. The praise of the octave is genuine as well as generous, but the impact is in the concluding couplet, with its echoes of *Lyc*, lines 119 and 128. (This is the only sonnet in English by Milton that ends with a couplet, although it is an Italian sonnet.

Sonn 17. The original *TM* title, afterwards deleted, was: "To Sʳ Henry Vane the younger." Before this sonnet appeared in 1694 in *Letters of State*, it was printed anonymously in *The Life and Death of Sir Henry Vane* (1662), pp. 93–94, where the author, George Sikes, introduced it thus: "The Character of this deceased Statesman, . . . I shall exhibit to you in a paper of Verses, composed by a learned Gentleman, and sent him [Vane], July 3. 1652." Sir Henry Vane the younger (1613–1662) was executed by the government of the newly restored Charles II, in part because of his involvement with the regicides of Charles I, on June 14, 1662, and soon afterwards *The Life and Death of Sir Henry Vane* was published as a tribute to the Puritan statesman. That Milton's authorship of the sonnet to Vane should have been kept secret at the time is hardly surprising. The date of 1652 given in *The Life of Vane* accords with the references in lines 5 and 6 to the negotiations, in which Vane played a prominent part, between England and the Netherlands in May and June of 1652 before the outbreak of war in July.

This has been connected with the preceding sonnet, given Milton's renewed concern in 1652 with liberty of conscience and Vane's known advocacy of a policy of religious toleration, but apart from the reference in line 10 to "spirituall powre & civill, what each meanes" and the implications in the lines that follow, there is nothing like the definite plea to Cromwell of 16. "Though the sonnet betrays no signs of a personal connection we may be sure that Milton and Vane knew each other well" (Honigmann, p. 155), and it may be considered more a personal tribute than an appeal to a public figure. The structure is unusual, in that there is no clearly defined break between octave and sestet, though one may be detected halfway through line 9. This is far from being a defect; the sonnet moves with an ease and fluency that indicate mastery of a form transcending mere mechanical requirements.

Sonn 18. "On the late Massacher in Piemont." The appalling massacre of the Vaudois, or Waldensian Christians, inspired by an edict of the Duke of Savoy

requiring conformity to Roman Catholicism, took place in April 1655. News of this seems to have reached England in May, and there was widespread indignation, reflected in official letters (in the drafting of which Milton probably had a hand) from the Commonwealth to various European governments. The Vaudois were commonly regarded as proto-Protestants, rather like the Hussites in Bohemia and the Lollards in England, and in *Eikon* (5:230) Milton indicates his belief in the great antiquity of their "heresy," going back to at least the time of Constantine. It is reasonable to date the sonnet in May 1655; the only text available is that of 1673. The sonnet has been justly praised for its power, and is another example of Milton's mastery of the form. As in 17, the transition between octave and sestet is not readily apparent, though there is a shift from the impassioned narrative of lines 6–10 to a further appeal to God in lines 10–14. The appeal for divine justice recurs throughout: "Avenge"; "forget not"; "record." The sonnet, however, is less devoted to its topical occasion, the massacre of the Waldensians, than it is to a plea for people to leave the Roman Catholic Church, dominated by a "tyrant" pope, and join the Protestant fold before its fall and destruction ("the *Babylonian* wo") and the often-assumed fast-approaching millennium.

Sonn 19. It is generally agreed that Milton is here responding to his blindness, but the exact date is problematic; since it follows the sonnet on the Piedmontese massacre in the 1673 *Poems* (the only text available), where there seems to be chronological ordering of the sonnets, and since it is succeeded in the 1673 text by 20, which can be dated in late 1655, it seems reasonable to assume a date of 1655 for this sonnet. But Parker proposed a date of 1651, based on the assumption that in using the phrase *E're half my days* Milton was thinking of his own father, who lived to eighty-four or older; in 1651 Milton was forty-two. In his *Milton,* however, Parker moved to a tentative date of 1655 because of its "biographical *rightness*" (pp. 1042–43). The dates of 1642 and 1644 have also been advanced, but these seem highly improbable.

Part of the difficulty in dating the sonnet is the use of the expression *E're half my days,* which cannot be a literal reference to the "threescore years and ten" of Psalm 90:10, if a date in the 1650s is accepted. Dorian (*Explicator* 10 [1951], item 16) suggests that "days" means "working days," and Shawcross proposed that the allusion is to Isaiah 65:20, where a life-span of one hundred years is mentioned.

A further difficulty of interpretation is that blindness is not specifically referred to in the poem. (The title "On His Blindness" was created by Bishop Newton in 1751.) Even if it is assumed that the sonnet is essentially an attempt by Milton to come to terms with his blindness, the question agrees as to the exact nature of the poet's response to the central problem: how can he continue to serve God, and is it indeed just of God to require his service? His well-known answer is that one serves by being ready to act upon call or occasion, not only by constant doing. The poem is one, thus, of resolution.

Sonn 20. This pleasant poem of friendship and invitation, addressed to

Lawrence, whose father was President of the Council of State, probably dates from the winter of 1655–56, though earlier periods have been suggested. Various critics have noted its Horatian tone; a similar English example is Ben Jonson's Epigramme 101. If, as the context seems to require, one takes *spare* in 13 to mean "spare time," rather than "refrain" or "forbear," the sonnet can be seen as advocating frequent indulgence in moderate and temperate pleasures, which is certainly Horatian.

Sonn 21. Like the previous sonnet, which it resembles in tone and manner, this reads like an invitation to a convivial evening, and reminds one that the mature Milton was not necessarily always grave and staid in demeanor. The date is uncertain, but it may well be the same as that of 20. The "Grandsire" of Cyriack Skinner, to whom this sonnet is addressed, was the celebrated jurist Sir Edward Coke; Skinner himself, who was one of Milton's pupils in 1640–1645, became a lawyer; he was quite clearly a friend and confidant of Milton, and was for a time a neighbor. He is the presumed author of the so-called Anonymous Biography of Milton, and the MSS of this sonnet and 22 are in his hand. The references to "the Swede" and "the French" in line 8 are to the campaign of Charles X of Sweden in Poland and its aftermath (1655–56) and to relations in the 1650s between England and France, and France and Spain. The intentions of the French would be particularly interesting to supporters of Cromwell's regime, who wished for the explusion from France of the future Charles II and his court. Like 20, it suggests the urbanity of Horace as well as Ecclesiastes 3:1–9, with its emphasis on appropriate activities at appropriate times.

Sonn 22. It is often assumed that this sonnet, addressed, like 21, to Cyriack Skinner, must, because of its place in *TM*, follow 21 in time of composition; it is therefore assigned a date in the winter of 1655–56 by some editors. However, the reference in the opening lines to the anniversary of Milton's total blindness creates a problem. If one accepts French's date for total blindness (*Life Records*, 3: 197–98) of about February 28, 1652, then this sonnet should be dated 1655; Parker argues (*Milton*, p. 988) for "early November of 1651" as the time when blindness became complete, but somewhat illogically goes on to place Sonnet 22 "in June 1654" (p. 1044), rather than November. The position in the order of the sonnets may well be due to a deliberate pairing of those addressed to Skinner, but the generally accepted date of 1655 seems reasonable.

In a sense, the subject matter here is similar to that of 19, since both sonnets allude to Milton's blindness, but the resemblance is superficial; here, the emphasis is not on the workings of divine providence but on the writer's loss of eyesight "in libertyes defence." The reference is usually considered an explicit one to *1 Def*.

Sonn 23. There has been considerable controversy over the subject and hence the date of this poem. Is the "late espoused Saint" Milton's first wife or his second? It used to be taken for granted that the reference was to Katherine Woodcock, the second wife, who died in 1658, but this was challenged in 1945 by Parker, in an article in *Review of English Studies* 21 (1945): 235–38, where he

asserted that Milton was writing about his first wife, Mary Powell, who died in 1652. Despite the early difficulties in the first marriage, there was a reconciliation that was apparently lasting; therefore (Parker implies) there is no reason why Milton should not have yearned for Mary after her death. Significantly (see line 5), Mary died in childbirth and Katherine did not. The article elicited a number of responses favoring the traditional assumption. The debate may favor the candidacy of Mary Powell, though all editors are not convinced. Even if one assumes that Milton was speaking of Mary Powell in the sonnet, it could still have been composed at any time after her death in May 1652; Shawcross (*Complete Poetry*, p. 246) suggests 1656–1658, and this is certainly appropriate to the position of the poem in *TM*.

Despite difficulty over detail, the main emphasis of the poem is plain enough: the poet dreams of his dead wife, who appears to him like one returned from the grave; as she leans forward to embrace him, he awakes, aware once again of his blindness and of his wife's death. It is the essential simplicity of statement that gives the sonnet much of its force, summed up in the painful monosyllabic directness of the final line: "I wak'd, she fled, and day brought back my night." [JD]

UPON THE CIRCUMCISION. This twenty-eight-line poem appeared in both the 1645 and 1673 editions of Milton's poems. A transcript of it in Milton's hand also appears in *TM*. The poem's dating involves complex issues—as does that of the manuscript itself. Scholars have generally assumed that Milton began the manuscript in the early 1630s and that *Circum* was written during that period. On the other hand, John T. Shawcross has argued that Milton did not begin *TM* until 1637 and that *Circum* was composed between January and September of that year, although it was not transcribed in the manuscript until later (*Modern Language Notes* 75 [1960]: 11–17).

Whenever it was written, *Circum* was probably the last of three works that Milton wrote in fulfillment of what seems to be a plan to commemorate each major feast day of the Christian year with a poem. Having completed a highly successful ode on Christ's nativity, he had confidently turned to Christ's passion, only to find it "above the yeers he had . . . and nothing satisfi'd with what was begun, [he had] left it unfinisht." With *Circum*, he took up his plan again for the last time. His reasons for abandoning it are not clear, but the fact that this last attempt produced less than memorable results may have contributed to his decision.

If *Circum* is not memorable, it is nevertheless more successful than *Passion*. In its opening lines, as in those of the latter poem, Milton alluded to the "Musick, and triumphant song" that had been so important an element in the *Nat*; in the remainder of the poem, however, he avoided the emphasis on himself that had proved his undoing in *Passion*. The first half of it addresses the angels who produced the "Musick": they are asked to join humanity in mourning for Christ, who "now bleeds to give us ease. . . ." Thus begins the pro-

cess—to be completed with the crucifixion—whereby love will triumph over the law. The second half extols this triumph, one that Milton had already touched upon in *Nat* and that was to be the central issue in the dialogue between God and Christ in Book 3 of *PL*. By thus concentrating on an issue that was important to him both early and late, he was able to finish the poem creditably.

The metrics of *Circum* derive from Milton's study of Italian poetry. Ants Oras has pointed out the poem's similarity in structure to Tasso's *canzone* on the Madonna of Loretto, but F. T. Prince has demonstrated that the two fourteen-line stanzas into which *Circum* divides "reproduce as closely as possible the stanza used by Petrarch in his *canzone* to the Blessed Virgin." Milton's phrasing is awkward in places, and it is noteworthy that he never again undertook a comparable imitation of an Italian model. Still, his metrical achievement itself—the exact rendering of a strict Italian form into English—is significant. [ERG]

SELECT BIBLIOGRAPHY

N.B.: See also bibliography within the essays themselves, only some of which reappears here. Numerous important essays for individual poems are included in collections listed under Studies of the Poetry.

Bibliography

Fletcher, Harris F. *Contributions to a Milton Bibliography, 1800–1930.* Urbana: University of Illinois Press, 1931. Reprint. New York: Russell and Russell, 1967. Addenda to Stevens.

Huckabay, Calvin. *John Milton: An Annotated Bibliography, 1929–1968.* Pittsburgh: Duquesne University Press, 1969.

Stevens, David H. *Reference Guide to Milton from 1800 to the Present Day.* Chicago: University of Chicago Press, 1930. Reprint. New York: Russell and Russell, 1967. Through 1928.

Collected Works

Fletcher, Harris F., ed. *John Milton's Complete Poetical Works, Reproduced in Photographic Facsimile.* 4 vols. Urbana: University of Illinois Press, 1943–48.

Patterson, Frank A., gen. ed. *The Works of John Milton.* 18 vols. in 21. New York: Columbia University Press, 1931–38.

Wolfe, Don M., gen. ed. *Complete Prose Works of John Milton.* 8 vols. New Haven: Yale University Press, 1953–82.

Biography

Darbishire, Helen, ed. *The Early Lives of Milton.* London: Constable, 1932. Reprint. 1966. Included are John Aubrey's notes, the Anonymous Biographer's brief life, Anthony Wood's, Edward Phillips's, John Toland's, and Jonathan Richardson's.

French, J. Milton. ed. *The Life Records of John Milton.* 5 vols. New Brunswick, N.J.: Rutgers University Press, 1949–58. Reprint. Stapleton, N.Y.: Gordian Press, 1966.

Masson, David. *The Life of John Milton.* 7 vols. London: Macmillan, 1881–94. Reprint. New York: Peter Smith, 1946.

Parker, William Riley. *Milton: A Biography.* 2 vols. Oxford: Clarendon Press, 1968.

Reference

Hunter, William B., gen. ed. *A Milton Encyclopedia.* 9 vols. Lewisburg: Bucknell University Press, 1978–83.

Ingram, William, and Kathleen Swaim. eds. *A Concordance to Milton's English Poetry.* Oxford: Clarendon Press, 1972.

Le Comte, Edward S. *A Milton Dictionary.* New York: Philosophical Library, 1961.

A Variorum Commentary on the Poems of John Milton. 3 vols. in 5 (to date). New York: Columbia University Press, 1970– . Still forthcoming are *Paradise Lost* and *Samson Agonistes.*

General

Banks, Theodore. *Milton's Imagery.* New York: Columbia University Press, 1950.

Barker, Arthur. *Milton and the Puritan Dilemma, 1641–1660.* Toronto: University of Toronto Press, 1942. Reprint. 1956, 1977.

Christopher, Georgia B. *Milton and the Science of Saints.* Princeton: Princeton University Press, 1982. Attention particularly to *Paradise Lost* and *Samson Agonistes.*

Danielson, Dennis. *Milton's Good God: A Study in Literary Theodicy.* Cambridge: Cambridge University Press, 1982.

Fixler, Michael. *Milton and the Kingdoms of God.* Evanston, Ill.: Northwestern University Press, 1964. Includes an important analysis of *Paradise Regain'd.*

Hanford, James Holly. *John Milton, Poet and Humanist.* Cleveland: Case Western Reserve University Press, 1966. Reprints of major articles including those on "Lycidas" and the major poems.

Havens, Raymond D. *The Influence of Milton on English Poetry.* Cambridge: Harvard University Press, 1922. Reprint. London: Russell and Russell, 1961.

Hill, Christopher. *Milton and the English Revolution.* London: Faber, 1977; New York: Viking, 1978.

Kranidas, Thomas. *The Fierce Equation: A Study of Milton's Decorum.* The Hague: Mouton, 1965.

Le Comte, Edward. *Yet Once More: Verbal and Psychological Pattern in Milton.* New York: Liberal Arts Press, 1954.

Patrides, C. A. *The Grand Design of God: The Literary Form of the Christian View of History.* London: Routledge & Kegan Paul, 1972.

———. *Milton and the Christian Tradition.* Oxford: Clarendon Press, 1966.

Samuel, Irene. *Plato and Milton.* Ithaca: Cornell University Press, 1965.

Saurat, Denis. *Milton: Man and Thinker.* Revised edition. London: Dent, 1944, 1946. Reprint. Hamden, Conn.: Archon Books, 1964.

Shawcross, John T. *Milton: The Critical Heritage.* 2 vols. London: Routledge & Kegan Paul, 1970, 1972.

Sprott, S. Ernest. *Milton's Art of Prosody.* Oxford: Blackwell, 1953.

Svendsen, Kester. *Milton and Science.* Cambridge: Harvard University Press, 1956.

Wittreich, Joseph A. *The Romantics on Milton: Formal Essays and Critical Asides.* Cleveland: The Press of Case Western Reserve University, 1970.

Wittreich, Joseph A., ed. *Milton and the Line of Vision.* Madison: University of Wisconsin Press, 1975. Eight essays by various authors examine Milton as a visionary (or prophetic) poet, and the tradition into which he thus falls. Discussed are Chaucer, Spenser, Sidney, Blake, Wordsworth, Percy and Mary Shelley, Byron, Wallace Stevens, and other contemporary American poets.

Woodhouse, A. S. P. "Notes on Milton's Early Development." *University of Toronto Quarterly* 13 (1943):66–101.

Studies of the Poetry

Allen, Don Cameron. *The Harmonious Vision: Studies in Milton's Poetry.* Baltimore: Johns Hopkins Press, 1954. Chapters on the "Nativity Ode," "L'Allegro" and "Il Penseroso," "Comus," "Lycidas," *Paradise Regain'd,* and *Samson Agonistes.*

Brooks, Cleanth, and John E. Hardy, eds. *Poems of Mr. John Milton: The 1645 Edition with Essays in Analysis.* New York: Harcourt, Brace, 1951. Reprint. New York: Gordian Press, 1968.

Burnett, Archie, *Milton's Style: The Shorter Poems, Paradise Regained, and Samson Agonistes.* London: Longman, 1981.

Condee, Ralph W. *Structure in Milton's Poetry: From the Foundation to the Pinnacles.* University Park: Pennsylvania State University Press, 1974.

Daniells, Roy. *Milton, Mannerism and Baroque.* Toronto: University of Toronto Press, 1963.

Finney, Gretchen L. *Musical Backgrounds for English Literature, 1580–1650.* New Brunswick, N.J.: Rutgers University Press, 1962.

Hyman, Lawrence W. *The Quarrel Within: Art and Morality in Milton's Poetry.* Port Washington, N.Y.: Kennikat Press, 1972.

Ide, Richard S., and Joseph A. Wittreich, eds. *Composite Orders: The Genres of Milton's Last Poems.* Special issue of *Milton Studies,* vol. 17. Pittsburgh: University of Pittsburgh Press, 1983.

Kermode, Frank, ed. *The Living Milton: Essays by Various Hands.* London: Routledge & Kegan Paul, 1960.

Labriola, Albert C., and Michael Lieb, eds. *"Eyes Fast Fixt": Current Perspectives in Milton Methodology.* Special issue of *Milton Studies,* volume 7 (Pittsburgh: University of Pittsburgh Press, 1975).

Lawry, Jon S. *The Shadow of Heaven: Matter and Stance in Milton's Poetry.* Ithaca: Cornell University Press, 1968. Discussions of the three major poems as well as the "Nativity Ode," the companion pieces, "Arcades," "At a Solemn Music," "Comus," and "Lycidas" explore extraliterary beliefs behind the poems and Milton's participation in those beliefs through the poems.

Leishman, J. B. *Milton's Minor Poems.* Pittsburgh: University of Pittsburgh Press, 1971.

Martz, Louis L. *Poet of Exile: A Study of Milton's Poetry.* New Haven: Yale University Press, 1980.

Milton Studies in Honor of Harris Francis Fletcher. Urbana: University of Illinois Press, 1961.

Nelson, Lowry. *Baroque Lyric Poetry.* New Haven: Yale University Press, 1961.

Nicholson, Marjorie Hope. *John Milton: A Reader's Guide to His Poetry.* New York: Farrar, Straus, 1963.

Prince, F. T. *The Italian Element in Milton's Verse.* Oxford: Clarendon Press, 1954. Reprint. 1962.

Radzinowicz, Mary Ann. *Toward Samson Agonistes. The Growth of Milton's Mind.* Princeton: Princeton University Press, 1978.

Rajan, Balachandra. *The Lofty Rhyme: A Study of Milton's Major Poetry.* Coral Gables, Fla.: University of Miami Press, 1970.

Rajan, Balachandra, ed. *The Prison and the Pinnacle.* Toronto: University of Toronto Press, 1973. Essays on *Paradise Regain'd* and *Samson Agonistes.*

Reesing, Johns. *Milton's Poetic Art: A Mask, Lycidas, and Paradise Lost.* Cambridge: Harvard University Press, 1968.

Sims, James H. *The Bible in Milton's Epics.* Gainesville: University of Florida Press, 1962.

Sims, James H., and Leland Ryken, eds. *Milton and Scriptural Tradition: The Bible into Poetry.* Columbia: University of Missouri Press, 1984.

Steadman, John M. *Milton and the Renaissance Hero.* Oxford: Clarendon Press, 1967.

Tayler, Edward W. *Milton's Poetry: Its Development in Time.* Pittsburgh: Duquesne University Press, 1979.

Tillyard, E. M. W. *Milton.* London: Chatto and Windus, 1930. Revised 1966. Biographically and somewhat psychologically oriented criticism of the works.

————. *The Miltonic Setting: Past and Present.* Cambridge: Cambridge University Press, 1938. Various subjects, including "L'Allegro" and "Il Penseroso" and epic.

————. *Studies in Milton.* London: Chatto and Windus, 1951. Among the poems discussed are *Paradise Lost, Paradise Regain'd,* and "Comus."

Tuve, Rosemond. *Images and Themes in Five Poems by Milton.* Cambridge: Harvard University Press, 1957. The poems are the "Nativity Ode," "L'Allegro" and "Il Penseroso," "Lycidas," and "Comus."

Watkins, Walter B. C. *An Anatomy of Milton's Verse.* Baton Rouge: Louisiana State University Press, 1955. Reprint. Hamden, Conn.: Shoe String Press, 1965. Three Essays on Sensation, Creation, and Temptation offer readings of the three major poems and "Comus" (with most emphasis on *Paradise Lost*) to demonstrate that Milton's poetry is "simple, sensuous, passionate."

Whiting, George. *Milton and This Pendant World.* Austin: University of Texas Press, 1958. Reprint. New York: Octagon Books, 1967. Extensive discussion of *Paradise Lost,* "Comus," and "Lycidas."

Whiting, George. *Milton's Literary Milieu.* Chapel Hill: University of North Carolina Press, 1939. Reprint. London: Russell and Russell, 1964.

Wittreich, Joseph A., ed. *Calm of Mind: Tercentenary Essays on Paradise Regain'd and Samson Agonistes in Honor of John S. Diekhoff.* Cleveland: The Press of Case Western Reserve University, 1971.

Studies of Individual Works

Another on the Same

Holmer, John Ozark. "Milton's Hobson Poems: Rhetorical Manifestations of Wit." *Milton Quarterly* 11 (1977): 16–21.

Arcades

Brown, Cedric C. "Milton's *Arcades*" Content, Form, and Function." *Renaissance Drama* 8 (1977): 245–74.

Demaray, John G. *Milton and the Masque Tradition: The Early Poems, Arcades, and Comus.* Cambridge: Harvard University Press, 1968.

Hunter, William B. "The Date and Occasion of *Arcades.*" *English Language Notes* 11 (1973): 46–47.

Shawcross, John T. "The Manuscript of *Arcades.*" *Notes and Queries* 6 (1959): 359–64.

Wallace, John M. "Milton's *Arcades.*" *Journal of English and Germanic Philology* 58 (1959): 627–36.

At a Solemn Musick

Heyworth, P. L. "The Composition of Milton's *At a Solemn Musick.*" *Bulletin of the New York Public Library* 70 (1966): 450–58.

Pecheux, Sister M. Christopher. "'At a Solemn Musick': Structure and Meaning." *Studies in Philology* 75 (1978): 331–46.

An Epitaph on the Marchioness of Winchester

Moloney, Michael F. "The Prosody of Milton's *Epitaph, L'Allegro* and *Il Penseroso.*" *Modern Language Notes* 72 (1957): 174–78.

Oras, Ants. "Metre and Chronology in Milton's 'Epitaph on the Marchioness of Winchester,' 'L'Allegro,' and 'Il Penseroso.'" *Notes and Queries* 198 (1953): 332–33.

West, Michael. "The Consolatio in Milton's Funeral Elegies." *Huntington Library Quarterly* 34 (1971): 233–49.

Wilson, Gayle E. "Decorum and Milton's 'An Epitaph on the Marchioness of Winchester.'" *Milton Quarterly* 8 (1974): 11–14.

Horace, The Fifth Ode of

Harding, Davis P. *The Club of Hercules: Studies in the Classical Background of Paradise Lost.* Urbana: University of Illinois Press, 1962.

Shawcross, John T. "Of Chronology and the Dates of Milton's Translation from Horace and the New Forcers of Conscience." *Studies in English Literature* 3 (1963): 77–84.

———. "The Prosody of Milton's Translation of Horace's Fifth Ode." *Tennessee Studies in Literature* 13 (1968): 81–89.

L'Allegro and Il Penseroso

Babb, Lawrence. "The Background of 'Il Penseroso.'" *Studies in Philology* 37 (1940): 257–73.

Bateson, F. W. "The Money-Lender's Son: *L'Allegro* and *Il Penseroso.*" *English Poetry, A Critical Introduction.* London: Longmans, 1950, pp. 149–64.

Brisman, Leslie. "'All before them where to choose': *L'Allegro* and *Il Penseroso*." *Journal of English and Germanic Philology* 71 (1972): 226–40.

Brooks, Cleanth. "The Light Symbolism in 'L'Allegro' and 'Il Penseroso.'" *The Well Wrought Urn: Studies in the Structure of Poetry.* New York: Reynal & Hitchcock, 1947, pp. 47–61.

Carpenter, Nan C. "The Place of Music in *L'Allegro* and *Il Penseroso*." *University of Toronto Quarterly* 22 (1953): 354–67.

Council, Norman B. "*L'Allegro, Il Penseroso,* and the Cycle of Universal Knowledge." *Milton Studies* 9 (1976): 203–19.

Dorian, Donald C. "The Question of Autobiographical Significance in *L'Allegro* and *Il Penseroso*." *Modern Philology* 31 (1933): 175–82.

Fish, Stanley E. "What It's Like to read *L'Allegro* and *Il Penseroso*." *Milton Studies* 7 (1975): 77–99.

Fixler, Michael. "The Orphic Technique of *L'Allegro* and *Il Penseroso*." *English Literary Renaissance* 1 (1971): 165–77.

Geckle, George L. "Miltonic Idealism: *L'Allegro* and *Il Penseroso*." *Texas Studies in Language and Literature* 9 (1968): 455–73.

Leishman, J. B. "*L'Allegro* and *Il Penseroso* in their Relation to Seventeenth-Century Poetry." *Essays and Studies* n.s. 4 (1951): 1–36.

MacKenzie, Phyllis. "Milton's Visual Imagination: An Answer to T. S. Eliot." *University of Toronto Quarterly* 16 (1946): 17–29.

Miller, David M. "From Delusion to Illumination: A Larger Structure for *L'Allegro—Il Penseroso*." *PMLA* 86 (1971): 32–39.

Moloney, Michael F. "The Prosody of Milton's *Epitaph on the Marchioness of Winchester, L'Allegro* and *Il Penseroso*." *Modern Language Notes* 72 (1957): 174–78.

Oras, Ants. "Metre and Chronology in Milton's *Epitaph on the Marchioness of Winchester, L'Allegro,* and *Il Penseroso*." *Notes and Queries* 198 (1953): 332–33.

Røstvig, Maren-Sofie. *The Happy Man: Studies in the Metamorphosis of a Classical Ideal, 1600–1700.* Oxford: Blackwell, 1964, pp. 152–60.

Stringer, Gary, "The Unity of *L'Allegro* and *Il Penseroso*." *Texas Studies in Language and Literature* 12 (1970): 221–29.

Swaim, Kathleen M. "Cycle and Circle: Time and Structure in *L'Allegro* and *Il Penseroso*." *Texas Studies in Language and Literature* 18 (1976): 422–32.

Watson, Sara R. "Milton's Ideal Day: Its Development as a Pastoral Theme." *PMLA* 57 (1942): 404–20.

Williamson, Marilyn. "The Myth of Orpheus in *L'Allegro* and *Il Penseroso*." *Modern Language Quarterly* 32 (1971): 377–86.

Lycidas

Alpers, Paul. "*Lycidas* and Modern Criticism." *ELH* 49 (1982): 468–96.

Austin, Warren B. "Milton's *Lycidas* and Two Latin Elegies by Giles Fletcher, the Elder." *Studies in Philology* 44 (1947): 41–55.

Brett, R. L. "Milton's *Lycidas*." *Reason and Imagination: A Study of Form and Meaning in Four Poems.* London: Oxford University Press, 1960, pp. 21–50.

Creaser, John. "*Lycidas:* The Power of Art." *Essays and Studies* 34 (1981): 123–47.

Elledge, Scott. *Milton's Lycidas: Edited to Serve as an Introduction to Criticism.* New York: Harper and Row, 1966.

Fixler, Michael. " 'Unexpressive Song': Form and Enigma Variations in *Lycidas:* A New Reading." *Milton Studies* 15 (1981): 213–55.

Hunt, Clay. *Lycidas and the Italian Cities.* New Haven: Yale University Press, 1979.

Lloyd, Michael. "The Two Worlds of *Lycidas.*" *Essays in Criticism* 11 (1961): 390–402.

Patrides, C. A., ed. *Milton's Lycidas: The Tradition and the Poem.* New and revised edition. Columbia: University of Missouri Press, 1983.

Shawcross, John T. "Establishment of a Text of Milton's Poems through a Study of *Lycidas.*" *Papers of the Bibliographical Society of America* 56 (1962): 317–31.

Thompson, Claud Adelbert. " 'That Two-Handed Engine' Will Smite: Time Will Have a Stop." *Studies in Philology* 59 (1962): 184–200.

Turner, Alberta. "The Sound of Grief: A Reconsideration of the Nature and Function of the Unrhymed Lines in *Lycidas.*" *Milton Quarterly* 10 (1976): 67–73.

Wallerstein, Ruth. "*Iusta Edouardo King.*" *Studies in Seventeenth Century Poetics.* Madison: University of Wisconsin Press, 1950, pp. 96–114.

Wittreich, Joseph A. "Milton's 'Destin'd Urn': The Art of *Lycidas.*" *PMLA* 84 (1969): 60–70.

———. *Visionary Poetics: Milton's Tradition and His Legacy.* San Marino, Calif.: Huntington Library, 1979.

Woodhouse, A. S. P. "Milton's Pastoral Monodies." *Studies in Honor of Gilbert Norwood.* Toronto: University of Toronto Press, 1952, pp. 261–78.

A Mask

Arthos, John. *On "A Mask Presented at Ludlow-Castle."* Ann Arbor: University of Michigan Press, 1954.

Breasted, Barbara. "*Comus* and the Castlehaven Scandal." *Milton Studies* 3 (1971): 201–24.

Brown, Cedric B. "The Shepherd, the Musician, and the Word in Milton's Masque." *Journal of English and Germanic Philology* 78 (1979): 522–44.

Demaray, John. *Milton and the Masque Tradition.* Cambridge: Harvard University Press, 1968.

Diekhoff, John S., ed. *A Maske at Ludlow: Essays on Milton's Comus.* Cleveland: The Press of Case Western Reserve University, 1968.

Fletcher, Angus. *The Transcendental Masque: An Essay on Milton's Comus.* Ithaca: Cornell University Press, 1972.

Haun, Eugene. "An Inquiry into the Genre of *Comus.*" *Essays in Honor of Walter Clyde Curry.* Nashville: Vanderbilt University Press, 1954, pp. 221–39.

Hunter, William B. *Milton's Comus: Family Piece.* Troy, N.Y.: Whitston, 1983.

Klein, Joan Larsen. "Some Spenserian Influences on Milton's *Comus.*" *Annuale Mediaevale* 5 (1964): 27–47.

Maxwell, J. C. "The Pseudo-Problem of *Comus.*" *Cambridge Journal* 1 (1948): 376–80.

Neuse, Richard. "Metamorphosis and Symbolic Action in *Comus.*" *ELH* 34 (1967): 49–64.

Rajan, Balachandra. "Comus: The Inglorious Likeness." *University of Toronto Quarterly* 37 (1968): 113–35.

Sensabaugh, George F. "The *Milieu* of *Comus*." *Studies in Philology* 41 (1944): 238–49.

Shawcross, John T. "Certain Relationships of the Manuscripts of *Comus*." *Papers of the Bibliographical Society of America* 54 (1960): 38–56, 293–94.

Sprott, S. Ernest. *A Maske: The Earlier Versions.* Toronto: University of Toronto Press, 1973.

Steadman, John M. "Milton's *Haemony:* Etymology and Allegory." *PMLA* 77 (1962): 200–207.

Swaim, Kathleen M. "Allegorical Poetry in Milton's Ludlow Mask." *Milton Studies* 16 (1982): 167–99.

Wilkenfeld, Roger B. "The Seat at the Center: An Interpretation of *Comus*." *ELH* 33 (1966): 170–97.

Wilkinson, David. "The Escape from Pollution: A Comment on *Comus*." *Essays in Criticism* 10 (1960): 32–43.

On the Death of a Fair Infant Dying of a Cough

Cope, Jackson I. "Fortunate Falls as Form in Milton's 'Fair Infant.'" *Journal of English and Germanic Philology* 63 (1964): 660–74.

Jones, William M. "Immortality in Two of Milton's Elegies." *Myth and Symbol: Critical Approaches and Applications*, ed. Bernice Slote. Lincoln: University of Nebraska Press, 1963, pp. 133–40.

MacLean, Hugh N. "Milton's Fair Infant." *ELH* 24 (1957): 296–305.

Shawcross, John T. "Milton's Nectar: Symbol of Immortality." *English Miscellany* 16 (1965): 131–41.

On the Morning of Christ's Nativity

Barker, Arthur. "The Pattern of Milton's Nativity Ode." *University of Toronto Quarterly* 10 (1941): 167–81.

Butler, Christopher. *Number Symbolism.* London: Routledge & Kegan Paul, 1970, pp. 140–43.

Cook, Albert S. "Notes on Milton's 'Ode on the Morning of Christ's Nativity.'" *Transactions of the Connecticut Academy of Arts and Sciences* 15 (1909): 307–68.

Davies, H. Neville. "Laid Artfully Together: Stanzaic Design in Milton's 'On the Morning of Christ's Nativity'." *Fair Forms: Essays in English Literature from Spenser to Jane Austen*, ed. Maren-Sofie Røstvig. Totowa, N.J.: Rowman & Littlefield, 1975, pp. 85–117, 213–19.

Entzminger, Robert L. "The Epiphanies in Milton's *Nativity Ode*." *Renaissance Papers* (1981): 21–31.

Jacobs, Laurence H. "'Unexpressive Notes': The Decorum of Milton's Nativity Ode." *Essays in Literature* 1 (1974): 166–77.

Kastor, Frank S. "Miltonic Narration: 'Christ's Nativity.'" *Anglia* 86 (1968): 339–52.

Kingsley, Lawrence W. "Mythic Dialectic in the Nativity Ode." *Milton Studies* 4 (1972): 163–76.

MacLaren, I. S. "Milton's Nativity Ode: The Function of Poetry and Structures of

Response in 1629 (with a Bibliography of Twentieth-Century Criticism)." *Milton Studies* 15 (1981): 181–200.

Maddison, Carol. "The English Ode." *Apollo and the Nine: A History of the Ode.* London: Routledge & Kegan Paul, 1960, pp. 318–30.

Morris, David B. "Drama and Stasis in Milton's 'Ode on the Morning of Christ's Nativity.' " *Studies in Philology* 68 (1971): 207–22.

Pecheux, Mother M. Christopher. "The Image of the Sun in Milton's 'Nativity Ode.' " *Huntington Library Quarterly* 38 (1975): 315–33.

Romano, J. R. "Heaven's Youngest Teemed Star." *Milton Quarterly* 15 (1981): 80–88.

Røstvig, Maren-Sofie. "Elaborate Song: Conceptual Structure in Milton's 'On the Morning of Christ's Nativity.' " *Fair Forms: Essays in English Literature from Spenser to Jane Austen,* ed. Maren-Sofie Røstvig. Totowa, N.J.: Rowman & Littlefield, 1975, pp. 54–84, 206–12.

———. "The Hidden Sense: Milton and the Neoplatonic Method of Numerical Composition." *The Hidden Sense and Other Essays.* New York: Humanities Press, 1963, pp. 43–51.

Shullenberge, William. "Christ as Metaphor: Figural Instruction in Milton's Nativity Ode." *Notre Dame English Journal* 14 (1981): 41–58.

Swaim, Kathleen M. " 'Mighty Pan': Tradition and an Image in Milton's Nativity Hymn." *Studies in Philology* 68 (1971): 484–95.

On the University Carrier

Holmer, Joan Ozark. "Milton's Hobson Poems: Rhetorical Manifestations of Wit." *Milton Quarterly* 11 (1977): 16–21.

Shawcross, John T. "A Note on Milton's Hobson Poems." *Review of English Studies* 18 (1967): 433–37.

On Time

Hardison, O. B., Jr. "Milton's 'On Time' and Its Scholastic Background." *Texas Studies in Language and Literature* 3 (1961): 107–22.

Paradise Lost

Addison, Joseph. "Critique of *Paradise Lost.*" *The Spectator,* (31 December 1711, 5 January 1712–13, May 1712). Often reprinted.

Babb, Lawrence. *The Moral Cosmos of Paradise Lost.* East Lansing: Michigan State University Press, 1970.

Barker, Arthur. "Structural Pattern in *Paradise Lost.*" *Philological Quarterly* 28 (1949): 16–30.

Berek, Peter. " 'Plain' and 'Ornate' Styles in the Structure of *Paradise Lost.*" *PMLA* 85 (1970): 237–46.

Berry, Boyd M. *Process of Speech, Puritan Religious Writing and Paradise Lost.* Baltimore: Johns Hopkins Press, 1976.

Blessington, Francis C. *Paradise Lost and the Classical Epic.* London: Routledge & Kegan Paul, 1979.

Bodkin, Maud. *Archetypal Patterns in Poetry: Psychological Studies of Imagination.* London: Oxford University Press, 1934.

Broadbent, John B. *Some Graver Subject: An Essay on Paradise Lost.* London: Chatto & Windus, 1960.

Burden, Dennis H. *The Logical Epic: A Study of the Argument of Paradise Lost.* London: Routledge & Kegan Paul, 1967.

Bush, Douglas. *Paradise Lost in Our Time.* Ithaca: Cornell University Press, 1945.

Carnes, Valerie. "Time and Language in Milton's *Paradise Lost.*" *ELH* 3 (1970): 517–39.

Chambers, A. B. "Chaos in *Paradise Lost.*" *Journal of the History of Ideas* 24 (1963): 55–84.

Cirillo, Albert R. "Noon-Midnight and the Temporal Structure of *Paradise Lost.*" *ELH* 29 (1962): 372–95.

Colie, Rosalie L. "Time and Eternity: Paradox and Structure in *Paradise Lost.*" *Journal of the Warburg and Courtauld Institute* 232 (1960): 127–38.

Condee, Ralph W. *Milton's Theories Concerning Epic Poetry: Their Sources and Their Influence on Paradise Lost.* Urbana: University of Illinois Press, 1949.

Cope, Jackson I. *The Metaphoric Structure of Paradise Lost.* Baltimore: Johns Hopkins Press, 1962.

Crosman, Robert. *Reading Paradise Lost.* Bloomington: Indiana University Press, 1980.

Crump, Galbraith M. *The Mystical Design of Paradise Lost.* Lewisburg: Bucknell University Press, 1974.

Davies, Stevie. *Images of Kingship in Paradise Lost.* Columbia: University of Missouri Press, 1983.

Demaray, John G. *Milton's Theatrical Epic: The Invention and Design of Paradise Lost.* Cambridge: Harvard University Press, 1981.

Diekhoff, John S. *Milton's Paradise Lost, a Commentary on the Argument.* New York: Columbia University Press, 1946. Reprint. New York: Humanities Press, 1958.

Dobbins, Austin C. *Milton and the Book of Revelation: The Heavenly Cycle.* University: University of Alabama Press, 1975.

Duncan, Joseph E. *Milton's Earthly Paradise: A Historical Study of Eden.* Minneapolis: University of Minnesota Pres, 1972.

————. "Archetypes in Milton's Earthly Paradise." *Milton Studies* 14 (1980): 25–58.

Emma, Ronald David, and John T. Shawcross, ed. *Language and Style in Milton.* New York: Frederick Ungar, 1967.

Evans, J. M. *Paradise Lost and the Genesis Tradition.* Oxford: Clarendon Press, 1968.

Ferry, Anne Davidson. *Milton's Epic Voice: The Narrator in Paradise Lost.* Cambridge: Harvard University Press, 1963.

Fiore, Peter Amadeus. *Milton and Augustine: Patterns of Augustinian Thought in Paradise Lost.* University Park: Pennsylvania State University Press, 1982.

Fish, Stanley. *Surprised by Sin: The Reader in Paradise Lost.* New York: St. Martin's Press, 1967.

Freeman, James A. *Milton and the Martial Muse: Paradise Lost and European Traditions of War.* Princeton: Princeton University Press, 1980.

Frye, Northrop. *The Return of Eden: Five Essays on Milton's Epics.* Toronto: University of Toronto Press, 1965.

Frye, Roland Mushat. *Milton's Imagery and the Visual Arts: Iconographic Tradition in the Epic Poems.* Princeton: Princeton University Press, 1978.

Fuller, Elizabeth Ely. *Milton's Kinesthetic Vision in Paradise Lost.* Lewisburg: Bucknell University Press, 1983.

Gardner, Helen. *A Reading of Paradise Lost.* Oxford: Oxford University Press, 1965.

Gilbert, Allan H. *On the Composition of Paradise Lost. A Study of the Ordering and Insertion of Material.* Chapel Hill: University of North Carolina Press, 1947.

Grose, Christopher. *Milton's Epic Process: Paradise Lost and Its Miltonic Background.* New Haven: Yale University Press, 1973.

Hamilton, G. Rostrevor. *Hero or Fool? A Study of Milton's Satan.* London: Allen & Unwin, 1944.

Hamilton, Gary D. "Milton's Defensive God: A Reappraisal." *Studies in Philology* 69 (1972): 87–100.

Hamlet, Desmond M. *One Greater Man: Justice and Damnation in Paradise Lost.* Lewisburg: Bucknell University Press, 1976.

Hanford, James Holly. "The Dramatic Element in *Paradise Lost.*" *Studies in Philology* 14 (1917): 178–95.

Harding, Davis P. *The Club of Hercules: Studies in the Classical Background of Paradise Lost.* Urbana: University of Illinois Press, 1962.

Howard, Leon. " 'The Invention' of Milton's 'Great Argument': A Study of the Logic of 'God's Ways to Men.' " *Huntington Library Quarterly* 9 (1946): 149–73.

Hughes, Merritt Y. "Milton and the Symbol of Light." *Studies in English Literature* 4 (1964): 1–33.

Hunter, William B. "Prophetic Dreams and Visions in *Paradise Lost.*" *Modern Language Quarterly* 9 (1948): 277–85.

Hunter, William B., C. A. Patrides, and J. H. Adamson. *Bright Essence: Studies in Milton's Christology.* Salt Lake City: University of Utah Press, 1971.

Jacobus, Lee A. *Sudden Apprehension: Aspects of Knowledge in Paradise Lost.* The Hague: Mouton, 1976.

Jones, Putnam F. "Satan and the Narrative Structure of *Paradise Lost.*" *If by Your Art: Testament to Percival Hunt,* ed. Agnes Lynch Starrett. Pittsburgh: University of Pittsburgh Press, 1948, pp. 15–26.

Kastor, Frank S. *Milton and the Literary Satan.* Amsterdam: Rodopi, 1974.

Kelley, Maurice W. *This Great Argument: A Study of Milton's De doctrina christiana as a Gloss upon Paradise Lost.* Princeton: Princeton University Press, 1941.

Kerrigan, William W. "The Heretical Milton: From Assumption to Mortalism." *English Literary Renaissance* 5 (1975): 125–66.

———. *The Prophetic Milton.* Charlottesville: University Press of Virginia, 1974.

———.*The Sacred Complex: On the Psychogenesis of Paradise Lost.* Cambridge: Harvard University Press, 1983.

Kirkconnell, Watson. *The Celestial Cycle: The Theme of Paradise Lost in World Literature.* Toronto: University of Toronto Press, 1952.

Kranidas, Thomas. "Adam and Eve in the Garden: A Study of *Paradise Lost, Book V.*" *Studies in English Literature* 4 (1964): 71–83.

Kranidas, Thomas, ed. *New Essays on Paradise Lost.* Berkeley and Los Angeles: University of California Press, 1969.

Lewalski, Barbara K. "Structure and the Symbolism of Vision in Michael's Prophecy, *Paradise Lost*, Books XI–XII." *Philological Quarterly* 42 (1963): 25–35.

Lewis, C. S. *A Preface to Paradise Lost*. London: Oxford University Press, 1942.

Lieb, Michael. *The Dialectics of Creation: Patterns of Birth and Regeneration in Paradise Lost*. Amherst: University of Massachusetts Press, 1970.

———. *Poetics of the Holy: A Reading of Paradise Lost*. Chapel Hill: University of North Carolina Press, 1981.

Low, Anthony. "Milton's God: Authority in *Paradise Lost*." *Milton Studies* 4 (1972): 19–38.

MacCaffrey, Isabel G. *Paradise Lost as "Myth"*. Cambridge: Harvard University Press, 1959.

MacCallum, H. R. "Milton and Sacred History: Books XI and XII of *Paradise Lost*." *Essays in English Literature from the Renaissance to the Victorian Age Presented to A. S. P. Woodhouse*, ed. Millar Maclure and F. W. Watt. Toronto: University of Toronto Press, 1964, pp. 149–68.

McColley, Diane Kelsey. *Milton's Eve*. Urbana: University of Illinois Press, 1983.

McColley, Grant. *Paradise Lost: An Account of Its Growth and Major Origins, with a Discussion of Milton's Use of Sources and Literary Patterns*. Chicago: Packard, 1940; rptd., New York: Russell and Russell, 1963.

Madsen, William G. *From Shadowy Types to Truth: Studies in Milton's Symbolism*. New Haven: Yale University Press, 1968.

Marilla, E. L. *The Central Problem of Paradise Lost: The Fall of Man*. Cambridge: Harvard University Press, 1953.

Mohl, Ruth. "The Theme of *Paradise Lost*." *Studies in Spenser, Milton and the Theory of Monarchy*. New York: Columbia University Press, 1949. Reprint. New York: Frederick Ungar, 1962.

Mulder, John R. "'Ambiguous Words and Jealousies': A Secular Reading of *Paradise Lost*." *Milton Studies* 13 (1979):145–79.

Northrop, Douglas A. "The Double Structure of *Paradise Lost*." *Milton Studies* 12 (1978):75–90.

Ogden, H. V. S. "The Crisis of *Paradise Lost* Reconsidered." *Philological Quarterly* 36 (1957):1–19.

Pecheux, Mother M. Christopher. "Abraham, Adam, and the Theme of Exile in *Paradise Lost*." *PMLA* 80 (1965):365–71.

Peter, John. *A Critique of Paradise Lost*. London: Longmans, 1960.

Prince, F. T. "On the Last Two Books of *Paradise Lost*." *Essays and Studies* 11 (1958):38–52.

Qvarnström, Gunnar. *The Enchanted Palace: Some Structural Aspects of Paradise Lost*. Stockholm: Almquist and Wiksell, 1967.

Rajan, Balachandra. *Paradise Lost and the Seventeenth Century Reader*. London: Chatto and Windus, 1947, 1966.

Reichert, John. "'Against His Better Knowledge': A Case for Adam." *ELH* 48 (1981):83–109.

Revard, Stella Purce. *The War in Heaven: Paradise Lost and the Tradition of Satan's Rebellion*. Ithaca: Cornell University Press, 1980.

Ricks, Christopher. *Milton's Grand Style*. Oxford: Clarendon Press, 1963, 1968.

Riggs, William G. *The Christian Poet in Paradise Lost*. Berkeley and Los Angeles: University of California Press, 1972.

Rollin, Roger B. *"Paradise Lost:* 'Tragical—Comical—Historical—Pastoral'." *Milton Studies* 5 (1973):3–37.

Rosenblatt, Jason P. "The Mosaic Voice in *Paradise Lost.*" *Milton Studies* 7 (1975):207–32.

Ryken, Leland. *The Apocalyptic Vision in Paradise Lost*. Ithaca: Cornell University Press, 1970.

Samuel, Irene. *Dante and Milton: The Commedia and Paradise Lost*. Ithaca: Cornell University Press, 1966.

———. "The Dialogue in Heaven: A Reconsideration of *Paradise Lost* III. 1–417." *PMLA* 72 (1957):601–11.

Seaman, John E. *The Moral Paradox of Paradise Lost*. The Hague: Mouton, 1971.

Shawcross, John T. *With Mortal Voice: The Creation of Paradise Lost*. Lexington: University Press of Kentucky, 1982.

Smith, Hallett. "No Middle Flight." *Huntington Library Quarterly* 15 (1952):159–72.

Steadman, John M. "Archangel to Devil: The Background of Satan's Metamorphosis." *Modern Language Quarterly* 21 (1960):321–35.

———. *Epic and Tragic Structure in Paradise Lost*. Chicago: University of Chicago Press, 1976.

———. *Milton's Epic Characters: Image and Idol*. Chapel Hill: University of North Carolina Press, 1968.

Stein, Arnold. *Answerable Style: Essays on Paradise Lost*. Minneapolis: University of Minnesota Press, 1953.

———. *The Art of Presence: The Poet and Paradise Lost*. Berkeley and Los Angeles: University of California Press, 1977.

Summers, Joseph H. *The Muse's Method: An Introduction to Paradise Lost*. Cambridge: Harvard University Press, 1962.

Toliver, Harold E. "Complicity of Voice in *Paradise Lost.*" *Modern Language Quarterly* 25 (1964):153–70.

Waddington, Raymond B. "Appearance and Reality in Satan's Disguises." *Texas Studies in Language and Literature* 4 (1962):390–98.

———. "The Death of Adam: Vision and Voice in Books XI and XII of *Paradise Lost.*" *Modern Philology* 70 (1972):9–21.

———. "Here Comes the Son: Providential Theme and Symbolic Pattern in *Paradise Lost*, Book 3." *Modern Philology* 79 (1982):256–66.

Waldock, A. J. A. *Paradise Lost and Its Critics*. Cambridge: Cambridge University Press, 1947.

Webber, Joan Malory. *Milton and His Epic Tradition*. Seattle: University of Washington Press, 1979.

Webber, Joan. "Milton's God." *ELH* 40 (1973):337–41.

Weber, Burton J. *The Construction of Paradise Lost*. Carbondale: Southern Illinois University Press, 1971.

Werblowsky, R. J. Swi. *Lucifer and Prometheus: A Study of Milton's Satan*. London: Routledge & Kegan Paul, 1952.

West, Robert H. *Milton and the Angels*. Athens: University of Georgia Press, 1955.

Whaler, James. *Counterpoint and Symbol. An Inquiry into the Rhythm of Milton's Epic Style.* Copenhagen: Rosenkilde and Bagger, 1956.

Wilding, Michael. *Milton's Paradise Lost.* Sydney: Sydney University Press, 1969.

Wilkes, George A. *The Thesis of Paradise Lost.* Melbourne: Melbourne University Press, 1961.

Williamson, George. "The Education of Adam." *Modern Philology* 61 (1963):96–109.

Woodhouse, A. S. P. "Pattern in *Paradise Lost.*" *University of Toronto Quarterly* 22 (1953):109–27.

Wooten, John. "Satan, Satire, and Burlesque Fables in *Paradise Lost.*" *Milton Quarterly* 12 (1978):51–58.

Wright, B. A. *Milton's Paradise Lost: A Reassessment of the Poem.* London: Methuen, 1962.

Paradise Regained

Barker, Arthur E. "Structural and Doctrinal Pattern in Milton's Later Poems." *Essays in English Literature from the Renaissance to the Victorian Age Presented to A. S. P. Woodhouse,* ed. Millar MacLure and F. W. Watt. Toronto: University of Toronto Press, 1964, pp. 169–94.

Chambers, A. B. "The Double Time Scheme in *Paradise Regained.*" *Milton Studies* 7 (1975):189–205.

Clark, Ira. "*Paradise Regained* and the Gospel According to John." *Modern Philology* 71 (1973):1–15.

Condee, Ralph W. "Milton's Dialogue with the Epic: *Paradise Regained* and the Tradition." *Yale Review* 59 (1970):357–75.

Cope, Jackson I. "*Paradise Regained:* Inner Ritual." *Milton Studies* 1 (1969):51–65.

Cox, Lee Sheridan. "Good-word Imagery in *Paradise Regained.*" *ELH* 28 (1961):225–43.

Fisher, Alan. "Why Is *Paradise Regained* So Cold?" *Milton Studies* 14 (1980):195–217.

Frye, Northrop. "The Typology of *Paradise Regained.*" *Modern Philology* 53 (1956):227–38.

Gilbert, Allan H. "The Temptation in *Paradise Regained.*" *Journal of English and Germanic Philology* 15 (1916):599–611.

Guss, Donald L. "A Brief Epic: *Paradise Regained.*" *Studies in Philology* 68 (1971):223–43.

Hamilton, Gary D. "Creating the Garden Anew: The Dynamics of *Paradise Regained.*" *Philological Quarterly* 50 (1971):567–81.

Hughes, Merritt Y. "The Christ of *Paradise Regained* and the Renaissance Heroic Tradition." *Studies in Philology* 35 (1938):254–77.

Hunter, William B. "The Double Set of Temptations in *Paradise Regained.*" *Milton Studies* 14 (1980):183–94.

Jordan, Richard D. "*Paradise Regained* and the Second Adam." *Milton Studies* 9 (1976):261–75.

Kelsall, Malcolm. "The Historicity of *Paradise Regained.*" *Milton Studies* 12 (1978):235–51.

Kermode, Frank. "Milton's Hero." *Review of English Studies* 4 (1953):317–30.

Le Comte, Edward. "Satan's Heresies in *Paradise Regained.*" *Milton Studies* 12 (1978):253–66.

Lewalski, Barbara K. *Milton's Brief Epic: The Genre, Meaning, and Art of Paradise Regained.* Providence: Brown University Press, 1966.

———. "Theme and Structure in *Paradise Regained.*" *Studies in Philology* 57 (1960):186–220.

McCaffrey, Phillip. "*Paradise Regained:* The Style of Satan's Athens." *Milton Quarterly* 5 (1971):7–14.

Marilla, E. L. "*Paradise Regained:* Observations on Its Meaning." *Studia Neophilologica* 27 (1955):179–91.

Meadowcourt, Richard. *A Critique on Milton's Paradise Regain'd.* London: Henry Lintot, 1732. Reprint in facsimile by Joseph A. Wittreich. Gainesville, Fla: Scholars' Facsimiles & Reprints, 1971.

Nelson, Carey. *The Incarnate Word: Literature As Verbal Space.* Urbana: University of Illinois Press, 1973, chapter 4, pp. 80–100.

Orange, Linwood E. "The Role of the Deadly Sins in *Paradise Regained.*" *Southern Quarterly* 2 (1964):190–201.

Pope, Elizabeth. *Paradise Regained: The Tradition and the Poem.* Baltimore: John Hopkins Press, 1947.

Renaker, David. "The Horoscope of Christ." *Milton Studies* 12 (1978):213–33.

Revard, Stella. "Vision and Revision: A Study of *Paradise Lost* 11 and *Paradise Regained.*" *Papers on Language and Literature* 10 (1974):353–62.

Sackton, Alexander H. "Architectronic Structure in *Paradise Regained.*" *University of Texas Studies in English* 33 (1954):33–45.

Safer, Elaine B. "The Socratic Dialogue and 'Knowledge in the Making' in *Paradise Regained.*" *Milton Studies* 6 (1975):215–26.

Schultz, Howard. "Christ and Antichrist in *Paradise Regained.*" *PMLA* 67 (1952):790–808.

———. "A Fairer Paradise? Some Recent Studies of *Paradise Regained.*" *ELH* 32 (1965):275–302.

Shawcross, John T. "The Structure and Myth of *Paradise Regained.*" *The Laurel Bough,* ed. G. Nageswara Rao. Bombay: Blackie & Son, 1983, pp. 1–14.

Steadman, John M. " 'Like Turbulencies': The Tempest of *Paradise Regain'd* as Adversity Symbol." *Modern Philology* 59 (1961): 81–88.

———. "*Paradise Regained:* Moral Dialectic and the Pattern of Rejections." *University of Toronto Quarterly* 31 (1962): 416–30.

———. "The 'Tree of Life' Symbolism in *Paradise Regain'd.*" *Review of English Studies* 11 (1960): 384–91.

Stein, Arnold. "*Paradise Regained.*" *Heroic Knowledge: An Interpretation of Paradise Regained and Samson Agonistes.* Minneapolis: University of Minnesota Press, 1957, p. 3–134.

Stein, Robert A. "'The Sources and Implications of the Jobean Analogies in *Paradise Regained.*'" *Anglia* 86 (1970): 323–33.

Sundell, Roger H. "The Narrator as Interpreter in *Paradise Regained.*" *Milton Studies* 2 (1970): 83–101.

Taylor, Dick. "The Storm Scene in *Paradise Regained:* A Reinterpretation." *University of Toronto Quarterly* 24 (1955): 359–76.

Teskey, Gordon. "Balanced in Time: *Paradise Regained* and the Centre of the Miltonic Vision." *University of Toronto Quarterly* 50 (1981): 269–83.

Weber, Burton J. *Wedges and Wings: The Patterning of Paradise Regained.* Carbondale: Southern Illinois University Press, 1974.

Widmer, Kingsley. "The Iconography of Renunciation: the Miltonic Simile." *ELH* 25 (1958): 258–69.

Wilkes, George A. "*Paradise Regained* and the Conventions of the Sacred Epic." *English Studies* 44 (1963): 35–38.

Woodhouse, A. S. P. "Theme and Pattern in *Paradise Regained.*" *University of Toronto Quarterly* 25 (1956): 167–82.

Zwicky, Laurie. "Kairos in *Paradise Regained:* The Divine Plan." *ELH* 31 (1964): 271–77.

The Passion

Gallagher, Philip J. "Milton's 'The Passion': Inspired Mediocrity." *Milton Quarterly* 11 (1977): 44–50.

Via, John A. "Milton's *The Passion:* A Successful Failure." *Milton Quarterly* 5 (1971): 35–38.

Psalms, Milton's Translations from the

Baldwin, Edward C. "Milton and the Psalms." *Modern Philology* 17 (1919): 457–63.

Boddy, Margaret. "Milton's Translations of Psalms 80–88." *Modern Philology* 64 (1966): 1–9.

Hunter, William B. "The Sources of Milton's Prosody." *Philological Quarterly* 28 (1949) 133–44.

Hunter, William B. "Milton Translates the Psalms." *Philological Quarterly* 40 (1961): 485–94.

Studley, Marian H. "Milton and His Paraphrases of the Psalms." *Philological Quarterly* 4 (1925): 364–72.

Samson Agonistes

Baum, Paull Franklin. "*Samson Agonistes* Again." *PMLA* 36 (1921): 354–71.

Bennett, Joan S. "Liberty Under the Law: The Chorus and the Meaning of *Samson Agonistes.*" *Milton Studies* 12 (1978): 141–63.

Beum, Robert. "The Rhyme in *Samson Agonistes.*" *Texas Studies in Language and Literature* 4 (1962): 177–82.

Boughner, Daniel C. "Milton's Harapha and Renaissance Comedy." *ELH* 11 (1944): 297–306.

Chambers, A.B. "Wisdom and Fortitude in *Samson Agonistes.*" *PMLA* 78 (1963): 315–20.

Cox, Lee Sheridan. "The 'Ev'ning Dragon' in *Samson Agonistes:* A Reappraisal." *Modern Language Notes* 76 (1961): 577–84.

242   Select Bibliography

Curry, Walter Clyde. "*Samson Agonistes* Yet Again." *Sewanee Review* 32 (1924): 336–52.

Damico, Helen. "Duality in Dramatic Vision: A Structural Analysis of *Samson Agonistes.*" *Milton Studies* 12 (1978): 91–116.

Ebbs, John Dale. "Milton's Treatment of Poetic Justice in *Samson Agonistes.*" *Modern Language Quarterly* 32 (1961): 377–89.

Ellis-Fermor, Una. "*Samson Agonistes* and Religious Drama." *The Frontiers of Drama.* London: Methuen, 1945, pp. 17–33.

Entzminger, Robert L. "*Samson Agonistes* and the Recovery of Metaphor." *Studies in English Literature* 22 (1982): 137–56.

Fell, Kenneth. "From Myth to Martyrdom: Towards a View of Milton's *Samson Agonistes.*" *English Studies* 34 (1953): 145–55.

Furman, Wendy. "*Samson Agonistes* as Christian Tragedy: A Corrective View." *Philological Quarterly* 60 (1981); 169–81.

Gossman, Ann. "Milton's Samson as the Tragic Hero Purified by Trial." *Journal of English and Germanic Philology* 61 (1962): 528–41.

———. "Samson, Job, and 'the Exercise of Saints'." *English Studies* 45 (1964): 212–24.

Harris, William O. "Despair and 'Patience as the Truest Fortitude' in *Samson Agonistes.*" *ELH* 30 (1963): 107–20.

Hawkins, Sherman H. "Samson's Catharsis." *Milton Studies* 2 (1970): 211–30.

Jebb, Sir R. C. *Samson Agonistes and the Hellenic Drama.* London: H. Frowde, 1908.

Kirkconnell, Watson. *That Invincible Samson.* Toronto: University of Toronto Press, 1964.

Krouse, F. Michael. *Milton's Samson and the Christian Tradition.* Princeton: Princeton University Press, 1949.

Lewalski, Barbara K. "*Samson Agonistes* and the 'Tragedy' of the Apocalypse." *PMLA* 85 (1970): 1050–62.

Low, Anthony. *The Blaze of Noon: A Reading of Samson Agonistes.* New York: Columbia University Press, 1974.

Marilla, E. L. "*Samson Agonistes:* An Interpretation." *Studia Neophilologica* 29 (1957): 67–76.

Miriam Clare, Sister. *Samson Agonistes: A Study in Contrast.* New York: Pageant Press, 1964.

Mueller, Martin E. "*Pathos* and *Katharsis* in *Samson Agonistes.*" *ELH* 31 (1964): 156–74.

Parker, William R. "The Date of *Samson Agonistes.*" *Philological Quarterly* 28 (1949): 145–66.

———. *Milton's Debt to Greek Tragedy in Samson Agonistes.* Baltimore: Johns Hopkins Press, 1937.

Radzinowicz, Mary Ann Nevins. "Eve and Dalila: Renovation and the Hardening of the Heart." *Reason and Imagination: Studies in the History of Ideas, 1600–1800,* ed. J. A. Mazzeo. New York: Columbia University Press, 1962, pp. 155–81.

Sadler, Lynn Veach. *Consolation in Samson Agonistes: Regeneration and Typology.* Salzburg: Institut für Anglistik & Amerikanistik, University of Salzburg, 1979.

Sellin, Paul R. "Milton's Epithet *Agonistes.*" *Studies in English Literature* 4 (1964): 137–62.

Stein, Arnold. *Heroic Knowledge: An Interpretation of Paradise Regained and Samson Agonistes.* Minneapolis: University of Minnesota Press, 1957, pp. 137–202.

Stollman, Samuel S. "Milton's Samson and the Jewish Tradition." *Milton Studies* 3 (1971): 185–200.

Tinker, Chauncey B. "*Samson Agonistes.*" *Tragic Themes in Western Literature,* ed. Cleanth Brooks. New Haven: Yale University Press, 1955, pp. 59–76.

Tung, Mason. "Samson Impatiens: A Reinterpretation of Milton's *Samson Agonistes.*" *Texas Studies in Language and Literature* 9 (1968): 475–92.

Wilkes, George A. "The Interpretation of *Samson Agonistes.*" *Huntington Library Quarterly* 26 (1963): 363–79.

Wilkinfeld, Roger B. "Act and Emblem: The Conclusion of *Samson Agonistes.*" *ELH* 32 (1965): 160–68.

Woodhouse, A. S. P. "*Samson Agonistes* and Milton's Experience." *Transactions of the Royal Society of Canada.* Third Series, 43, Section 2 (1949): 157–75.

————. "Tragic Effect in *Samson Agonistes.*" *University of Toronto Quarterly* 28 (1959): 205–22.

Sonnets

Baldi, Sergio. "Poesie italiane di Milton." *Studi secenteschi* 7 (1966): 103–50.

Honigmann, E. A. J. *Milton's Sonnets.* London: Macmillan, 1966.

Hunter, William B. "Milton and the Waldensians." *Studies in English Literature* 11 (1971): 153–64.

McCarthy, William, "The Continuity of Milton's Sonnets." *PMLA* 92 (1977): 96–109.

Mengert, James G. "The Resistance of Milton's Sonnets." *English Literary Renaissance* 11 (1981): 81–95.

Nardo, Anna K. *Milton's Sonnets: The Ideal Community.* Lincoln: University of Nebraska Press, 1979.

Shawcross, John T. "Milton's Italian Sonnets: An Interpretation." *University of Windsor Review* 3 (1967): 27–33.

————. "Milton's Sonnet 19: Its Date of Authorship and Its Interpretation." *Notes and Queries* n.s. 4 (1957): 442–46.

Shullenberger, William A. "The Power of the Copula in Milton's 'Sonnet VII.'" *Milton Studies* 15 (1981): 201–12.

Smart, John S. *The Sonnets of John Milton.* Glasgow: Maclehose, Jackson, 1921. Reprint. Oxford: Clarendon Press, 1966.

Upon the Circumcision

Chambers, A. B. "Milton's 'Upon the Circumcision': Backgrounds and Meanings." *Texas Studies in Language and Literature* 17 (1975): 687–97.

Oras, Ants. "Milton's *Upon the Circumcision* and Tasso." *Notes and Queries* 197 (1952): 314–15. [JTS]

CONTRIBUTORS AND CONTRIBUTIONS

ACL   Albert C. Labriola
          On Shakespeare

BKL   Barbara K. Lewalski
          Paradise Regained

BR   Balachandra Rajan
          Lycidas

DB   Douglas Bush
          Paradise Lost

EBS   Elaine Safer
          On the Morning of Christ's Nativity

ERG   E. Richard Gregory
          Another on the Same
          At a Solemn Musick
          At a Vacation Exercise
          Epitaph on the Marchioness of Winchester, An
          Horace, The Fifth Ode of
          On the University Carrier
          On Time
          Passion, The
          Song: On May Morning
          Upon the Circumcision

JD   James Dale
          Sonnets, Milton's

JGD   John G. Demaray
          Arcades

JTS   John T. Shawcross
          Biography, Milton's

LN   Leonard Nathanson
                L'Allegro and Il Penseroso
                On the Death of a Fair Infant
ML   Michael Lieb
                On the New Forcers of Conscience
MPB   Margaret Pearse Boddy
                Psalms, Milton's Translations from the
RBW   Roger B. Wilkenfeld
                Mask, A
TK   Thomas Kranidas
                Samson Agonistes

INDEX

Page references in boldface type indicate main entries.

Milton's
English Poetry